Denise Kimber Buell

■

# WHY THIS NEW RACE

■

## Ethnic Reasoning in Early Christianity

■

Columbia University Press
New York

Columbia University Press

*Publishers Since 1893*
New York    Chichester, West Sussex
Copyright © 2005 Columbia University Press
All rights reserved

Library of Congress Cataloging-in-Publication Data
Buell, Denise Kimber, 1965–
Why this new race : ethnic reasoning in early Christianity / Denise K. Buell.
p.    cm. —
Includes bibliographical references and indexes.
ISBN 0–231–13334–0 (cloth : alk. paper)
1. Race—Religious aspects—Christianity—History of doctrines—Early church,
ca. 30–600.  2. Ethnicity—Religious aspects—Christianity—History of doctrines—Early
church, ca. 30–600.  3. Identification (Religion)—History of doctrines—Early church,
ca. 30–600.  I. Title.  II. Series.
BR195.R37B84 2005
270.1'089—dc22
2005041278

∞

Columbia University Press books are printed on permanent
and durable acid-free paper.

Printed in the United States of America

c 10 9 8 7 6 5 4 3 2 1

*Designed by Lisa Hamm*

# Contents

# Abbreviations

## Ancient Literary Works

| | |
|---|---|
| AA | Acts of Andrew |
| Adv. Haer. | (Irenaeus) Against All Heresies |
| 1 Apol. | (Justin Martyr) First Apology |
| 2 Apol. | (Justin Martyr) Second Apology |
| Apol. | (Aristides, Tertullian) Apology |
| Dial. | (Justin Martyr) Dialogue with Trypho the Jew |
| Eccl. Hist. | (Eusebius) Ecclesiastical History |
| Embassy | (Athenagoras) Embassy on Behalf of the Christians |
| Ep. Diog. | Epistle to Diognetus |
| Exc. Theod. | (Clement of Alexandria) Excerpts of Theodotos |
| First Princ. | (Origen) On First Principles |
| GosPhil | The Gospel of Philip |
| Herm. Sim. | Shepherd of Hermas, Similitudes |
| Herm. Vis. | Shepherd of Hermas, Visions |
| M. Just. | Martyrdom of Saints Justin, Chariton, Charito, Evelpistus, Hierax, Paeon, Liberian, and their Community |
| M. Lyon and Vienne | Acts of the Martyrs of Lyon and Vienne |
| M. Perp. and Fel. | Martyrdom of Perpetua and Felicitas |
| M. Poly. | Martyrdom of Polycarp |
| Nat. D. | (Cicero) On the Nature of the Gods |
| Or. | (Aelius Aristides) Orations |
| P. Giss. | Papyrus Gissen |
| Prot. | (Clement of Alexandria) Protreptikos |

| | |
|---|---|
| *Rec.* | (Pseudo-Clement) *Recognitions* |
| *Rom. Ant.* | (Dionysios of Halicarnassus) *Roman Antiquities* |
| *Scill. Mart.* | *Acts of the Scillitan Martyrs* |
| *SophJesChr* | *Sophia of Jesus Christ* |
| *Strom.* | (Clement of Alexandria) *Strōmateis* |
| *Tetr.* | (Ptolemy of Alexandria) *Tetrabiblos* |
| *TriTrac* | *The Tripartite Tractate* |

## Modern References

| | |
|---|---|
| *ANRW* | *Aufsteig und Neidergang der römischen Welt* |
| *BG* | *Codex Papyrus Berolinensis* |
| *HTR* | *Harvard Theological Review* |
| *JBL* | *Journal of Biblical Literature* |
| *JECS* | *Journal of Early Christian Studies* |
| *JTS* | *Journal of Theological Studies* |
| *NHC* | *Nag Hammadi Codex* |
| *n.s.* | *new series* |
| *SC* | *Sources chrétiennes* |

# Preface

Why do we need another book on early Christian self-definition? Many excellent studies already argue that early Christians defined themselves using a range of categories and strategies, comparing themselves with philosophical schools, households, other Jews, and modes of government. These studies all insist on interpreting early articulations of who and what Christians are in their specific historical, cultural, and political settings.

In part, this book is a variation on such studies. Scant attention has been paid to the ways that Christians defined themselves in terms of larger corporate collectives, which have been variously called "ethnic groups," "races," or "nations" ("barbarian," "gentile," as well as Greek, Roman, Jew, Egyptian, etc.). I call this mode of self-definition "ethnic reasoning." Early Christians developed ethnic self-comparisons in relation to other kinds of self-comparisons, including familial and civic ones. Ethnic reasoning helps us to explain early Christian self-definition in ways that contribute to current scholarly attempts to rethink both how we understand the relationship between "Christians" and "Jews" in Roman antiquity and how we understand early Christian participation in ancient ways of thinking about identity and difference.

But I do not merely seek to situate early Christians more fully in their ancient context. By itself, this goal is problematic because it does not ask how the interpreter knows when (or that) she understands the ancient context and how she makes sense of materials from a different time and place. To address this concern, I also turn the spotlight on the interpretive framework. In my view, contemporary methodological as well as sociopolitical circumstances help to explain the reasons why most historians steer clear of speaking about "ethnicity" with respect to early Christians and strongly resist the applicability of "race" for antiquity overall. The presuppositions and frameworks that continue to dominate mainstream reconstructions of Christian origins have both racist and anti-Jewish consequences—even when interpreters explicitly seek to avoid these consequences.[1] We need to change our ways of thinking about early Christian history, which means also changing our ways of thinking about what race, ethnicity, and religion are.

At the same time, my methodological and sociopolitical commitments also condition the possibilities for and importance of interpreting some forms of early Christian imagination and practice as "ethnic reasoning." I argue that by strategically using the modern categories of race and ethnicity to speak about early Christian self-definition, we will be better able to resolve a problematic paradox in the way these concepts have informed historical reconstructions of early Christians. Specifically, I challenge the view that ethnicity and race were irrelevant to early Christians—an argument that has been used to accomplish important modern antiracist work yet relies on and perpetuates anti-Judaism in the process. To support an interpretation of Christianity that can help end both racism and anti-Judaism, I revisit scholarship and early Christian texts that destabilize the prevailing view that Christian universalism can be understood as mutually exclusive with "particularity"—a split that is often correlated with the nonethnic/ethnic binary.

In sharing drafts of this project, I regularly encountered two kinds of responses, both of which underscore the point that studying early Christian history and self-definition has much contemporary relevance. To paraphrase the first kind of response: "Why has no one said this before? It seems so obvious now." This suggests that my argument emerges out of and seems useful for tackling issues perceived to be of pressing concern today, especially regarding Christian anti-Judaism (in the past and present) and the complicated ways that Christianity has been shaped both to resist and be complicit with racism, especially in North America.

The second kind of response is quite different: "Why on earth are you using the category of 'race'?" European respondents in particular have viewed this as a highly problematic recuperation of a category that is spurious, has caused too much death and suffering already, and is anyway a modern concept. North American responses in this vein tend to emphasize the last factor, its modernity. I am not naïve about the modernity of the concept. It is no coincidence that it is race, not other modern concepts central to this book—ethnicity and religion—that evokes the strongest reaction. This selective response indicates how loaded "race" remains in our current lives. Far from seeking to rehabilitate the concept, I use it precisely because of the damage this modern concept has wrought and continues to wreak. If we want to get beyond race, we have to grapple with how it informs historical interpretation even when it is excluded. By provocatively using race interchangeably with ethnicity in this book, I am challenging readers to be accountable to the terms we use for interpreting cultural differences in antiquity.

To understand the elusive but entrenched presence of race in contemporary scholarly models, we need to cultivate a prismatic vision that can reimagine the relevance of race and ethnicity to ancient articulations of Christianness in light of the continued political, social, ideological, and theological challenges posed by modern racism and anti-Judaism.[2] To aim for diffraction in how one sees—to see prismatically—is to value the production of patterns of difference and to resist the "false choice between realism and relativism."[3] By taking into account not just our own social and ideological locations and the early Christian texts under consideration but also the history and locatedness of the fields in which we work, we move from a double vision (now versus then) to at least a triple vision. That is, we need to modulate between a critical consideration of the present, for how our commitments and social location condition our historical analyses; of the recent historical past, for how it has shaped and constrained both our interpretive frameworks and our present commitments; and of the ancient historical period in which early Christian texts were produced, to gauge their interests and constraints. This approach builds on Elisabeth Schüssler Fiorenza's call to develop an "ethics of interpretation" and her analysis that embraces "the rhetoric of interpretation in the present and the rhetoric of interpretation in the past."[4] In so doing, we can recognize how the practices of historical interpretation have implications for the present and evaluate their adequacy both in terms of the limits of the material under consideration and in terms of the approach used to make sense of this material.

I bring together a range of scholarship where related but often independent conversations are taking place (contemporary feminist theory, critical race theory, cultural anthropology, postcolonial theory, Jewish studies, ancient history, classical studies, as well as the study of religion). These fields all include scholars who attend to the relation of self/other and relations of power, often with explicit aims for transforming how we think (if not also how we live). For example, a recent work in classics offers a perspective that resembles aspects of Schüssler Fiorenza's complex approach. Simon Goldhill argues that studies of ancient "Greekness" tell us more about the fluidity and complexity of both scholarly method and cultural identity than about the precise content of Greekness:

> There have always been writers, ancient and modern, who have thought that there is an essence of Greekness. That there is evident and wholesale disagreement about what such an essence is, makes it easy enough, these days, to concede that the idea of Greekness is differently constructed by different writers in different eras (including in ancient Greece). But that cautious relativism has far-reaching implications for contemporary historians, who cannot help finding their own reconstructions of those differences becoming *part* of the history being related. . . . Especially on a topic like 'cultural identity,' the historian's narration has to go back and forth between present and past, like a weaver's shuttle, to make up a picture.[5]

Contemporary discussions about early Christian self-definition are also linked with questions of cultural identity in the present. The classification of Christianity in relation to modern categories like religion, nation, race, or ethnicity does not tell us what the essence of Christianity is. This insight about the complex interrelation of interpreter to interpreted has been voiced in a number of earlier forms, from early hermeneutics to contemporary feminist and postcolonial theory. The latter two kinds of critical stances differ from Goldhill's perspective because feminist and postcolonial critics insist that attention to the complexity and fluidity of historical analysis and cultural identities requires us to go beyond a recognition of one's own role in reconstruction to the defense of particular, historically specific interpretations. In other words, it is possible not only to acknowledge the specificity and limitations of one's interpretation, but also to advocate for it—even provisionally—on the basis of its particular, contingent implications for the present and future.

As a historian of early Christianity, I am convinced that the way we retell the origins of Christianity matters for those struggling for racial justice and for overcoming anti-Judaism in the present. This claim builds upon traditions of abolitionist, civil rights, and Jewish-Christian dialogue in America. But I am insisting that we need to bring together two kinds of discussions that have largely been kept distinct: discussions about the relationship between Jewishness and Christianness and discussions about the relationship between Christianity and race, which in America especially has been dominated by a black/white binary.[6] In so doing, I question the value of distinguishing ethnicity from race and assess how the present informs historical analysis.[7]

I am equally concerned to show why those interested in Christian origins need to consider questions of race and ethnicity more thoroughly than we have and how both scholarship and activism can benefit from doing so. This call is directed primarily to mainstream theology and historical scholarship on Christianity, which still has much to gain from the challenges and visions offered by voices marginalized by ideology and/or social location.[8]

I offer an interpretation of early Christian strategies of self-definition that resonates both with ancient interpretations of cultural difference and modern ones. My hope is that contemporary readers will find this interpretation valuable for rethinking the metaphors and methods that continue to influence reconstructions of early Christianness and for rethinking how to grapple with ongoing efforts to address Christian anti-Judaism and racism. If future generations of readers find that this project no longer speaks to their contemporary situation, I hope it will be because we will have transformed our world for the better.

This book would not have been possible without generous support, encouragement, and sometimes prodding from many people and institutions. I owe a great debt to my teachers John Gager, Bernadette Brooten, and Elisabeth Schüssler Fiorenza for the ways they sparked my thinking about Christian anti-Judaism and its implications for historical analysis. My colleague Denise McCoskey helped enormously in the early phases of imagining how and why we need to bring critical race theory into conversation with antiquity. There is no substitute for colleagues and friends who understood what I was attempting and pushed me in just the right ways. Caroline Johnson Hodge, Melanie Johnson-DeBaufre, and Laura Muench-Nasrallah know this project from the inside out; one could not ask for better friends (and colleagues). Special thanks for enthusiasm, support, and valuable feedback to: Gay Byron, Elizabeth Castelli, Karen King, Wendy Lochner, Larry Wills, and my anonymous reader from Columbia University Press.

I was able to benefit from feedback on specific portions of the book-in-progress, thanks to opportunities to present my work at Colgate University, Harvard Divinity School, and Occidental College, as well as the North American Patristics Society, the American Philological Association, and the Society for Biblical Literature. More intimate settings also provided timely and valuable input; for this, I warmly thank all the participants in the Brown University Seminar on Culture and Religion in the Ancient Mediterranean World, the Models of Piety in Late Antiquity Group, the Boston Patristics Group, and the Oakley Faculty Seminar on Martyrdom in the Ancient Mediterranean World at Williams College.

Much of my early writing was made possible by the support and community of the Radcliffe Institute for Advanced Study, where I held a fellowship in 2000 and 2001; Cathy Silber, Francesca Sawaya, Augusta Rohrbach, and

Lisa Herschbach, fellow members of an intrepid writing group, valiantly read early versions of a number of chapters. An additional semester's leave from Williams College allowed me to maintain my writing momentum at a crucial time. Ideas in the book have appeared in two earlier articles: "Race and Universalism in Early Christianity"[9] and "Rethinking the Relevance of Race for Early Christian Self-Definition."[10] Thanks to the journals for permission to reprint portions of the articles here.

# WHY
# THIS
# NEW
# RACE

■

# Introduction

"Why this new race [*genos*]?" is a question posed by an early Christian about Christians.[1] The very presence of this question challenges conventional ways of thinking about the relationship between Christian origins and race/ethnicity. Most people—Christian or not—do not think of Christianity as *necessarily* linked with race or ethnicity. Indeed, most historical reconstructions published in the last twenty years depict earliest Christianity as an inclusive movement that *rejected* ethnic or racial specificity as a condition of religious identity. "Christianity swept racial distinctions aside," proclaims classicist Frank Snowden Jr.[2] Similarly, Anthony Smith, writing for anthropologists as well as historians, states that earliest Christianity "helped to . . . transcend existing ethnic divisions."[3] Feminist theologian Rosemary Radford Ruether asserts that "class, ethnicity, and gender are . . . specifically singled out as the divisions overcome by redemption in Christ."[4] And in his recent study of early Christianity, Guy Stroumsa baldly states: "Ethnic terms were deeply irrelevant for the Christians."[5] These four examples are typical in making the rejection of race or ethnicity a defining feature of earliest Christianity.

But if early Christians defined themselves in terms of being able to transcend ethnicity or race, then what is an early Christian text doing defining Christians in terms of a *genos*? *Genos* is a term widely used for Greeks, Egyptians, Romans, and *Ioudaioi*—groups often interpreted as ethnic groups or their ancient equivalents. How does this square with the widespread evidence that early Christians also made universalizing claims about Christianness—that anyone could become a Christian? The central argument of this book is that early Christian texts used culturally available understandings of human difference, which we can analyze in terms of our modern concepts of "ethnicity," "race," and "religion," to shape what we have come to call a religious tradition and to portray particular forms of Christianness as universal and authoritative.

Whether translated as "race," "ethnicity," "people," "lineage," "kind," "class," or "sex," *genos* is a term that ancient readers would have understood to signal a group classification. While it has a broad range of possible meanings in Greek,[6] it frequently demarcates groups whose members apparently share certain characteristics (which can include ancestors, rights of inheritance, knowledge, ritual practices, and ways of life, among other things). Christians also referred to themselves using other language that their contemporaries would have understood as positioning Christians as comparable to groups such as Jews, Greeks, and Romans: the terms *ethnos, laos, politeia* (Greek), and *genus* and *natio* (Latin) pepper early Christian texts.

While the vocabulary of peoplehood and human difference offers an important entry point for examining early Christian self-definition, even more important than the presence of specific terms are the *rhetorical situations* in which early Christian texts use ideas about peoplehood to communicate and persuade readers about Christianness. "Ethnic reasoning" refers to the modes of persuasion that may or may not include the use of a specific vocabulary of peoplehood.[7] Early Christians used ethnic reasoning to legitimize various forms of Christianness as the universal, most authentic manifestation of humanity, and it offered Christians both a way to define themselves relative to "outsiders" and to compete with other "insiders" to assert the superiority of their varying visions of Christianness.

## Four Strategic Uses of Ethnic Reasoning for Early Christians

Early Christians found ethnic reasoning useful in their projects of self-definition for many reasons. This book explores four especially significant reasons for and applications of ethnic reasoning. First, race/ethnicity was often deemed to be produced and indicated by religious practices. Early Christians adapted existing understandings of what ethnicity and race are and how they relate to religiosity by reinterpreting the language of peoplehood readily available to them in the biblical texts they shared with (other) Jews, as well as political and civic language used broadly to speak about citizenship and peoplehood in the Roman Empire. Nonetheless, early Christians were consistent with the views of their contemporaries when they emphasize a close link between religious practices, cult membership or participation, and ethnoracial identity. Ethnic reasoning offered Christians one way to negotiate their identities in the imperial landscape.

Second, although ancient authors frequently refer to membership in a *genos*, *ethnos*, *laos*, and *phylon* as a matter of one's birth and descent (that is, as fixed or ascribed), such membership was nonetheless seen to be mutable. Early Christians capitalized on this dynamic character of ethnicity/race as being both fixed and fluid in a range of ways. The common description of conversion as rebirth illustrates one central way in which Christians depicted Christianness simultaneously in terms of "essence" and transformation.

Third, this juxtaposition of fluidity and fixity enabled early Christians to use ethnic reasoning to make universalizing claims, arguing that everyone can, and thus ought to, become a Christian. By conceptualizing race as both mutable and "real," early Christians could define Christianness both as a distinct category in contrast to other peoples (including Jews, Greeks, Romans, Egyptians, etc.) and also as inclusive, since it is a category formed out of individuals from a range of different races.[8]

Finally, early Christians also used ethnic reasoning polemically, especially to compete with one another. In the first few centuries of the common era, Christianity was a work-in-progress with no official form; those whom we study as early Christians actually make up a broad range of different groups, practices, and beliefs. Either by condemning the religious practices and beliefs of rival Christians to encapsulate Christianness (point one, above), by accusing rival Christians of overstating the "fixity" of one's identity and thus limiting the possibilities for transformation (point two), or by construing rival Christian groups as particular rather than universal (point three), early Christians wielded ethnic reasoning both to authorize their own visions of Christianness and to caricature and exclude competing alternatives. Christians could tailor each of these arguments to criticize non-Christian groups as well.

Using ethnicity and race as analytical categories reveals a multivalent set of rhetorical strategies for early Christian self-definition that cuts across and interrupts conventional classifications of early Christian literature. Attention to ethnic reasoning requires us to consider apologetic treatises in relation to martyrdom narratives, writings of "church Fathers" in the same breath as Nag Hammadi treatises, apocryphal acts with pedagogical treatises, and so on. But in addition to breaching the generic classifications of literature, attention to ethnic reasoning helps to provide alternative historical explanations for the relationship among varieties of early Christians and between Christians and non-Christians.

To reconceptualize early Christian self-definition in terms of ethnic reasoning sheds new light on Christian-Jewish, Christian-imperial, Christian-local, and intra-Christian relations. In the case of Christian-Jewish relations, attention to ethnic reasoning resists the impulse to reconstruct Christianness over and against Jewishness and resists periodizations that mark an early and decisive split between Christianity and Judaism.[9] And since ethnic reasoning also resonates with non-Jewish cultural practices of self-definition, it offers an analytic point of entry that requires attention to both Jewish and non-Jewish frames of reference, not to one at the expense of the other, and to both as being integrally part of Christian self-definition, not as its "background."[10]

Viewing Christian strategies of self-definition in relation to the power of the Roman Empire is also vital for evaluating the possible meanings and ramifications of ethnic reasoning. As formulations of those not in power, pre-Constantinian Christian texts that employ ethnic reasoning can be read as attempts to consolidate and mobilize geographically, theologically, and organizationally disparate groups under one banner—figured as a people, "the Christians." Conceptually, early Christians share some strategies in common with local populations in the empire who also seek to define and negotiate their collective identities in relation to a larger imperial "whole." Early Christians in specific cities or regions (for example, Sardis or Asia Minor), like Lydians, sometimes define themselves in relation to a larger whole: for Christians, this larger whole could be "Christians" conceived as a translocal phenomenon in relation to and encompassing "Greeks," the Roman Empire, or the human race; for Lydians, this larger whole could be Asia Minor or Greeks.[11] Yet, also like the Lydians, early Christians most frequently claim an identity that remains distinctive and coherent in relation to a larger whole. Not all Christians took the same approach. Some Christians devised a discourse of peoplehood that functioned to construct a sense of a unified community and claim political legitimacy despite and sometimes in response to persistent local differences, while other Christians invoked ethnic reasoning to define Christianness as particular and distinct from other communal identities, including other forms of Christianness.

One way to consider the question of the relation between ethnicity, race, and Christianness is to chart the range of ethnic groups who joined the emerging forms of Christianity and to explore how ethnic identities would have affected the character and development of particular Christian communities across the Mediterranean basin. I am not attempting this kind of analysis. Christianity did develop in regionally specific ways, and the heterogeneity of its adherents is clear from the evidence for Christian communities scattered across the Roman Empire and beyond. Such studies complement my own insofar as they illuminate the ways that Christianness comes into being in local, particularized forms,[12] even as some Christian writers craft textual idealizations of Christianness as universal. But I am not trying to link particular, local forms of Christianness to any preexisting ethnic or civic identities. I argue that specific contexts in which early Christians define themselves matter *not* because, for example, Galatians were inescapably shaped by their "Celtic" heritage (and thus produced corresponding forms of Christianness).[13] Instead, a consideration of the particular social, political, and historical conditions of Galatia can illuminate the significance of early Christian uses of certain rhetorical strategies of ethnoracial self-definition—the same strategies used in Alexandria, Carthage, or Rome might resonate quite differently.

## Rethinking the Apparent Fixity and Particularity of Race and Ethnicity: Questions of Definition

We have failed to recognize the importance and functions of ethnic reasoning in early Christian self-definition largely because of how dominant *modern* ideas about race, ethnicity, and religion inform our approaches to and presuppositions about the meanings of those three terms (including their possible relationships). We cannot avoid reckoning with modern ideas about race, ethnicity, and religion, so the problem is not that modern ideas are distorting historical analysis, since we can only interpret the past from the vantage point of the present. As long we continue to read texts from antiquity, it is necessary to tackle the interpretive and ethical challenges of making our readings intelligible to modern readers and persuasive within the parameters of the ancient text. These tasks are intertwined, of course, to the extent that our ability to measure of the persuasiveness of a reading for its context cannot be separated from our present assessment of the historical context. Noting some of the ways in which race and ethnicity currently inform interpretations of early Christianity will clarify why I take a different approach.

There is no single way that all people think or speak about race and ethnicity today. Most of us are familiar with the perception that race and ethnicity are "given." Whether defined in terms of biology, our family background, cultural inheritance, and so on, race and ethnicity are often spoken of as attributes about which we have no say, something we are born with.

At the same time, most are also probably familiar with the view that race and ethnicity are social constructions, meaning that they exist and have real significance in our lives because the societies in which we live organize and classify humans into "races" and "ethnicities." This classification process is social and cultural. Even if race and ethnicity seem to point to "real" and fixed human differences, changes in how races and ethnicities are defined over time indicates that they are in fact social creations and not eternal realities.

In contrast, most people speak about religious identity as voluntary, even when many of us experience religion as "given," either as part of our racial or ethnic identities or minimally as an involuntary part of our upbringing. This perception of voluntariness is reinforced by widespread perceptions that it is possible to convert from one religion to another, on the basis of strongly held personal views. This is despite the fact that in Northern Ireland, the terms "Catholic" and "Protestant" have functioned as seemingly fixed affiliations for many in speaking about political divisions. Furthermore, most of us can also think of recent and ongoing conflicts where religion and ethnicity are treated as fundamentally intertwined—such as among Albanians, Serbs, and Bosnians in the former Yugoslavia or between Palestinians (primarily equated with Muslim, despite the presence of Palestinian Christians) and Israelis (primarily equated with Jews, although there are non-Jewish Israeli citizens, including Palestinians).

In many interpretations of early Christianity, race and ethnicity continue to be treated as if they connote a fixed or given facet of identity, while religion is primarily viewed as voluntary. When these assumptions are unquestioned, race and ethnicity appear to be in tension with Christianity because Christianity is understood to be not only a "religion" but also a category open to all people and gained through conversion. Universalism and conversion both imply a fluidity that race and ethnicity seem to lack (when viewed as "fixed"). An understanding of race and ethnicity as concepts that are fluid and subject to change even when they are depicted as fixed allows for a different interpretation of the relationship between race/ethnicity and religion in early Christian texts and imagination.

## An Alternative View

As I shall discuss in more detail (especially in chapter 1), instead of viewing race or ethnicity as ascribed or fixed, I suggest that we view each as concepts to which fixity is *attributed* but that are nevertheless malleable. I draw this approach especially from anthropologist Ann Stoler's argument that "the force of racial discourse is precisely in the double-vision it allows, in the fact that it combines notions of fixity and fluidity in ways that are basic to its dynamic."[14] What Stoler argues about race is more widely accepted as applicable to ethnicity. While *appeals* to ethnicity and especially race as fixed are indeed a common feature of modern ways of thinking and often correlated with oppressive policies and practices, both ethnicity and race also always entail fluidity. What do I mean by this? Simply that these concepts are always unstable—they are not always defined in the same ways in all contexts, and considerable energy and anxiety have been expended to "secure" stable meanings for race/ethnicity in colonial and racist regimes. Certainly some fundamental "essence" such as blood, flesh, or seed is often asserted as the basis for reckoning membership in an ethnoracial group and is traceable through means such as genealogy and kinship. But ideas about race and ethnicity gain persuasive power by being subject to revision while purporting to speak about fundamental essences.

The fluidity of race and ethnicity may be revealed in change over time, in the active competition over the meaning of race/ethnicity in a particular moment, or in specific arguments about the fluidity of the two terms. In the introduction to a collection of essays on ancient perceptions of Greek ethnicity, Irad Malkin notes that most sociologists and anthropologists, and now also many classicists and ancient historians, reject the notion that there is any fundamental essence to ethnicity in favor of the view that ethnicity is a contingent, social construction.[15] Stoler identifies a similar trend in contemporary historical studies of race, a trend she calls an "attack on immutability."[16] Stoler and Malkin want to resituate scholarly discussions away from the question of whether or not race/ethnicity is fixed or mutable to analyses of how discourses of race and ethnicity rely upon the notion of fixity or primordiality even while they are also always under negotiation and flux.[17]

Gerd Baumann also develops this view, arguing that two discourses coexist in the practice of ethnicity as well as religion: the first being an essentializing discourse that emphasizes ethnicity or religion as having some inherent, eternal core (fixity); and the second a "processual" discourse that emphasizes change and transformation of cultural phenomena (fluidity). Members of ethnic and religious groups (particularly those who hold less cultural power), as well as the media, are more likely to assert a fixed (also known as "primordialist") view of ethnicity or religion, while academics and members of "unmarked" or dominant ethnic groups are more likely to espouse the view that ethnicity and religion are either mutable or strategic (which correlates with what is known as the "instrumentalist" or processual view).[18]

But instead of offering these two discourses as mutually exclusive, Baumann shares with Stoler and Malkin the view that they regularly function together as a "dual discursive construction." He gives a hypothetical example of a person wishing to "strengthen the sense of solidarity and unity among a group of followers." To do so,

> The leader needs to preach an essentialist theory of culture: "Our group will act and will be, and deep down has always been, united in its thinking and identity." Yet employing this essentialist rhetoric is in fact a creative act. The rhetoric is essentialist, yet the activity is processual. Culture is said . . . to be rooted in an unchangeable past, yet the leader can hope to create it *because* he or she knows culture to be malleable and pliable, open to change. . . . What the culture-forging leader preaches is the essentialist theory; what he or she practices is the processual theory.[19]

These two positions function together to reinforce the notion of ethnicity as ascribed even as the very terms by which this ascription is defined are changed. This insight removes both the need to explain away claims for the reality of ethnic or racial identities as false consciousness and the need to "prove" their reality by biological or physiological means.

Baumann distinguishes between ethnicity and religion, depicting them as two parallel cultural constructions that offer competing strategies for making claims to individual and collective rights in the nation-state.[20] Nevertheless, he also notes that they can intersect in a number of ways, ranging from a state-imposed equation of religious and ethnic boundaries (Bosnian Muslims) to a rhetorical definition of one as the other (he views the sectarian conflicts in Northern Ireland as a case of national and ethnic conflicts being translated into a religious register).[21]

While aimed at studies of modern cultures, these suggestions are valuable for historical studies as well. He rightly contends that we can accomplish a more subtle understanding of what religion, ethnicity, and nationality can mean in a given context and how these categories converge and diverge in people's lives by deliberately researching against the grain of reifying discourses and across the social cleavages said reifying discourses seek to produce and maintain.[22]

Approaching race/ethnicity, as well as religion, as characterized by a double-sided discourse of fixity and fluidity allows us to revise prevailing interpretations of the significance of race/ethnicity for early Christians. Many early Christian texts depict Christians as members of a people, like Jews. "Race" does not mark the dividing line between Jews and Christians. Christians depicted Christianness as having an "essence" (a fixed content) that can be acquired. Christians could define conversion as both the transformation of one's ethnicity and the restoration of one's true identity. By portraying this transformation as available to all, Christians universalized this ethnoracial transformation. Instead of positioning Christianness as *not-race*, or aracial, many early Christian texts defined their version of Christianity as a race or ethnicity, sometimes in opposition to other rival articulations of Christianness, and sometimes in contrast to non-Christian groups and cultures (including, but not limited, to those defined as "Jews").

It is fair to say that the majority opinion about ethnicity among anthropologists and sociologists, as well as by other scholars who draw upon their work, is that ethnicity entails claims of common kinship or descent from a common group or ancestor. That is, such claims are generally viewed as a necessary criterion of ethnicity—if we find these claims, we might have "ethnicity"; if we do not, then we do not have ethnicity.[23] If we use this definition of ethnicity, then we find that early Christians do largely conform to it, insofar as many wrote about Christians as united by common ties of kinship to a range of figures—God, Christ, Abraham, Seth—and to other groups, such as the Hebrews or Israelites.

Without minimizing the prevalence of ancient appeals to kinship and descent in formulating claims of collective identity, I depart somewhat from this limited definition of ethnicity. Following Stoler, I define the necessary criterion of ethnicity/race as the dynamic interplay between fixity and fluidity. Appeals to kinship and descent are one significant way in which the "reality" and "essence" (or fixity) of ethnicity/race is articulated. Just as "blood" is a powerful *symbol* for the relationship implied by the concept "kinship" in our culture, but is not in fact its essence, so too are "kinship" and "descent" symbols for the fixity or enduringness implied by the concept of "ethnicity."[24] When kinship and descent participate in the fluid aspect of ethnicity, insofar as descent and kin relations shift and can be redrawn (discursively or ritually) to exclude and include individuals and groups, these signs of fluidity are often accounted for by asserting that ethnic claims of descent and kinship are "fictive" rather than "real." But this distinction falsely implies that there is an intrinsic content to kinship or descent, when in fact these are analytical categories created by scholars to account for a diverse range of social organizations, practices, and cultural symbols.[25]

Most definitions of ethnicity acknowledge that other factors (language, religion, place, foodways) may be claimed by a given community as more central than kinship or descent. Nonetheless, when kinship and descent are privileged as necessary to ethnicity, these other factors are dismissed as mere "markers" or attributes of ethnicity, rather than being ethnicity's constitutive elements.

Foregrounding fixity/fluidity, rather than some specific content like kinship and descent, risks making ethnicity/race indistinguishable from other cultural categories, such as religion and citizenship, since both of these could also be said to share this dynamic of fixity and fluidity. I invite the reader to explore rather than predetermine their interrelationships.

## Implications of Viewing Race and Ethnicity as "Fixed"

The almost unanimous view that early Christians defined themselves over and against ethnic or racial specificity (that is, as a movement open to all humans regardless of ethnicity and race) relies on an understanding of race/ethnicity as ascribed or fixed. Race and ethnicity are positioned as irrelevant to early Christian self-definition because they seem to contrast with universalism. In this way of thinking, racially or ethnically specific forms of Christianity may exist, but these variations are viewed either as incidental (not affecting a perceived underlying essence of Christianity) or as problematic (obstructing the achievement of a Christian ideal to dissolve racially or ethnically linked forms of religion and society). This interpretation of the relationship of race/ethnicity to Christianity was especially elaborated in modern historical contexts in light of arguments that race/ethnicity are natural, biological traits.

The contemporary resistance to thinking about early Christian self-definition in terms of race is partly a response to the legacy of modern notions of race as they emerged in Romanticism and scientific racism. The interpretation of Christian origins formulated by the nineteenth-century French philologist Ernest Renan illustrates the kind of legacy that scholars concerned with promoting civil rights, such as Snowden and Reuther, have sought to challenge. Renan's 1863 *Life of Jesus* was hugely popular. It went through more than sixty-one editions in French, was translated into English and German, and was widely commented on within a year of its publication.[26] His work has been credited with introducing "racial categories into theological discussion." For Renan, Jesus was an *Aryan* Jew, and his main rivals, the Pharisees, were Semitic Jews.[27] This racial mapping allows Renan to portray Christianity as arising naturally out of Judaism, while his category "Aryan Jew" also permits him to write that Christianity "over time rid itself of nearly everything it took from the race, so that those who consider Christianity to be the Aryan religion par excellence are in many respects correct."[28]

By the end of the nineteenth century, Renan's attempt to align Christians with a particular race was largely undone—at least in the academy—

and was replaced by a widespread view of Christianness as emphatically not a race. In the study of Christianity, and especially Christian origins, this shift has translated into an emphasis upon defining the difference between Christianity and Judaism as that of an ideally universal religion versus a religion of a particular people.

This legacy has been both positive and negative. On the positive side, at least since the early nineteenth century, the notion of Christian origins as racially inclusive and egalitarian has supported opposition to Christian and non-Christian practices that sanction differential treatment on the basis of "race." Especially in North America, certain biblical passages have been crucial in formulating the transcendence of racial difference as an original Christian ideal, especially within the African American biblical interpretation, to combat white Christian racism. "God is no respecter of persons: But in every nation one who fears [God], and works righteousness, is accepted with [God]" (Acts 10:34–35); "For [God] has made of one blood all the nations of the world to dwell on the face of the earth" (Acts 17:26); and "There is neither Jew nor Greek, neither slave nor free, male and female: for you are all one in Christ Jesus" (Gal. 3:28) are three of the most well-known New Testament passages cited to challenge racist forms of Christianity.[29] The interpretation of these New Testament passages as indicative of explicitly nonracialized Christian origins depends on a historical model of Christian history that moves from "pure" origins to less pure realizations of Christianity over time. When Christian practices and structures contribute to racist and ethnocentric oppression, this outcome has often been interpreted as a failure to realize the universalistic and egalitarian ideals inherent in earliest Christianity.[30] This argument presupposes a sharp distinction between universalism and ethnic/racial particularity. While important for antiracist interventions, especially the North American civil rights efforts, defining Christianness in contrast to race has not solved the problems of modern racism. This construction of universalism also paradoxically perpetuates anti-Judaism in the name of antiracism.

Appeals to earliest Christianity's universalism have also had a negative legacy, because claims that earliest Christianity transcended ethnoracial distinctions have often been formulated over and against a definition of Jewishness. "Ethnicity" in particular continues to surface as a crucial explanation for differences between Jews and Christians, both in the Roman period and in the present. The authors of a recent book on the religions of the Roman Empire, for example, state bluntly: "Christianity lacked the ethnic links of Judaism."[31] That is, modern understandings of ethnicity as inherent and immutable have been used especially to differentiate early Christians from other Jews. In Christian interpretations, this kind of distinction most often conveys a negative view of Judaism because Christianity's universalism is defined as an improvement on the exclusive particularity of Judaism.[32]

I live in a country that is still deeply racist, and one in which anti-Judaism also persists, as the controversy over Mel Gibson's 2004 film *The Passion of Christ* has made clear. Furthermore, violence and genocide perpetrated along ethnic lines escalated in the latter part of the twentieth century in many parts of the world (for example, in Rwanda and Burundi as well as the former Yugoslavia). My desire to formulate an interpretive framework that resists both racism and anti-Judaism leads me to favor a view of race and ethnicity not typically used to interpret early Christian self-definition. I am trying to accomplish two things simultaneously: first, to join current efforts to dismantle racist logic in the present, especially as it plays out in American deployments of white supremacy, by offering a reading of Christian origins in which alternative constructions and contestations of race and ethnicity are at play; and second, to join efforts to dismantle Christian anti-Judaism by calling into question readings that naturalize the differences between Christianness and Jewishness along an axis of ethnic/nonethnic, where ethnicity is defined as a given, biological category. These goals form part of my larger feminist commitment to the notion that racism and anti-Judaism are produced and sustained in relation to other webs of oppression, especially sexism, heterosexism, and classism.

I am convinced that interpretive frameworks that implicitly or explicitly make race or ethnicity a primary site of difference between Jewishness and Christianness in the ancient world will continue to produce a harmful modern paradox. If Christianness gets defined as ideally nonracial or nonethnic, in contrast to Jewishness, then even critiques *within* Christianity about the tradition's failure to realize this ideal may unintentionally reinforce a form of racially inflected Christian anti-Judaism. In other words, definitions of Christianity's racially inclusive ideal will perpetuate a racially loaded form of anti-Judaism if the implied point of contrast to Christianity's inclusiveness is Jewishness.[33] Furthermore, this model risks sustaining white privilege by positioning Christianity as intrinsically separate from ethnicity/race and by offering a problematic loophole for whites to avoid examining the ways that racism has infused dominant forms of Christian theology and practice.[34]

To help remove this paradox, I reread of a range of early Christian texts that understand Christianness as always implicated in broader cultural struggles over forms of affiliation and identification. Instead of presuming that ethnicity and race are fixed aspects of identity, I approach these concepts as dynamic and characterized by an interaction of appeals to fluidity and fixity. This is not the last word, but is intended to open up new lines of conversation and debate among historians and those interested in these contemporary issues. I find a double-sided conceptualization of race and ethnicity compelling not only for our time but also for antiquity. This is not because it is the only way to speak about these concepts, or because I see modern and ancient ideas as the same. This approach allows us to render early Christian discourse "knowable," but does not require that we collapse historical differences.

My argument is twofold: it is necessary to explain why and how early Christians used notions of peoplehood to define themselves as well as to scrutinize our current habits of thought and assumptions about race, ethnicity, and religion in writing history. Our understandings of race and ethnicity have their own modern histories that require both investigation and exorcism.

## The Use of "Race" in This Study

Those who feel comfortable speaking about race and ethnicity with regards to early Christianity usually insist that early Christianity was defined in opposition to these categories. Others, however, insist that "race" is an inappropriate category to use for early Christian history. Especially since the publication of Martin Bernal's first volume of *Black Athena* in 1987, "race" has fallen out of favor as an analytical category for classical antiquity.[35] The arguments against using race rely on a definition of race as clear, immutable, grounded in biology, and especially indicated by skin color. Thus defined, race (in contrast to "ethnicity") is deemed irrelevant for antiquity because it is anachronistic. Since this particular formulation does not appear in surviving ancient Mediterranean texts, so the logic goes, one should not import "race" into the study of antiquity. These scholars insist that modern biological definitions of race are just that—modern—and imply that "race" as a category cannot be defined in any other manner. As a result, they advocate that "we should strive to see that it is eliminated from both public and private usage."[36] In contrast, these scholars tend to view "ethnicity" as a suitable category for analysis of Mediterranean antiquity.[37]

At stake in these objections and this solution are at least three things: the view that "ethnicity" is sufficiently distinct from "race" and consequently that the former can serve as a relevant category for historical analysis while the latter ought to be dismissed; concern about avoiding a historical method that makes the past conform to the terms of the present; and concern over the noxiousness of "race" because of its relationship to racism.[38]

We can see these points clearly in a 2001 issue of the *Journal of Medieval and Early Modern Studies* devoted to race as an analytical category for medieval history. In his concluding essay to the issue, William Chester Jordan expresses skepticism about the usefulness of the term: "I cannot prove," he writes, "but I do not believe that readers will sufficiently shed their modern notions of race simply because scholars redefine the concept against the modern grain, so that medieval race can encompass change and independent nonbiological markers."[39] Jordan suggests that race can only be thought of as an "allegedly fixed category" whereas ethnicity is preferable because it "can be (not always is, but can be) understood as a process."[40] He is certainly not alone in this view about the differences between race and ethnicity.[41] Jordan does not say that scholars *cannot* redefine race, but he questions whether readers will take up such alternative interpretations of race. He makes an important point about the pernicious effects of associating race in particular with immutability—a problem he thinks ethnicity can potentially avoid.

In the rest of this section, I respond to these concerns with three main points. First, I am not convinced by the way that most scholars differentiate "race" from "ethnicity" to justify the exclusion of "race" for historical analysis. While this book intentionally uses the terms interchangeably, this is not because I think they are necessarily synonymous;[42] rather, I am provoking attention to their inexactness—both in the contemporary moment and in their relationship to ancient categories of cultural difference. "Ethnicity" is also a modern category, so its appropriateness for the interpretation of early Christianity (or medieval history) is no more or less obvious than "race." Second, we need to reconsider the charge of anachronism in light of broader questions about how we write history. "Race," "ethnicity," and "religion" are all modern categories. The question of the viability of using these categories to speak about ancient self-understandings is partly about how to formulate an interpretive framework that accounts for historical difference while still being intelligible to the interpreter. But it is also about how to define these concepts now by asserting a difference between the present and the past. We can place modern categories into conversation with ancient ones without effacing their differences, even while we must also acknowledge that we can only understand those differences through the lens of our present. Third, while I share the concern to avoid perpetuating the noxious effects of racism, I do not think we avoid them by avoiding the term "race." In an era of genocidal "ethnic cleansing" in Rwanda and the former Yugoslavia, ethnocentrism has proven as noxious as racism. Furthermore, replacing race with ethnicity has obscured the racist aspects of using ethnicity to distinguish Jews from Christians.

■

One of the most familiar arguments about the irrelevance of "race" to early Christians was made famous by Frank Snowden Jr., who argued that by making differentiations among humans that we might call "racial," ancient inhabitants of the Mediterranean nonetheless differed radically from modern Americans and Europeans in that they did not attach a value judgment to skin color. Although she does not use the term "race" herself for antiquity, Gay Byron has posed a significant challenge to Snowden's thesis, as well as to historical reconstructions of Christianity as a religion in which "race" was irrelevant, by demonstrating a broad range of early Christian texts that employ "blackness" or "Ethiopians" in loaded ways.[43] Byron does not argue that there is no difference between modern racism and the rhetoric she interprets in early Christian texts, but her work rules out the comforting idea that there was a "golden age" of early Christianity in terms of the ways that ancient understandings of human difference functioned. She examines how blackness as well as persons classified as "Ethiopian" and "Egyptian" are woven into early Christian language—both positively (to indicate the universality of Christianity, that it includes even the "exotic" other from the ends of the earth) and negatively (to indicate the problematic "other" within). Snowden's and Byron's work offer good examples of how modern concerns about the formulation and deployment of race influence the topics the historians address. This book complements Byron's by examining a different set of rhetorical practices. I show how Christians conceptualized themselves not only as a group formed out of members of other peoples, but also as a people themselves.

Even if one is sympathetic to the view that it might be difficult to get readers to "shed their modern notions of race" to entertain the possibility that "medieval race can encompass change and independent nonbiological markers," it is vital to remember that this difficulty exists partly because *today* many people think of race as something that people in the past *used* to think about as fixed. Narratives about the history of race generally reinforce this perception. Such histories of race frequently seek to identify the historical "origins" of the concept. Even though agreed upon as a modern concept, there is very little consensus about precisely when and where "race" began. In an argument that scholars and students of early Christianity will find quite familiar, Ann Stoler notes that these quests for the origins of race serve authorizing functions for the present more than they secure knowledge about "race." Even more applicable to this study is Stoler's point that, regardless of when and where they identify the beginning of "race," these narratives depict race as initially invested with fixity. As she explains, "this adherence to the notion of fixity rests on the assumption that fixity was rooted in a commonly shared biological model of race, that some notion of 'immutability' was crucial to it, and that race was a concept unproblematically conceived as 'natural.' "[44] Histories of race often narrate the change over time in understandings of race from "fixed" to "constructed." This narrative arc positions the interpreter among those who have come to recognize the spuriousness of race's fixity while construing fixity as a fundamental feature of race in the past.

Stoler's research on the colonial Dutch Indies demonstrates that the notion that race is mutable is not, however, the result of twentieth-century challenges to scientific racism. In the colonies, she argues:

> Race could never be a matter of physiology alone. Cultural competency in Dutch customs, a sense of 'belonging' in a Dutch cultural milieu, a 'distance' and disaffiliation with things Javanese, as well as appropriate domestic arrangements, parenting styles and moral environment made up the ethnography of race. Each of these, to different degrees, and with strategic priority, were crucial to defining in law and everyday practice who was to have access to what privileges and who was to be considered European.[45]

That is, even when racial classifications are presented as "fixed," the range of colonial practices and institutions established to manage these allegedly fixed differences as well as the "slippage" in how individuals are classified minimally suggest that race was perceived to be fluid even if this fluidity was denied. Stoler persuasively suggests that "the porousness we assign to the contemporary concept of race may be a fluidity fundamental to the concept itself and not a hallmark of our postmodern moment."[46]

A number of scholars support Stoler's alternative approach to race by noting ways that "race" has, in the past, been viewed as mutable: "Lamarckian notions that acquired traits could be inheritable, and that human variation was responsive to environmental conditions were as much a part of nineteenth-century racial thinking and practice as those focused more squarely on the immutability and permanence of traits."[47] As Peter Harrison puts it: "In our present age, in which a Darwinian view of the influence of heredity and environment is taken for granted, we tend to forget that, prior to the nineteenth century, belief in the inheritance of acquired characteristics was widespread." This logic, often called "Lamarckian," after Darwin's famous rival, also extended to religion. One could also acquire and transmit good or false religiosity: "The most common hereditary religious affliction was idolatry."[48]

Harrison's work not only supports the perception of race as mutable but also complicates distinctions made between race, ethnicity, and religion. In early modern Britain and Europe, questions about human diversity (prompted especially by the "discovery" of the Americas, colonization, trade, and slavery) were discussed by Europeans as questions of religious diversity; in turn, religious diversity could be used to explain or correlated with racial difference.[49] For seventeenth-century Europeans interested in tracing the origins both of European peoples as well as "newly discovered" peoples, biblical narrative guided the analysis. Peoples were classified in relation to Noah's children,[50] and it was the link between Noah's children and their religious practices that were viewed as determinative of other national or racial features.[51] Thus, long before preachers of the American South linked Ham's "hereditary affliction" to race and racially based slavery,[52] European Christian authors defined this affliction in terms of *religion*: "Idolatry had, in modern parlance, a genetic basis, and as a result was characteristic of certain races—those races descended from Ham."[53]

Historians of North America have also shown that racial differences in the European colonies were defined along religious lines before the labor arrangements of slavery and eventually the biological sciences became the privileged sites for defining race.[54] In other European colonies such as India, it is not until the mid-nineteenth century that "race comes to replace religion as the defining characteristic of the British nation and its right to imperial rule."[55] Even so, religion and ethnicity/race remain closely interconnected in colonialism, since religious conversion could be perceived and intended to have ethnic/racial effects, especially as a challenge to modern discourses about the fixity of ethnic or cultural identities.[56]

Since race has been defined in many ways over time, we must ask what is at stake for modern scholars in excluding race from a historical analysis of classical antiquity by delimiting the meaning of "race" according to one particular modern definition, especially since classicists (among others) have begun to examine how the very tools for studying ancient history have their own modern histories that include both complicity in and resistance to modern racism and ethnocentrism.[57]

Despite the fact that both ethnicity and race are modern concepts, many scholars view ethnicity but not race as a viable analytical category for interpreting the ancient Mediterranean world, including the Hellenistic and Roman imperial periods.[58] How can one modern concept be ruled in and another ruled out? This apparent contradiction has everything to do with how they are defined relative to each other in the present.

Ethnicity cannot be understood without reference to race insofar as it is a term coined in the mid-twentieth century specifically as an alternative to biologically based understandings of race. The very distinction between these concepts must also be seen in light of the circumstances—especially World War II and the civil rights movement—that made desirable the formulation of a category like ethnicity to stand as an alternative to the biological ideas about race that were invoked to classify humans in ways that supported programs of genocide, colonialism, slavery, and class exploitation. In twenty-first-century America, we are still struggling with the nineteenth- and twentieth-century legacy of ideas about race as a biological or natural concept and the racist social policies these ideas continue to undergird. The claim that ethnicity can be perceived as mutable while race can only be perceived as immutable does not hold up. Biological definitions of race have largely come to be seen as the product of particular historical and social circumstances in modern European and American history; this paradoxically suggests that race is a sociocultural category, even as its "naturalized" associations are actually foregrounded by the coining of "ethnicity." Nonetheless, both ethnicity and race continue to *seem* "natural," and ethnicity is often used with biological or genetic connotations when used to convey identity linked to birth (not just upbringing, preferred food, clothing, or music).

We also need to remember that "religion" is a modern construction, by which certain phenomena are identified as belonging to the species "religion." Classifying phenomena within that species is a relatively recent enterprise.[59] So even if one argues that second-century Christians produced and practiced a different kind of religion than Coptic Christians or twentieth-century Lutherans, the persuasiveness of the argument rests not in the historical "proof" one cites but rather in the conceptualization of what religion can entail and how one interprets and classifies historical sources within the concept.

I am suspicious of the ways that certain modern concepts seem to be viewed as unproblematic for analysis of antiquity—religion, ethnicity, and gender, for example—whereas others have become "off-limits" ("race" and increasingly also "sexuality"). The use of familiar categories does not preclude analyses that destabilize modern meanings. Studies abound that attend to the differences between our modern understandings of family, gender, and social status (such as created through slavery) and ancient ones. Increasingly, sexuality is viewed as a modern concept without a direct correlation in antiquity; nonetheless, many studies explore the "prehistory" of the concept or still employ the modern term. The value of using our modern categories of race and ethnicity to talk about early Christian self-definition lies in the modern context for and consequences of historical interpretation.

In his introduction to an anthology of theories of ethnicity, Werner Sollors concludes by indirectly highlighting the need for further attention to how we study ethnicity and race in relation to religion. While noting the uncertainty about the philological origin of the English term "race," he speculates on the hypothesis that it derives from the Spanish and Castilian term *raza*:

> It was used in Castilian . . . to describe (and expel from Spain) people "tainted" by Jewish and Moorish blood—hence "race" in the "physical" and "visible" sense, we might think. Yet the list of people to which the doctrine of purity of blood (*limpieza de sangre*) was applied went on and included descendants of heretics and of "*penitenciados* (those condemned by the Inquisition)." Thus at this terrible beginning, "race" was hardly based on perception of "phenotypal" difference but on a religiously and politically, hence "culturally," defined distinction that was legislated to be hereditary, innate, and immutable.[60]

I am not interested in whether or not Sollors has in fact identified the origin of the term race. Rather, I want to underscore two points: first, we ought not to overstate the distinctions between race and ethnicity—since in this example *raza* "was what we would now call an 'ethnic' distinction."[61] Second, in spotlighting the cultural basis for defining *raza* in the context of the Spanish Inquisition and its aftermath, we find an example of how religion and race/ethnicity can interrelate. In this example, the definition of *raza* intersects with the definition of religion: to define who counted as an authentic Christian, as well as an authentic Spaniard, Christian authorities also formulated ideas about race. This project of classification was part of a larger political and colonial project with implications for defining gender, colonial and political status, as well as race/ethnicity and religiosity.[62] In the medieval and early modern Spanish context on the continent and in the colonies, religiosity and race are intertwined.

I am not suggesting that our modern understandings of race and ethnicity, which can themselves range quite broadly, were shared by inhabitants of the ancient Mediterranean world. The important differences between the discourses that produced the modern nation-state and those that produced the Roman Empire, and between the discourses that produced the variety of movements we analyze under the common rubric "early Christian" and those that serve modern Christians, raise questions about how we use historical readings in service of contemporary arguments. Our very ability to assert that there *are* important differences (or continuities) is always determined in the present and always has consequences for the present. If I insist on disjuncture between the Mediterranean world of late antiquity and today, these differences also underscore the contingent character of present-day modes of thought.

In order to evaluate the strengths and limitations of historical analysis we need to consider at least three things: the history of the interpretive frameworks we are using to make sense of the ancient sources, the present context in which we are writing, and the historical period in which early Christian texts were produced. This threefold consideration of historical interpretation has important implications for the ways we draw the boundaries around concepts like "race," "ethnicity," and "religion," as well as "gender," "sexuality," and "identity."

What Stoler suggests is fundamental to the concept of race, a combination of rhetorical and material fluidity and fixity,[63] is precisely what many ancient historians and classicists are now articulating as characteristic of ancient ethnicity and "cultural identity."[64] Indeed, her description of the ethnography of race in the Dutch Indies resembles the network of concerns that appear in texts that attempt to define Romanness, Greekness, Jewishness, as well as Christianness. For example, Greg Woolf has forcefully argued that Romans "valued common descent hardly at all, and regarded material culture and morality as much more central constituents of their sense of self."[65] Romans were also characterized by an ingathering of previously disparate peoples: "Roman identity was based to an unusual degree on membership in a political and religious community with common values and *mores* (customs, morality, and way of life)."[66] And crucially, the Roman *mos maiorum* was itself a double-edged concept, invoking stability ("ancestral ways") while nonetheless continuously under revision: "It was not an option to freeze an inherited identity of the Roman, based on the *mos maiorum*; the ancestral way was always disputed and changing."[67] Like Romans, early Christians do not view descent as a bar to (or a precondition of) becoming Christian; nonetheless, Christians also develop and ritually elaborate claims of primordial descent as a basis for defining the Christian community. Increasingly, studies of ancient materials are taking into account rhetorical claims that these categories of collective identification have some fundamental reality while also noting ways that they are malleable.[68]

Finally, I want to address the "avoid race because it's noxious" argument. Some classicists, such as Jonathan Hall, acknowledge the similarity between contemporary views of race as a socially constructed category and his definition of ancient ethnicity. Despite this, Hall expresses uncertainty as to "whether the term 'race' has yet outgrown its troubled past sufficiently to re-enter current social-scientific discourse."[69] If we want to move beyond racism, we cannot wait for it to outgrow its troubled past on its own; rather, we need to confront the elusive elasticity of race, since racism persists even when race has been exposed as a construct.[70]

Because our interpretive models for studying the ancient past have been formulated and revised within racist cultures, we need to keep the term active so as to be able to examine how our interpretive models encode, and thus perpetuate, particular notions about race.[71] By using the terms race and ethnicity interchangeably I signal my view that neither term has a one-to-one counterpart in antiquity; moreover, this choice indicates that these terms cannot be neatly distinguished even in modern parlance. I also want to keep modern readers alert to the contemporary stakes of historical work. By excluding the category of race from work on classical antiquity, we risk implying that our modern legacy of racial thinking can be shut off when we examine ancient texts and that our versions of ancient history are either irrelevant or alien to the ways that we handle questions of human sameness and difference in the present.

## The Modern Study of Religion Meets the Modern Study of Race and Ethnicity

We are used to thinking of science, especially the biological sciences, as the site for authoritative knowledge about race. But we have seen that "religion" had already been a domain for the production of ideas about racial difference.[72] The study of religion came into its own as a distinct discipline, with its own academic departments at the end of the nineteenth century, precisely at the moment when modern scientific disciplines were being formed and were cornering the market on cultural authority. What changes with the construction of religion as an academic discipline is not so much the interconnection of ways of thinking about race and religion than the dominant epistemological framework for doing so. This shift occurs in part alongside and through the consolidation of modern academic disciplines.[73] To be sure, this shift is monumental because it results in an apparent severing of the discourses of race and religion. Religion itself gets produced as an object of scientific inquiry, *parallel* to race, rather than the site of production of "race." I do not mean to suggest that religion was not already a discursive and cultural domain before academics so dubbed it, but rather that the perception of the category shifted.

Scholars shaping the study of religion recognized that this fledgling discipline would gain the greatest clout if its practitioners presented their work as scientific in method and approach. They not only named their pursuits as scientific, but they also embraced the ideal of value-neutral, empirical inquiry that aimed to produce ever-expanding "objective form[s] of knowledge."[74] This ideal of the detached observer who produces objective facts is the hallmark of modern scientific practices and disciplines. As Nancy Leys Stepan and Sander Gilman among others have noted, one troubling consequence of this epistemology is that it decentered and often disabled political and moral questions because this regime of knowledge claimed that it could offer "objective, neutral answers" about human difference.[75] Because late nineteenth-century scholars honed this epistemology through the science of race, sex, and sexuality and because the study of religion was at great pains to assert itself as a humanistic science, it would be surprising *not* to find ideas about race and sex in the models used to construct "religion" and its study.

These scientific practices authorized as objective knowledge ideas about race and ethnicity that were constructed in and through organic metaphors of sex, reproduction, and blood—ideas that were already in the air and especially salient in constructions of nationalism. The notion of nation as coterminous with race, and the Romantic idea of race as immutable and determined by "earth and particularly blood,"[76] were central to the articulation of German nationalism, for example, but in turn also mapped onto readings of history, especially the historical development of other peoples and nations—of Israel as well as other ancient peoples including Dorians and Greeks.[77] Regina Schwartz gives a clear example of how the well-known biblical critic Julius Wellhausen relied on such metaphors:

> Familiar nineteenth-century organic metaphors govern his discourse: innate tendencies "grow," a seed "flowers" into a nation. . . . Whether as the growth of an organism or the accretion of geologic deposits, this is the picture that he quickly applies not only to the development of the text, but to its plot, that is, to the biblical narrative's own account of history. Deftly, almost without our noticing, the story of Germany becomes the story of Israel.[78]

Not only do heterosexuality, sex, and race all become naturalized through mutually constituting organic metaphors; more ominously, these naturalized concepts take on both a vivid, concrete life *and* a covert life that sustains them. Concretely, they are institutionalized by social and political policies, legal rulings, and the like—this is most obvious in occupational and residential segregation.[79] Covertly, these metaphors lurk in the foundations of most academic frameworks for defining and studying history, science, anthropology, and religion, among other fields. In these contexts, organic metaphors may appear in disguise, as assertions of the totality of history, as evolutionary discourse, and as typologies of religion.[80] The metaphoricity with which these concepts and models are imbued has often gone unremarked as scientific experiments on organic matter—bodies—can function to transmute organic metaphors into perceived truths about organisms.

In the academic study of religion, race serves as a marker for distinguishing among types of religions. In the late nineteenth century, scholars tussled over how to define and classify religions, but often agreed that there were two basic types—even if they disagreed about the defining features of these types. William Whitney described the twofold division as that of "race-religion" and "a religion proceeding from an individual founder";[81] that is, for Whitney, race serves as primary basis for the two largest classifications of religion. In contrast, Whitney's contemporary Cornelius Tiele advocated an alternative dichotomous classification—between "nature" and "ethical" religions. In many respects, Tiele's alternative closely resembles Whitney's. For both, the former variety of religion ("race" or "nature") corresponds to local, indigenous religions, whereas the latter (from a single founder or "ethical") has a "revealed" or prophetic component.[82]

What Tiele's classification accomplishes, however, is a resituation of the significance of race. Far from disappearing, race now appears as the salient factor in distinguishing *between* "ethical" religions. For Tiele, nature religions are tied to specific races, states, or nations; but he thinks that this also holds true for almost all ethical religions. Tiele writes, "Most religions limit themselves to a particular people or nationality, it is as part and parcel of the civilisation to which they belong; but these two alone [Christianity and Buddhism] address themselves, not to a single people, but to all men and to every nation in its own language."[83] Most ethical religions are ethnically or nationally linked, whereas a rare few transcend this limit. Thus Tiele uses race as a way to define a small group of religions, including Christianity, as exceptional in not being racially linked.

The distinction between religions viewed as ethnoracially linked (and usually geographically specific) and those that are universal (in aspiration if not in reality) does not imply a single kind of relationship between "race" or "ethnicity" and "religion" but does carry with it a value judgment, since universal religions are often depicted as the evolutionary successors to religions that are tied to a particular social or cultural group or region: the ideal is to transcend the particular.[84]

Race and ethnicity have not only been used to classify and compare religions with one another in a given moment but also to assert the relationships among religions over time. In a sociopolitical context that supports the institutionalized disciplinary methods dominated by the notion of progressive time and evolution, this means that religions often get arranged developmentally as progressing from least developed to more developed.

Universalization and individualization (and secularization) are privileged as signs of cultural progress. In the study of Christianity, and especially Christian origins, this has translated into an emphasis upon defining the difference between Christianity and Judaism as that of an ideally universal religion versus a religion of a particular people. It has also allowed a masking or dismissal of the significance of how Christian congregations today still often correlate with ethnoracial communities (Irish Catholics, Greek Orthodox, Norwegian Lutherans, "Black church," and so on). That is, ideas about race and ethnicity have been used to define Christianity as a special *kind* of religion, one that is universal because it is not tied to a cultural marker of particularity, most notably race, despite acknowledged links in social arrangements.

While race and ethnicity may be used to define Christianity, Christianity has often served, explicitly or not, as the measuring stick for defining religion as a whole. The most obvious examples of this are the ways that belief (or faith), the idea of divinity (or God), and scripture have often been made essential criteria for determining whether or not something counts as a religion at all (Buddhism has sometimes not counted as a religion because a belief in god[s] is absent), or for determining what kind of religion it is (such as distinctions between practice- or ritual-centered religions and belief-centered ones, or religions that assert that there is only one God in contrast to those that assert that there are many gods, or religions that have a set body of authoritative texts like a Bible versus those that do not). In this way of thinking, aspects that are considered central to Christianity, especially Protestant Christianity, have often served as the basis for producing theories about religion overall. Just as "religion" is a construction whose contours have owed much to assumptions imbued with Christian resonances, so too "Christianity" is a construction with no singular manifestation. What counts as Christian has always been a matter of negotiation, argument, and revision. Christianity's privileged place as the unmarked referent for "religion" with its idealized construction as transcending race has meant that race and ethnicity function as indices of particular, marked religions.[85]

Scholarship since World War II has sought to dismantle approaches that reinscribe Romantic, social-evolutionist, and positivist readings of race and ethnicity and historical development of peoples and religions, as well as approaches to religion that privilege Christianity (especially in its Protestant forms). Regina Schwartz's work on biblical monotheism offers an important recent example; in her interpretation of Israel and biblical history she tries to account both for a "narrative that tends to construct identity as someone or some people set apart, with boundaries that could be mapped, ownership that could be titled" and the persistent instability of this identity: "if . . . the parameters of Israel's identity are always very much at issue, if which God is allowed and which is not, and which woman is allowed and which is not forever being contested, then the identity of the nation and the people is not already mapped, but in the process of being anxiously drawn and redrawn."[86] Most importantly for this study, Schwartz proceeds to link the questions raised by this tension with historiographical method and its implications:

> The biblical narrative's effort to construct Israel's past may well be an effort to construct Israel, but this is not a German historian's project, not a construction in the sense of building a building, or national spirit unfolding, or an organic personality flowering. Instead, the notion of "Israel" is an inconsistent, fractured, and multiple concept: a people who are bound by a law that they refuse to obey, a people who are defined by their nomadism but who are promised a land to settle in and embark on its conquest, a people who remember (or adopt) a shared history only to constantly forget it, a people who promise fidelity to their God only to go astray. And even these formulations are misleadingly stable, for each presupposes a "people" when defining them is very much a part of the task of this history.[87]

In reconstructing early Christian history, we need to heed Schwartz's insistence on identifying the slippages both between the historian, the text, and the historical reconstruction, as well as between the rhetoric of the text and the historical situation being conjured.

## Race and Ethnicity in the Modern Study of Christian Origins

Definitions of peoplehood, race, and ethnicity as natural, heritable, and immutable have left their mark on the study of Christian origins. Religion has no intrinsic or necessary relation to race or ethnicity. The ways in which ethnicity and race have been defined and interpreted in relation to the development of Christianity prior to its legalization in 313 vary widely, but have generally served to build and reinforce an understanding of Christianity as a universal religion. Both elements of this description, "universal" and "religion," are loaded; their connotations, both apart and when combined, have been forged at least partly in relation to the production of modern ideas about race and ethnicity, as well as gender and social status.

This section briefly outlines how organic and evolutionary metaphors about race and human difference lurk in the way scholars often reconstruct early Christian history, thereby creating an interpretation of the past that perpetuates modern habits about race, ethnicity, and religion that we would do well to break. By asking what kinds of assumptions about race, ethnicity, and religion shape our approaches to ancient history, we can understand why mainstream interpretive frameworks and presuppositions shape interpretations in such a way that the vast majority of historical accounts explain as absent or aberrant early Christian self-definition either in terms of race or ethnicity, or *as a race*.

Specialists in the study of Christian origins have produced their own kinds of classifications of religion. We find echoes of Tiele's framework in early twentieth-century explanations of early Christianity's relationship to its contemporary religious setting. In his influential 1933 study of conversion in antiquity, for example, Arthur Darby Nock distinguishes between two primary varieties of religion. He classifies most ancient Mediterranean religions as linked to particular communities and/or peoples, whereas he defines Judaism and Christianity, as well as Greek philosophical schools, as "prophetic" religions (characterized by the possibility of conversion).[88] In this work, prophetic religions correspond to what Tiele calls ethical religions.

The basic differences between Nock's two types of religion come down to this: the older, particularized type is ascribed, given, transmitted in culture, maintained through practices, and tied to or dependent upon a population group.[89] The second, prophetic type of religion is always acquired, and as such taken up as a matter of individual choice. It is belief-centered, and not inherently tied to any population group or culture. Nonetheless, Nock distinguishes *among* prophetic religions on the basis of the scope of their prophetic vision; that is, like Tiele's ethical religions, prophetic religions differ as to whether they are universal or restricted to a particular group/people. In this way, he distinguishes Judaism from Christianity. Nock sees Judaism as having universal potential but primarily restricted in practice to one people. Christianity, in contrast, he views as having emerged from Judaism precisely by departing from a national, ethnic restriction to include gentiles actively in its prophetic vision.[90] For Nock, it is not prophetic vision per se that makes Christianity separate from Judaism, but rather its fully actualized universal scope.

Reconstructions of early Christian history have generally been framed in relation to two central questions: "What is the original form of Christianity?" and "How and why did Christianity 'succeed'?" Although it may not appear so at first glance, both of these questions rely on modern ideas about race for answers. These questions have been problematized by many scholars of early Christianity for the last few decades. My work contributes to this impulse both by calling attention to the submerged ways that ideas about race support these framing questions and by outlining the benefits of devising alternative framing questions that tackle the deployment of ideas about race and ethnicity in early Christian texts.

The first question, regarding the original form of Christianity, is genealogical (in the non-Foucauldian sense). It presupposes that we can determine essence by looking at origins—and that there is a fundamental essence to be traced. It also contains within it a prior question: what makes Christianity different, distinct, or unique (that allows us to even speak about it having an origin)? Christianity is then studied implicitly in organic terms as a life form, with the presupposition that there is a fundamental essence or structure to this life form that may be altered in subsequent strains but which can be uncovered by tracing Christianity back to its original roots.[91] Within this line of questioning, the relationship between Christianity and Judaism becomes especially pressing: if Jesus was a Jew and his first followers were Jews—that is, if Christianity is itself traceable to Judaism—then what is the essence of Christianness that is not Jewishness?[92]

I want to underscore two points about the complex ways in which this question has been answered. First, this question demands an answer that defines Christianity as specific and different from Judaism, if not also from everything else in its day. Since the late nineteenth century, a privileged marker for distinguishing among phenomena, including religion, has been organic, biologized race. This means that there would be a strong tendency to define Christianity in racially inflected terms, to model the essence of Christianity's difference using organic metaphors associated with constructing racial differences among humans. So we might expect modern ideas about racial difference to support genealogical answers about Christianity's original essence.[93]

My second point, however, is that a racially informed model for Christianity had to be denied, even as it returns to haunt. This denial rests on the mapping I mentioned earlier, of Christianity as a kind of religion that is defined by its being *not* linked to race, and the higher value accorded to Christianity on this basis. Ironically, we may fail to see how, in the deployment of a developmental framework, Christian history is treated precisely *as the history of a people*.[94] That is, we fail to see that many of the structuring categories and explanations used to chart the development of Christianity or to analyze the differences among Christians rely on metaphors of sexual reproduction.[95] Moreover, these metaphors encode organic notions of racial and sexual difference that appear in preoccupations with what we might call miscegenation.

Three concepts in particular signal this concern with early Christianity's sexual/racial purity: "syncretism," "Judaizing," and "heresy." All three are used to explain differences within Christianity in terms of improper "mixing" of some original essence of Christianity with allegedly external elements.[96] Some feminists have noted how these concepts rely on sexual metaphors to explain the mixing process, and are gendered. Women, for example, are viewed as especially susceptible to heresy and Judaizing.[97] Others have noted that the search to identify the authentic core of Christianity serves the interest of those conducting the search and often "discovers" as the core that which has already been established as authentic by dogma and institutions.[98] Nonetheless, these important interventions do not call attention to the presence of modern ideas about race in the very framing of Christian history.

There is an irony here. Naturalized ideas about race help to structure the very classifications of religions despite the insistence on defining Christianity as not-race.[99] This racially linked notion of what religion is helps to explain why anti-Judaism persists in the face of reconstructions of Christian origins that are quite explicit about seeking to avoid this implication. By distinguishing Christianity as universal and racially unmarked, Judaism is constructed as its constitutive other—the racially marked particular. Furthermore, when these two complexes are located in a historical sequence, first Judaism, then Christianity, an evolutionary progression from particular to universal is implied.[100]

The second question that drives many scholarly reconstructions of early Christian history, "how did Christianity succeed?" is forward-looking, or teleological.[101] It takes success for granted and works backwards to seek causal explanations and contributing factors. The question of Christianity's original form is usually implied in the teleological question of Christianity's success. The teleological question has a negative twin: "When and how did Christianity go astray?" A negative teleology can be developed using a model of Christian degeneration—one that often relies on the idea of mixing (as seen in the concepts of syncretism and heresy) noted above.[102]

Answering the teleological question, either positively or negatively, means not just stating how Christianity is distinct, but especially how it is distinct from Judaism. How and when does this movement associated with the Jewish Jesus and his Jewish followers get to be something else? This means that one of the continuing questions in scholarly reconstructions is "when did Christianity break from Judaism?" Even scholars who actively resist producing histories that trumpet Christianity's history as one of triumph remain obsessed with this question.

Although the responses to this question vary in terms of timing and circumstance, the very formulation of the question implies that Christianity's coherency, if not success, depends upon having established a definitive break with Judaism.[103] What has remained strikingly consistent in the last century of mainstream scholarship is the assertion that Christianity's success (as well as its "break" with Judaism) correlates with its "going universal." But when we inquire about this universalism, it turns out that it is measured by the extent to which Christianity becomes a *gentile* movement that has transcended its particular roots in Judaism.[104] This is an odd measure of universality, since it depends on ancient dichotomies of self-other (Jew/gentile), adapted loosely so that "gentile" becomes "self" and the Jew becomes the "other" by which the self is defined.

In holding up for scrutiny the biologized assumptions that pervade the metaphors with which historiographical narratives have been devised, we are better able to inquire into their limits and implications. We need instead to view religion (including Christianity) as well as race and ethnicity, as strategic, contingent, and mutable concepts. As others have argued (without paying specific attention to ideas about race), we need to approach Christianity not as an essence but as a contested site—one defined and claimed by competing groups and individuals—and Christian history not as an evolving totality but rather as a series of ongoing struggles, negotiations, alliances, and challenges.[105] Our interpretive models should seek not an original essence for Christianity but rather highlight the processes and strategies of negotiation and persuasion that permeate the very creation of Christianness. By exposing the subtle persistence of a "fixed" and naturalized understanding of race in modern interpretive frameworks and by self-consciously producing interpretive frameworks that imagine race and ethnicity as discourses that rely on appeals to both fixity and fluidity, new ways of reconstructing Christian history emerge that *neither* insist that differences are natural and essential—and thus fundamentally incommensurable and unbridgeable—*nor* that all difference must be dissolved into one ultimate sameness.

# Toward an Alternative Reconstruction of Early Christian History

So how do these broader historiographical and epistemological issues affect the interpretation of early Christian texts? The *Epistle to Diognetus*, the writing that contains the question "Why this new race [*genos*]?", offers a glimpse of how a different approach to early Christian history can work, an approach that does not rely on either a genealogical or teleological framework.

The *Epistle to Diognetus* is a tantalizing early Christian text because of its unknowns: we do not know who wrote it, nor when or where it was written. The content suggests that it predates the legalization of Christianity; it might have been composed in Alexandria, Egypt about 200 C.E. These guesses themselves indicate the extent to which any interpreter of this (or any other) text always brings expectations and assumptions to the text that shape her interpretation. But in addition to questions of authorship and historical context, of course, our reading of texts also depends upon broader epistemological and theoretical choices, as this chapter has emphasized.

The *Epistle to Diognetus* opens with a series of questions about Christianity that the reader expects to have answered:

> I perceive, most excellent Diognetus, that you are exceedingly eager to learn about the piety (*theosebeia*) of the Christians and you are asking very clear and careful questions about them: who is the god in whom they believe, and how do they worship (*thrēskeuein*) it . . . and why this new race (*genos*) or practice (*epitēdeuma*) has come to life at this time, and not formerly.
>
> (*Ep. Diog.* 1.1).

By implying that the addressee of the text has already posed these questions, the narrator gives the impression that the discussion to follow is guileless, aiming only to answer Diognetus's "very clear and careful questions." These questions intrigue but they also raise further interpretive questions: how does the author control the depiction of Christianness by depicting these as the most salient issues—the details of this piety, concern with justifying its novelty? What is the significance of juxtaposing "race" with "practice"? How does the text address the question of Christians being considered a *genos*, the Greek term that I have translated as "race"?

Before addressing the specifics of the Christians in question, the narrator first offers a criticism of "Greeks" and "Jews," focusing specifically on their respective practices. Thus, the structure of the narrative makes Christians comparable with and parallel to Greeks and Jews, and then portrays Greekness and Jewishness especially via "religious" ideas and actions. Rhetorically, this positions Christians as comprising a *genos*, like Greeks and Jews; moreover, it implies that the salient content of a *genos* for this text is "religion," depicted in terms of both appropriate practices and the appropriate understanding of the object of worship. This structure raises the possibility that this text is defining "race" in quite a different way than is familiar to most modern readers. I develop these points further in chapter 1.

The speaker then turns to consider Christians, situating the topic in terms of the question of difference—what makes Christians distinct? The narrator's framing indicates that language, customs, and place of residence (if not origin) are among the accepted means of distinguishing people from one another. Nonetheless, he or she insists that these categories *fail* to determine Christian difference: "For the distinction between Christians and the rest of humanity is neither country nor language nor customs [*ēthe*]. For they do not dwell in cities in some place of their own, nor do they use any strange variety of dialect, nor practice an extraordinary kind of life" (*Ep. Diog.* 5.1–2). Since language and customs, as well as territory, were then, as they have sometimes been in the modern period, possible indexes of ethnicity and race, the narrator seems to unsettle the question of whether Christians are, in fact, a new race or a new practice.

But if Christians are not distinct in their manner of language, customs, or habitation, what—if anything—makes them different from non-Christians? Distinctiveness, it seems, is to be found in their political or civic status:

> Yet while living in Greek and barbarian cities, depending upon their respective situations, and following the local customs, both in clothing and food and in the rest of life, they display the wonderful and admittedly strange character of the constitution of their own citizenship (*politeia*). They dwell in their own homelands (*patria*), but as if visitors (*paroikoi*) in them; they share all things as citizens (*politai*) and suffer all things as foreigners (*zenoi*). . . . They pass their time upon the earth but have their citizenship in heaven.[106]
>
> (*Ep. Diog.* 5.4–5, 9)

What can we make of this? This text initially links Christians with a race (*genos*), but when we ask what this means, we find the notion of citizenship at the center. For the *Epistle to Diognetus*, this defining feature makes it possible to portray Christianness in at least partially universalizing terms—as an identity that, like other forms of citizenship, is potentially accessible to all free male people, something that sets Christians apart yet allows them to otherwise "fit" into the status quo. In the process, the text articulates and rejects other ways to define peoplehood in antiquity, such as territory, language, and customs. Nonetheless, the prior sections of the text, condemning the religious practices of Greeks and Jews, suggest that religious practices are central to the distinctive *politeia* embodied by Christians.

This text does not employ the concept of race as particularity in order to pit the notion of the universal over and against the notion of the particular, where Christianness is not-race because it is defined as universal. Instead, *genos* is redefined as that which is a marker of difference but potentially (if never actually) universal, like Roman citizenship. This slippage between ideas of ethnicity, race, and civic status would have been especially clear to ancient readers in relation to being Roman since Romanness is both a civic identity (linked to the city of Rome) and a broader ethnoracial one (in the context of the Roman Empire). Furthermore, the idea that a people can be spread out across a vast geographical area and not necessarily bound by one language, was one already published by Roman-period Jewish writers such as Philo and Josephus. Chapters 1 and 4 especially explore ways that ethnicity and race in antiquity were seen to be acquirable (like citizenship) yet "real." Chapter 5 builds upon these concepts, analyzing early Christian universalizing strategies as a form of ethnic reasoning.

Within the framework built upon genealogy and teleology, the reading I have offered is impossible. In that framework, only two main options are available. The first option is to insist that the *Epistle to Diognetus* raises the question "why this new race?" only to reject it. We find this interpretation in the French-Greek critical edition of the text. The editor, Henri-Irénée Marrou, interprets the author's answer to this question by stating that "the author protests with vigor" this notion of Christians being a new race. Marrou explains: "the Christians are not a people, a specific human race, like the Jews are."[107] For Marrou, the narrator's assertion that place, language, and customs do not distinguish Christians from non-Christians is the proof that the narrator is protesting the equation of Christianness with race. But Marrou's explanation is unsatisfying. As I have argued, the narrator does not stop here but instead affirms this equation, by defining *genos* primarily in terms of citizenship or civic membership as well as implicitly in terms of religious practices according to the overall organization of the text. Instead of protesting with vigor the idea that Christians constitute a *genos*, the *Epistle to Diognetus* answers in the affirmative even while defying Marrou's (and perhaps also some ancient readers') expectations about the meaning of *genos*.[108]

The second option is to argue that the text is exceptional, that is, not representative of "mainstream" Christian thought—an interpretive move that has embedded in it the presupposition that there is an identifiable essence to early Christian thought. Is the *Epistle of Diognetus* exceptional? Not especially. It closely resembles other early Christian texts that also seek to explain and defend Christianness (such as Aristides' *Apology* and Athenagoras's *Embassy on Behalf of the Christians*. See chapter 1 for further discussion). Furthermore, as we see happening in the *Epistle to Diognetus*, a number of other early Christian authors define Christianness through similar juxtapositions of peoplehood, religiosity, and citizenship by depicting Christians as foreigners or strangers in the world or as citizens of heaven (for example, *Odes of Solomon*, Hebrews, and 1 Peter). These texts presume a correlation between religious practices and participation in a civic whole.[109] As such, they preserve and perpetuate a long tradition of Jewish thought—both in terms of imagining a peoplehood that ultimately embraces all and in terms of articulating this vision of universal citizenship still in terms of a people.

## Plan of the Book

I advocate a prismatic approach to the study of the past, which requires a consideration of at least three vantage points: the present, for how our commitments and social location condition our historical analyses; the recent historical past, for how it has shaped and constrained both our interpretive frameworks and our present commitments; and the ancient historical period in which early Christian texts were produced, to gauge their interests and constraints. Because of this, each chapter tackles questions about modern interpretive frameworks and their implications as well as offering close readings of ancient materials. Each chapter touches on most of the four strategic uses of ethnic reasoning (defining ethnicity through religious practices, viewing ethnicity as mutable even if "real," universalizing ethnicity and religion, and using ethnic ideas as polemic), while emphasizing a cluster of implications that ethnic reasoning has for our understanding of early Christian self-definition. In all of these chapters, we see that approaching ethnicity/race as a dynamic concept characterized by fixity and fluidity helps to complicate and rethink our assumptions about early Christian self-definition.

Chapter 1 explores how religious practices were already closely associated with ethnicity in the early Roman imperial period, reading selected early Christian apologies and martyr narratives to show how early Christians used this connection to construct the boundaries and legitimacy of Christianness. This chapter also calls for rethinking the ways that scholars have defined Christianity in relationship to other ancient forms of religiosity.

Chapter 2 explores the scholarly treatment of Christians as a historically new movement, and the function this serves for our own understanding of the relation between the past and the present. Here, I show how early Christians used ethnic reasoning to give themselves a past as well as a distinctive present and future. By looking at writings by Justin Martyr, Clement of Alexandria, and Origen, as well as the Pseudo-Clementine *Recognitions* and *The Tripartite Tractate*, we can see how ethnic reasoning informs the ways that early Christians appropriate and (re)write the past and create a universalizing future for their "new" people.

Chapter 3 addresses the broad question of how to reconstruct Christian-Jewish relations in the first few centuries of the common era. My contribution includes a close reading of Justin Martyr's *Dialogue with Trypho the Jew*, showing how claims to ethnic fluidity and fixity can be manipulated to differentiate between Christians and Jews while defining both Christians and Jews as members of ethnic groups.

Chapter 4 problematizes the persisting temptation to speak about early Christian diversity along the lines of heretical or sectarian and orthodox or proto-orthodox. It hones in on how attention to ethnic reasoning not only helps us to understand early Christian depictions of conversion but also the internal disputes among Christians. I especially examine anti-Valentinian polemic in Clement and Origen's writings as well as the rhetoric in *The Gospel of Philip*.

Finally, chapter 5 reflects on the implications of how universalism is defined—what it means for early Christians, how they used ethnic reasoning to make universalizing claims, and what it means for modern interpreters to define early Christianity as a universal religion. I give special attention to what we learn from the visionary text *The Shepherd of Hermas* while also considering examples from Clement, Justin, Tertullian, and the apocryphal *Acts of Andrew*. Because universalizing claims presuppose the possibility of individuals becoming members of this movement, I also examine the implications that ethnic reasoning might have for theorizing conversion.

# 1

■

# "Worshippers of So-Called Gods, Jews, and Christians"

## Religion in Ethnoracial Discourses

Despite an increasingly nuanced body of scholarship on ethnicity in antiquity, religion remains surprisingly undertheorized in relation to ethnicity/race and pre-Constantinian Christianity virtually absent from a consideration of these terms.[1] Christians are too often viewed as exceptional or irrelevant by those interested in ancient ethnicity. Even studies that emphasize the diversity of early Christianities and foreground their *realia* do not interpret these in relation to ancient ways of thinking and speaking about race or ethnicity. When ethnicity is discussed, scholars are more likely to ask how Christianity developed in relation to preexisting ethnicities than to consider how Christians variously define themselves in ethnoracial terms.[2]

Ethnic reasoning is a valuable rhetorical strategy for early Christian authors in part because religiosity and race were already conceivable as interrelated in Roman-period texts, institutional practices, and policies, as well as in earlier texts used by Roman-period authors. While not omnipresent, religion serves as a persistent feature of ethnoracial and civic discourse and practices. Traditional definitions of Christianity as a religion of belief detached from the notion of an ethnoracial group need to be radically revised.

Many early Christians define Christianness as a membership in a people characterized especially by religious practices, in contrast to historical reconstructions that portray Christianness as a category that transcends or dissolves ethnoracial difference. The Greek version of Aristides' second-century *Apology*, for example, classifies Christians as a *genos* and proclaims their superiority to other kinds of humans. "For it is clear that there are three kinds (*genē*) of humans in this world: worshippers of so-called gods,[3] Jews, and Christians" (Aristides *Apol.* 2.2). While it may not have been obvious to all second-century or later readers that humanity should be divided into these three groups,[4] the Greek version of this early Christian text shows how an early Christian could imagine the relationship between race/ethnicity and religiosity. The description of the first *genos*—"worshippers of so-called gods"—suggests that, for Aristides' *Apology*, religious practices are the primary means for differentiating *genē*.

Aristides' approach resembles that of the *Epistle to Diognetus*. As we have seen,[5] the *Epistle to Diognetus* also defines Christians as members of a *genos*; *genos* is juxtaposed with "practice" (*epitēduema*) or encapsulated by the more abstract concept of "god-fearing" (*theosebeia*) (*Ep. Diog.* 1.1). Although the *Epistle to Diognetus* does not offer any blunt statement classifying all humans, its narrative structure implies a similar tripartite classification: Greeks, Jews, and Christians. Like *Diognetus*, the *Apology* unfolds through an examination of each *genos* in turn. In both writings, the most salient characteristic distinguishing these races is their piety, embodied especially in their religious practices.

The first section of this chapter demonstrates that, by analyzing ancient constructions and negotiations of ethnicity in terms of a dialectic between fixity and fluidity, we can account for both the wide range of elements invoked to define ancient ethnicity/race and the functions of these elements. Ancient authors appeal to religion at times to define ethnoracial affiliations as fixed and at other times as fluid. Early Christians frequently portray religiosity and ethnicity/race as mutually constituting and, like their contemporaries, treat ethnicity/race as both fixed and fluid.

The second section of the chapter overlaps with the first, but focuses more closely on the range of ways that ancient authors appeal to and define religion in ethnoracial discourse. Developing the more general observations from the previous section, I identify four different roles that religion plays: to assert the fixity of ethnoracial differences between groups, to accomplish ethnoracial fluidity (as a means by which one can change membership), to make links between two or more distinctive ethnoracial groups, and to make differentiations within a group.

In the third and fourth sections I examine a few early Christian writings at greater length for how they define Christians as constituting an ethnoracial group especially characterized by religious practices and beliefs (Athenagoras's *Embassy on Behalf of Christians*, the *Acts of the Martyrs of Lyon and Vienne*, and the *Acts of the Scillitan Martyrs*.) The chapter closes by reflecting on some of the implications for how we classify and compare early Christian "religion(s)" alongside their contemporaries.

## The Fixity and Fluidity of Ethnicity/Race in Antiquity

Ethnicity/race and religion are durable yet flexible concepts in antiquity. They do not have a necessary or singular relationship in ancient writings; nonetheless, early Christians like Aristides and the author of the *Epistle to Diognetus* are not aberrant in appealing to religious practices when defining Christians as members of a people.

There was no "mainstream" view of ethnicity to which those seeking to define Christianness could respond. Like their contemporaries, Christians defined themselves through selective interaction with existing social practices and interpretations of how these practices pertained to identification. If we imagine culture as a dynamic "product of the practice of meaning, of multiple and socially situated acts of attribution of meaning to the world, of multiple interpretations both within society and . . . between societies,"[6] then we should expect a range of meanings—including assertions of essential and distinctive meanings—attributed to concepts and practices that overlap. For example, the boundaries between religion, ethnicity, civic identity, and philosophy were often blurred in antiquity. How and why these identity formations get produced and differentiated is worth examining not because they *are* intrinsically different from one another but because they shed light on the social contexts and power relations at work in the establishment and transformation of cultures and identities.

Irad Malkin writes, "Greek ethnicity appears to have been something that was always both traditional and negotiable":

> Each time we find a statement involving ethnicity it reformulates the concept or expresses some position about it. . . . In attempting a response to the question "Who is a Greek?" [most ancient writers] would play with acceptable conventions, choosing to emphasize particular aspects or even invent new ones.[7]

As Malkin hints, there were a range of conventions from which one could select when formulating a position about ethnicity. Many scholars cite Herodotus (*Histories* 8.144.2) to identify at least one important cluster of ancient conventions, which include five criteria for Greekness: "common purpose (avenging the burning of temples by Persians), kinship (having the same blood, *homaimon*), shared language (*homomglōsson*), shared sanctuaries of the gods and sacrifices (*theōn hidrumata koina kai thusiai*), and similar ways of life or customs (*ēthea homotropa*)."[8]

While a common goal, kinship, language, shared religious practices, and way of life continue to be invoked in various combinations in ancient definitions of Greekness long after Herodotus, we should not presume that these criteria are either *essential* to Greek ethnicity or the only criteria ever cited.[9] In other texts, territory and climate are deemed more significant forces in defining an *ethnos* or *genos*.[10] Some authors divide the world into climatic zones that determine human differences such as temperament and skin color.[11]

This range of possibilities extends also into the Roman imperial period. The second-century C.E. astronomer Ptolemy of Alexandria, for example, prognosticates the bodily and social (*ethika*) characteristics (among which he includes religious practices) that belong to an entire group (for example, an *ethnos*, *chōra*, or *polis*) due to regional climate and the influence of astral bodies (*Tetr.* 2.1).[12] Geographical and climatic differences also form the basis for one kind of ancient physiognomy, whereby human appearances and behaviors could be classified and evaluated as ethnic differences: "Define Greece and Ionia as the geographical center of the earth, partition off north from south and east from west, define moral and physical excellence as the mean between extremes, and—presto—the "pure Greek" becomes the ideal."[13] This model is used by the second-century C.E. physiognomist Polemo even though "Polemo prefaces his own rendition of the material with the observation that in this day and age, when one finds Syrians in Italy and Libyans in Thrace, hair and skin color are hardly determinate in physiognomy anymore—indeed it is sometimes difficult to determine who belongs to what race!"[14]

Polemo's difficulty in using geography or physical planes of the body to securely establish ethnoracial identity does not mean that he or other authors cease to find ethnicity/race a meaningful category. It does suggest, however, the instability of this mode of classification. The emperor Caracalla's edict calling for the expulsion of "Egyptians" from the city of Alexandria (in lower Egypt) in 212 C.E. demonstrates both this instability and the ongoing relevance of ethnicity/race.[15] The edict orders that "All Egyptians who are in Alexandria, and particularly country folk who have fled thither from elsewhere and can easily be identified, are absolutely by every means to be expelled," but then goes on to qualify this comprehensive ban, permitting "dealers in pigs and river-boat men and those who bring in reeds for heating the baths" and those who come into the city for religious festivals and sacrifices to enter and leave the city as usual.[16]

When we look more closely to see how the edict seeks to define and limit "Egyptian," it appears that that "country folk" without jobs are the primary targets, and the latter portion of the text confirms this suspicion: "The ones who are to be prevented are those who flee the countryside where they belong in order to avoid farmwork."[17] These excerpts suggest that most Egyptians fit status- and geography-linked stereotypes of rural yokels abandoning the country for the bright lights of the city but bringing no vital skills to it.

Furthermore, the opening states that Egyptians "can easily be identified." But as we read further in the edict, the situation turns out to be more complicated than mere physical identification: "Amongst the linen weavers the true Egyptians can easily be recognized by their speech, which reveals that they are affecting the appearance and dress of others. What is more, in the way they live, their manners, the opposite of urbane behavior, reveal them to be Egyptian rustics."[18] The document reveals a tension between the presuppositions that Egyptianness ought to be marked on the body in obvious ways (through occupation, dress, manners, and religious practice) and the acknowledgment that it is not necessarily so. In the case of linen weavers and perhaps others, one must listen to their speech—but even this may not also prove effective. Egyptianness can apparently be defined in the early third century especially by occupation, religious practices, spoken accent, and perhaps social behavior. Ultimately, this text most narrowly defines "Egyptian" with residents of the *chōra* "who flee the countryside where they belong in order to avoid farmwork," thereby eliding an occupational category with a stereotype about lazy peasants.

Caracalla's edict reveals that to qualify as Egyptian in this context one must be identifiable through occupation and social habits (dress, manners, way of speaking, etc.). Further, it indicates that some "Egyptians" have become or might become sufficiently "not-Egyptian" enough to warrant exception from the expulsion (in this case, those who come to seek a more "cultured" existence in the city). Not surprisingly, what is salient for determining race and ethnicity shifts according to the context.

Thus, a list of possible conventions takes us only so far in understanding race or ethnicity in antiquity. We need to ask not only what criteria are being emphasized but also "why, and under what circumstances, ethnic claims are rhetorically mobilized."[19] David Konstan, for example, persuasively suggests that Herodotus frames his fivefold definition to address intra-Hellenic tensions, specifically the possibility of Athenian dominance, by emphasizing collective Hellenic unity in the wake of the Persian Wars.[20] Centuries later, in the Roman imperial period, Greekness is defined and negotiated especially in relation to Romanness;[21] conversely, existing discussions of Greekness served as both a model and foil for definitions of Romanness.[22] Similarly, ideas about what constitutes a *Ioudaios* shifts over time and needs to be evaluated in context.[23] The same holds true for identifying the different circumstances that underlie the range of early Christian uses of ethnic reasoning.

We ought then to treat ethnicity as a concept that is contested and revised through speaking and writing, as Jonathan Hall convincingly argues in his study of ancient Greek ethnicity.[24] Instead of assuming that ethnicity is either filled with some specific content at all times (otherwise known as a primordialist view, which is a carryover from Romanticism) or is merely a self-serving tool constructed in service of political gain (otherwise known as an instrumentalist view), Hall stands with a number of anthropologists and sociologists who have tried to mediate between these extremes.[25]

My approach diverges from Hall's in one crucial way. I agree with Hall that "any quest . . . for an objective definition of an ethnic group is doomed to failure simply because the defining criteria of group membership are socially constructed and renegotiated."[26] Hall's discursive approach to ethnicity implies that "one ought to apply the name of ethnic discourse" to whatever means are used to assert ethnic identity, "whether common blood or customs or gods or language."[27] But Hall limits the scope of ethnicity, singling out genealogies (and territory) as that which allows a scholar to identify a discourse as "ethnic" rather than some other cultural discourse (such as religious discourse).[28] Instead, I suggest we take seriously the broader implications of his approach, which allows for the flexibility of ethnicity.

*Genos* is etymologically linked to descent. Genealogical appeals do indeed appear across a range of social and historical contexts, and a number of the texts examined in chapter 2 illustrate how Christians found genealogical claims valuable in locating themselves in relationship to the past. Nonetheless, it would be a mistake to interpret claims of kinship or common ancestry as a necessary feature of ethnicity or race. Neither are genealogical claims a sufficient indicator of ethnoracial discourse. Romans give little attention to common ancestry or language in defining Romanness in the imperial period, favoring instead factors such as education, observance of Roman laws, morality, piety, and citizenship.[29] Perpetuation of (ever-shifting) traditions (*mos mairorem*) was more valued than issues of kinship.[30] What is crucial is the *function* that genealogical claims play: namely, they imbue ethnoracial identities with a sense of stability, essence, and longevity.

We can avoid the tendency to strangle a definition of ancient race/ethnicity if we imagine a spectrum running between two poles: fixity and fluidity. Genealogical claims function to support assertions of identity as fixed, inherent, primordial, and ascribed. This is the case even when genealogies are patently fabricated. It is not a genealogical argument or an appeal to "shared blood" that is the point, but an appeal to the "essence" of ethnicity or race. When skin color is invoked in the present, it functions analogously, to reinforce the perception that ethnoracial differences are "fixed." Appeals to common territory can fulfill a comparable role since the idea of a shared connection with place, or the effect of a place on individuals, can also function as a fixed criterion for ethnoracial membership. Genealogy and place can be combined as well, as in claims of autochthony or descent from a particular territory.[31]

Although ethnicity and race are concepts frequently constructed through appeals to fixity (essences, including lineages and "nature"), they can also be constructed through appeals to malleability. That is, definitions of ethnoracial membership can foreground "achievement" (not merely "ascription"). If seeking to portray ethnicity as attainable, one might stress the centrality of common purpose, common language or education (*paideia*), way of life, or religious practices.[32] Even claims of fixity are subject to fluidity in practice. Hall rightly notes that appeals to descent are performances of cultural negotiation that *produce* fundamental ties, rather than revealing preexisting ones.[33] Nonetheless, by overemphasizing genealogy he discounts an important strand in Greek *self*-definition since there are other means—notably by education—by which Greekness is said to be achieved (in contrast to assertions of Greekness as ascribed).

Ancient definitions of ethnicity do not necessarily occupy one of the extreme ends of the ascribed/achieved (or fixed/fluid) spectrum I have mapped. Frequently, they exhibit some combination of appeal to both fixity and fluidity, as does Herodotus's definition.

Religious practices can be used to support either end of the spectrum or, more often, to connect them.

## The Roles of Religion in Defining Ethnicity/ Race in Antiquity

Religion is a swing category within ancient definitions of ethnicity and race, useful in construing ethnoracial affiliation as fixed, fluid, or both. I see four primary ways that religion functions in ethnoracial discourse: (1) to mark differences between groups, helping to produce a collective civic or ethnoracial identity—especially under conditions of colonialism and diaspora; (2) to enable ethnoracial transformation; (3) to establish connections between otherwise distinctive groups; and (4) to assert and regulate differences within groups. While these functions cannot always be neatly distinguished and are often intertwined in a given text, it is useful to note how religion gets defined in ways that make it suitable for both asserting fixity and enacting and negotiating ethnoracial fluidity.

## Religion as Ethnoracial Difference

Early Christians could draw upon biblical traditions in which *ethnē* are defined "as dynasties with separate geopolitical and religious boundaries, demarcated by the worship of different deities."[34] The association of a people with particular deities and religious practices was also longstanding in Greek and Roman cultures: "Just as in describing a strange people you spoke of *chresthai nomois* (using or having customs), so you spoke of *chresthai theois* (having gods). The gods of a people were one of its attributes."[35] Cicero, for example, writing on the brink of the Roman imperial period, anticipates early Christian assertions of their own superiority as a people on the basis of their piety: "If we care to compare our characteristics with those of foreign peoples (*externis*), we shall find that, while in all other respects we are only the equals or even the inferiors of others, yet in the sense of religion (*religio*), that is in worship of the gods (*cultus deorum*), we are far superior" (Cicero *Nat. D.* 2.8).[36]

When writing about "others," religion is often singled out as a site of ethnoracial difference.[37] Egyptians were especially ridiculed and critiqued by Romans, Greeks, and Jews alike for their religious practices—veneration of animals in particular.[38] Greeks condemned Persians not only for alleged immorality but also for illicit religious practices, notably magic. Jews condemned their gentile contemporaries on religious grounds, as idolaters (for example, in Pseudo-Philo and *Sibylline Oracles*). Christians defined themselves fully within these conventions: "Do not worship . . . as the Greeks . . . neither worship as the Jews. But we, who worship [God] in a new way, in the third way (or form) (*genei*), are Christians" (Clement of Alexandria *Strom.* 6.39.4; 41, 2; 41.6).[39] Recalling the classification of humans that we have seen in *Diognetus* and Aristides' *Apology*, this passage is formulated as an admonition against the religious practices of the other kinds of humans.[40]

While religious practices can be adopted or rejected, and can be used to illustrate the fluid end of the spectrum, they were also understood to be closely tied to the fixed end because religious practices (especially sacrifices) both produced and reinforced kinship. This relationship between religion and kinship has usually been described in reverse terms—that is, that kinship results in shared religious practices. For example, Robert Parker explains Herodotus's appeal to shared worship in defining Greekness by making kinship the starting point: "the connection in Greek society between who you are and who you worship is absolutely pervasive. . . . I would insist that a Greek would normally assume that *shared blood would have as a consequence shared religious practices.* . . . One sacrifices with one's kinsmen, near and remote."[41] However, Nancy Jay's work on sacrifice shows that religious practices like sacrifice accomplish the very determination of socially significant kinship;[42] that is, sacrifice produces kinship and secures lines of descent. "Sacrificial ritual can serve in various ways as a warrant of, and therefore as a means of creating, patrilineal descent."[43]

The observance of particular religious practices can create or indicate group identity that can also be asserted through genealogical connections to deities. Abraham's covenant with God and adoption of circumcision creates a relationship that was simultaneously genealogical and religious, a tradition that early Christians adapted to define themselves.[44] The dynamic function of religiosity in ethnoracial discourse is also evident in Hellenistic and Roman-period texts that discuss Jewishness (or Judaeanness). Piety and observance of customs and law reinforce both ends of the fluid/fixed spectrum, and are interwoven with other criteria for defining membership, including appeals to kinship and ancestry. In the book of Judith, for example, Israelites are described as a people (an *ethnos* and a *genos*).[45] The "essence" of this people is largely defined by their relationship to a deity, which is intertwined with genealogical definitions. The character Achior, the leader of the Ammonites, describes Israelites as a "breakaway" people: "they are descended from the Chaldeans; and at one time they settled in Mesopotamia because they refused to worship the gods their fathers had worshipped in Chaldaea. They abandoned the ways of their ancestors and worshipped the God of Heaven, the god whom they now acknowledge" (Jth. 5:6–8). Although the backdrop here is genealogy, the "fixity" of ethnoracial essence is only ensured by the preservation of ancestral customs, notably the worship of the same god(s). When Chaldaeans (obviously referring to Abram in Genesis 12) switch their customs and religious allegiances, they cease to be Chaldeans and become a new *ethnos*. Religious practices and beliefs are thus among the factors that both embody ethnoracial fixity and permit fluidity. In Judith, religious observances can be cited as that which preserves and marks the differences between ethnoracial groups.[46] Religion serves as that which "fixes" ethnoracial differences. The next chapter explores in greater detail the way that Christians and others appeal to the past to secure claims of ethnoracial coherency in the present. For the moment, however, I want to consider further how religion functions as a mechanism for change.

## Religion as Means for Ethnoracial Transformation

Religion helps to shore up group boundaries (serving the ends of "fixity") but, as Judith's narrative suggests, this may be accomplished by a fluid sleight of hand, which acknowledges the porousness of ethnoracial boundaries. The second function of religion is as a vehicle for ethnoracial fluidity. This function overlaps with the first, insofar as religious practices are closely linked with ethnoracial membership, but the emphasis differs. In the first function, fixity is stressed; in the second, one highlights the possibility of crossing ethnoracial boundaries.

The adoption of particular religious practices, as in the case of becoming a Jew, could produce ethnoracial transformation. In Jewish and Christian writings, this fluidity is positively construed when the adoption of religious practices and beliefs means becoming a Jew or Christian respectively. Similarly, Roman vitriol against Druids indicates that, in some instances, religious transformation is deemed a necessary component for becoming a Roman— that is, although it is not the only factor, the transformation from "barbarian" to "Roman" could include or even require a shift in religious practices.

Judith locates this fluid role for religiosity in the past, at the origins of the Israelite people, but also in the present: Achior himself exchanges his Ammonite identity for membership in the Israelite community near the end of the text by swearing allegiance to the god of the Israelites and becoming circumcised (Jth. 14:10). In turn, his conversion is portrayed as not merely the act of a single individual; instead, like the move from Chaldaean to Israelite, Achior's transformation has ongoing consequences: his descendants are also members of Israel. That is, Achior's acquired religiosity becomes a hereditary trait for his descendants.

Shaye Cohen argues that during the Hellenistic period there is a shift in how being a *Ioudaios* is defined, from an emphasis on birth to shared religious practices.[47] He interprets this shift as a move from an ethnic to a religious (or "cultural") understanding of *Ioudaios*. My approach to race/ethnicity as dynamic concepts calls into question any sharp distinction between ethnicity/race and "cultural identity." If we do not suppose that ethnicity necessarily entails a privileging of the "fixed" end of the spectrum, we can say instead that the shift Cohen identifies entails a transformation in how ethnicity/race is defined, with a greater emphasis on its fluidity, such as we find in the emphasis on piety in Judith, culminating in Achior's conversion.[48] Naomi Janowitz supports this view, emphasizing that Jews redefine Jewishness partly by adapting "Greek" ideas and about practices of membership in an *ethnos*:

It was not so much the clash between Judaism and Hellenism as the very nature of the *ethnos* that opened up the possibility of non-Jews becoming 'Ioudaioi' (Cohen 1999, 105). Affiliating with an *ethnos* was not a complex undertaking, since ancient *ethnē* had more permeable boundaries, than, for examples, the tribal units familiar from Hebrew scriptures.[49]

The possibility of crossing ethnoracial boundaries requires viewing ethnicity/ race as potentially fluid, even though crossing such a boundary may be viewed as the acquisition of a permanent identity.[50]

My challenge to Cohen extends also to some recent work on Greek identity in the Roman period that distinguishes between Greekness as an ethnicity and Greekness as a cultural identity. When "Greekness" is defined as sufficiently fluid as to be potentially available to all (even if it is in fact attained only by few), in contrast to definitions of Greekness that appeal to "the polis of one's birth," Tim Whitmarsh declares, "whatever might have been the case in earlier Greece, the notion of 'Greekness' was not by now coterminous with ethnicity: it was a socially constructed style, one strand in a skein of valorized concepts (civilization, intelligence, manliness) which could not be disentangled meaningfully."[51] But to argue that definitions of Greekness shift over time and include in the Roman period definitions that foreground *paideia*, Atticizing accents, and past cultural achievements does not necessitate the conclusion that Greekness becomes a cultural identity and ceases to be conceivable as an ethnoracial identity. This interpretation only follows if one presumes that the meaning of ethnicity inheres solely in fixed criteria such as claims of common descent or territory. Ethnicity/race is a possible (though not necessary) *feature of cultural identity*, one that is always entangled with and produced in relation with other social concepts and categories.[52] So, while not synonymous, I analyze ethnicity/race under the broader umbrella of cultural identity, rather than position cultural identity as mutually exclusive with ethnicity/race.

The linking of religious practices with ethnoracial transformation and coherency appears in "Christian" texts as early as 1 Peter.[53] This text describes the addressees (in "Pontus, Galatia, Cappadocia, Asia, and Bithynia") as ones who have given up "the futile ways inherited from [their] fathers" (1 Pet. 1:18) and taken up a new holy code of conduct from another father (1:14–17). The result of this moral and religious change is portrayed ethnoracially: "Once you were no people (*ou laos*) but now you are God's people" (2:10). The results of this transformation are communicated partially through images of rebirth (1:3, 23) that suggest the fixity of this transformation: it produces kinship (with God and with one another). This transformation is also partially conveyed by situating this "chosen *genos*, royal priesthood, holy *ethnos*, God's own people (*laos*)" (2:9) in relation to their social context as "visiting strangers" and "resident aliens" (1:1, 2:11) among the various *ethnē* to which they once belonged (4:4).[54] The content of these distinctions is largely faith- and belief-based (clearly pertaining to ideas about resurrection and the power of God), and are to be demonstrated through moral conduct and willingness to suffer. In 1 Peter, religious and moral practices, and belief in the Christian God both signal the fluidity of ethnicity/race (the possibility of changing one's ethnoracial identification) and embody what ought to be stable and essential about one's identity as a member of this new chosen *genos*.

Aristides' *Apology* offers another kind of example of how religion can moderate between the notions of ethnicity/race as fixed and fluid. Aristides portrays Christians as kin to an eponymous ancestor who established the religious practices that continue to perpetuate the kin bonds and collective identity of its participant members: "those who conform to the righteousness of this preaching[55] are called Christians" (*Apol.* [Greek] 15.2). Christians are "those who, more than all other *ethnē* on earth, have discovered the truth" (15.3). The text thus complicates the perception that a *genos* is reckoned by birth even when genealogies and kinship are invoked. The Syriac manuscript tradition, which may predate the surviving Greek manuscript tradition, supports this interpretation. According to the Syriac, "the Christians reckon the beginning of their race from Jesus Christ" (2.4). Jesus himself is said to have been "born of the race of the Hebrews" (2.4), but the Christian race consists of those "who today believe in this teaching [about Jesus]" (2.4). The *Apology* foregrounds "righteousness" or assent to "teaching" about Jesus as crucial for being counted in Jesus' lineage.

Birth, genealogy, belief, and practice are all ways that the *Apology* defines a *genos*. Assent to religious teachings is imagined as the essence that constitutes a *genos*. While this *genos* is understood to be real, membership in it is fluid to the extent that one can become a member of the *genos* by adopting the piety of the Christians. This argument plays upon familiar appeals to *ta patria*, or ancestral customs,[56] where the identifying practices of a group are linked to a common ancestor (as we have also seen in Judith and 1 Peter). Paul similarly formulates an argument for how gentiles can acquire Abraham as their ancestor through Christ.[57] Aristides' rhetoric also makes vivid that the adoption of such practices can be interpreted as gaining ancestors.

The role of religion in ethnoracial transformation invites reconsideration of the concept of conversion. As the previous examples indicate, this fluidity is not portrayed as a private matter of individual conscience resulting in an individual's affiliation with a religious movement, but explicitly as becoming a member of a people, with collective and public consequences. For example, Judith's piety not only defines her as an individual Israelite[58] but as the one able to save her people from a political/religious shift that would have the effect of ethnic annihilation. The intertwined connection of religiosity with ethnoracial identification is what allows Judith's actions to be interpreted as the work of Israel's God to preserve the Israelites from ethnoracial others (for example, Assyrians).

Using ethnic reasoning, some Christian authors argue that individuals need to transform themselves, for example, into members of a saved, righteous, immovable, or true *genos*, a holy or special *laos*.[59] That is, the idea of ethnic mutability appears in early Christian texts to speak about crossing the threshold from outsider to insider as the assumption of a new ethnoracial identity. In addition, some texts also describe the spiritual transformations one undergoes after becoming an insider in terms of further changes in one's *genea/genos/ethnos*. Alongside a wealth of other imagery (especially developmental and educational), Clement of Alexandria, Origen, and the authors of the *Tripartite Tractate* and the *Gospel of Philip* use ethnoracial imagery to depict the progression of insiders from a less to a more spiritually advanced or perfect condition. When focusing on contexts that stress fluidity (*becoming* a Christian, developing as an "insider"), our attention is especially drawn to boundaries—how they are crossed, of what they consist.

At the same time, early Christian texts often build upon an understanding of ethnicity/race as a stable and often primordial aspect of oneself (recalling the first function of religion discussed above). Because race and ethnicity are invoked as fundamental categories, early Christians sometimes construe calls for ethnoracial transformation in terms of return to or restoration of an essential, primordial identity that is identified variously as authentic humanness or absorption into a divine unity (for example, Justin Martyr's *First Apology*, Tertullian's *Apology*, the *Apocryphon of John*, and the *Tripartite Tractate*). Whether ethnoracial change is considered complete upon crossing a specific threshold or continues afterward, texts that explain this change in terms of restoration or perfection clearly illustrate the double-sidedness of ethnicity/race: the "elect," "immovable" or "spiritual" *genos* is primordial and yet needs to be (re-)constituted through the transformations of individual humans.

## Religion as a Link Between Distinct Ethnic/Racial Groups

We have seen that religion can function as a means of ethnoracial transformation as well as a method by which ethnoracial groups can be distinguished (Chaldaeans from Israelites in Judith, "so-called worshippers of gods" and Jews from Christians in Aristides' *Apology*). A third way that ancient texts use religion in ethnoracial discourse plays upon the fixed/fluid dynamic by using religion to link groups that are presented as ethnoracially distinct. In the book of Judith, for example, Israelites are portrayed by Achior the Ammonite as renegade descendants of Chaldaeans; Josephus restates this connection approvingly (*Against Apion* 1.71) in contrast to an alternative story, that Jews are Egyptians by *genos*.[60] Dionysius of Halicarnassus, a Greek from Asia Minor who lived in Rome at the beginning of the imperial period and wrote in Greek for a Greek-speaking audience, attempts to trace Roman origins to Greeks, not barbarians, via alleged similarities in religious practices (see, for example, *Rom. Ant.* 7.70.1–5). At first glance, Dionysius's project resembles the tales about Jews as formerly Chaldaeans or Egyptians. But there is an important difference. While Josephus uses religion to mark or define ethnoracial differences, Dionysius appeals to religion in order to make a link between Romans and Greeks; that is, religion is used to make connections across groups otherwise considered to be ethnoracially different.[61]

As one of the building blocks for the construction, display, and negotiation of Romanness, *religio* could serve in the imperial period as a means both to connect diverse ethnoracial groups and to signify their distinctiveness.[62] Although religious practices continue to be correlated with race, ethnicity, and civic membership throughout the imperial period, Augustan cultic innovations lay the groundwork for a universalizing rhetoric that serves to hold together the diverse and regionally operated cults, especially ruler cults.[63] While the universalizing effect of discourse on people's lives should not be overstated,[64] and "imperial cult" should not be equated with Roman religion,[65] the adoption and pursuit of a range of cultic observances constitute one facet of signifying Romanness. Even in the absence of cultic unity, "piety" is a criterion for Romanness that can be invoked in the crossing and demarcating of ethnoracial and civic boundaries.

## Using Religion to Regulate Intraethnic Differences

Finally, in addition to helping to produce collective unity, differentiating and linking ethnoracial groups, and offering a mechanism for changing ethnicity/race, religiosity could also be employed to police or negotiate what was to count as "authentic" membership in an ethnoracial group. To this end, religion is presented as not only fixed but also as central to ethnoracial identity. Any perceived or unsanctioned variations of religious belief or practice—any fluidity—is decried as a potential threat to the coherency of the group. That is not to say that religious practices or beliefs remain fixed in practice, but rather that the ideological framework insists that even innovations or changes be explained in terms of a rhetoric of fixity (or continuity). This is an issue familiar to anyone in a religious community that has discussed or undertaken liturgical changes (for example, to use more inclusive language and terminology), organizational changes (for example, ordination of women, gays, and lesbians), or doctrinal changes (such as alteration of views about how the religion views divorce).[66] In identifying this function of religion in ethnoracial discourse we find that, like ethnicity/race, "religion" (*eusebeia, theosebeia, thrēskeia, pietas, cultus*) was also both traditional and negotiable.

Religion played a key role in the imperial period as a central marker of "what was to count as 'Roman' and what was not."[67] Since the content of the rituals and festivals used to demonstrate Romanness could and did shift over time, we should recognize this connection as something to be argued for, not merely uncovered.[68] In the late republican period, Romans increasingly attempt to differentiate "religion" from nonreligion.[69] "Nonreligion" was a moving target but was most commonly embraced by the concepts of *supersititio* and atheism. *Superstitio* in particular comes to function both as a term for improper religious worship by Romans and for foreignness.[70] Thus, religion could be used to highlight differences within an *ethnos* or *genos* or to locate apparent insiders as outsiders.[71]

By the first century C.E., religion was well established as a public discourse that was especially useful for asserting, contesting, and transforming ethnoracial as well as civic identities across the Mediterranean basin. How and who one worshipped could indicate or create one's ethnoracial and/or civic membership, even as it was viewed as a product of that membership.

Ethnicity/race could be defined in a broad range of ways in antiquity. I have suggested that by analyzing ethnoracial claims and definition in terms of a fixed/fluid spectrum we can make sense of appeals to ethnicity/race as fixed or fluid (or both). Ethnoracial discourses are dynamic. I have established the presence of religion in a number of instances of ethnoracial definitions and discussions, showing that religion is discursively relevant to ethnicity in many ancient texts, Christian and non-Christian.[72] The next two sections develop these insights with close readings of early Christian apologetic and martyr texts.

## Ethnic Reasoning in Apologetic Writings: The Case of Athenagoras

The second-century treatise *Embassy on Behalf of the Christians* by Athenagoras[73] is framed as a letter that requests rights and recognition for Christians on the same terms that the other ethnic and civic groups in the empire receive. It is generally classified as an apologetic text, which Frances Young has persuasively described as one in which "a group regards itself *as a people* in fighting for social and political recognition."[74]

The text opens by comparing Christians with other categories of people in the empire, specifically as they constitute *ethnē* and cities:

> The inhabitants of your empire, greatest of kings [Marcus Aurelius and Commodus], follow many different customs [*ethoi*] and laws [*nomoi*], and none of them is prevented by law or fear of punishment from cherishing their ancestral ways [*ta patria*]. . . . All these both you and the laws permit, *since you regard it as impious [asebēs] and irreligious [anosios] to have no belief at all in a god and think it necessary for all to venerate as gods those whom they wish*, that through fear of the divine they may refrain from evil. . . . We, however, who are called Christians, you have not given the same consideration.

(*Embassy 1.1, 2, 3, my emphasis*)

Athenagoras depicts Christians as a people who should, according to the logic of the empire, have the same rights to worship their own god in their own way, as any other people might.[75]

The logic to which Athenagoras appeals is significant: that Roman law permits a variety of "customs and laws" or "ancestral ways" in order to avoid impiety and irreligion. This link presumes that the reader knows that customs, laws, and ancestral ways entail religious practices, the belief in and veneration of gods. Athenagoras further explains that the consequence of piety ("fear of the divine") is good conduct—which sustains a peaceful and orderly empire. He credits Roman policy with favoring piety but only to argue that Roman treatment of Christians contradicts their own principles; he suggests that, if various *ethnē* and cities can worship the gods of their choice, then Christians ought to have the same rights.

To explain Christianity as group with its own form of piety could have made sense to ancient readers since it put allegiance to the Christian god with its attendant customs, laws, and forms of worship in an intelligible social framework. Nonetheless, it would have been unlikely to satisfy a Roman official since Romans might have been flexible about *which* gods were worshipped, but were less flexible about *how* gods were worshipped.[76] In accounting for the different form their piety takes, Christians had to handle this imperial concern.

In the remainder of the *Embassy*, Athenagoras develops two kinds of defenses for Christianness. He first elaborates Christianness in light of the concept of proper religiosity (piety) and its consequences for the stability of the empire, arguing that Christians are pious. Then he goes further, asserting that Christians are *the* pious members of the empire, in contrast to members of other *ethnē* and cities. He notes that the accusation of atheism against Christians arises because most people "measure piety by the rule of sacrifices" and thus charge Christians "with not acknowledging the same gods as the cities." He counters this by asserting that the Christian God demands a different kind of sacrifice, "bloodless sacrifice and 'the service of our reason'" (*Embassy* 13).

Athenagoras does not merely fit Christians into ancient conceptualizations about religion and its relation to ethnoracial or civic groups (which were not static anyway). He also criticizes existing ideas and structures. To do so, Athenagoras returns to his opening argument about people in different places having different gods, this time developing the point in a new way:

> As to the other complaint, that we do not pray to and believe in the same gods as the cities, it is an exceedingly silly one. Why, the very people who charge us with atheism for not admitting the same gods as they acknowledge, are not agreed among *themselves* concerning the gods. . . . If, then, we are guilty of impiety because we do not practice a piety corresponding with theirs, then *all* cities and *all* peoples (*ethnē*) are guilty of impiety, for they do not all acknowledge the same gods.
>
> (*Embassy 14.1, 3*)

Athenagoras brackets the question of how Christians interrelate with their non-Christian neighbors,[77] focusing his attention upon differences between cities and *ethnē*. He contends that intercity differences in religious worship, rather than alleged *Christian* atheism, signal impiety. His argument obscures how Christians, as inhabitants of these cities and among these *ethnē*, live in *disjunction* with the local customs. He holds up religious differences between cities as a sign of mass confusion about the true nature of the divine. Athenagoras thus inverts the position he attributes to the emperors in the opening, implying that their decision to protect ancestral customs for all peoples but the Christians in the name of peace may paradoxically produce social instability. His argument may seem strained, but it is made possible by positioning the inscribed reader as able to grasp how fundamental religious practices are to civic, ethnoracial, and imperial coherency.[78]

# The Race of the Righteous and Pious: Martyrdom and the Christian *Genos*

*There were punished the Christians, a* genus *of people characterized by a novel and maleficent superstition.*

(Suetonius *Nero* 16.2)

The popular accounts of early Christian martyrs offer an excellent site for examining how early Christian texts construct a collective identity in which race and religiosity are mutually constituting. These narratives also demonstrate the overlap between ethnoracial discourses and other ancient modes of collective identification (by city, family, status, and gender). Martyrdom narratives, and their close counterparts, stories of apostles' lives, vividly relate brave and harrowing deaths or brushes with death. Although persecutions against Christians before 250 C.E. were small-scale, sporadic, and locally based, directly touching the lives of relatively few, written tales of these persecutions were widely known and admired. Judith Perkins has suggested that suffering became the best-known defining feature of Christians, especially to non-Christians.[79] The continued valorization and composition of these narratives after the legalization of Christianity suggests that martyrdom forms an important node of Christian self-definition, especially in retrospect.[80]

Martyr narratives presuppose and play upon the notion that one's identity is embedded in a multiply inflected social network (that is, gender, status, age, citizenship, language, and ethnicity/race are all salient). Through torture and suffering, but also through resituating identity, these texts produce an idea of Christianness that applies to both the individual martyr, the witnesses to the martyrs in the narrative, and the reading/hearing community. The texts help to produce a collective identity that offers an alternative social network, in part through remembering the martyrs. In martyrdom narratives, Christianness is presented as distinctive from other collective identifications but able to incorporate individuals from many peoples and backgrounds by means of resituated allegiances and especially via the adoption of "true" religiosity.

Judith Lieu is, to my knowledge, the only other scholar who has called attention to the connection between martyr texts and Christian self-definition through ideas about "race" or "nation."[81] She analyzes the *Martyrdom of Polycarp* for its collective identification of Christians as the "race of the righteous (*tou genous tōn dikaiōn*)" (14.1; 17.1) and as the "God-loving, God-fearing race (*tou theophilous kai theosebous genous Christianōn*)" (3.2). Lieu persuasively interprets *Polycarp* in light of Maccabean writings as well as Judith and the *Sibylline Oracles*.[82] In these texts proper religiosity is the central issue—both for the persecutors and for the martyrs. Membership in an *ethnos* or *genos* is produced and demonstrated through proper religiosity, and charges of improper religiosity (atheism, impiety, idolatry) both structure the confrontation between state and martyr and the martyrs' responses to the state. The hostile crowds in *Polycarp*, subdivided into "the many *ethnē*" and the "Jews of Smyrna," charge that Christians destroy the gods and fail to sacrifice and revere the gods (12.2). Narratively, the text responds by depicting Polycarp as a proper sacrificial offering to the true God.

Lieu underscores the political function of martyrs: "when the martyrs are called 'father' or 'mother' (4 Macc. 7.1, 9; 15.29), this is a civic not a familial title."[83] Not only did the emperor receive this epithet, but so too did community leaders. She suggests that it is in this sense that we should understand the reference to Polycarp as "the father of the Christians" (*M. Poly.* 12.2). So too can we read the function of figures like Blandina (*Martyrs of Lyon and Vienne*) and Perpetua and Felicitas (*Martyrdom of Perpetua and Felicitas*) as not only exemplars but also as founders of a people that is imagined both in terms of kinship/descent and in terms of religious practices. These lineages are established by memorializing these figures as kin—again revealing a blurring among kinship, religiosity, civic, and ethnic identities.

In martyr narratives, racial, civic, and national identities are defined not simply through a willingness to suffer but specifically through a willingness to suffer in order to remain pious and maintain religious integrity. Lieu discusses only the *Martyrdom of Polycarp*, in which *genos* is explicitly used to describe Christians. We can also see ethnic reasoning at work in martyr texts that do not explicitly name Christians as a *genos* or *ethnos*. The *Acts of the Martyrs of Lyon and Vienne* and the *Acts of the Scillitan Martyrs*, both set in the last quarter of the second century, offer two additional examples of how Christianness could be constructed in terms of peoplehood. The *Martyrs of Lyon and Vienne* illustrates a negotiation between the levels of imagined community, provincial city, and empire, while the *Scillitan Martyrs* compares Christianness directly with Romanness, even though the setting is also a provincial city.[84] Ethnic reasoning partly accounts for how and why martyr texts (and other kinds of writings) rhetorically craft the distinctiveness of Christianness.

In 177 C.E., Christians came under attack in two towns in southern Gaul (now France): Lyon and Vienne. This local persecution is memorialized in the martyrdom narrative, *The Acts of the Martyrs of Lyon and Vienne*. Eusebius preserves the only copy of this narrative.[85] Lyon and Vienne were both known as centers of Roman cultic activity, and some of the most vigorous construction of temples in these cities happened during the late second century.[86] The larger city, Lyon, was home to one of the first sites for the imperial cult in the West; its Altar of Roma and Augustus offered a way for Gallic provincial aristocrats to negotiate their relationship with Rome and to compete for honors in their local communities.[87] Vienne, though smaller, featured a monumental religious complex (the "Sanxay") and an advantageous location at the mouth of the Rhone.[88] The martyr account sets the latter phase of trials and tortures at the beginning of a festival with international draw (*M. Lyon and Vienne* 47); this accords with the imperial cult center of Lyon (the Tres Galliae) being both the venue for sacrifices and gladiatorial games and for an annual assembly of representatives "from every state in the three northern Gallic provinces, an assembly at which cult honors would be paid to Rome and Augustus."[89] As homes or gathering places for a broad range of people from Gaul and elsewhere, especially known for cultic practices and honors tying Gaul to Rome, Lyon and Vienne would have been geographical and symbolic sites for early Christians—as well as provincials—to work through how to define themselves in relation to local and imperial identifications.[90]

The text emphasizes the endurance of a handful of Christians and the baleful wavering of many others. One of the few pillars of fortitude is Sanctus, said to be a deacon from Vienne. Sanctus's special strength lies in his virtual muteness under torture—all he will say is "I am a Christian." What is interesting about this for our purposes is how the narrator frames this testimony. We are told that his torturers try to get him to say "something that he *ought not*" but that Sanctus was so determined that he "would not even state his own name or *ethnos* or native city, or whether he was slave or free. But to every question he replied in Latin: 'I am a Christian.' This he confessed again and again, instead of name and city and *genos* or anything else" (*M. Lyon and Vienne* 20).[91]

For an early Christian listener or reader, this aspect of the narrative could have been both ironic and inspirational—the irony and inspiration stemming from the radically different meanings of the phrase "say something you ought not" in the eyes of the Roman torturers versus the eyes of the Christian audience. From the perspective of a non-Christian, Sanctus plays right into Roman hands merely by confessing that he is a Christian. That is, Sanctus does indeed say something he ought not to by asserting *Christianus sum*. But this irony is mitigated by the fact that, from the perspective of a Christian, his response is inspirational: Sanctus holds firm to his Christianness while others in the narrative lapse. The narrative generates tension by the raising the possibility that Sanctus might fail to hold firm to the name Christian, as do so many of his peers (*M. Lyon and Vienne* 11–12).

Concern over the name "Christian" permeates many early Christian texts.[92] In the early second century, Pliny the Younger, a Roman provincial governor in the eastern empire, developed an approach to judging accused Christians in which confession of being a Christian (confession of the name) was deemed a sufficient measure of guilt (Pliny's *Letter to Trajan*).[93] In Christian texts, the argument generally runs that it is unjust for Christians to be charged or tried as wrongdoers merely on the basis of the name; for example, Athenagoras writes:

> If indeed, any one can convict us of a crime, be it small or great, we do not ask to be excused from punishment but are prepared to undergo the sharpest and most merciless inflictions. But if the accusation relates merely to our name . . . it will devolve on you, illustrious and benevolent and most learned sovereigns [that is, the emperors], to remove this despiteful treatment by law.
>
> (*Embassy* 2)

Athenagoras and other apologists give the appearance that accusations using the name "Christian" are scandalous and not sparked by anything but the name. Yet even if Christians might have been called to public attention for illegal deeds rather than by (or for) their name alone, Athenagoras and many other early Christian writers seek to gain recognition and rights as "Christians"; that is, the name is actually central to their aims.[94]

The martyr narratives likewise stress the significance of the name "Christian." Far from being held up as the unfair object of attack, the name is precisely the point. It is the distillation of the martyr's identity: "I am a Christian" is "a ritualized and performative speech act associated with a statement of pure essence [that] becomes the central action of the martyrology."[95]

In the *Martyrs of Lyon and Vienne*, Sanctus's two-word statement, "Christianus sum," is construed as a subversion of expected ways of locating oneself socially. He aligns himself solely with this illegal name, the very reason for which he has been arrested. Christianness thus replaces conventional statements of identity, including that of membership in a *genos* or *ethnos*. When learning that Sanctus would not even say whether he was "slave or free," ancient readers of this text might have been reminded of the very passage that *modern* scholars appeal to most frequently when defending the position that ethnicity did not matter to early Christians—Galatians 3:28 (and its parallels):[96] "There is neither Jew nor Greek; there is neither slave nor freeperson; there is no male and female. For you are all one in Christ Jesus" (Gal. 3:26–28).[97] So one way to read Sanctus's assertion is that identity markers, including race or ethnicity, do not matter once one is a Christian.

This type of reading, however, draws our attention away from the function of the contrast between "I am a Christian" and the apparently expected type of response: Christianness is being defined by means of such a contrast. While the *Martyrs of Lyon and Vienne* does not limit the meaning of Christianness to race or ethnicity, locating it rather in the crisscrossing of social identifications, this martyr narrative depends upon an understanding that Christianness can be meaningfully compared with ethnoracial as well as civic status, and the name "Christian" is invoked to do their work.[98] Christianness fulfills, among other things, the function of an ethnoracial marker.[99] This function is not mutually exclusive with, but rather supported by the universalizing rhetorical thrust of martyr narratives: in these texts, anyone, even the most socially marginal, can embody Christianness.

The martyr narrative depicts Christianness as not simply affirmed but in fact produced in and through public display. The performative statement "I am a Christian" is a public and political action rather than solely the statement of an individual's personal beliefs. This statement does not just make Sanctus a Christian; it also implicates the reader/listener in a corporate identity. The reader/listener is invited to stand either with the suffering Christians or with the wavering ones (*M. Lyon and Vienne* 25–26, 32–35, 45–46, 48),[100] while the opposition is embodied in the official torturers and the angry mob. The text attempts to secure the fixity of identities against a backdrop of fluidity—embodied in the lapsed but also in the potential for new Christians to be created.

Piety marks membership in provincial city and empire and the text "exposes" those allied with Rome as savagely impious, a move that depicts Christians as a distinct group on the basis of their contrasting piety. That this collective identity is understood as inextricably religious, political, civic, and ethnoracial is clear from the framing of the confrontations. For example, the vicious beating of Potheinos, a local leader described as the "entrusted with the *diakonia* of Lyon's *episkopē*" (*M. Lyon and Vienne* 29) highlights how religiosity differentiates Christians from non-Christians: "everybody acted as though it were a serious fault and impiety to fall short in their viciousness towards him, for they thought that in this way they could avenge their gods" (31). This martyr narrative thus differentiates Christianness starkly from the practices and values of provincials and Roman officials.

In the brief *Acts of the Scillitan Martyrs*, set in 180 C.E. Carthage, the provincial capital of Roman Africa, we find Christianness directly juxtaposed with Romanness. Despite its provincial setting, this text differs from the *Acts of the Martyrs of Lyon and Vienne* by making no mention of provincial or local characters or conflicts. This Latin text features the trial and execution of twelve Christian women and men.[101] In the opening dialogue, competing political notions of peoplehood, expressed in and through religiosity, quickly emerge as central. The Christian spokesperson, Speratus, puts the Roman official, Saturninus, on the defensive:

> The proconsul Saturninus said: "If you return to your senses, you can obtain the pardon of our lord the emperor." Speratus said: "We have never done wrong; we have never lent ourselves to wickedness. Never have we uttered a curse; but when abused, we have given thanks, for *we hold our own emperor in honor.*" Saturninus the proconsul said: "*We too are a religious people,* and our religion is a simple one: we swear by the Genius of our lord the emperor and we offer prayers for his health—as you also ought to do."
>
> (*Scill. Mart.* 2–3, my emphasis)

Not only does Speratus signal the political and public implications of Christianness by referring to Christians honoring "our own emperor," but Saturninus's response indicates that he understands this as a religious statement too: "we too are a religious people." The narrative positions Romanness in relation to Christianness by means of religiosity.

Speratus then offers to instruct Saturninus about simplicity,[102] implying that the official's notion of a "simple" religion is misguided. Saturninus responds defensively, on the assumption that such instruction will entail criticism of Roman "sacred rites." He demands instead that Speratus "swear rather by the Genius of our lord the emperor" (*Scill. Mart.* 5). Predictably, Speratus rejects this demand, but the formulation of his rejection again emphasizes the *political* character of Christianness: "I do not recognize the empire of this world. Rather, I serve that God whom no one has seen" (6). In this text, both the religion of Christians and that of Romans are depicted as conceptually equivalent, although Christianity is held up as true.

After a little more back and forth, Saturninus offers the Christians a thirty-day reprieve to reconsider their allegiances and practices. In apparent response to this offer, "once again Speratus said, 'I am a Christian!' And all the others agreed with him" (*Scill. Mart.* 13). This compact statement leads to their immediate execution.

We can push our reading further by examining the judgment pronounced by Saturninus just before the executions are meted out. His proclamation highlights the importance of religious practices, locating their significance in relation to the collective identities of Christian and Roman, respectively:

> Saturninus . . . read his decision from a tablet: "Whereas Speratus, Nartzalus, Cittinus, Donata, Vestia, Secunda, and the others have confessed that they have been *living in accordance with the rites of the Christians* (*ritu Christiano*), and though given the opportunity to *return* to the usage of the Romans (*Romanorum morem*) they have persevered in their obstinacy, they are hereby condemned to be executed by the sword."
>
> (Scill. Mart. 14, my emphasis)

This passage is fascinating. Here we have a Christian text depicting the Roman perspective on Christianness as membership in a people. "Living in accordance with the rites of the Christians" not only indicates that practices are the means by which one identifies Christians, but also positions them as a non-Roman people. The wording of the decision implies that all had followed the customs of the Romans at one time but have since become something else, "Christians," by having adopted the "rites of the Christians." This phrasing recalls Achior's tale about how some Chaldaeans became Judaeans and his own transformation from Ammonite to a member of the community of Israel (Jth. 5:6–8; 14:10). Once again, ritual practices establish ethnoracial boundaries, while also serving as evidence for how such boundaries can be crossed.

The phrasing of Saturninus's judgment, allowing the Christians the chance to "return" to Roman ways, need not mean that they were all Roman citizens, but rather obedient subjects of the imperial order, regardless of background. Nevertheless, the earlier contrast between the empire of this world and the allegiance of the Christians to a "lord who is the emperor of kings and of all nations" (*Scill. Mart.* 6) suggests that the adoption of Christian rites defines (and creates) Christians as an alternative ethnopolitical grouping to Roman imperial classifications.

It is not just Christianness that gets constructed in the *Acts of the Scillitan Martyrs* but also Romanness, including Roman religion. Saturninus declares to Speratus and the others that Romans are religious people, and, as in many other early Christian texts, veneration of the emperor and adherence to "ancestral customs" form the core elements of Roman religion. Indeed, attempts to make Christians accede to these points through action or speech is central to the plotting of many martyrdom narratives, as in the scenes between the martyr-in-waiting Perpetua and her distraught non-Christian father: after a few unsuccessful attempts to reason with her in jail, he appears at her public hearing with her infant son crying "Perform the sacrifice!" (*M. Perp. and Fel.* 6.25).[103] It is important to note, however, that these constructions of Romanness in martyr texts create the impression that Roman religion and identity forms the major contrasting option for a unified Christianity. On the ground, local or regional cultic practices and the identities they indexed may well have been more salient than "Roman-ness"; moreover, Christianness itself was not a unified whole—a fact that martyr texts hint at.[104]

## Implications for Defining Early Christianity as a Religion

Seeing some of the ways in which early Christians defined themselves as an ethnoracial group characterized especially by their religiosity permits us to reconsider how Christianity has been defined in relation to other forms of ancient religion.

There are two main facets to most modern characterizations of religion in Mediterranean antiquity: (1) religion in antiquity was practice-centered, not belief-centered; and (2) religion was embedded in, not distinct from, a larger social matrix (that is, it is difficult to speak of distinct religious communities that are not fully implicated in the rest of one's life). This twofold understanding of ancient religion is understood to be closely associated with race/ethnicity and civic identity, as these concepts connote social particularity (often marked by practices). I find this twofold view useful as a heuristic device, but it too often serves as a foil for defining Christianity as contrastingly belief-centered and universal. As a consequence of this oppositional definition, Christian uses of ethnic reasoning remain unread and unreadable in most reconstructions of Christian origins.

Christianity used to be frequently depicted as a transhistorical and transcultural phenomenon, constituted by a focus on belief. To be sure, most recent studies of forms of Christianity in the Roman period are very careful to situate their interpretations in relation to rhetorical, regional, and/or material contexts. Nonetheless, Christianity is still often distinguished from other ancient religions in making belief, rather than practice, the core of the religion. Keith Hopkins, a very sensitive interpreter of antiquity, rather uncharacteristically perpetuates this view: "The very existence, from early on in Christian history, of brief statements of Christian beliefs set Christianity apart from Judaism and paganism. Put crudely, the contrast is that *Christianity* became a *religion of belief*, whereas *Judaism and paganism were religions predominantly of traditional practice*, with settled adherents."[105] What is striking about this formulation is the work that "belief" does. Placing belief at the center of Christianity, in explicit contrast to "traditional practice, with settled adherents," reinscribes a modern western dichotomy between mind and body; it implies that Christianity is not intrinsically linked to historical and social context. Even if one views some early forms of Christianity as proportionately more belief-centered than contemporary religious cults and movements, it is still necessary to explain how these forms could have been intelligible to ancient peoples from within their own social contexts. John North helps to mitigate this problem by proposing that ancient views about religion shifted over time "from embedded in the city-state to religion as a choice of differentiated groups," such that Christianity would be intelligible as one of these.[106] For North, it is not so much "belief" as individual choice to affiliate with a group not already primarily aligned with family and city that marks a shift in the definition of ancient religiosity.[107] While recognizing that religious groups formed alternative collective identities, North emphasizes the significance of individual choice in membership, a position that echoes the implications of "belief."

While Roman religion may be especially linked with key religious practices (dubbed as ancestral custom), the martyr narratives do not employ a contrast between practice and belief to distinguish Christian religiosity from other forms of religiosity. Rather, Christians refuse participation in practices such as ritual sacrifices or offerings on behalf of the emperor but make actions such as martyrdom itself, prayer, sexual abstinence, and the performative declaration "I am a Christian" central to their definitions of Christianness. Likewise, the apologetic texts do not make a sharp distinction between belief and practice. Athenagoras argues that Christians should be granted the right, like other peoples, not only to worship the god of their choice but also to worship this god in their own manner. His extensive attention to how Christians behave and contrasting condemnation of the behavior of others indicates that practices were as central to Christianness as beliefs.[108] As Lieu notes, religious integrity in early Christian texts is often elaborated with reference to *eusebeia* or *theosebeia*, which she translates as piety and god-fearing. *Eusebeia* is one of the central Greek terms for religiosity and *theosebeia* is prevalent in Jewish literature.[109] Because these terms are concretely related to how one lives and what one does, these cannot be interpreted as only pertaining to belief or faith.

The implications of rethinking this sharp division between belief and practice extend to ongoing discussions of the relationship between Christianity and Judaism. Katharina von Kellenbach has suggested that "antithetical juxtaposition" constitutes one of three "rules of formation" of Christian discourse about Judaism:[110] belief versus practice and detachment from social structures versus social embeddedness (more commonly referred to as universal versus particular) constitute two key antitheses. Although the "profoundly simplistic" but pernicious contrast between Judaism as a religion of law (or practice) and Christianity as a religion of freedom or grace (or belief) has been challenged in a number of ways,[111] such contrasts remain troublingly pervasive. I suspect that "practice" often functions as a shorthand for "ethnic" and "belief" for "universal."

The second element of modern definitions of ancient religion, that religion was embedded in a larger social matrix, is also often contrasted with Christianity. Christianity is often depicted as a movement that breaks the conventional embeddedness of religion in society and politics.[112] This break is spoken of in three overlapping ways: (1) Christianity is universal—addressed to all individuals, not to specific civic, ethnoracial, or regional groups; (2) Christianity has an otherworldly, rather than this-worldly focus;[113] and (3) Christianity is a religion of conversion or volunteerism, rather than of birth. These three arguments presuppose that ethnicity/race in antiquity is never part of a universalizing rhetoric and always ascribed.

Thankfully, many scholars today recognize that the context in which Christianity emerged was one in which the social matrix was characterized by significant diversity, resulting from colonization, migration, travel, and war. Most people were not embedded in a static matrix, but rather a dynamic and cosmopolitan one.[114]

Many Christian texts do make universalizing claims. Nonetheless, as I shall explore more fully in chapter 5, saying that Christianity is open to all people is not mutually exclusive with defining Christians as members of an ethnoracial group.[115] Many early Christians certainly do appeal to "otherworldly" phenomena such as a heavenly ruler, city, and citizenship, but they frame these appeals in culturally specific concepts such as imperial rule and political enfranchisement (for example, in *Acts of the Scillitan Martyrs*). Furthermore, as I have suggested with respect to Judith and 1 Peter, conversion need not be interpreted as mutually exclusive with ethnicity—in these texts, religious conversion is inextricably linked with ethnoracial transformation. Reading early Christian texts for how they seek to craft a communal identity within and among alternative cultural identities makes central the questions of ethnicity, gender, and status.

The martyrdom narratives suggest that Christianness is being imagined as an alternative collective identification, but we should not mistake this to mean it is context-free. Furthermore, alternative forms of embeddedness were available before Christians began to define themselves as Christians. The cult of Dionysius as introduced into Italy,[116] philosophical schools, and the geographically and socially distinctive communities of *Therapeutai/ Therapeutrides* and at Qumran offer other obvious alternative forms of structure and embeddedness.

Early Christian movements are not simply interpreted over and against these two defining features of religion. Christian origins are also situated in a temporal framework. The proposed contrast between Christianity and other ancient religions has often been interpreted in the context of a temporal framework that presumes an (ideal) development of religion over time from local to universal (a version of the teleological approach discussed in the introduction). When this ideal of progress and universalization informs historical reconstructions, Christian origins can be reconstructed to support historical or theological claims that ethnicity and race were irrelevant to early Christian self-definition, as well as to support claims about Christianity's uniqueness (usually implying superiority) relative to other ancient religions. Presuming a positive change from socially embedded to "universal" religions implies Christianity's difference from and superiority to Judaism and polytheistic cultic traditions while obscuring the ways that Christianity has always been embedded in particular sociohistorical contexts. This framework's most recent manifestation has been summarized by Guy Stroumsa as a shift of "the main criteria of identity . . . from ethnicity to culture, and then to religion," which is interpreted as a trend towards universalism because religion is understood as unmoored from the messy specificities of "ethnicity" and "culture."[117] Using this rubric, interpreters of Christianity will be likely to devalue or ignore references to ritual practices (or will attribute them to Jewish or pagan influence).[118] It also means that Christian self-definition as a *genos*, *ethnos*, or *laos* is more likely to be ignored or explained as "mere" metaphor, rather than in terms of sociopolitical embeddedness. We do not have to make this sharp either/or distinction between "particular" and "universal" or between "practice" and "belief" in reconstructing early Christian self-understandings.

# 2

## "We Were Before the Foundation of the World"

### Appeals to the Past in Early Christian Self-Definition

*Unlike the Egyptians, Babylonians, Phoenicians, and Jews, the
Christians did not comprise a distinct national or racial group whose
history could be written. Even so, this did not stop such writers as
Aristides, the anonymous author of the Epistle to Diognetus, and
Eusebius from describing Christianity as a* triton genos *or "third
race" distinct from Greeks and barbarians.*[1]

In the last chapter, we saw that early Christians used ethnic reasoning to portray Christianness as an ethnic identity especially
characterized by religious beliefs and practices. But it might still
seem obvious that they lacked a fundamental basis for supporting an
ethnoracial self-understanding: a past. More than that, they had no
unified identity; before legalization, what we tend to group under the
heading "Christian" covers a broad range of groups, some of whom
did not even call themselves Christians. Amazingly, this historical
novelty and lack of unanimity did not prevent some Christ-believers
from describing themselves as a people, as this opening citation from
Arthur Droge notes. For Droge, this is a problem to be explained.
Even though he notices early Christian uses of ethnic/racial language,
he classifies Christians as something other than a "national or racial
group." This chapter resolves Droge's conundrum, arguing that the
puzzle of Christian self-description as a "race" or "ethnicity" disap-
pears if we approach histories as mobile constructions that rhetorically produce and recast, rather than describe, collective identities.
That mobility includes the choices modern historians make to select
materials as "Christian" and give meaning to that concept.

The historical arguments of early Christian authors strikingly echo
the strategies and presuppositions of earlier Jewish, Greek, and
Egyptian historiographers, as Droge's careful study demonstrates.[2]
But these arguments also resonate with the ways their contemporaries used the past to reimagine themselves for purposes of the present.[3] Christians take a page out of the book of other minority groups

to authorize themselves. They especially use strategies of (other) Jews and Roman-period Greeks as they stand relative to Rome: asserting greater antiquity and claiming to be the source of authentic wisdom for other peoples. Christians also borrow from hegemonic groups such as the Romans by claiming both to be the superior descendants of a degenerate, once glorious people and to be a people potentially open to all. Early Christian texts may not have always persuaded ancient readers that Christians constitute a people with an ancient pedigree, but that does not mean that the attempts were disingenuous or merely metaphorical.

Early Christians were not the only ones inventing themselves in the early Roman imperial period. So too were Romans, Greeks, Judeans, Lydians, and Aphrodisians, among others. Unlike the term "Christian," other names such as Hellene, Egyptian, and Judean were terms that had been in the Greek linguistic repertoire by the Roman imperial period. Nonetheless, it is misleading to think that these terms (or the groups to whom they referred) were stable. Their meanings underwent continual negotiation and revision in antiquity. The past was a crucial site for authorizing the values and practices by which one could claim and demonstrate one's present identity. But the past itself was contested—how one framed the past conditioned how one measured "Greekness," "Jewishness," "Romanness," etc., and the interrelations of such collective categories in the present. Attention to ethnic reasoning in appeals to the past illuminates the local and imperial political-rhetorical contexts within which early Christians defined themselves.

Early Christian authors create Christians as a people no less than Romans, Lydians, Judeans, and other groups in appealing to the past to depict their identities as coherent, historically continuous, and superior to, if also linked with, other peoples. But the persuasiveness of these constructions depends on their ability to convince readers that they speak of real groups. That is, appeals to the past participate in the double-sided dynamic of ethnoracial discourse—that fixity and fluidity are both conditions for imagining ethnicity/race. By portraying a people as continuous over time, historical ethnographies or mythic tales make ethnicity or race seem fixed. At the same time, historical accounts often display the fluidity of ethnicity/race by suggesting, for example, that one people can be transformed into another (that Romans emerged from the Greeks, Christians from Jews) or that different peoples can emerge from a common ancestor (Jews and Spartans from Abraham, Ilians and Romans from Aeneas). As we shall see, appeals to ancestral ties of kinship are central for Christians, as they had long been for other inhabitants of the ancient Mediterranean world.[4]

An analysis of early Christian uses of the past raises questions about our own uses of the past. Modern and ancient interpreters often emphasize that what makes early Christians distinct is that they are a "new" phenomenon in the Roman imperial period. How do claims of novelty function in reconstructions of early Christian history? And what bearing do conceptualizations of novelty have upon the identification and interpretation of ethnic reasoning in early Christian texts? The next section takes up these questions since their answers shape any interpretation of early Christian materials.

The remainder of the chapter explores some of the ways that Christians invented a past—and also a destiny—for themselves. Two sections consider a range of early Christian examples. Finally, I situate Christian uses of the past in terms of the Roman imperial context of power relations. I suggest that we can interpret early Christian uses of the past not only as indebted to available historiographic and ethnographic practices but also as participating in contemporary imperial and regional efforts to establish who's who in the empire.

## Novelty in the Construction of Difference

Being "new" or not is a recurring theme in early Christian writings, as we see in the *Epistle to Diognetus*'s opening rhetorical question about "why this new race (*genos*) or practice (*epitēdeuma*) has come to life at this time, and not formerly" (*Ep. Diog.* 1.1). How do pronouncements of early Christian novelty function in modern scholarship about early Christians? Most modern interpretations of early Christian texts stress that Christianity was a new phenomenon in antiquity, somehow different from existing socioreligious formations. What are the implications of interpreting Christianity as "new" in the Roman period? Is Christianity to be considered new and different in a relative or essential sense?[5] Most scholars resist assertions of Christian absolute uniqueness, although essential novelty has been attributed especially to the person and teachings of Jesus, as well as to the gospels as a literary genre and the concept of "eschatology."[6]

In historical narratives that stress the novelty of early Christians, novelty marks and enacts the possibility of difference. Because "novelty" is a time-linked assertion of difference, it functions minimally in historical reconstructions to mark a point of rupture or change. But the question of novelty is not only about how to situate early Christians in relation to their non-Christian contemporaries but also about how the interpreter situates herself in relation to antiquity.

Broadly speaking, an interpreter can position herself in overall continuity with the historically "new" phenomenon of Christianity or emphasize her own difference (hence novelty) in time and worldview relative to early Christians and the Roman period. These are oversimplications, however. Most of those who might be classified under the first option do not deny historical change, and accept that Christianity has changed over time. And most of those who might be classified in terms of the second option acknowledge that modern interpretations flatten some of the differences between the present and past in making the past meaningful and "knowable" in the present.

Nonetheless, when the modern reader or interpreter positions herself in continuity with that which is defined as "new" in an earlier historical context, a claim to "novelty" may be used in service of creating sameness across time. Christians today, for example, are more likely to accept the idea of historical otherness with regard to Jews and "pagans" than with regard to early Christians precisely because these Jews and pagans are already thought of as "other." What is "new" and different about Christians in antiquity is thus structured as potentially the "same" between ancient and modern Christians. Because Christians today in all of their diversity see themselves in continuity with the "Christians" of ancient texts (at least Christian Testament texts), any historical narrative about early Christians has the possibility of being read in a broader framework of continuity and sameness.

What are the consequences of this framework for discussing the relationship between "religion" and race/ethnicity for Christians? As I discussed in the previous chapter, modern interpreters have frequently argued that a central feature of early Christians' novelty was the severing of a connection between ethnicity/race and religion. Many scholars agree that early Christianity should be classified as a "religion," and that its distinctiveness inheres in its emphasis on belief and its (at least conceptual) break from the conventional embeddedness of religion in society and politics. In his influential study at the beginning of the twentieth century, Adolf Harnack argued that when Christians defined themselves as a *genus/genos* (notably a "third" *genus/genos*), they had in mind not an ethnic or racial collective idea but a "religious" one.[7] Much more recently, Frances Young has explained the ethnic reasoning of early Christian apologists in terms of such a shift. When apologists like Athenagoras "claimed [Christians] to be a people or a race, alongside others to whom rights were given . . . they initiated the trend that would eventually turn religion into a belief system rather than traditional ethnic customs."[8] These arguments make early Christians the precursors of modern ideals about Christianity and about "religion," even when modern forms of Christianity or religion are not viewed as identical with those of antiquity.

Because the consumers of histories of Christianity are most often themselves Christian, historical reconstructions can be deployed within an interpretive framework of sameness/continuity to spark reform in the present among communities that identify themselves as continuous with the communities of biblical texts.[9] For these communities, novelty *within* Christianity is deemed problematic, so innovation is especially effective when framed as a restoration or reform by appeal to the past. Modern debates over women's leadership and ordination in Christian communities, for example, frequently look to historical interpretation to justify exclusion or inclusion of women's religious leadership. In other words, Christians today are reinventing their own past to serve the needs of the present. While appearing to be fixed, the past (the content of Christian tradition) is flexible in practice, and able to accommodate a range of interpretations.

The malleability of the past, despite the apparent continuity in "tradition," means that it should be possible to reimagine the past to serve the present goal of fighting racism without perpetuating Christian anti-Judaism. I am suggesting that this requires grappling with the unacknowledged ways that modern histories of early Christianity have been racialized. The denial of the saliency of race masks its centrality to the framing of Christian history. This is a primary concern of Shawn Kelley's *Racializing Jesus: Race, Ideology and the Formation of Modern Biblical Scholarship*. Kelley focuses on scholarship about Jesus; we should extend this to include the racialization of interpretive frameworks for reconstructing Christian history.[10]

What about an approach to early Christianity that emphasizes a break between the modern interpreter and the ancient Christians? The still influential historical-critical method as well as the more recently popular Foucauldian-inspired new historicist approach both insist on a gap between ancients and moderns. These approaches may position Christianity as "new" in its historical context, but tend to emphasize two things: that there is a greater difference between the interpreter and antiquity than between early Christians and their contemporaries, and that the novelty of early Christians can be explained by context rather than uniqueness (such as the uniqueness of Jesus).

Averil Cameron, for example, situates her approach to early Christian rhetoric in sharp contrast to what she calls the "extravagant claims" of Christian novelty made by some "New Testament" critics.[11] She implies that contemporary Christian interests inform explanations of how and why Christianity was novel. Her work instead emphasizes the *relative* novelty of Christians. In order to explain how "this 'new' Christianity was able to develop . . . a means to ensure its place as a rival to and then inheritor of the old elite culture," Cameron argues that "Christian discourse . . . made its way in the wider world less by revolutionary novelty than by the procedure of working through the familiar, by appealing from the known to the unknown."[12] This perspective is widely shared today.

Interpreting Christianity as a concept and set of social groups that emerges in the early Roman imperial period foregrounds the importance of historical context. This approach implies that early Christian rhetorical and material practices were (and must be rendered) intelligible within a specific historical context. Cameron's approach thus relativizes the novelty of Christianity by framing it as creative adaptation of available epistemologies and rhetorical techniques. Although Cameron does not reveal the contemporary underpinnings for her own interpretive commitments, her emphasis on the continuities between Christians and non-Christians in the Roman period implicitly challenges assumptions of similarities between ancient and modern interpreters.

While this approach avoids the notion of essential difference between early Christians and their contemporaries, it still often preserves a notion that there is some essential essence to peoplehood of which Christians did not partake because they were a historically emergent group in the Roman period. Like Arthur Droge, who asserts that early Christians were not an ethnicity/race/nation like other groups because they have no comparable past, Frances Young seems to share Droge's distinction between "real" non-Christian peoples with "ethnic cultures" and Christians who claim "that they are an *ethnos*, a people, despite the evident fact that they have no common ethnic roots."[13] In her view, "the problem for Christians was that they were not assimilated into the Jewish *ethnos*, while apparently abandoning their own ethnic cultures."[14] Droge and Young take the important step of situating Christian historical ethnographic claims in relation to their contemporaries, but the perception that early Christians lacked the common past necessary to be an *ethnos* still limits their interpretations of Christian ethnic reasoning.[15]

Even when framed with a strong emphasis on a disjuncture between past and present (including *within* "Christianity"), contemporary questions and interests govern historical reconstructions and framing. On this point, traditional historical critical methods and Foucauldian historiography part company. While a historical critic aims to interpret other times and places on "their own terms" while seeking to remove his own "biases" from the interpretation, Foucault was quite emphatic that genealogical studies begin from questions in the present.[16] But both these frameworks have to contend with the problem of how to proceed from "the known" of the present to "the unknown" of the past in a way that does not do violence to the difference of the past. Modern interpreters can only make sense of ancient texts and perspectives to the extent that we are first able to see them as "known" and knowable in our own terms. Only then can we proceed to argue for how they differ.[17]

When the modern reader or interpreter positions herself in discontinuity with the Roman period, including with early Christians, she risks masking the process by which she determined what constitutes the difference of the past. In order to be accountable to the possible implications of one's own rendering of the past, it is necessary to make this process visible. As I have discussed in both the introduction and chapter 1, I find a fluid/fixed approach to race/ethnicity compelling for making sense of race/ethnicity not only in our time but also for antiquity. This is not because it is the only way to speak about these concepts or because I see modern and ancient ideas as the same. This dynamic approach to race/ethnicity strikes me as more useful than other approaches to race/ethnicity for critiquing racist and ethnocentric mental habits and material practices without denying the rhetorical and material effects that these concepts continue to exert.

For the study of antiquity, this approach allows us to render early Christian discourse "knowable," but does not require that we make early Christians seem "like us." By interpreting ancient discourses of collective identity in terms of this fixed/fluid dynamic, we can chart a difference between ancients and moderns that can be used as a resource for contemporary Christians. Because history writing is fundamentally an activity of and for the present, any difference I assert between modern and ancient people does not exhaust the range of ways in which "now" and "then" differ. Other differences will continually interrupt and reveal the provisionality of my own interpretation. If the next generation of scholars occupies a world in which we have moved beyond racism, I would happily consign this focus to irrelevance.

If we adopt an approach to ethnicity/race as fluid *despite* early Christian reliance on a rhetoric of fixity, it is no longer necessary to sharply differentiate early Christian appeals to being an *ethnos* from those of any other group. Appeals to the past conform to this fixed/fluid character, because the past is claimed as a site of fixity (where things happened), yet this claim always exposes the fluidity of the past and the instability of its meaning in relation to the present (which of the many things that happened are noticed? What is their significance?). Since inhabitants of the Mediterranean basin during the Roman period did not have one specific way of defining *ethnos* and *genos*, the very concept of "common ethnic roots" is slippery, with a variety of different possible meanings. The contents of the "Jewish *ethnos*" and other "ethnic cultures" as well as any purported "common ethnic roots" are themselves contested and dynamic. Christians were quite conventional in developing historical arguments that served to define themselves as a people; and, like their contemporaries, early Christian claims about being members of an *ethnos, laos,* or *genos* are idealizing and ideological, not descriptive.[18] I do not mean, however, that Christian claims to embody a people are "fictive" in contrast to the claims of others. All such claims are "fictive" to the extent that they are constructions, but "real" to the extent that their adherents do not treat them as fiction but reality.

## The Rhetoric of Restoration and the Rhetoric of Descent: Novelty and Heritage in Early Christian Texts

It has become a modern scholarly cliché that ancients valued tradition and disparaged novelty and that early Christians had to defend themselves against charges of abandoning tradition and spreading dangerous innovations.[19] The mid-second-century Christian Theophilus of Antioch states that his three volume work *To Autolycus* aims to demonstrate that "[the Christian] message is not recent in origin, nor are our writings, as some suppose, mythical and false" (*To Autolycus* 3.29). If we take change rather than continuity for granted, it is possible to argue that Christians were not unique in being "new" in the sense of historically recent. Romanness, as defined in the late republican and early imperial period, offers a provocative point of comparison. Just as Augustan innovations were clothed in the language of restoration, so too did Christians manage perceptions about their teachings and practices in the language of restoration—of Israel and/or all humanity.

A rhetoric of restoration accommodates change within an ideal of continuity. This section explores two primary ways that followers of Christ used appeals to the past to portray themselves: as promoting restoration rather than innovation and as living in accordance with their true origins. I examine a variety of early Christian texts that employ such arguments. All of these arguments address pressing issues of how to live in the present and future, and each are formulated using ethnic reasoning: restoration of a people or of the entire human race in its original form. In the subsequent section, I explore a different kind appeal to the past, which emphasizes the positive aspects of novelty by linking them to a rhetoric of realizing one's potential.

For some early Christians, the best defense is a good offense. In his *Apology*, the late second-century Christian author Tertullian dismisses accusations of Christian novelty by arguing that it is the *Romans* who abandon the ancestral customs they claim to venerate:

> You are forever praising antiquity and every day you improvise some new way of life. . . . In fact, as to that very point of ancestral tradition which you

think you most faithfully guard, which above all else you have used to designate the Christians as lawbreakers—I mean the passion for worshipping
gods. . . . I will show instead that you despise, neglect, and destroy that tradition, totally against the authority of your ancestors.

(*Apol.* 6.9–10)

In this passage, Tertullian portrays innovations to tradition as problematic,
charging the Romans with hypocrisy.

To defend Christians, Tertullian suggests that all humans contain the
"essence" of Christianness (in the soul), and adapts the history of Israel to
explain why it is only recently that God made it possible for this essence to
be fully realized—through Christ. This adaptation relies on the idea that the
source of true knowledge and true worship, though incipient in all humans,
historically belonged to one people (*gens*)—the Jews (and *not* the Romans)—but has now become available, through Christ, to all humans.
Christians might be historically recent, but their teachings and way of life
are in continuity with the God historically linked with the Jews. Tertullian
appeals to the greater antiquity of Jews to trump Roman claims to antiquity. By making Christians heirs to this antiquity, he can imply also the superiority of the "new" Christians.[20]

Late second- and third-century Christian texts in eastern parts of the
empire manage perceptions of early Christian novelty less aggressively than
Tertullian. The Pseudo-Clementine *Recognitions*, Clement of Alexandria's
*Protreptikos*, and Origen's *Against Celsus* offer a diverse range of early
Christian texts that all employ a rhetoric of restoration to explain how followers of Christ constitute a people with a past, despite their apparently historic novelty.

For the late second- or early third-century Pseudo-Clementine *Recognitions*, followers of Christ are Hebrews. This text explicitly situates Jesus as
the Christ, whose primary role is to restore the Hebrew people by restoring
its cultic practices. For this text, the pressing problem is a rift among Hebrews as a result of misunderstanding Jesus's nature and function. By framing Jesus as the second prophet sent to restore the Hebrews rather than as
an unauthorized innovator, the Pseudo-Clementine narrative situates followers of Christ as authentic Hebrews.

The narrative appeals to the past both to explain this current rift and to
authorize its own solution: that of accepting Jesus as the Christ and replacing sacrifice with baptism. The *Recognitions* traces the followers of Jesus to
Abraham (and all humans to Noah). The two fourth-century versions of the
Pseudo-Clementine *Recognitions* that survive (in Latin and Syriac) explain
ethnoracial distinctions as having first emerged according to the particular

virtues, knowledge, and behavior of Noah's three sons (*Rec.* 1.30.2–31.2). We learn that the Hebrews constitute one people who can trace themselves to Abraham; he is identified as the progenitor "from whom our race, the Hebrews, who are also called Jews, multiplied" (1.32.1). For this text, this self-description includes the followers of Christ. Instead of presuming that the author of this text must have been Jewish "by birth," I want to explore briefly how the text characterizes the concept of membership in a *genos*. Membership entails the notion of belonging to a genealogically continuous people, but this belonging is indexed by state of mind and actions, not simply "birth." Furthermore, for those not born into membership, it is achievable—at least upon the historical arrival of the second prophet, Jesus.

The *Recognitions* distinguishes the Hebrew *genos* from other descendants of Abraham by the conditions of knowledge under which it began.[21] Once he has learned the "truth" about God and his destiny, Abraham asks for and receives a son—Isaac. Hebrews are the descendants of Abraham via Isaac (*Rec.* 1.34.1–2; see also 1.33.3). Prior to gaining this true knowledge, Abraham has two sons, Ishmael and Eliezer, "from whom the tribes of Arabs and Persians descended" (Syriac) or "from [Ishmael] the barbarian nations descend, while from [Eliezer] the peoples of the Persians descend" (Latin) (1.33.3). Other groups can thus also claim Abraham as their ancestor but cannot trace a genealogical connection to this "truth." The text explains the relationship between these different ethnoracial groups as descent-based, where descent is defined by the conditions of Abraham's knowledge (about divine truths) at their origins. The descendants of Abraham's other sons do not differ due to a difference in their mothers but because of their relation to "truth" and "custom" (1.33.1; 1.34.1; 1.35.1).[22]

Abraham's own state of knowledge sets in motion ethnoracial distinctions among the peoples associated with his sons. Nonetheless, the text makes clear that the ensuing nations, named ethnoracially and characterized by practices, do not remain static over time. Practices (especially piety) shape and potentially transform them. Offering an extended interpretation of the biblical narrative, the *Recognitions* argues that the Hebrews, after their extended habitation in Egypt, needed to spend forty years in the desert to remove "the vices that had been added to them in Egypt" (Syriac, 1.35.1). The Latin version is even more explicit about how proximity and habit can transform the self: "by a series of exercises for forty years a renewal by changed custom might destroy the evils that had grown into them from the customs of the Egyptians by usage for a long time" (Latin, 1.35.1). In other words, Hebrews had become transformed by adopting Egyptian practices for generations. In the *Recognitions*, Moses helps to accomplish this remediation by instituting a temporary corrective measure of sacrifices in God's name (1.36.1–2). Having established a precedent for change (both negative and positive), the text defines Jesus as the prophet of truth who teaches the Hebrews to stop sacrificing—replacing sacrifice with baptism (1.39.1–2).

If sacrifice was the compromise measure taken to wean Hebrews from their Egyptian habits, then Jesus's anti-sacrificial teachings are consistent with the original essence of "Hebrewness." This claim to authentic "Hebrewness" is then deployed to address a larger concern of the *Recognitions*: healing the split within the Hebrew *ethnos* that ensues in response to Jesus. Interestingly, the *ethnos* can be unified not only by Hebrews adopting the correct teaching against sacrifice but by those previously outside the *ethnos* doing so as well. Thus, the boundaries of Hebrewness are porous. By instruction and action one can become a member.

This interesting text has received the greatest attention from scholars wanting to make sense of the relationship between Jewishness and Christianness in the third and fourth centuries. It is most often classified as an example of "Jewish Christianity" in part because the narrative never uses the term "Christian" and locates the followers of Christ as "Hebrews." The presence of ethnic language in the narrative has been explained in terms of Jewish influence: "Since Christianity is considered by the author to be the true Judaism, he finds it necessary to explain the discontinuity [between Jews and Christians] with respect to race."[23] In this view, the presence of arguments that explicitly define followers of Christ as those Hebrews who "restore" the people to its "original" and authentic manifestation is only explicable if it is viewed as a "Jewish" kind of argument. This view implies that "race" would not otherwise be expected to form part of Christian self-definition. This assumption needs to be questioned. What happens if we presume that ethnic reasoning was a regular feature of early Christian self-definition—how might this complicate the way we reconstruct the meaning of "Christian" in relation to "Jew"?

If we turn to consider works by early Christian authors who are more well known today, we also find the rhetoric of restoration in Clement of Alexandria and Origen. In his *Protreptikos*, a treatise ostensibly written "to the Greeks," Clement portrays Christianness as the newest but also the most original form of human existence.[24] In this text, he emphasizes not the continuity between Christianness and the biblical past identified with the history of Israel (as does the author of the *Recognitions*) but reaches back to the origins of human creation to explain the antiquity of Christian novelty. He argues that since the recent historical appearance of Christ, original human unity can be restored (for example, see *Prot.* 1.6.4–5; 9.88.2–3). While the term "Christian" might be new, it actually represents the most ancient form of humanness, including the oldest and truest form of worship. He compares Christians with other peoples who contend for the title of most ancient human race (in this case, Egyptians, Arcadians, and Phrygians):

> Not one of these [peoples] existed before our world (*kosmos*). But we were before the foundation of the world, we . . . were begotten beforehand by God. We are the rational images formed by God's Logos, or Reason (*logika*), and we date from the beginning because of our connection with him, because "in the beginning was the Word." Since the Logos was from the first, he is the divine beginning of all things, but because he lately took a name— . . . the Christ—I have called him a new song.
>
> (Prot. 1.6.4–5).

This passage anticipates the direction of Clement's subsequent argument: this particular new group, "Christians," comprises the original humans even though Christ only appeared recently. Christians, according to Clement, are not just the oldest people but are in fact the *only* human race.

Just as there is one authentic race, so also he thinks there is only one true form of worship. He uses the universalizing claim that Christians are members of a *genos* that encompasses *all* humans in order to ground his claim that Christian worship—as he defines it—is the only true form of religion. According to Clement's argument, the recent historical appearance of Christ offers the opportunity for humanity to be restored and reunited. This argument allows Clement to acknowledge that becoming a Christian entails abandoning ancestral customs but also to argue that this is desirable because they are replaced by something older and truer.

Clement's younger contemporary Origen also walks a fine line between claiming antiquity for and emphasizing the novelty of Christians. In *Against Celsus*, Origen responds to a treatise composed a generation earlier by the philosopher Celsus. Origen describes Celsus as having lambasted Christians in ethnoracial terms, implying that Celsus questions their legitimacy both as a philosophy and as a people. Celsus dismisses Christians as either renegade Jews (*Against Celsus* 3.5) or as a mishmash of troublemakers or idiots who have abandoned their various collective identities: "since the Christians have forsaken their traditional laws (*patria*) and do not happen to be some one people (*hen ti tynchanontas ethnos*) like the Jews they are to be criticized for agreeing to the teaching of Jesus" (5.35).[25] The accusation that Christians neglect "ancestral customs" (including those of *Ioudaioi*) locates Christians within both a contemporary ethnoracial (or civic) framework and a historical one. It also implies that Christians engage in dangerously different practices—ones that break with the past.

To counter Celsus's allegation that Christians abandon ancestral customs—whether customs of Jews or others—Origen appeals to biblical narratives to argue for a historical period of human unity before there was a multiplicity of individual nations with their corresponding ancestral customs. As in Clement's *Protreptikos*, this move implies that all ancestral customs are trumped by an earlier historical moment.

Nonetheless, Origen also positions Christians as a historically recent *ethnos* composed of members of a range of peoples, a collective identity formed in relation to the God of Israel, after the people of Israel largely "failed" to remain obedient to God. In this sense, he concedes but revalues Celsus's arguments that Christians are very similar to *Ioudaioi* and also not one singular *ethnos* but rather a collective one made up of people who have "abandoned" their various ancestral customs. Origen thus locates Christians within a framework of restoration that accounts for their novelty while legitimizing them by linking their new identity to an ancient human unity.

## The Importance of Kinship Claims

We shall return to these works by Clement and Origen in the next section, because they both also draw on the rhetoric of realizing one's potential. But to conclude this section, I want to call attention to how genealogies function in the rhetoric of restoration.

In the *Recognitions*, the argument that Jesus restores authentic Hebrew practices is located within a larger narrative that stresses the genealogical continuity of the Hebrew people with the ancestor Abraham. As I argued in the last chapter, genealogical appeals are important for ethnic reasoning not because kinship and descent are ubiquitous or necessary aspects of how ethnicity or race were conceptualized in antiquity, but because they offer a central way of communicating a sense of ethnic/racial "fixity," essence, and continuity. Nonetheless, arguments from kinship were an important means of communicating this fixity in antiquity, so it is not surprising to see Christians using them. Genealogical lists can function as a shortcut for tracing ethnoracial essence over time. Appeal to descent from particular ancestors is among the favored techniques for shaping claims to a common past. Many ancient texts create both a history and a destiny for groups by styling them as descendants of particular individuals.

Followers of Christ regularly defined themselves as descendants of key figures such as Abraham (Paul, Justin, Pseudo-Clementine *Recognitions*),

Seth (*Gospel of the Egyptians*, *Apocryphon of John*), Norea (*Hypostasis of the Archons*), as well as Jesus (Aristides' *Apology*, Justin's *Dialogue with Trypho*). In such texts, one's future—specifically one's access to salvation—depends on membership in the correct descent group.

In appeals to the past, descent and kinship may especially connote continuity, but can also serve to explain discontinuity. Abraham is central for Jews, including followers of Jesus. The author of 1 Maccabees links Jews and Spartans to a common ancestor, Abraham, drawing upon an element of Greek culture that Greeks *also* value so that "Jews could now partake of it. Indeed, better than partake of it, they could take credit for it. Abraham was ultimately responsible."[26] Here we see how appeal to a purported common ancestor could serve to promote common cause between two or more groups perceived as different in the present. This strategy may serve a range of goals. In the case of 1 Maccabees, the goal may be not simply to position a key ancestor of the Jews as one shared also by Spartans, but also to create a link that would allow Jews to benefit from the favor Spartans received from the Romans.[27]

In the letter to the Galatians, Paul extends to "gentiles" the possibility of becoming descendants of Abraham, as Jews already are.[28] Paul argues that gentiles (or "Greeks") can acquire the honorable ancestry of other Jews by becoming descendants of Abraham through Christ.[29] Simply having Abraham as a common ancestor does not erase the differences between Jews and gentiles, however; placing these two groups under one larger umbrella still allows Paul to rank gentiles (or Greeks) and Jews hierarchically, according to the rhetorical situation. Simultaneously, this genealogical argument allows Paul to redefine Jewishness, suggesting a range of possible ways of understanding what it means to be a *Ioudaios*.

Alternatively, appeal to a common ancestor might be used as the basis for making an argument about why two or more groups are different now, thereby providing a historical "explanation" for contemporary differences. As we shall see in more detail in the next chapter, Christian authors devise or use genealogies to trace their roots to ancestors also claimed by Jews (such as Abraham), sometimes with the explicit purposes of differentiating "Christians" from "Jews."[30]

This legacy persists in later writings, including Eusebius's famous *Ecclesiastical History*. Eusebius relies on the kind of logic articulated by authors like Clement and Origen. In the early fourth century, Eusebius draws on the history of Israel to answer the question of who the Christians are in the first book of his "history" of the Church. While acknowledging that Jesus's ministry in the flesh was in the recent historical past, and that Christians constitute an "admittedly new *ethnos* (*neon homologoumenōs ethnos*)" (*Eccl. Hist.* 1.4.2), Eusebius stresses that

> even if we are clearly new, and this really new name of Christian is recent-
> ly known among the *ethnē*, nevertheless our life and method of conduct, in
> accordance with the precepts of religion, has not been recently invented by
> us, but from the first creation of humans, so to speak, has been upheld by
> the natural concepts of the ancient people who were friends of God.
>
> (*Eccl. Hist.* 1.4.4)

For his proof, Eusebius turns to the Hebrew *ethnos*, known for its antiquity, and especially the figure of Abraham, "whom the children of the Hebrews boast as their own originator and ancestor" (1.4.5). Eusebius handily
appropriates Abraham for Christians, saying, "If the line be traced back
from Abraham to the first man, anyone who should describe those who
have obtained . . . righteousness as Christians, in fact, if not in name, would
not shoot wide of the truth" (1.4.6). In other words, he concludes this section of the introduction:

> At the present moment it is only among the Christians throughout the
> whole world that the manner of religion that was Abraham's can actually
> be found in practice. What objection can there then be to admitting that
> the life and pious conduct of us, who belong to Christ, and of the God-
> loving men of old is one and the same? Thus we have demonstrated that the
> practice of piety handed down by the teachings of Christ is not new or
> strange but, if one must speak truthfully, is primitive, unique, and true.
>
> (*Eccl. Hist.* 1.4.14–15)

Here we can see the sinister supersessionary implications of using a rhetoric of restoration to articulate the distinctiveness of the Christian *ethnos*. It
is precisely because Eusebius defines Christians as an *ethnos* that his argument is coherent. This example suggests that one difference between ancient and modern Christian anti-Judaism turns on the presence or absence
of Christian self-comparison to a people. Eusebius makes Christians a superior people to the Jews, whereas modern Christians have sometimes argued that Christians are superior to Jews because Jews are a people while
Christians exceed these boundaries. Yet as we shall see in the next section,
the argument that Christians exceed the boundary of a single people was
also one that early Christians made using ethnic reasoning. Indeed, by collapsing Christianity with humanity, early Christians could argue that Chris-

tians constitute the ideal form of the human race, whereas all other peoples (and their forms of piety) fall short.

## Realizing Your Potential: Rhetoric of Universal Humanity in Appeals to the Past

Early Christian texts could foreground fixity to negotiate change, either by appealing to restoration of ancient practices or continuity of descent, but they could also highlight ethnic fluidity while nonetheless presupposing a kind of common essence to humanity. Specifically, Christians as different as those who valued Justin Martyr's *First Apology* and the *Tripartite Tractate* could understand Christians as belonging to a people who had realized humanity's "true" potential. Although such arguments seem to emphasize the value of change, they share in common with the rhetoric of restoration the idea that what is new is actually the fulfillment of an original plan or reality.

In this section as in the last, I consider both more and less well-known second- and third-century Christian texts to show that a broad range of early Christians employed this form of ethnic reasoning. Justin's *First Apology*, Clement's *Protreptikos*, and Origen's *Against Celsus* offer familiar examples, whereas the *Sophia of Jesus Christ*, Theophilus of Antioch's *To Autolycus*, and the *Tripartite Tractate* serve as less well-known examples. These examples are not exhaustive and do not have some hidden coherence. But this selection does indicate that this form of Christian argument is not limited to one form of early Christian literature or worldview; as such, it reinforces my overall argument that examination of ethnic reasoning can sustain scholarly efforts to resist reinscribing prescriptive distinctions among varieties of early Christians.

Appeals to the past shape one's claims about the present. For some texts, appeals to the past are used to destabilize one's apparent identity in the present; things might not be what they appear to be at first glance. In a number of texts produced by followers of Jesus, we find motifs that serve to challenge conventional readings of the past in an effort to reread the significance and meaning of one's present collective identifications. For example, Paul famously interprets Jesus in light of Adam (1 Cor. 15). Other texts, such as the *Sophia of Jesus Christ*, *Hypostasis of the Archons*, and the *Apocryphon of John* reread Genesis 1–3 to define a people (*genea*) in relation to a cosmic drama of creation and salvation. Knowing one's origins, one's "root," is necessary for salvation.

The rhetoric of having a "root" nature or essence, like the rhetoric of patrilineages (for example, tracing one's ancestry back to Abraham), relies on the notion of fixity while the injunction to discover or trace one's root, or to "awaken," to be enlightened, to become perfect, or to be reborn all offer different expressions of instability/fluidity/dynamism. Justin Martyr's concept of the *logos spermatikos*, a seed of the divine logos implanted in the souls of all humans (*2 Apol.* 8.1), is probably the best-known early Christian example of how the past could be cited to justify present Christian beliefs and practices as fulfilling the unrealized potential in humans.

In his mid-second-century *First Apology*, Justin Martyr appeals to the past specifically to explain the present: "In the beginning [God] made the human race with the power of thought and of choosing the truth and acting rightly, so that all people are without excuse before God; for they have been born capable of exercising reason and intelligence" (*1 Apol.* 28.3). The *logos* is this shared capacity. For Justin, Jesus is the incarnation of the entire *logos*—so those who follow his teachings follow the Logos in its entirety: "Whatever we say as having been learned from Christ, and the prophets who came before him, are alone true, and older than all the writers who have lived" (23.1). Most broadly, he claims that Christ came "for the conversion (*allagē*) and restoration (*epanagogē*) of the human race" (23.2).

Humanity requires conversion and restoration for two main reasons: first, the people who transmitted the truth about the *logos*, the Jews, went astray—as evidenced by their colonization by Romans in Justin's day;[31] and second, although all humans have the *logos* implanted in them, most peoples have not had access to unsullied teachings about the truth. The teachings that Justin attributes to Jesus both allow "gentiles" to have access to the entire *logos*[32] and offer a way to restore the legacy of the *logos* that the "Jews" have let slip. This reasoning builds on the assumption that the *logos* is a fixed essence, and accounts for its unrealized potential in many humans by implying that what varies are the ways people teach about the *logos*.[33]

Justin offers a version of philosophical debates common in the second century in which Greek philosophers, especially Middle Platonists, sought to demonstrate their philosophy as the oldest, the basis for others:

Like Numenius, Justin traces Platonic philosophy back to an ancient oriental theology, but whereas Numenius allow that this primitive theological tradition was handed down by the 'most famous nations,' Justin contends that Moses was the exclusive source. . . . It is nothing other than the revelation of the *logos* to Moses and the prophets contained in scripture. Christianity is not one, or even the best, philosophy among many; it is the *only* philosophy insofar as it is the reconstitution of the original, primordial philosophy.[34]

As we shall see in the next chapter, Justin renders this argument in his *Dialogue with Trypho* to mean that Christianity is the authentic form of Israel now—not simply the only *philosophy* but the only *people* of God.

As for many Christian authors, Justin depicts the process of becoming a Christian as one of rebirth (*1 Apol.* 61; *Dial.* 85.7–9). Nonetheless, his view that Christ was the historical incarnation of the preexistent *logos* allows him to claim that "[Christ] is the *logos* of which every *genos* of humans partakes. Those who lived in accordance with *logos* are Christians, even though they were called godless, such as, among Greeks, Socrates and Heraclitus and others like them; among the barbarians, Abraham, Ananiah, Azariah, and Mishael, and Elijah and many others . . . " (*1 Apol.* 46.2). Thus, for Justin, the novelty of Christianity is tempered by positioning it in relation to the antiquity of the *logos*. Furthermore, the novelty of individual conversion is moderated by framing it as activating and perfecting the seed of the *logos* already implanted in one's soul.

In Justin's *First and Second Apologies*, the Jews are the people who have historically transmitted the truth about the *logos* even though all humans contain its "seed." In the *Sophia of Jesus Christ*,[35] all humans also seem to contain the "drop" from above, but not everyone understands this. Those that possess the drop and know it understand that they belong to an "unruled" people (*genea*) (*SophJesChr* 99.17–19) and activate their membership to ensure that this becomes their destiny.

The *Sophia of Jesus Christ* is framed around clarifying "the underlying reality of the universe and the plan," which the disciples are struggling to determine before the post-resurrection appearance of Jesus (91.2–9; 92.3–5). The distinction between those who are saved and those who are not seems to turn on one's ability to understand that everything will return to its roots: "everything that came from the perishable will perish, since it came from the perishable. But whatever came from the imperishable does not perish but becomes imperishable" (98.1–6). Those that do not learn or understand this difference go "astray" and "die" (98.7–9).

The disciples learn from Jesus that their "roots" are "in the infinities" (*SophJesChr* 108.20–23) and that Jesus has come to awaken and perfect those who have their origins from "above" yet have been born into this world (106.24–108.23). The disciples ask Jesus about their origins, their destiny, and instructions for how to live: "Mary said to him, 'Holy Lord, where did your disciples come from and where are they going and (what) should they do here?' " (114.8–12). Jesus's reply begins with the actions of the cosmic power Sophia, implying that the disciples come from the perfect realm of Sophia, not this imperfect realm that has been created by her imperfect offspring. Although the end of the text does not spell this out, it seems that the destiny of the disciples and all those who "awaken" and come to understand their "root" is the perfect realm of their origin. Jesus instructs the disciples to live in ways that defy the false gods of this imperfect world, and the text concludes by having the disciples imitate Jesus in going to "tell everyone about the God who is above the universe" (118.24–25). In this text, like Justin's *Apologies*, we find the rhetoric of restoration firmly intertwined with the notion of a potential to be realized in humans.

Clement's *Protreptikos* contains a similar impulse.[36] Especially in the latter part of the work, Clement suggests that those who become Christians undergo a transformation that does not simply restore but actually fulfills previously unrealized potential in all humans. The various forms into which humans have been divided have resulted in a fragmentation of truth. But Christ now makes it possible for this fragmentation to be healed. As if to emphasize both the potential in Greek thought as well as the inability of the potential to be realized in "Greek" terms, Clement cites Homer, attributing his words to the *logos*:

> "Listen, you myriad peoples (*phyla*)" (*Iliad* 17.220), or rather, all reason-endowed humans, both barbarian and Greeks; the entire human race (*to pan anthrōpōn genos*) I call, I who was their creator by the father's will. Come to me that you may be marshaled under one God and the one Word of God.
>
> (*Prot.* 12.120.2–3)

The appearance of Christ has made it possible for the "whole human race . . . both barbarians and Greeks," to be (re)unified as the one *genos* that they actually are (120.2). But this reunification requires the transformation of individual members of various races, notably through the adoption of proper religious attitudes and practices.

Origen also makes use of the argument that Christians fulfill the unrealized potential of humans. This strategy emerges in response to Celsus's apparent allegation that Christians are *unoriginal* in their novelty. As Origen writes, "[Celsus] thinks he can criticize our ethical teaching on the grounds that it is commonplace and in comparison with the other philosophers contains no teaching that is impressive or new" (*Against Celsus* 1.4).[37] When Celsus accuses Christians of unoriginality in condemning idolatry, for example, Origen writes, "in this instance also, as in that of other ethical principles . . . moral ideas have been implanted in humans, and . . . it was from these that Heraclitus and any other Greek or barbarian conceived the notion of maintaining this doctrine" (1.5). The lack of novelty that Celsus views as a liability of Christian teaching and organization Origen positions as proof of its universality; as he puts it, the truths of Christianity are only possible for humans to accept because they resonate with universal ideas all human share:

> There is therefore nothing amazing about it if the same God has implanted in the souls of all humans the truths which God taught through the prophets and the Savior; [God] did this so that every person might be without excuse at the divine judgment, having the requirement of the law written on their heart (Rom. 2:15).
>
> (*Against Celsus*, 1.4)

By locating this universalism within a historical narrative of human development, Origen can speak of Christians as both a universally true philosophy and a historically recent *ethnos* that is authorized and legitimized by original human unity. This universalizing argument relies on rather than opposes ethnic reasoning because Origen portrays Christians as the *ethnos* that embodies these universal truths—an *ethnos* that humans from all other *ethnē* can and should join.

By emphasizing the common origins of humanity (via Adam, Noah, or Seth), followers of Jesus—like other Jews—could formulate universalizing visions of the future of their people by imagining a way for the original unity of human to be reunited in the destiny of a single people. Even when genealogies serve to differentiate groups of humans in the present, these universalizing frameworks for human history support claims that Christ comes to reunify humanity, bringing together individuals from "every human race" into a variously named people (for example, "Hebrew," "Israel," "Christian," "seed of Seth," "immovable *genea*," etc.). The mid-second-century Christian Theophilus of Antioch, for example, locates the original ancestors of all humanity in the scriptures. Theophilus writes that humanity is descended from Seth (*To Autolycus* 2.30) because after six generations, the "seed of Cain" sank "into oblivion" because of his fratricide.[38] Nonetheless, he views Christians as descended from a particular people: "the Hebrews . . . are . . . our ancestors" (3.20). He links Christians with Hebrews both via shared scriptures and a specific ancestor: Abraham, "our patriarch" (3.24).

A final example offers a different form of Christian argument about realizing one's potential. In the *Tripartite Tractate*, preserved in the Nag Hammadi corpus, original unity is identified with divinity: humans intrinsically consist of multiple essences. Nonetheless, the text depicts human salvation as a process whereby humans are ideally transformed (and transform themselves) so that divine unity can ultimately be restored. For this text, salvation is potentially universal, but is imagined as the restoration not of initial human unity but rather of initial divine unity. Humanity changes to become assimilated to and reincorporated into the divine.

As its title suggests, the *Tripartite Tractate* is divided into three main sections that roughly cover the prehistory of the world, the creation of the humanity, and a third part that comprises a range of topics including anthropology, incarnation, and salvation. The entire work is shaped around the premise that the "church" offers the site for the restoration and reunification of humanity with its divine origins. Belief in Christ is portrayed as the means to achieve the ideal of unity:

> For when we confessed the kingdom which is in Christ, [we] escaped from the whole multiplicity of forms and from inequality and change. For the end will receive a unitary existence just as the beginning is unitary, where there is no male and female, nor slave and free, nor circumcision and uncircumcision, neither angel nor human, but Christ is all in all.
>
> (*TriTrac* 132.16–28)

This unification involves "the restoration to that which used to be a unity" through a progression of kinds of teaching tailored to the "form" of the believer.[39]

But it is crucial to note that this unity is not something that individual humans have from the outset. As the second section of the text makes clear, humans were created with a "mixed" nature; the task is to cultivate the "best" portion of one's mixed human nature, the part that comes from the perfect kingdom. According to the *Tripartite Tractate*, "the first human being is a mixed formation, and a mixed creation, a deposit of those of the left and those of the right, and a spiritual word (*logos*) whose attention is divided between each of the two substances from which it takes its being" (106.19–25). This mixture of "left" with "right" substances and the presence of a third element, the spiritual (pneumatic), mirrors the three levels of cosmological organization discussed in the first part of the text. It also foreshadows the subsequent division of humanity into three *genē*, distinguished by a prevailing element (pneumatic—from the spirit, psychic—from the soul, or hylic—from matter).[40] With the arrival of the savior in the world:

> Humanity came to be in three essential types [*rēte kata ousia*], the pneumatic, the psychic, and the hylic. . . . Each of the three essential types [*ousia genos*] is known by its fruit. . . . The pneumatic race [*genos*], being like light from

light, and like spirit from spirit, when its head appeared, it ran toward him immediately. . . . It suddenly received knowledge in the revelation.

(*TriTrac* 118.14–17, 21–23, 28–36)

In contrast to the eager response to the savior that characterizes the pneumatic *genos*, the psychic race emerges as those who are more hesitant in their responses (118.37–119.8), and the hylic race consists of those who "hateful toward the Lord at his revelation" (119.8–16).

How should we understand these *genē*? For Einar Thomassen these three *genē* are "religious qualities, that is to say, ethical and intellectual [ones]" not "genetic composition,"[41] based on the various human responses to the "coming of the Savior" (*TriTrac* 118.24–28). The coming of the savior induces the division of humanity into three *genē* "as people actualize the different potentialities of their souls."[42] I would sharpen Thomassen's reading, following Elaine Pagels and Harold Attridge. Instead of distinguishing between "religious" and "genetic" definitions of a *genos*, they convincingly suggest that these two are combined in the text's ontology: "the soteriology of this text is . . . clearly consistent with its basic ontology, for, on every level of being, *act determines essence*. . . . The coming into being of three kinds of human being is a response to the coming of the Savior and is a result of different attitudes towards him."[43] That is, for the *Tripartite Tractate*, "genetic" composition is the *result* of the "religious" qualities one acts upon—they are inextricably linked. Ethnic membership is defined in terms of religiosity. Each of the three *genē* is a distillation of the initially mixed components of humans. Those who distill the pneumatic component are on the best track, but because humans intrinsically contain all three elements, one can potentially shift between these *genē*. The *Tripartite Tractate*, like some other early Christian texts we have seen (for example, 1 Peter), imagines the ethnoracial consequences of responses to the savior and the adoption of new religious practices.

The universalizing tendency in the texts considered in this section is striking. Early Christians regularly portrayed themselves as the people who embody this universal vision. That is, Christian self-definition as a people was not mutually exclusive with universalism. By locating themselves in a historical narrative whose trajectory moved in an arc from one kind of human (either unified or internally composite) to many kinds of humans, Christians could claim to represent the future reunification or perfection of the entire human race. This argument sought its authority in the past and was especially elaborated in terms of peoplehood.

We now need to examine how both this universalizing tendency and the rhetoric of restoration, with its emphasis on continuity with practices and lineages of the past, formed part of in the fabric of larger Roman-period views and practices of collective identity.

■

# Who's Who in the Roman Empire?

It was not only the Christians who were defining themselves. In both the republican and early imperial periods, the following questions were pressing for many: "Who are the Romans? Are they Barbarians or are they Greeks?" as well as "And *we Greeks*, who were we? . . . What place can we expect today and on what basis?"[44] And to these we should also add questions of regional, local, and civic identities: "Who are the Lydians? Who are the Aphrodisians? Who are the Egyptians?" and so on. Equally important for other inhabitants of the empire was the question "Who are the people of God?" Appeals to the past play a crucial role in the possible answers to these questions of collective identity and difference.

For some authors such as Dionysius of Halicarnassus, Romans are Greeks by origin, which he "proves" by telling the history that both Greeks and Romans have "forgotten," a tale of migration, colonization, preservation and loss of ritual practices, morals, and education. As François Hartog observes, this "solution was favoured by a number of Roman intellectuals—at least for a while—and, of course, also by the Greeks."[45] Hartog carefully attends to how the same claim (Romans are Greeks) might have had significantly different meaning when articulated by a Roman intellectual like Cato and a Greek intellectual like Dionysius. Hartog comments on Cato's history of Rome:

> In Cato, who was the first to choose to write a history in Latin, it [the claim that Romans are Greeks] may have served as a symbolic instrument of emancipation, which made it possible to escape from the Greeks-Barbarian dichotomy, or rather to subvert it, "You Greeks, you classify us among the Barbarians, but we are certainly not Barbarians as our ancestors were Greek."[46]

While Dionysius drew heavily upon Cato, Hartog notes that the context for Dionysius's assertion of the continuity between Romans and Greeks is very different. Not only is he writing in Greek "for a Greek readership," but in his day, at "the beginning of the Augustan period, no Greek can have still believed that the Romans were purely and simply to be classified as Barbarians. After all, at this very moment Strabo was recognizing the Roman's historic mission to take over from the Greeks in the task of civilizing the *oikoumenē*."[47] Hartog convincingly suggests that Dionysius uses the claim that Romans are Greeks primarily for the purposes of answering questions about *Greek* self-definition and meaning in the Roman-dominated world:

The meaning of "The Romans are Greeks" now surely became "We Greeks are also, in a way, Romans. We are their parents, or rather their grandparents, so their empire is, in a way, also ours." In short, genealogy is used to legitimate not only the indisputable existence of this Graeco-Roman empire, which, with the advent of Augustus, established itself even more firmly, but also the place that Greek figures of note claimed within it: "their" place, fully acknowledged.[48]

As Hartog shows in the different cases of Cato and Dionysius, very different motivations may explain an emphasis on genealogical continuity. And when genealogical connections are made between or among groups perceived as different in the present, they serve a range of possible functions. Cato's goal may be to authorize Romans in the face of powerful Greek taxonomies. Dionysius may have hoped to secure a place for "Greeks" in the present Roman Empire by appealing to their common stock at a moment when Romanness could be defined as the fulfillment of the potential of Greekness, a definition implying that contemporary "Greeks" fall short by contrast as a degenerate trajectory of a shared past with Romans.[49]

Other authors, like Dionysius's contemporary Virgil, preferred a different answer to the question of Romanness: for Virgil, Romans are neither Greek nor barbarian. Rather, using a "Greek" historical framework, Virgil constructed a third option for Romans:

> The thesis of Rome's Trojan origin, magnified by Virgil, was to break away from that view and set up Rome as a third group, from the "very start." This was all the more acceptable given that, as Thucydides had pointed out, the dichotomy between Greeks and Barbarians had, at that point, not been introduced. The Trojans may not have been Greeks, but they certainly were not Barbarians either.[50]

By the middle of the second century C.E., yet another solution to the Roman question emerges, embodied in a Greek rhetor's speech in praise of Rome. For Aelius Aristides,

> the old division, long since obsolete, between the Greeks and the Barbarians must now be replaced with one that is all-encompassing and more relevant: between Romans and non-Romans. For the Romans are not simply one "race" (*genos*) among others, but the one that counterbalances the rest. Their name, overspilling the boundaries of a city, designates a "common race": the *genos* of Roman citizens.[51]

Early Christian self-designations as a *genos, ethnos,* or *laos* are frequently quite analogous to the kind of description of Romanness that Aelius Aristides offers here.

Early Christians produced variations on the "Roman question." For example, centuries after the "Roman question" has been most fiercely debated, Eusebius revives it to frame his exposition of the newly legalized Christians: "Anyone might naturally want to know who we are . . . Are we Greeks or barbarians? Or what can there be intermediate to these?" (*Preparation for the Gospel* 1.2.1).[52] In Eusebius's day, this question is no longer a pressing one for Romans, although it remains a shorthand way to speak about all humans. By positioning Christians in the place of Romans, Eusebius may be inviting reflections about the relationship between Romanness and Christianness. While he does not explicitly equate Christians with Romans by this substitution, his framing invites this equivalence.

Most often, Christians either worked from another powerful and totalizing taxonomy: *Ioudaios/ethnē* ("Jew"/"gentile") or combined it with the Greek ones. Hartog's point about motivation is significant here. For a text like Luke-Acts, the followers of Jesus are situated primarily in relation to the Jew/gentile taxonomy, though the text defines them as a third option. Virgil's *Aeneid* is indebted to an overarching Greek framework but resists locating Romans precisely in terms of either Greek or barbarian; similarly, the author of Luke-Acts clearly situates Christians in terms of the past of Israel while creating a narrative distinction between "Christians," "Jews," and "gentiles."[53] But the rhetoric of Luke-Acts may even more closely resemble that of Aelius Aristides in its universalizing vision. Furthermore, as many have noted, the two-part work shifts its geopolitical and theological center from Jerusalem to Rome, permitting an interpretation of the destiny of the Christians as somehow connected with Romanness.

Attempts to define Romans in relation to the longstanding dichotomous convention Greek/barbarian provide a useful point of reference for rethinking Christian texts that position Christians as a third option, even when Jew/gentile replaces Greek/barbarian as the salient antinomy. The same Christian author can define Christians in more than one way: as "true Jews" (or Israelites or Hebrews), as a distinct third option, or—as Aelius Aristides does for the Romans—the common *genos* that counterbalances the rest.

While Dionysius offered one possible answer to the question of who Greeks are in the empire by way of addressing the question of who the Romans are, his was not the only contribution to the question of Greekness in the early imperial period. An important study by Antony Spawforth sheds light on one way that Greekness was negotiated in a provincial context.[54]

Some inhabitants of Asia Minor in the early Roman imperial period used ethnic reasoning to negotiate the meaning of "Greek" in relation to "Lydian" identity. In this example, differences are managed in order to allow individuals to identify as Lydians, Greeks, and sometimes also Sardians simultaneously. Without collapsing the differences between these categories, genealogies serve in part to define Sardians and Lydians as "true" Greeks—indeed, as the ancestors of the Greeks.

Although we should not presume that being Greek *prior* to the Roman period was a transparent, unambiguous identity,[55] Greek self-definition underwent a major shift during the first two centuries C.E. This shift was partly a response to Roman policies in the provinces as well as to Roman perceptions and idealizations of Greekness (perceptions and idealizations that contributed to Roman self-definition). Roman policy and literature redefined Greekness in relation to a particular territory (Achaia) and time period (classical), a move that served Roman interests and to which Roman-period "Greeks" had to respond.[56] Rome also reclassified residents of its provinces, so that some "Greeks" no longer counted as such for Roman political purposes (notably in Egypt and Asia Minor).

Inhabitants of Asia Minor had long had an ambivalent relation to Greekness. "Lydians" were among the regional groups that had been characterized in various relations to Greekness. In some classical Greek sources[57] Lydians are stereotyped as "barbarian," and Strabo also considered them non-Greek.[58] Nonetheless, they were also sufficiently associated with Greekness by Strabo's day to have been subject to "ethnic downgrading" by Romans (from Greek to barbarous "Lydian").[59] More complex still, this Roman demotion failed to translate fully into policy since the Lydian cities of Sardis and Thyatira "appear as members of the *koinon* 'of the Hellenes who live in Asia' " under Augustus and "gained admission into the Panhellenium" under Hadrian.[60]

Spawforth convincingly argues that Lydians, among others, managed this complexity by positioning themselves in relation to Greekness: they "offered themselves as heirs, as living embodiments, of the prestigious brand of Hellenism so admired by their philhellene Roman rulers."[61] They accomplished this in a range of ways, especially including modes of speech, but also through genealogical practices that linked their regional identities to Achaia. Instead of merely asserting their authentic Greekness, however, the Lydians defined themselves *both* as a distinct ethnic group *and* as Hellenes; moreover, the citizens of Sardis were able to assert themselves as simultaneously Sardians, Lydians, and Greeks. The association of key ancestors with all three groups supported these multiple claims.

Here we find civic and ethnic identities blurring: "The names of the citizen tribes of the Sardian polis . . . all consciously invoke Lydian history, myth, or geography."[62] More significantly, two of these names link the Sardians/Lydians to larger collectives. Specifically, " 'Pelopis,' after Pelops, [is the] eponym of the Peloponnese and founder of the Olympian games . . . [and] 'Asias,' after Asies . . . [is the] eponym—after a Lydian tradition known to Herodotus—of continental Asia."[63] By the second century C.E., these tribe names inform "the official titulary that Sardis adopted under Hadrian: 'first mother city of Asia and all Lydia and Hellas.' " As Spawforth notes, the claim to be the "mother city of Hellas" depends on the "Lydian origins of Pelops" and positions the Peloponnese, equated with Hellas, as a Lydian colony.[64]

These genealogical claims fulfill a range of functions. Locally, they serve to bolster civic (Sardian) claims to be the first city of the region and province by positioning Greeks, as defined in Roman territorial terms, as the descendants of the Sardians. While perhaps useful for negotiations with Rome, this claim may have been primarily directed at intercity and regional rivalries of Roman period Asia Minor.[65] Linked genealogies also allow one to claim more than one ethnicity (Lydian, Hellene), highlighting the situational and strategic character of identification.[66] This multiplicity is one manifestation of the fluidity of ancient notions of ethnicity.

From this example, we can take away a few valuable lessons for the study of early Christian self-definition. Appeals to the past exceed literary forms. They also played out in domains of epigraphy, civic organization, and cultic practices. It also suggests that early Christians raised or based in the eastern part of the Roman Empire may have negotiated collective identities first and foremost with respect to local/regional identities and Helleneness, and less directly with Romanness. It is worth noting that definitions of Romanness are not explicitly on the table in this Lydian/Hellene/Sardian context. They may be implicitly so, to the extent that inhabitants of Asia Minor were dealing with Roman perceptions of Greekness.

Of course, "Greeks" and "Romans" were not the only ones trying to claim and negotiate collective identities in the empire. Claims of historical ties between peoples, especially when these peoples are perceived to be different in the present, were used in a range of contexts. In the first century B.C.E., for example, Diodorus of Sicily skeptically recounts a claim he attributes to fourth-century B.C.E. Hecataeus of Abdera about Egyptians— that Athenians and Judaeans descend from Egyptians.[67] Diodorus reports: "The Egyptians say that . . . a great number of colonies were spread from Egypt all over the world," including "Babylon," where they established priesthoods and astrology, and "practically the oldest city in Greece, Argos" (*Diod.* 1.28.1, 2). Furthermore, Egyptians allegedly claim "that the *ethnos* of the Colchi in Pontus and that of the *Ioudaioi* in between Arabia and Syria, were founded as colonies by certain emigrants from their country; and this is the reason why it is a long-established custom among these *genē* to circumcise their male children" (1.28.2–3). "Even the Athenians, they say, are colonists from Saïs in Egypt," offering such proofs as etymology for the city's name, political organization, alleged Egyptian background of early Athenian kings, appearance, manners (*ēthē*), and religious practices (specifically, the veneration of Demeter and "swearing by Isis") (1.28.4–29.4).

Diodorus's source, Hecataeus of Abdera, used the "Greek ethnological method," which "tried to understand the common past of mankind historically,"[68] including by attributing Greek ancestry to "barbarians." Many non-Greeks also accepted Greek interpretations of their national origins or some of the basic premises of Greek historiography and adapted them to produce their own origin stories (as is the case of linking Romans with Greek history via Aeneas and the Trojans).[69] Some non-Greeks tailor Greek claims of antiquity and cultural superiority to offer competing unifying historical narratives of humanity: in addition to Hecataeus, Xanthus renders Lydians as the progenitors of the Greeks, and a number of Jewish authors similarly reconstruct cultural history to make Jews the predecessors of the "best" of Greek culture.[70] As in debates over the Roman question, when asking whether to forge alliances, seek support, justify colonization, or authorize power, motivation matters.

## Conclusion

Celsus accuses Christians of unoriginality. In some respects he is absolutely right. Not only does Christian teaching resemble elements of contemporary philosophy, but even Origen's strategy of defending what is distinctive and historically recent about Christian teaching and practice with reference to an original human unity is indebted to both biblical and classical Greek models. Early Christians used biblical sources (and traditions of biblical interpretation) as well as what Elias Bickerman called the "Greek ethnological method" of imagining human history in universalizing terms (and traditions of its interpretation) to define themselves. From both biblical and "Greek" explanations about human history (and their respective adaptations and interpretations by Judaeans, Greeks, Egyptians, and Romans among others), Christians learned ways of classifying human groups in historic relation to one another that emphasized an original unity ("universal history") while also explaining differences among human groups despite original unity. By producing variations on this totalizing framework, Christians explained their recent historical emergence, asserted their superiority, and articulated universalizing ideals (that the diverse, particular communities were/should be a unified *ekklēsia* and that humanity ought to be reunified in and as the "Christian" people, or whichever descriptive is used to define this people).

Were early Christians simply borrowing the frameworks of their "others," asserting that they had a place within these stories? And if so, why invent on someone else's terms? These questions, while provocative, are misleading because they assert a self/other divide that may be the outcome of ethnoracial historical discourses rather than its starting point. Although early Christians are generally interpreted as the "others" to Jews, Greeks, Romans, etc., it is important to remember that the individuals who began to think about themselves as members of a category "Christian" were not in fact "others" to all from the outset.[71] Those we retrospectively include under the umbrella of "early Christian" invent themselves and their "others," as well as their possible interrelations, through a process of negotiating the flexible discourses that were already part of the sociopolitical and rhetorical-imaginative contexts they inhabited.

Irad Malkin gives a modern example that illuminates both the flexibility of ethnoracial discourses and the strategic uses of a minority group using the dominant group's "master narrative." Both Jewish Israeli intellectuals and Palestinian Arabs have used biblical narratives of Israelite occupation of Canaan in order to re-present Jewish and Palestinian identities, respectively, as "Canaanite," with drastically different degrees of success. In linking modern Jewish Israelis with Canaanites, the goal was "to convince the native Arab populations (and the Jews themselves) of their common regional heritage so as to live happily together."[72] In contrast, identifying Palestinians as the descendants of biblical Canaanites "provides a natural right to Palestine, standing in the same relation to modern Jews as the Canaanites did in antiquity to the Hebrews. It is used here not to integrate but to distinguish and create a hierarchy between peoples in relation to the same land."[73] While identifying today's Israelites with Canaanites of the past has failed to win broad support (especially in the face of a more successful alternative Zionist narrative), equating Palestinians with Canaanites has become popular since the 1980s. These two adaptations of the same biblical narrative, suggests Malkin, have had such different receptions because of their relative persuasive power to insiders and outsiders in light of the contemporary political situation.

Even if the interpretive identification of modern Jewish Israelis with ancient Canaanites might seem surprising, it is unsurprising to find Jewish Israelis drawing on an ethnic myth produced within their sacred literature.

But what about the Palestinian Arabs? Malkin notes, "Just as the ancient Romans appropriated the Trojan side of the Greek myth of Troy to account for (and validate) their national origins, the Palestinian 'Canaanites' use the Hebrew myth of the Old Testament. In both cases, myths of *origines gentium* depend on a notion of a 'full' story adopted from the Other."[74]

Malkin cites the Palestinian use of the broad contours of Jewish history as an instance of a people accepting "the Other's view of themselves," albeit for the purposes of promoting pro-Palestinian political goals. "Peoples often accept the Other's view of themselves. Sometimes, reacting against it, they retain the discourse but change the roles. Such adoptions, which emphasize a connection and a distinction at the same time, are particularly significant . . . when one party convinces the Other that to be valid and credible that Other's past must be *interdependent* with its own."[75] What Malkin calls attention to is not merely the hegemony of particular ways of thinking about the past but also the *mobility* of ethnoracial discourses. The asymmetrical distributions of cultural, material, and political power may indeed account in part for the macronarrative that at least some members of a nondominant group use to define the group, but they do not predetermine the way such a narrative is interpreted and used.

Instead of thinking of ethnographic histories as narratives wielded by those with political and/or cultural power to which nondominant groups must either capitulate (assimilate) or subvert (resist), I suggest we think of the process as rather more complex. The emergence of a successful political and cultural power requires the consolidation of persuasive self-representations (for example, Virgil's *Aeneid* and its indebtedness to a "Greek" historical framework). Nonetheless, hegemonic narratives always presuppose excluded alternatives and these latter not only remain resources for contestation and resistance but also underscore the contingency of power and the possibilities for new definitions.

Origin stories about a nondominant group that appropriate the discourses and conceptual apparatus of the culturally and/or politically dominant may serve as a means of subversion, not simply an indication of subordination or assimilation.[76] But these polarities only represent the extreme ends of the spectrum of possibilities. Such appropriations may more frequently serve to produce new definitions of minority and majority groups that strengthen the coherency, comprehensibility, or even the *possibility* of a given minority group in a changing sociocultural and political landscape.

Early Christians adapted available "master narratives." But we should not interpret these adaptations as evidence that early Christians were merely derivative or intentionally deceptive. Rather, by imagining early Christians as comparable to other groups in seeking to negotiate their collective identities with reference to the past we gain further appreciation for how and why early Christians found ethnic reasoning important for self-definition. Christian appeals to the past share with non-Christian appeals an attempt to authorize a collective identity in the present by devising a common past.

Some early Christians undertook to define Christianness partly in and through historical narratives that both claim illustrious and ancient origins of the (apparently new) Christian people and locate Christianness in relation to other ethnoracial groups and their associated glories or reputed shortcomings. The double-sided character of ethnoracial discourse benefited early Christians in their attempts to define Christianness as an authentic identity that was nonetheless newly emerging in the sociocultural landscape of Roman Empire. Justin Martyr, Theophilus of Antioch, Clement of Alexandria, Origen, and the authors of the Pseudo-Clementine *Recognitions*, the *Sophia of Jesus Christ*, and the *Tripartite Tractate* all build arguments that account for historical change either as the preservation, restoration, or perfection of authentic truth(s) of the past or as the corruption and confusion of such truth(s). In appeals to the past, the teachings (or texts) and ways of life associated with particular ethnoracial groups are the vehicles of this preservation or corruption. By adapting literary and rhetorical techniques employed by authors seeking to legitimize, define, or locate particular ethnoracial groups in historicizing terms, early Christians could portray themselves as a people with a respected pedigree (emphasizing stability over time) with historical ties to other peoples (notably "Hebrews" but also Greeks and various "barbarians"). Moreover, they could also position Christians as a distinct people because they embody the best preservation or perfection of the truth(s) (thereby accounting for change and ethnoracial difference).

By means of historical narratives and cosmological narratives, early Christians sought to offer compelling stories of who they are (their "essence") by speaking about their collective origins and the transmission of truth. At the same time, early Christians implicitly or explicitly undergirded their claims for the essence of Christianness by presupposing the malleability of identity: ethnoracial groups and/or individuals devolve or evolve in relation to the criteria for Christianness. The next two chapters elaborate this complicated dynamic and illuminate its implications for how we reimagine both the relations between Christianness and Jewishness and the relations among varieties of Christianity.

# 3

■

# "We, Quarried from the Bowels of Christ, Are the True *Genos* of Israel"

## Christian Claims to Peoplehood

As we have seen, ancient definitions of ethnicity and race were disputed and changeable. Even when some fundamental "essence" like blood, flesh, or seed is asserted as the basis for reckoning membership in an ethnoracial group and traceable through means such as genealogy and kinship, ideas about race and ethnicity gain persuasive power by being subject to revision (flexible) while purporting to speak about fundamental essences (fixed). Early Christians participated in this dynamic treatment of ethnicity/race, adapting it to define Christianness.

Approaching ethnoracial discourse as doubled-sided in early Christian texts calls into question how we use ethnoracial categories to reconstruct Christian-Jewish relations and imagine the differences between Christians and Jews in antiquity. Besides the identification of Jesus as the Christ, Christianness is most often distinguished from Jewishness in ethnoracial terms: "Christianity lacked the ethnic links of Judaism."[1] That is, Christianness is often defined by ethnoracial contrast with Judaism—Judaism has "ethnic links" but Christianity does not.[2] This statement implies that what is meant by "ethnic links" is transparent and agreed upon. But unspoken assumptions that "ethnic links" are ones of biological kinship obscure the ways that reckoning race or ethnicity *even by descent* is a social process, for individuals and for groups.[3]

The previous chapter discussed how followers of Christ mitigated the widespread suspicion of new groups either by claiming descent from Hebrews (Theophilus of Antioch and the author of the Pseudo-

Clementine *Recognitions*) or by presenting themselves as a new people who were prophesied and planned from ancient days (Clement of Alexandria's *Protreptikos*). This chapter develops the insight that early Christians used ethnic reasoning to locate themselves as an ethnoracial group with an esteemed historical pedigree (despite their recent arrival on the historical scene). Doing so has implications for how we imagine the relationship between Christianness and Jewishness in antiquity. Using Justin Martyr's *Dialogue with Trypho the Jew* (ca. 160 C.E.),[4] I argue that reconstructions of ancient Jewishness and Christianness cannot turn on the axis of ethnoracial/non-ethnoracial.

In the first, second, and third centuries C.E., neither Christianness nor Jewishness corresponded to a clear, unified social formation or ideological conception. In addition, their relationship to one another was dynamic and often blurry. Ethnic reasoning could be used to define and contest both Christianness and Jewishness as well as to differentiate between them. In his *Dialogue with Trypho*, Justin Martyr uses ethnic reasoning to define Jews and Christians as members of different *ethnē/laoi/genē* that share a common deity, scripture, and some common ancestors (most notably, Abraham and Jacob). Justin distinguishes "Jews" from "Christians" by making the former appear a relatively more "fixed" kind of people and the latter a relatively more "fluid" kind of people.

Before turning to a detailed analysis of the text, however, it is worth previewing the complex ways that Justin makes use of the double-sided dynamic of ethnoracial discourse in defining Christians and Jews. Justin's definition of Christianness foregrounds fluidity, making acquisition of membership universally available through a change in beliefs and practices.[5] By contrast, Justin seems to bind his Jewish interlocutors to notions of fixity, alleging that they define membership and salvation through flesh and blood lineages. He states that his Jewish interlocutors view themselves as "Abraham's seed according to the flesh" while Justin and his ilk are those who share "the faith of Abraham."[6] In such passages, Justin seems to reinforce the perception that Jewishness is a "fixed" affiliation established by birth, whereas Christianity is a voluntary affiliation established by "faith."

At first glance, then, Justin seems to fulfill modern expectations about the content of ethnicity/race (determined by claims to physical ancestry) and to locate ethnicity/race as a defining feature of Jewishness that is absent from Christianness. But Justin's argument resists such a reading: not only does he define Christianness in terms of ethnicity, but he also treats ethnicity/race as double-sided (fixed and fluid). That is, Justin's argument does not rely solely on a contrast between fluidity (Christian) and fixity (Jewish). These more obvious emphases are counterbalanced by more subtle subcurrents in the *Dialogue*. Justin at times portrays Christians as having a fixed essence and, especially through his characterization of Trypho, indicates a view of Jewishness as fluid.

His depiction of Christianness may foreground fluidity, in the sense of being open to all, but Justin also seeks to present it essential (that is, fixed) terms. He does this in three ways. First, Justin genealogically links all humans through Noah, implying that all share an essence that gives us the capacity to become members of this new people of God.[7] His second technique is also genealogical: Justin describes the results of becoming a Christian as having become a descendant of Abraham, Jacob, or Christ.[8] Justin's third way of "fixing" Christianness is to demarcate its boundaries and essence by, for example, stating that "there is no other way" to gain salvation than to "know our Christ" and "be baptized."[9] Yet even as Justin seems to stabilize the criteria for Christianness, he indicates that his definition of what constitutes Christianness differs from that of other followers of Christ.[10] Whether pertaining to eating practices, attitudes towards observance of Mosaic law, Christology, resurrection, identification of authentic teachers, or prophecy, it is clear that Justin's view of Christianity is one among many in his day. Through his use of ethnic reasoning, Justin asserts some coherency and legitimacy to the varied practices and beliefs of individuals and small groups who did not necessarily all view themselves as "Christians," let alone as members of a universal and united movement. At the same time, his definition of Christianness implicitly critiques rival Christian alternatives.

Justin's construction of Jewishness also includes this combination of fixity and fluidity. Although Justin says that Jews claim that their salvation is secured by descent "according to the flesh," nowhere in the text does Trypho affirm this view. The first time that Justin makes such a claim, Trypho "responds" by saying that he must interrupt to ask a "very urgent question," which proves to be about the relation between *practice* and salvation (*Dial.* 45.1–2); he ignores the issue of descent. Instead, Trypho embodies a notion of peoplehood that also foregrounds fluidity: he exhorts Justin to adopt his way of life (8.4) and he stresses the centrality of observances for defining membership as a Jew and ensuring salvation.[11]

The complex dynamism within and overlap between Christianness and Jewishness in Justin's rhetoric make sense if we think of the mid-second century as a time when these identities are neither uniform nor wholly distinct. Justin is staking out a distinct domain and meaning for Christianness when these are murky and contested. This perspective requires revising some of the ways that the *Dialogue* has been interpreted.

Justin is frequently cited as evidence for Christianity having become a predominantly gentile movement by the mid-second century. Marcel Simon's hypothesis that Christians and Jews were in active competition with each other for members remains popular as an explanation of the general historical setting for Justin's *Dialogue*.[12] Because its rhetorical setting is that of a dialogue between a Christian and a Jew, Justin's *Dialogue* also interests scholars as evidence of contact between Jews and Christians in second-century Asia Minor. The difficulty with interpreting Justin's text and its historical situation in this way is twofold. First, it presupposes a clear and meaningful distinction between gentile and Jew in relation to Christianness. The fact that Justin comments that Christ-believing gentiles who observe the law are likely to be saved suggests that such a distinction was not obvious to all (*Dial.* 47.4). We do not need to imagine that Justin has a coherent group in mind to deduce that the question of the relation between observance of Mosaic law, gentiles, and enacting one's belief in Christ is unsettled. Second, even if individuals are calling themselves "Jews" and "Christians" in Justin's day,[13] what is meant by these terms is also far from clear—so we cannot extrapolate to imagine discrete social groups behind each rhetorical statement about Jews and Christians.

Instead, I see Justin presupposing the fluidity of the borders between Jews and Christians.[14] We should not envision Justin drawing on an established Jewish framework or social formation as a foil for his own process of Christian self-definition. Rather, contemporaneous with Justin's own construction of Christianness (with its internal and external borders), Jewishness is also being constructed.[15] Both "Jews" and "Christians" could draw upon the same scriptures, symbols, and surrounding social institutions to craft themselves.[16] As the following analysis demonstrates, ethnic reasoning was one means by which Christianness and Jewishness was articulated and contested.

This fixed/fluid dynamic of ethnic reasoning functions to reveal and conceal the fuzziness of the boundaries between Jewishness and Christianness. While seeking to differentiate them (to declare their differences as real), Justin also repeatedly blurs their boundaries, by defining Christians as Israel and by negotiating the range of possible practices he deems acceptable for membership. Belief in Jesus as the Christ seems to be the only factor that consistently distinguishes "Christians" from "Jews" in this text,[17] and Justin does not even insist on a single understanding of Christ's nature.[18]

This chapter has two main parts. In the first section, I examine some of the ways that Justin defines Christians as a people. Justin uses ethnic reasoning fluidly to reinterpret scripture and construe Christianity as universal. At the same time, he stabilizes this fluidity by appearing to speak about a coherent, distinct group: the true Israel, a new race, or the descendants of Abraham. The second part of the chapter reveals the significant tensions between Justin's allegations that Jews define themselves (and their relation to salvation) "according to the flesh" and his more fluid characterization of Jewishness.

Justin's portrayal of Jews as believing that Jewishness is determined by physical relationship ("according to the flesh") correlates with what most modern readers expect to find in a definition of ethnoracial membership. As a result, most interpreters fail to see that "race" continues to be central to Justin's definition of *Christianness*, including the idea of an ethnoracial essence.[19]

Justin does not reject but rather redefines the concept of ethnoracial membership for Christians in the *Dialogue*. By depicting an alternative definition of race as based on descent "according to the flesh," Justin constructs a foil for his argument that the Christian race is formed through faith in Christ and obedience to a "universal" law.[20] That is, the idea of Jewishness as physically determined follows rather than precedes Justin's assertion that Christians constitute a people. He claims that his Jewish interlocutors mistake flesh and blood for the *correct* essence of faith, spirit, and obedience to God. Justin resituates the notion of an ethnoracial essence (something "fixed") by defining faith, not blood, as the essence of Christianness. It is the conceptualization of peoplehood that undergoes transformation, not the notion of membership in a people.

The notion of descent *kata sarka* is a red herring for modern readers—and perhaps ancient ones—that distracts from the porousness between Jewishness and Christianness and from the internal variability of both Christianness and Jewishness. Recognizing the rhetorical function of descent "according to the flesh" in the *Dialogue* allows for the conclusion that Justin seeks to construct a Christianness that relies upon the idea of peoplehood. The distinction that Justin makes between Jews and Christians is one of degree and authenticity, not of kind.

## Christians as a People

In the *Dialogue*, Christians constitute a people (*genos, ethnos, laos*). Membership in the Christian *genos* is gained, Justin says, by changing one's state of life,[21] by following the commandments of Christ,[22] by becoming like Abraham in his faith,[23] and by belief in Christ.[24] He emphasizes that these criteria are transformative and universally applicable: by changing religious attitudes and practices, people of "of various colors (*poikilos*) and appearances (*polyeidos*) from every human *genos*" become members of another people (*Dial.* 134.5).

Justin offers a range of descriptions for this people including the true and spiritual Israelite *ethnos*, the *genos* of Judah, Jacob, Isaac, and Abraham,[25] the "true high priestly *genos* of God,"[26] another people (*laos heteros*),[27] another Israel,[28] the *ethnos* promised to Abraham,[29] and the *genos* headed by Christ.[30] Using such phrasing, Justin vacillates among three views: (1) Christians are *the* Israelite *genos* or *ethnos* (thereby effacing the right of any other group to this identity) or the people promised to Abraham; (2) Christians are a second, superior, Israelite people; and (3) Christians are a distinct people formed out of individuals from all human races, including Jews. Thus Justin at times competes for the title of *genos/laos/ethnos* of Israel or privileged ancestry with his Jewish interlocutors (encompassing the first two views),[31] while at other times he seems to carve out a space for Christians as a distinct people (the third view). Each of these views presumes that ethnoracial identification is mutable, yet "real." None of these treats Christian peoplehood as metaphorical.

## Christians as Israel

By exploring how Justin develops his claim that Christians are Israel, we can see how ethnoracial concepts get transformed even as their authenticity and coherency is asserted. On the one hand, the title "Israel" remains stable— along with its association of chosenness, inheritance of divine gifts, and salvation. On the other hand, its meaning is contested. Justin adapts the meaning of "Israel" but masks his own creativity under the guise of knowing its "true" meaning.

Near the opening of the *Dialogue*, Justin sets the stage for much of the *Dialogue's* subsequent arguments by claiming that "we, who have been led to God through this crucified Christ are the true spiritual Israel, and the descendants (*genos*) of Judah, Jacob, Isaac, and Abraham who, though uncircumcised, was approved and blessed by God because of his faith and was called the father of many *ethnē*" (*Dial.* 11.5). In this compact statement, Justin challenges the right of Trypho and others to the title "Israel" and asserts that followers of Christ are the true descendants of those whom Trypho might also claim as his ancestors. This genealogical appeal creates expectations in readers for Justin to address what it means to be a descendant of Judah, Jacob, Isaac, and Abraham and how this relates to following God's commandments, especially circumcision.

While he applies "Israel" to Christians at this early point of the *Dialogue* (11.5), Justin only develops this claim more fully near its conclusion, where he demands that Trypho and his companions explain "the significance of the name Israel" (125.1). From their silence, Tessa Rajak persuasively argues, "there could be no more graphic demonstration that they lack any title to the claim."[32] Justin confirms this lack not only by offering his own etymology for the name but also by accusing Jews of appealing to physical descent to define themselves and their soteriological status:

> Israel was [Christ's] name from long ago, which he conferred upon blessed Jacob when he blessed him with his own name, announcing thereby that all who come to the father through him are part of the blessed Israel. You, however, have comprehended nothing of this, nor do you make an effort to understand, but, expecting with assurance to be saved only because you are children of Jacob according to the flesh, you again deceive yourselves, as I have repeatedly shown.
>
> (*Dial.* 125.5)

To understand the force of Justin's criticism here, we have to look at the chapters immediately preceding this statement. What becomes clear is that Justin is not constructing salvation by descent as the problem, as it might appear from this excerpt. Rather, he is arguing for a different way of reckoning descent that ensures salvation. Indeed, Justin's allegation that Jews look to fleshly descent to define membership and salvation comes upon the heels of his having positioned Christians as descendants of Jacob and offspring of Christ: "As therefore from that one Jacob, who was also surnamed Israel, so also we who keep the commandments of Christ, by virtue of *Christ who begat us to God*, both are called and in fact are, Jacob and Israel and Judah and Joseph and David, and true children of God" (123.8). This citation is itself the climax of an extended section in which Justin uses Isaiah and Ezekiel to argue that scripture speaks of two Israels.

Justin asserts that God is angry with the Jews, and that they are "foolish and hard-hearted." (*Dial.* 123.4). Then he writes:

> By Isaiah, [God] says thus about *another Israel*: "In that day shall Israel be third among the Assyrians and Egyptians, blessed in the land which the lord of Sabaoth blessed, saying, blessed shall be my people which is in Egypt and among the Assyrians, and my inheritance is Israel" (Is. 19:24). When God blesses and calls this people (*laos*) Israel, and cries aloud that it is his inheritance, how is it that you do not repent, both for deceiving yourselves *as though you alone were Israel, and for cursing the people* (laos) *that is blessed by God*? For also when he was speaking to Jerusalem and the countryside around it, he added again, "And I shall beget men upon you, my people Israel, and they shall inherit you, and you shall be a possession for

them, and you shall no more be bereaved by them of children" (Ezek. 36:12).

(*Dial.* 123.6)

Justin situates these citations both to offer the unsupported claim that Isaiah speaks of two Israels and to anticipate objections to such an interpretation. Indeed, immediately upon the heels of the Ezekiel citation, Justin interjects Trypho into the monologue, essentially making him prove Justin's point that Jews think that they alone are Israel: " 'What follows?' said Trypho, *'Are you Israel, and does he say all this about you?'* " (123.7). Justin snipes that either Trypho is so thick that he really does not get it or is just wanting to be contentious, but allows that perhaps Trypho just wants more proof of Justin's claims (123.7). Trypho receives no more speaking lines in this section, but merely "nods in assent" that the latter is the case, and Justin plows ahead:

In Isaiah again, if you do listen . . . God, speaking about the Christ, calls him in a parable Jacob and Israel. Now he says in this way, "Jacob is my servant, I will help him; Israel is my chosen, I will set my spirit upon him and he shall bring forth judgment to the gentiles. . . . And on his name shall gentiles hope" (Is. 42:1–4). As therefore from that one Jacob, who was also surnamed Israel, *so also we who keep the commandments of Christ are, by virtue of Christ who begat us to God, both are called and in fact are, Jacob and Israel and Judah and Joseph and David, and true children of God.*

(*Dial.* 123.8)

Glossing Jacob and Israel as Christ, Justin defines Christ as the first ancestor of the people "Israel." As the last portion of this passage indicates, "keeping the commandments of Christ" is the key criterion of membership, although procreative imagery portrays the relationship between members and Christ.

When competing to be "Israel," Justin contends that "we, quarried from the bowels (*koilia*) of Christ are the true race of Israel (*Israelitikon to alēthinon genos*)" (135.3). This striking phrase leads Justin to elaborate why this "true race" differs from "your people," referring to Trypho. Using Isaiah 65:9–12, which distinguishes between God's chosen "seed of Jacob and Judah" and those destined for slaughter (135.4), Justin writes:

But you yourselves perceive that this seed of Jacob is here spoken of another kind (*allo ti*), for none of you would suppose that it was spoken about your people (*laos*). For it is not granted that they who are of the seed of Jacob can leave a right of entrance to them that are born of Jacob, nor that [God], when upbraiding the people as being unworthy of inheritance, should again promise it to them, as though he received them. But even as the prophet says, "And now, you house of Israel, come and let us walk in the light of the Lord. For he has dismissed his people (*laos*), the house of Jacob; because their place was filled, as at the first, with soothsayings and divinations" (Is. 2:5). So also here we must perceive *two seeds of Judah, and two races (*genē*), as two houses of Jacob, the one born of flesh and blood, and the other of faith and spirit.*

(*Dial.* 135.5–6)

Justin thus reads prophetic texts not as attempting to call a people back to order, but as about two rivals to the title "Israel." As the final sentence of this passage shows, he differentiates the two *genē* not only with regard to salvation but also by how they are constituted ("flesh and blood" versus "faith and spirit"). But these differences cannot be neatly mapped in terms of literal to metaphorical since what is at stake is the real Israel. Rather, Justin creates this opposition in order to rewrite what material practices as well as ideas will constitute the *genos* Israel. In so doing, he also authorizes his reading of scripture.

## Christians as an "Other" Race

Justin does not only depict Christians as *verus Israel*.[33] He also defines Christians as a people without explicit reference to Israel. Trypho is nevertheless positioned as a member of a contrasting people:

*For Christ, being the firstborn of every creature, has also become again the head of another race (*allo genos*), which was begotten anew of him by water and faith and wood,* which held the mystery of the cross, even as Noah also was saved in wood. . . . When therefore the prophet says "In the time of Noah I saved you," as I said before, he is speaking to *the people (*laos*) that was similarly faithful with God,* and had these symbols. Moreover Moses having a rod in his hand let your people through the sea. But *you suppose that he spoke only to your people (*genei hymōn*), or your land.* Yet in that the whole earth, as the scripture says, was flooded . . . it is clear that God did not say this to your land, but *to the people (*laos*) that obey him* . . .

(*Dial.* 138.2–3)

Instead of differentiating between two houses or seeds of Jacob, this passage uses scriptural references to Noah to support his interpretation of Christ as the progenitor of a new "other" people through baptism, faith, and the cross. This interpretation, positioned as the key for scripture, hides the ways that scripture undergirds this particular reading of Christ and functions to delegitimize the alleged scriptural interpretations of Trypho and his companions. Justin claims that "your people" misunderstand the scriptures; in particular, they misunderstand the people about whom the scriptures speak. This passage implies that Trypho belongs to a people disobedient to God, a theme which pervades the *Dialogue*.[34]

A different interpretation of scripture produces a reading that authorizes a "new people," but at the same time the competition for shared scripture is waged as an ethnoracial one: Justin implies that membership in different peoples results in different interpretations. Classifying biblical interpretation ethnoracially makes the interpretive process seem fixed when it is in fact variable—even among those who identify themselves as members of the same group.[35]

## Christians as Descendants of Abraham

As we have just seen, Justin defines Christians as a people especially through interpretation of biblical passages. In the process, he portrays Jews as those who use the wrong kind of logic to define themselves, while he, as a Christian, understands what peoplehood really means. Consequently, he claims that Christians are the people blessed by God and best capable of understanding scripture. When Justin introduces the identification of Christ-believers as "Israel" (*Dial.* 11.5), he also locates them in the *genos* of Abraham. He elaborates this connection to Abraham especially in the context of interpreting Deuteronomy 32:16–23, part of a speech given by Moses to the Israelites about the consequences of improper religious behavior:

> And the Lord saw, and was jealous and provoked because of the anger of his sons and daughters, and said: "I will turn my face away from them, and will show what shall happen to them in the last times, because they are a perverse generation, children in whom there is no faith. They made me jealous with a no-god, they made me angry with their idols. I will make them jealous with a non-people (*ouk ethnos*), with an *ethnos* that does not understand I will make them angry . . . " (Deut. 32:19–21)
>
> (*Dial.* 119.2)

Justin uses this in-group condemnation of Israelite faithlessness and idolatry as his opening to define Christians as the *ethnos* used to punish God's "sons and daughters." This citation's reference to a "non-people" might seem to support an argument that Christians do not constitute a people at all.[36] But Justin does not take this option. Instead, he combines a pastiche of other scriptural references to interpret this "non-people" as a new kind of people:

> After that righteous one [that is, Jesus] was slain, we sprouted up afresh as another people (*laos heteros*), and shot forth as new and thriving ears as the prophet said: "And many *ethnē* shall flee to the Lord in that day to become a people (*laos*) . . . " (Zech. 2:15). But we are not only a people, but also a holy people (*laos hagios*), as we have already proved: "And they shall call it a holy people, redeemed by the Lord" (Is. 62:12).
>
> (*Dial.* 119.3)

Justin emphasizes that Christians are a people, specifically a people brought into existence from many peoples after the death of Christ. The term "holy" for the people contrasts with the idolatry attributed to the Israelites.[37]

Justin continues by explicitly addressing how Christians compare with other peoples. He implies that chosenness is one distinguishing feature of his own people: "Thus we are not a people (*demos*) to be despised, nor a barbarian tribe (*phylon*), nor like the Carian or Phrygian peoples (*ethnē*), but God has chosen us, and has appeared to those who did not enquire after him. 'Behold, I am God,' God says, 'to the people (*ethnos*) who did not call upon my name' (Is. 65:1)" (*Dial.* 119.4).

The remainder of this passage suggests that the link between a people and a deity is not the only kind of difference between Christians and others; ways of reckoning descent also matter. He now contrasts Christians with other *ethnē*, especially those *ethnē* who can also define themselves as descendants of Abraham:

> For this [the Christian *laos*] is the *ethnos* that God long since undertook to give Abraham, and promised to make him the father of many peoples (*polloi ethnē*), not saying father of Arabs or Egyptians or Idumaeans. For he also became the father of Ishmael, a great *ethnos*, and of Esau, and there are still a great number of Ammonites. Noah was also the father of Abraham and in fact of every human race (*pantos anthrōpōn genos*), and others became ancestors (*progonoi*) of others [that is, other peoples].
>
> (*Dial.* 119.4)

Here, Justin establishes a distinction between God's promise to Abraham to be the father of many *ethnē* and the ability of multiple *ethnē*—including Ammonites and Ishmaelites—to trace their lineages back to Abraham. *Is-*

*raelitikoi* or *Ioudaioi* are, however, conspicuously absent from this example. Justin uses this definition of ethnoracial membership by descent to link the "non-people" of Deuteronomy 32:21 with the Christian people. Abraham is not just the ancestor of specific peoples, such as the Ammonites or Ishmaelites, but is also the ancestor of a *collective ethnos*, the Christians.

The fact that scripture does not name the "many *ethnē*" promised to Abraham is crucial for Justin's point: God did not say that Abraham would become the father of Arabs, Egyptians, or Idumaeans, nor is Abraham like Noah, who can be called the father of "every human race." For Justin, this vague "many *ethnē*" fathered by Abraham forms the basis for a single *ethnos*, equated with the new, holy people that sprout up after Christ's death.

Justin now gets to the heart of his point, specifying the terms of ethnoracial membership for the new holy people: the new race (of Christians), one promised long ago to Abraham, is formed out of those individuals who respond to Christ with faith and action (changing their life), as Abraham responded to God.[38] While Abraham can rightly be called their father, the terms of kinship are distinguished from those that allegedly define membership in other groups (Arabs, Egyptians, Idumeans, Ishmaelites, Ammonites, etc.):

> What more then does Christ here grant to Abraham? This, that by a similar calling he called him with his voice, telling him to go forth from the land in which he was living. And all of us God also called by that voice and *we went forth from the state of life (politeia) in which we were living* . . . And we shall inherit the holy land together with Abraham, receiving our inheritance for a boundless eternity, being *children of Abraham because we have a similar faith with him.*
>
> (*Dial.* 119.5)

Because the individuals who make up the new people come from many different peoples, Abraham can thus be understood as the "father of many nations," while Justin can still call the result a single "holy people." Without specifying the basis for other definitions of peoplehood, Justin here offers an apparently different measure—that of faith in Christ and a transformed way of life.

Justin's interpretation raises the question of the place of Jews in Justin's story about the formation of this new people since they too trace their ancestry to Abraham. He addresses this issue near the end of this textual unit, by contrasting the Israelites critiqued by Moses in the scriptural text and the new holy people, as Justin defines it. He concludes by reaffirming that what ties this holy people to Abraham is faith: "Therefore [God] does promise

[Abraham] the *ethnos* when it is of the same faith (*homoiopistos*) with him, pious (*theosebēs*) and righteous (*dikaios*), and pleasing to the father. But [God] does not include you, 'in whom there is no faith' (Deut. 32:20)" (*Dial.* 119.6). This sharp statement seems to explicitly exclude the "you"—by implication, Jews—from the *ethnos* promised to Abraham. But the force of the contrast applies more to the conceptualization of ethnicity, rather than to an unyielding categorical exclusion of a particular *genos* from this new *ethnos*. A little later, Justin allows that "some of your *genos* will be found children of Abraham, seeing that they are also found in the portion of Christ" (120.2; see also 33.2, 39.2, 130.2), but he stresses throughout the *Dialogue* that belief in Christ is necessary for being a "true" descendant of Abraham.

## Descent as a Red Herring:
## The Fluidity of Trypho's *Genos*

In Justin's use of ethnic reasoning to define Christianness, beliefs and practices enable membership in this people, but membership also entails acquisition of ancestors that one might not previously have had (in the case of gentiles, Abraham and Jacob).[39] Justin treats his ethnoracial claims for Christians as contested—he is not the only one to claim to be a member of Israel or a descendant of Abraham, for example. Sometimes Justin claims that Trypho (or his teachers) misunderstands scripture and uses ethnic reasoning to authorize his own readings; other times he attributes Trypho's interpretive differences to diverging ideas about descent. In reinforcing his claim that Christians are Israel, Justin incapacitates Trypho's implied objection by stating: "You, however, have comprehended nothing of this, nor do you make an effort to understand, but, expecting with assurance to be saved only because you are children of Jacob according to the flesh, you again deceive yourselves, as I have repeatedly shown" (*Dial.* 125.5). We now need to take a closer look at Justin's assertion that his interlocutors rely on physical descent or "fixity" as the primary marker of membership and measure for salvation.[40]

On three occasions, he explicitly states that Jews believe, or their teachers teach, that salvation is ensured by descent from Abraham or Jacob "according to the flesh" (*Dial.* 44.1; 125.5; 140.2). By refusing to link salvation to descent *kata sarka*, Justin seems to imply that Trypho views this as a vital criterion for salvation. But as I noted earlier, Justin never places such a claim in Trypho's mouth. Justin appears to accept that Trypho is a descendant of Jacob (and Abraham) *kata sarka* although he does not specify what this means. We should be cautious about interpreting descent "according to the flesh" as a transparent description of how membership or salvation is reckoned among "Jews." Instead, we should ask how Justin uses this idea in his arguments. In my view, the idea of descent according to the flesh functions as a kind of red herring in the *Dialogue*. That is, it draws attention away from the way that Justin uses this allegation to construct "fixity" by descent for Christians. The idea of descent through the spirit allows Justin to invest Christianness with a historical longevity and substance, even as he insists on its fluidity (its openness to all).

We also need to reckon with the way that Justin shapes Trypho's character and their discussions. Trypho's "self-presentation" in the *Dialogue* is at odds with these three pronouncements about Jewish self-definition and soteriology. This tension suggests that Justin views Trypho's *genos* and *bios* as both fluid and troublingly similar to his own. But instead of making Justin's arguments incoherent, Trypho's more fluid embodiment of Jewishness actually allows Justin to tackle the fluidity within his own *genos* and the porousness between it and that represented by Trypho.

## Genos Kata Sarka

The concept of descent *kata sarka* can be used in a relatively neutral sense, to indicate something like our modern sense of kinship.[41] In the *Dialogue*, however, descent "according to the flesh" has a primarily negative connotation, because of the way that Justin ties it to ideas about salvation. The example cited above functions to disown Jews of the title "Israel" and to dismiss alternative biblical interpretations while also providing a contrasting image for the definition of Christians as a people descended from Jacob in a superior manner (125.5).

The first occasion in the *Dialogue* in which Justin appeals to descent according to the flesh also emphasizes the soteriological consequences of ethnoracial membership:

> You are sadly mistaken if you think that, just because you are descendants of Abraham according to the flesh, you will share in the legacy of benefits that God promised would be distributed by Christ. No one can participate in any of these gifts except those who have the same ardent faith as Abraham, and who approve all the mysteries. . . . There is no other way but this: that you come to know Christ, be baptized with the baptism which cleans you of sins . . . and thus live free of sin.
>
> (*Dial.* 44.1–2, 4)

This passage accepts that Trypho can define himself as a member of the *genos* of Abraham *kata sarka*, but denies that this qualifies him for God's promises.[42] In this excerpt, "faith," knowledge of Christ, and baptism are Justin's eligibility requirements for receiving God's promises. Were we to consider only this passage, we might conclude that Justin is contrasting faith with kinship or ethnoracial identity (so that Christianity could be understood as a religion characterized by faith and Judaism as a religion characterized by "ethnic links"). But the larger context of this passage does not support such a reading. For Justin, sharing Abraham's faith, believing in Jesus as the Christ, and being baptized create "ethnic links" with Abraham as well as Judah, Jacob, Isaac, and Christ; Christians are members of a *genos/ethnos/laos*—the one that he thinks will be saved.

Indeed, Justin first introduces the idea of descent as a component of membership in a people with respect to *Christ-believers*, defining them as the "true spiritual Israel and the *genos* of Judah, Jacob, Isaac, and Abraham" (*Dial.* 11.5). This suggests that construing Jews as a people who also reckon descent from these ancestors is a strategy whereby Justin can bolster his definition of Christians. That is, his interest in presenting *Christians* as a people, the people of God, drives his characterization of Jews as a people who must be defined differently. Descent *kata sarka* serves as a foil for a contrasting Christian way of reckoning descent according to faith.[43] Both kinds of descent connote a kind of "fixity" to ethnoracial membership, even though we tend to interpret faith as producing a less binding affiliation than "flesh."

Descent according to faith is fluid for Justin, insofar as this kind of descent can be acquired—through belief in Christ, baptism, and following the commandments of Christ. But descent according to the flesh also appears to be fluid in the *Dialogue*. It is not just Christians who can acquire descent. This is most vivid in Justin's comments about the effects of circumcision on proselytes. According to Justin, Jews treat male converts as "native-born" (*autochthōn*) once they have been circumcised (123.1). It is not relevant to my point whether or not Justin is accurate or referring to any historical situation. What is relevant, however, is that he offers a specific instance of a ritual being interpreted to produce kinship and ethnoracial identity. This passage suggests that when Justin attributes to Jews the view that they merit salvation because of descent "according to the flesh" from Jacob or Abraham, he specifically has in mind descent reckoned by the practice of circumcision, not birth.

Circumcision occupies Justin's attention repeatedly in the *Dialogue*, in part because of its association with Abraham. He states early on that "the custom of circumcising the flesh . . . was given to you as a distinguishing mark to set you off from other *ethnē* and from us" (16.2).[44] This statement is not simply a comment on what makes Jews visibly distinct, but what produces a "Jew" at all. Justin plays on this later to define Christians, in the passage that describes circumcision as making a male proselyte a "native-born" Jew: "we who are deemed worthy to be called a people (*laos*) are likewise an *ethnos* because we are *uncircumcised*" (123.1). It is crucial for Justin's argument to parse the meaning of circumcision so that it remains that which produces a male Jew but not that which makes salvation possible. Justin stresses that Abraham's faith and not his circumcision is what engenders a lineage of salvation.[45] He also criticizes the practice of circumcision for its gender-specificity, pointing out that it is available only to males.[46]

In one additional passage near the very end of the *Dialogue*, Justin attributes a belief in salvation as the result of descent *kata sarka* not directly to Trypho but to his "teachers": "They deceive both themselves and you when they suppose that those who are descendants (*spora*) of Abraham according to the flesh will certainly share in the eternal kingdom . . . suppositions which the Scriptures show have no foundation in fact" (140.2). Justin supports these accusations with appeals to both scripture and gospel. On the one hand, he cites a combination of passages from Isaiah (1:9; 66:24) and Ezekiel (14:14, 18, 20) to support his position that not all descendants *kata sarka* will be saved. On the other hand, he cites Matthew 8:11–12 to support his view that other people will be saved.

While appearing to condemn an argument about salvation by descent, it is once again crucial to note that Justin does not reject genealogical arguments per se, having just defended the view that Christ calls all humans to salvation with reference to the descendants of Noah's sons, claiming that despite their different paths, both lineages are blessed and eligible for salvation (*Dial.* 139.1–5). But he condemns the view attributed to Trypho's teachers that lineage alone is sufficient for salvation "even though they be faithless sinners and disobedient to God" (140.2). Ironically, Justin's arguments share with these alleged rival teachers the importance of descent, but he implies that they do not give piety its due. While genealogical arguments certainly figure prominently in some rabbinic definitions of Jewishness, they do not function as Justin suggests. Instead, genealogical arguments at times appear to attempt to secure a fixity to Jewish identity that is not in fact clearly secured.[47]

## Trypho

If Justin uses descent *kata sarka* as a foil for defining *Christian* descent, so too does he craft Trypho's character to help him define Christianness. In particular, Justin foregrounds Christian universality (fluidity) even as he seeks to stabilize its content (fixity). Furthermore, he uses Trypho to acknowledge and negotiate the diversity (fluidity) within Christianness and the blurriness between Christianness and Jewishness (fluidity). Justin's character attributes fixity and particularity to Trypho even while Trypho emerges as a representative of a fluid and porous group.

To understand how Trypho can embody fluidity while also being pegged as a member of a fixed group, it is necessary to examine another binary construction important for Justin's rhetoric. This binary (particular/universal), like descent according to the flesh/according to faith, resonates with modern assumptions about race and ethnicity. A central reason why Jewishness and Christianness are often mapped as ethnic/nonethnic is because we tend to associate ethnicity/race with "particularity" and "fixity" and to define "universality" as its fluid opposite. Justin positions Trypho as representing a "particular" way of life, linked to his ancestors (*Dial.* 10.1, 11.1, 3), whereas Justin claims to offer a universal and eternal law for all humans (11.2, 4). So far, Justin does not trouble modern presuppositions.

Nonetheless, Justin also attributes an ethnoracial identity to those who follow this universal, eternal law: they are the "true and spiritual Israelite" people, the "*genos* of Judah and Jacob and Isaac and Abraham" (*Dial.* 11.5, also 135.3). The particular/universal asymmetrical binary is a structuring device whereby Justin can differentiate himself from Trypho despite considerable common ground. But the fulcrum of difference that separates the particular from the universal is *not* ethnic/nonethnic. Both groups are construed as peoples. Instead, the particular is construed as limited and temporally bound ("fixed"), whereas the universal is construed as eternal and more fluid, because anyone can adopt the universal law and join the universal people.

Justin defines his *genos* and correspondingly its law as a universal one, in contrast to the laws that apply to one particular *genos*: "the law given at Horeb . . . belongs to you alone, but that other [law] belongs to all people absolutely" (*Dial.* 11.2). This other law "must now be observed by all those who lay claim to the inheritance of God." Justin equates it with Christ: "as an eternal and final law was Christ given to us" (11.2).[48] In addition, Justin views adoption of this new law as what gives its followers the right to be called "the true spiritual Israel" (11.5).[49] This explanation suggests that Justin is not simply aiming to define his group as a universal people, but in fact competing for the right to *be* Israel, a specific people whose terms of membership are under contention.

Justin adds another quite different explanation for why he does not view circumcision and Mosaic law as criterion for membership in the Christian people. Instead of locating the law transmitted by Moses as good but super-seded, he defines it as a corrective for "your people showed itself to be wicked and ungrateful" (*Dial.* 19.5–6). He also defines the earlier covenant of cir-cumcision between God and Abraham as intended "to distinguish you from the other *ethnē* and from us Christians" for the purposes of future punish-ment (16.2, 3, see also 19.2). This second explanation, that circumcision marks off male Jews for punishment and the law was given in response to disobedi-ence, prepares readers for an oppositional definition of Christianness.

There is a tension between Justin's two explanations. Both define cir-cumcision and the Mosaic Law as particular, but the first explanation (law given at Horeb: particular; law of Christ: universal) links the two "laws" to-gether sequentially so that the latter can be defined as the true manifestation of the former (the same, only better),[50] while the second positions them op-positionally (Mosaic law is particular because it is corrective and temporary, while the law of Christ is universal because it is positive and eternal).

The law that Justin deems "universal" is of course his particular under-standing of the law rendered with the assertion of its global and eternal ap-plicability. For both Justin and Trypho, it is actually specific laws and prac-tices that indicate membership for *both* Christians and Jews. It is by no means clear that the "particular" is merely "fixed," since Justin describes Trypho as interested in converting Justin to his way of life (*Dial.* 8.4). But by locating Trypho on the "particular" side of the universal/particular bi-nary, Justin minimizes the fluidity of the identity Trypho represents.

Trypho criticizes the way of life Justin represents not because Justin is not descended *kata sarka* from Abraham or Jacob, but on the basis of piety (*Dial.* 8.3–4, 10.2–4). Trypho insists that Justin follows a way of life that falls short of proper piety, by not following the "whole written law" (8.4) and by justifying this lapse through an appeal to the man identified as the Christ:

> You place your hope in a crucified man and still expect to receive favors from God when you disregard his commandments. Have you not read that the male who is not circumcised on the eighth day shall be cut off from his people? This precept was for stranger (*allogenos*) and purchased slave alike. But you scorn this covenant, spurn the commands that come after, and then try to convince us that you know God, when you fail to do those things that every God-fearing person would do.
>
> (*Dial.* 10.3–4)

This criticism only makes sense if Justin seeks to define piety on the basis of the texts and traditions shared with Trypho; it structures Justin's subse-quent argument to be one of asserting difference in the context of common ground. This passage also implies that Trypho views "God-fearing" enacted through observing God's commandments as primary to membership in his *genos*—there is no indication here that salvation is assured without proper piety. Trypho does not invoke descent *kata sarka* but rather piety as the basis for salvation. Finally, it is worth noting that circumcision appears here as a fluid mechanism for bringing males into the "people."[51]

Justin may foreground Trypho's concerns about how to practice piety precisely because religious observances—obeying the commandments of Christ—are also central to Justin's definition of what it means to be a member of his holy *genos* (for example, see *Dial.* 11–16). This is not only a matter of negotiating differences between "Christians" and "Jews" but also among Christians, since Justin makes clear that observances are also a matter of contention among those who believe in Christ. This last point is discussed further below.

Religious practices play a double-sided role in Justin's ethnic reasoning. They can be used as evidence of either fixity or fluidity. In the case of Jewishness, Justin defines circumcision as a practice that distinguishes them from all other peoples, including Christians (*Dial.* 16.2), but he also sees it as a practice that can create Jews (123.1). In the case of Christianness, despite Trypho's charge that Christians do not follow a way of life (*bios*) separate from the gentiles (10.3), Justin holds up practices (baptism, not eating meat sacrificed to idols) as essential aspects of membership (fixed) whose performance can also create Christians (fluid). For Justin, this fluid acquisition of membership as a Christian can be described in "fixed" terms as acquiring descent from Abraham, Judah, Jacob, Isaac, and Christ.


## Fluidity Within Christianness and Between Christianness and Jewishness

Trypho asks whether "some" (*tines*) can be saved if they "desire to live keeping the institutions of Moses, and believe in this Jesus who was crucified, recognizing that he is the Christ of God . . . " (*Dial.* 46.1). Justin states: "In my opinion, Trypho, such a one will be saved . . . " (47.1). The logical implication of this exchange might seem to be that, so long as one believes in Jesus as Christ, one can continue to follow the customs particular to one's *ethnos* or *genos*. But this is not the point Justin wants to make, because he never entertains the possibility that a Phrygian, Egyptian, or Greek could maintain their ancestral customs after having becoming a follower of Christ. Rather, Justin insists that for "gentiles," becoming a member of the

Christian *genos* means giving up their former customs: "some among every (*genos*) have repented of the old evil manner of life belonging to each people (*genos*)" (121.3).[52]

Only followers of Mosaic law can continue with their former practices and adopt belief in Christ. This is an interesting exception for a couple of reasons. First, it calls attention to the emptiness of Justin's arguments that Mosaic law is to correct disobedience or is superseded by Christ. His concession indicates at least the likelihood that Christ-believers were not unanimously convinced by such arguments. Second, making an exception for Mosaic law underscores the blurriness among those using shared scripture and claiming common ancestors. What Justin elsewhere insists are two distinct peoples ("two seeds of Judah, and two races (*genē*), as two houses of Jacob, the one born of flesh and blood, and the other of faith and spirit" [*Dial.* 135.6]), are here potentially indistinguishable.

And, as the passage continues, we find that this blurriness extends to Christ-believers who come "from the gentiles." Justin adds a caveat to his affirmation that Christ-believing followers of Mosaic law will be saved: they will be saved "unless they try to persuade others—I mean those from the gentiles (*apo tōn ethnōn*) who have been circumcised by Christ and are free from error—to keep the commandments that they do, saying that one will not be saved without them" (*Dial.* 47.1). This statement has been interpreted as Justin's attempt to prevent "Jewish" converts to Christianity from making Mosaic law and circumcision necessary for gentile Christ-believers. Justin seems to object to the idea that gentiles who wish to join the people of Christ will be convinced that to become a "native-born" member of the *genos* that Justin proclaims is the true, spiritual Israel, one would adopt the practices many associate with being a member of the Israelite people—observance of the Sabbath, circumcision for men, as well as festivals and sacrifices (for example, 23.3–4). But the Christ-believers who follow Mosaic law and might attempt to persuade gentile Christ-believers to do likewise are not necessarily "Jews" or those who were observing Mosaic law prior to believing in Jesus as the Christ; these hypothetical individuals might also be "from the gentiles."[53] Indeed, he states that circumcised gentiles who observe Mosaic law within the Christian *genos* will likely be saved so long as they also believe in Christ (47.4).

For Justin, it is necessary and desirable to become a member of Christ's *laos*, but in seeking to control what this entails he reveals considerable overlap with Trypho's way of life and considerable diversity among Christ-believers. Justin differentiates between two kinds of intra-Christian diversity: dissenting but "pure" Christians[54] and Christians in "name only."[55] When Justin raises the issue of intra-Christian differences explicitly, only once is observance of circumcision or Sabbath the point of dispute (*Dial.* 47.2–3). In this context, the intra-Christian difference is elicited by a question from Trypho, who asks: "Why . . . did you say, 'in my opinion, such a one [who observes Mosaic law] will be saved'? There must be others who hold a different opinion" (47.2). This is a typical strategy for Justin. Trypho similarly precipitates comments on divergent Christian views about eating meat sacrificed to idols,[56] the nature of Christ,[57] and on the millennium.[58]

In remarking on the range of views held by those who see themselves as Christian, Justin situates his own attempts to "fix" Christianness within a situation of intra-Christian fluidity. Since he views some people as illegitimate bearers of the name "Christian," Justin must contend with alternative articulations of Christianness when defining what it means to be a member of the Christian people.[59] Justin does not use ethnic reasoning directly to confront alternative Christian perspectives, but other early Christians do. Indeed, what Justin does by attributing to his interlocutors deterministic definitions of race/ethnicity linked to soteriological claims, other early Christian authors do to condemn Christian rivals. As the next chapter explores, Clement of Alexandria and Origen depict their Christian rivals as holding rigid notions of how physical descent relates to salvation. They accuse so-called "gnostic" or "Valentinian" Christians of holding the position that some humans are saved by nature, and that these natures can be differentiated into *genē*.

## Conclusion

Justin's argument defies an easy distinction between ascription (fixity) and achievement (fluidity) as the basis for ethnoracial membership. Both are at play in the *Dialogue*. In this text, Justin seeks to resignify existing ethnoracial classifications. He does not contrast Christians to Jews in terms of figurative versus literal peoplehood, however. Justin presents his Christian *genos* as very "real."

Even though he disparages his Jewish interlocutors for their supposed emphasis on descent, Justin preserves the significance of physical descent and kinship by asserting the common lineage of the different human *ethnē* and *genē*. The consequences of the faith, behavior, and ritual (baptism) can be described in terms of descent, appearing to be "fixed." This claim supports his universalizing argument: individuals from all human *genē* are eligible to become members of the true Israelite race,[60] the new holy people,[61] because they are all "siblings" by nature and descendants of Noah.[62] Although Justin's definition of Christianness is universalizing and fluid to the extent that he envisions this people as open to all, membership must still be attained.[63] In keeping with Justin's *logos spermatikos* idea in the *Apologies*, each individual must activate their eligibility through faith and obedience to the new way of life (as understood by Justin) in order to gain salvation or "inheritance" from God.[64] As Christians, individuals *become* direct descendants of Christ (as they are reborn), and they also can be called descendants of "Judah, Jacob, Isaac, and Abraham" (*Dial.* 11.5). Additionally, the consequences of membership in the Christian people actually correspond to what he accuses Jews of believing: namely, that being a member of the Christian *genos* ensures salvation. For Justin, ethnoracial mutability is thus deeply intertwined with ideas about a fundamental essence, and ethnoracial membership bears directly upon individual salvation.

We should thus resist the temptation to draw the contrast between Judaism and Christianity as that between "an ethnic monotheism" (Judaism) and "a proselytizing monotheism that had cut loose from the ancestral ways" (Christianity).[65] Historical reconstructions of Christian/Jewish collective identities cannot turn on the axis of non-ethnoracial/ethnoracial or metaphorical/literal. As I stated earlier, it is the conceptualization of peoplehood that undergoes transformation, not the notion of membership in a people. This conceptualization does not merely happen in contrast to a static, preexisting Jewish sense of peoplehood, but rather it happens concurrently and overlapping with Jewish conceptualizations of identity and peoplehood.

When interpreting early Christian texts, we should distinguish between the rhetorical distance placed between Christianness and Jewishness by some authors and the dependency of these same authors on the conceptual framework drawn especially from biblical traditions and contemporary discourses to imagine Christians *as a people*. Whether the Christian people are said to be the authentic form of the "true Israel" or a "new people," Christian supersessionism can be understood in part as a product of the Christian claim to embody themselves authentically as the *people* of God precisely through their religious practices. This claim is consistent with ethnic reasoning and is not a sign of its absence.

# 4

—

# "A *Genos* Saved by Nature"

## Ethnic Reasoning as Intra-Christian Polemic

The idea of changing one's ethnicity or race may sound quite strange to modern ears, since we live in a world that accustoms us to view ethnicity and (perhaps even more so) race as "givens." Although it is still common to find "race" defined as a concept characterized by the belief in its immutability, I take an alternative approach drawn especially from Ann Stoler's argument that "the force of racial discourse is precisely in the double-vision it allows, in the fact that it combines notions of fixity and fluidity in ways that are basic to its dynamic."[1] Early Christians craft Janus-like arguments about ethnicity/race, as we have seen in Justin's *Dialogue with Trypho*. Whereas the last chapter calls for rethinking how we define Jewishness in relation to Christianness, this chapter highlights the implications of arguing that intra-Christian polemic exploits the double-sided character of ethnic reasoning.

Christian texts penned against rival Christian views regularly rely on ideas about race/ethnicity/kinship to create boundaries among forms of Christianness. For example, Christian writers such as Irenaeus, Clement of Alexandria, and Origen depict their own positions about Christianness as fluid because open to all, while caricaturing their rivals as holding rigidly essentialist and elitist notions about who can achieve gnosis or salvation based on their "racial" heritage. Although elaborated differently, their insistence upon fluidity in the face of alleged fixity recalls Justin's critique of alleged Jewish appeals to descent "according to the flesh" as the basis for salvation. Nonetheless, like Justin, Clement and Origen imagine Christians as members of a new people. We should not mistake their emphases on fluidity for an absence of ethnic reasoning in their own constructions of Christianness. It is not only their Christian rivals who use ethnic reasoning. Furthermore, despite charges to the contrary, those rivals who use ethnoracial language to differentiate among humans portray ethnoracial boundaries as permeable.

Texts classified by modern scholars as "gnostic" have long been recognized as sites for ethnoracial self-definition.[2] A large number of the texts in the Nag Hammadi Library as well as passages preserved in the writings of heresiologists like Irenaeus use ethnic reasoning to speak about salvation and define "insiders" and "outsiders." The "saved" are defined variously, including as descendants of Seth and members of the "immovable *genea*"; in other texts, humanity is divided into three *genē* (spiritual, soul-endowed, and material), with salvation being linked to the first two groups.

For some scholars, such ethnoracial language is a marker of sectarianism,[3] setting them apart from "mainstream" forms of Christianness. In such interpretations, modern assumptions about ethnicity, race, and kinship as innate or fixed combine with a "friendly" reading of the works of Irenaeus, Hippolytus, Clement, Origen, and Epiphanius to reinforce the theological binary of heresy/orthodoxy. Ethnoracial language is contrasted with universalizing language as sectarian (or "heretical" or "gnostic"[4]) is to "mainstream" or "proto-orthodox." These scholars largely accept the assertions made by Christian authors such as Irenaeus, Clement of Alexandria, and Origen when they claim that rival Christians view salvation as coming "from nature" (that is, innate or fixed) and classify a small group of humans as "elect" and "saved by nature" in contrast to all others.[5]

For example, Clement of Alexandria claims that a rival teacher, Theodotos, holds the view that humans come in three types—the "naturally" saved (the "pneumatics," named for their *pneuma* or spiritual element); those that have the free will to choose salvation or damnation (the "psychics," named for their *psychē* or souls); and those that are "naturally" excluded from salvation (the "hylics," named for their *hylē* or materiality): "The pneumatic is saved by nature (*physei*); the psychic, having free will (*autoexousia*), has the capacity for faithfulness (*pistis*) and incorruption or unfaithfulness and corruption according to its choice; the hylic is lost by nature" (*Exc. Theod.* 56.3).[6] Origen and Clement characterize some of their Christian rivals as sectarian and heretical not only by labeling them after a teacher—"Valentinians" after Valentinus, rather than "Christians,"—but also by claiming that people like Theodotos understand ethnoracial concepts as rigidly fixed in their views of criteria for salvation.

In order to avoid reinscribing the polemics of early Christian texts and to gain a more adequate reconstruction of the diversity within early forms of Christianness, we must ask not only what is at stake when these men portray the anthropology and self-understanding of their rivals as "fixed," but also look to see whether and how ethnic reasoning informs their own positions. Reading early Christian texts for their dynamic use of ethnic reasoning avoids an interpretive framework governed by the judgments of the historical winners of these theological debates. By attending to their common rhetorical strategies, we can better understand the process by which early Christians sought to explain salvation and anthropology while fighting with one another to produce authoritative teachings. Paying attention to the way that ethnic reasoning relies on the idea that ethnicity/race is both fixed and fluid offers a way to examine early Christian literature that is still often held apart, such as "gnostic" and "nongnostic." Indeed, my approach supports challenges to the viability of such distinctions. The view that "gnostics" believed in a form of "soteriological determinism" is one produced by a particular modern interpretation of ancient Christian polemic that uses ethnic reasoning.

I build on the work of scholars who have sought to interrupt the continuity between ancient heresiology and modern interpretations. The crucial importance of investigating these longstanding connections has been most recently and eloquently developed by Karen King.[7] Luise Schottroff initiated a skepticism about the characterizations of "gnostic" anthropology (and its implications for soteriology) as deterministic.[8] She set in motion further consideration of the rhetorical and polemical interests of authors like Irenaeus, Hippolytus, Clement, Origen, and Epiphanius, all of whom provide extensive negative comments about Christian rivals.[9] Building on Schottroff's work, Michael Williams has proposed that the idea that the catchphrase "immovable race (*genea*)," which appears in five Nag Hammadi texts to designate insiders,[10] can be interpreted as potentially open to all humans—not as a predetermined, elite, and fixed group.[11] Elaine Pagels and Harry Attridge similarly interpret the three ethnoracial distinctions of the *Tripartite Tractate* as referring to groups constituted by their actions rather than by ascription.[12] In my framework, this suggests that "gnostic" and "Valentinian" Christian texts fully engage the fixed/fluid dialectic of ancient ethnoracial discourse,[13] using ethnic reasoning to speak about the "real" differences between insiders and outsiders while also envisioning the possibility and ideal of ethnoracial mutability to enable outsiders to become insiders.[14] We ought to evaluate this polemical use of ethnic reasoning in light of intra-Christian struggles to secure authority and to categorize Christians into deceptively distinctive categories like "gnostics," which may distort more than reflect the social and historical character of the varied forms of early Christian communities.

This chapter first examines some of the ways that Clement of Alexandria and Origen use ethnic reasoning and related ideas about kinship to depict their Christian rivals, especially those they classify as followers of the teacher Valentinus, as holding "fixed"—and thus heretical—ideas about anthropology and salvation. I also show how their own perspectives deploy ethnic reasoning by emphasizing its fluidity. The second half of the chapter examines the *Gospel of Philip*, an early Christian writing that many scholars classify as "Valentinian." Based on Clement's and Origen's critiques, we should expect to find fixity characterizing its teachings about anthropology and salvation. Instead, we find that it also foregrounds fluidity in its ethnic reasoning. The uses of ethnic reasoning in the *Gospel of Philip* do not support the charges made by Clement and Origen.

## "Saved by Nature"? Clement's and Origen's Polemics Against Rival Christian Anthropologies

Valentinus, Clement, and Origen were all early Christian teachers who spent at least part of their careers in the cosmopolitan urban center of Alexandria in the eastern part of the Roman Empire. Valentinus flourished a generation before Clement; after beginning his career in Alexandria, he spent the latter part in Rome (active in the 140s). Like Valentinus, Clement (ca. 150–210) made his name as a Christian teacher in Alexandria. Although Clement has fared better in church historical tradition, there is no evidence that Clement had any more institutional authority than Valentinus for his teaching.[15] Both teachers gained their authority not from a local bishop but from persuading students that they offered the interpretive keys to scripture and Christian life.[16] Origen's situation was slightly different. Apparently Clement's student (though never called a "Clementine"), Origen first became a teacher in Alexandria at a time when the episcopacy (the bishop-led church structure) was gaining local power. After a conflict with a bishop, Origen relocated to Caesarea; his position there included public speaking in a church, although he continued to teach.

For this study, I am most interested in how Clement and Origen framed their anthropology and soteriology in the context of other Christian views. If we bear in mind that Clement and Origen were writing as teachers competing for students with other Christian teachers, it becomes easier to discern the polemical aspects of their arguments, including their use of ethnic reasoning. Clement and Origen both emphasized universal access to salvation, and they linked this to a universal human capacity for free will. They further linked this capacity to the idea of God as the creator of humanity. For both, becoming a Christian could be imagined as an ethnoracial transformation accomplished by using one's free will wisely. This transformation entails becoming a member of God's people. Clement contrasted this view with what he construes as its alternative: namely, the view that certain humans are "naturally" related to and thus saved by God. Origen similarly condemned the idea that God, as the creator of all humans, would have created some humans as naturally and permanently better than others (a difference in the nature of human souls). Thus, they relied on the argument that rival Christians hold "fixed" ideas about human differences—differences seen to be imposed at creation—and that these Christians correlate these fixed differences with salvation.

## "Salvation comes not from nature but from a change in obedience": Clement of Alexandria's Rhetoric

None of Clement's works is a sustained attack against rival Christians.[17] Yet he regularly locates his own views in relation to other Christian opinions, especially in his multivolume work, the *Strōmateis*.[18] The second book of Clement of Alexandria's *Strōmateis* repeatedly emphasizes that humans must actively acquire salvation—it is not a "given." What is given is the capacity to be faithful or unfaithful. For Clement, faith is the starting point of salvation: "This great change, that a person passes from unfaith to faith and comes to faith through hope and fear, comes from God. This is important: faith appears to us as the first leaning towards salvation; fear, hope, and penitence develop in the wake of faith, in association with self-control and patience, and lead us to love and knowledge" (*Strom.* 2.31.1). This progression is significant for Clement not only because he distinguishes between levels of Christian advancement (where knowledge, *gnōsis*, is acquired to reach the highest level), but also because he depicts this cumulative progression in stark contrast to alternative understandings of Christianity.

In particular, Clement condemns Christians who allegedly hold that salvation is based upon an innate connection between humans and God and distinguish between Christians who have faith and Christians who have knowledge. He depicts these views as problematically intertwined. He holds the students of Valentinus up for special criticism: "Valentinus's followers attribute faith to us in our simplicity, but arrogate knowledge to themselves as *saved by their nature*. They want it to dwell in them in accordance with the superiority of the *exceptional seed sown in them*. They claim it is very different from faith, as spirit is from soul" (*Strom.* 2.10.2, my emphasis). From this passage it seems that Valentinus's followers distinguish between levels of Christians: those like Clement who have faith and those like Valentinus who have knowledge. But Clement also distinguishes between Christians who have faith and those who go on to gain *gnōsis*, as 2.31.1 above suggests. So what is Clement's objection to these Christians? Is it that he claims to have not merely faith but also authentic knowledge? In this passage, Clement alleges that the distinction is that these Christians map these classifications as "fixed" by nature, rather than viewing Christians of "faith" and Christians of "knowledge" as different stages through which any individual can progress.

Clement objects to this alleged spiritual anthropology in two main ways: by appealing to the notion of free will and by insisting on the gap between divine and human natures. These two arguments appear together in the following passage: Clement insists that God "has no natural relation to us, as the founders of the heresies like to think" (*Strom.* 2.74.1, 4, 75.2) but makes Christians children if one responds correctly: "when a person freely rises to the knowledge of the truth by a process of self-discipline and learning . . . God calls them to the position of 'son' and that is the greatest progress of all" (2.74.2). This passage suggests that adoption is the model of sonship Clement has in mind for Christians.[19]

In Clement's view, God has created the conditions for individuals to act—that is, to respond to divinity. Nonetheless, Clement differentiates among levels of ability to respond:

> There is no benefit if the learner is not ready to receive it, or prophecy for that matter, or preaching, if the hearers are not open to persuasion. . . . So the divine Word has summoned everyone en masse in a loud voice knowing perfectly well those who will not allow themselves to be convinced. Nonetheless, because we have the power to respond positively or negatively, he has made a summons full of righteousness, and demands of each only that of which each is capable. There is one group for whom the capacity accompanies the will; they have developed this by practice; they have purified themselves. There is another, who may not yet have the capacity, but do already have the desire. Desire is the work of the soul, practical action requires the body as well.
>
> (*Strom.* 2.26.1, 3–4)

Clement divides those who wish to respond positively to the *logos* into two groups: both have the "will" or "desire" but only one group has trained the body sufficiently to be able to respond fully. The passage implies that with adequate "practice" everyone can potentially attain this more advanced level of response.

The fluidity that this implies does not, however, prevent Clement from using ethnic reasoning to describe the consequences of conversion. He emphasizes that faith and righteous action are the means by which such a transformation occurs. For example:

> "You have chosen God today to be your God, and the Lord has chosen you today to be his people" (Deut. 26:17–19). God makes his own the person who is eager to serve true reality and comes as a suppliant. Even if he is only one in number, he is honored on equal terms with the whole people. He is part of the people; he becomes the complement of the people, once he is reestablished out of his previous position, and the whole in fact takes its name from the part. This high birth is shown in excellence of choice and practice.
>
> (*Strom.* 2.98.1–3)

The biblical prooftext serves Clement's purposes because of its focus on choice.[20] His interpretation emphasizes that transformation occurs through the actions of both the human and the divine. Significantly, this change is construed as becoming a member of God's people and receiving a "high birth" as the result of good choices and actions.[21]

It is important to note that Clement does not pause to explain his use of high birth or ethnoracial membership (becoming a member of God's people) as that which can be attained during one's lifetime—these are presented as unproblematically fluid. Elsewhere, he depicts Christians as a whole as a people that is composed of other peoples; a transformation of religious practices and beliefs leads to an ethnoracial transformation.[22] Furthermore, he distinguishes between Christians according to their level of training and understanding, often using procreative or kinship language.[23] Yet, when procreative, kinship, or ethnoracial concepts are linked with rival teachings, they are held up as hallmarks of fixity and determinism, as signs that these Christians teach that salvation comes from "nature," not "obedience."

For example, Clement writes that Valentinus, like Basilides (another teacher), thinks that there is "a *genos* saved by nature (*physei . . . sōzomenon genos*)" and that "this different *genos* (*to diaphoron genos*) came to us from above in order to abolish death" (*Strom.* 4.89.4). He disputes this alleged view for how it undermines the view that it was Christ who came to abolish death (4.91.2). Clement also indicates that he and his followers come out looking inferior according to this way of thinking, apparently being excluded from this "saved *genos*" and reckoned instead in the category of humans known as "psychics," or soul-endowed. Clement exclaims, "Don't let those previously mentioned people [that is, Valentinians and Basilidians] call us 'psychics' in a negative way" (4.93.1). In this same context—indeed implicitly as a defense—Clement stresses that action, not essence, is what matters, implying that these other Christians would disagree, that his rivals do not consider ethical action integral to salvation:

> The perfect person (*teleios*) must practice love and so gain God's friendship by fulfilling the commandments from love. . . . Assuredly sin is an activity (*energeia*) not an essence (*ousia*): and therefore it is not the work of God. Sinners are called the enemies of God because they make themselves enemies by the commands which they do not obey, as those who obey become friends: ones (the latter) so-called because of their fellowship, the others (former) because of their estrangement, which is the result of free choice.
>
> (*Strom.* 4.93.2–94.1).

Although Clement elsewhere speaks approvingly about the ethical practices and teachings of so-called Valentinians,[24] in this context as well as in the second book of the *Strōmateis*, he contrasts a piety cultivated through righteous actions and love (fluid) with the idea that some are saved by nature (fixed), making them appear mutually exclusive.

## "Becoming Israelites": Origen and Ethnoracial Transformation as the Effect of Free Will

In the early third century, Origen also developed his understanding of human anthropology and salvation using the concept of free will. For Origen, as discussed in his *On First Principles*, ethnoracial distinctions as well as those of status, gender, and health can be explained as the embodied consequences of the better or worse exercise of free will. He states this in contrast to the alleged views of rival Christians, "those from the schools of Marcion, Valentinus, and Basilides" (*First Princ.* 2.9.5). That is, he suggests that these Christians deny the role of free will in favor of a kind of determinism. The state of one's soul is marked on the body, including by one's ethnoracial identity. Origen suggests that they appeal to the circumstances of birth, including ethnoracial identities as defined by physical descent, to explain human differences:

> The heretics oppose us as follows . . . [by arguing] that some receive a bet-
> ter [condition] at birth: one, for example, is begotten from Abraham and
> born according to the promise, another of Isaac and Rebecca—the latter
> even supplanting his brother at his mother's breast, and is said to be loved
> by God before birth. They further argue against us that one is born among
> the Hebrews, where one is raised in the divine law; another among the
> Greeks, wise men and competent scientists; another among the Ethiopians
> who are accustomed to eating human flesh; another among the Scythians
> where parricide is almost required by law; or among the Tauriens who
> burn strangers.
>
> (*First Princ.* 2.9.5)

Origen suggests that his rivals appeal to scripture and cultural stereotypes
to account for differences among humans. Biblical passages provide a
precedent for viewing certain individuals or lineages as favored by God due
to the circumstances of their birth. The latter examples range beyond scripture and rely upon stereotypes about various ethnoracial groups. The implication here is that one's ethnoracial affiliation is established at birth and
has significantly different effects upon one's future. "Hebrew" clearly represents the most favorable ethnoracial assignment, with "Greek" playing a
close second. According to Origen, his rivals explain these different human
conditions in terms of "a diversity in the nature of souls" or else by "acci-
dent or chance," so that "a soul of a bad nature is destined for a bad people
(*gens*), while a soul of a good nature [belongs] to a good one" (2.9.5). Although he does not say so explicitly, Origen depicts these rivals as holding
a fixed view about the nature of souls, which he implies correlates with fixed
ethnoracial identities, fixed not only in terms of their being determined at
birth but also in terms of their relative moral value.

Origen counters that "[God] created all creatures equal and alike. . . . But
since these rational creatures . . . were endowed with the power of free will,
it was this freedom that induced each one by its own voluntary choice either to make progress through the imitation of God or to deteriorate
through negligence" (*First Princ.* 2.9.6). By emphasizing the fluidity of souls
(and their embodied forms), Origen appears to offer an opposing view to
those of his rivals, one that not only places the responsibility for differences
among humans upon the individual (not the condition of their creation)
but also allows for mutability between types, including ethnoracial affiliations. Because the most explicit feature of Origen's point pertains to the
mutability of one's soteriological status, the reader could easily infer that
his rivals insist on the fixity of this status. However, it is important to note
that Origen does not contest the idea of diagnosing the condition of the

soul from the state of the body; this view he shares with many people in the ancient world.[25] Rather he tries to set himself apart from rival Christians in terms of the relative fluidity or fixity attributable to the condition of the soul that manifests itself in and on the body.

Origen returns to this topic later in the work, once again framing it in intra-Christian polemical terms:

> To those who fabricate "natures" (*physeis*) and who benefit from this teaching, we must say the following: if they preserve the view that only one lump (of clay) produces the lost and the saved, and that there is also the same creator for the lost and the saved; and if he is good, the one who makes not only the pneumatics but also the earthly (*choïkos*)—for this follows, then it is surely possible that that which is a vessel of honor now because of its good actions, but does not continue to act this way, in a manner that conforms to the dignity of a vessel of honor, will become in another time (*aiōn*) a vessel of shame.[26]
>
> (*First Princ.* 3.1.23)

In this passage, Origen appeals to the notion of a single creator to contest the idea that "lost" and "saved" humans have different origins. For him, a single creator means that human differences—soteriological and ethnoracial, among others—must be explained in terms of human actions.

If a good vessel can become bad, then the converse must be equally possible, Origen reasons, expanding his illustration of the ideal goal of this progression in ethnoracial terms: the goal is to become an Israelite, but not just any Israelite—specifically, an Israelite who has entered "into the church of the Lord" (*First Princ.* 3.1.23). Although this mutability contrasts with the apparently fixed view of ethnoracial membership that Origen attributes to those of the "schools of Marcion, Valentinus, and Basilides," Origen shares with them the view that some *genē* are better than others:

> And perhaps the present Israelites will be deprived of their *genos* for not having lived worthily of their noble birth, being changed as it were from vessels of honor to vessels of dishonor; while many of the present Egyptians and Idumaeans who have come near Israel will, when they have borne more fruit, "enter into the church of the Lord," no longer being reckoned as Egyptians or Idumaeans but for the future becoming Israelites.[27] Thus according to this view some people by the exercise of their wills make progress from worse to better, while others fall from better to worse.
>
> (*First Princ.* 3.1.23)

In this passage, Origen treats a *genos* as something that one can change through a better or worse exercise of one's free will. But he also relies on cultural stereotypes to imply that exercising one's free will can produce better or worse ethnoracial identities.

Origen redefines what it means to be a true Israelite as an ideal culmination of the exercise of free will, a redefinition that disenfranchises "present Israelites" who have not entered "the church of the Lord." But he does so for the purposes of intra-Christian polemic—the context is not a polemic against "present Israelites." This is clear from the rhetorical context in which Origen sets his view that humans can improve or diminish their soteriological standing through their own actions in contrast to unnamed Christian others who allegedly invent a teaching about (two or more) fixed human natures. By invoking the categories of "pneumatics" and "earthly," Origen implies that these are the two human natures specified by these Christian rivals.[28]

## Ethnoracial Fluidity in So-Called Valentinian Writings

The allegations of Clement and Origen against Christians associated with the Christian teacher Valentinus lead us to expect a fixed differentiation among kinds of humans according to their ability to be saved. But now that texts such as the *Tripartite Tractate* and the *Gospel of Philip* have come to light in the Nag Hammadi collection,[29] we find that their ethnic reasoning participates in the double-sided character of racial discourse, emphasizing mutability as much as "essences." The Nag Hammadi Library contains a collection of texts from different time periods, all copied and translated from Greek into Coptic by the middle of the fourth century. So although these texts were composed somewhat earlier, it is difficult to know precisely when; the *Tripartite Tractate* and the *Gospel of Philip* are often located in the third century.[30]

## A Brief Consideration of the *Tripartite Tractate*

In chapter 2, I discussed the *Tripartite Tractate*, showing that fluidity among three human *genē* is central to the text's soteriology, through an examination of the text's brief reference to the creation of the first human as "mixed" being (inherently composite), the arrival of the savior, and illustrations of how humans can change their *genos* in response to the savior. The *Tripartite Tractate* shares Clement's idea that humans respond to the *logos* according to their current capacity, and likewise frames the result of this response ethnoracially. The multiplicity of *genē* that results from the savior's appearance is a problem to be resolved ultimately by reunification into one spiritual unity; the ideal destiny of humans is a dissolution of the original human mixture and a transformation into the best of these *genē*, the pneumatic (which also means dissolution of the human into the spiritual Pleroma, or completeness). This is a universalizing ideal that presupposes the possibility and desirability of transformation, a far cry from the allegations of elitism or determinism of which Christians associated with Valentinus are accused by Clement and Origen (as well as some modern interpreters).

In the *Tripartite Tractate*, the church does not constitute a single *genos*, although belief in Christ is portrayed as the means to achieve the ideal of unity:

> For when we confessed the kingdom which is in Christ, [we] escaped from the whole multiplicity of forms and from inequality and change. For the end will receive a unitary existence just as the beginning is unitary, where there is no male and female, nor slave and free, nor circumcision and uncircumcision, neither angel nor man, but Christ is all in all.
>
> (*TriTrac* 132.16–28)

The context clarifies that this unification involves "the restoration to that which used to be a unity," through a progression of kinds of teaching tailored to the "form" of the believer.[31] This unity is not something that individual humans have from the outset—it has to be cultivated by emphasizing the "best" portion of one's mixed human nature. Describing the membership of the Church as comprising two *genē* offers the text a way to speak about differences among believers in Christ, much as developmental or educational imagery also accomplishes this for Clement and Origen. But it would be a mistake to assume that this *genos* language implies that the *Tripartite Tractate* views these differences as immutable. Instead, it closely resembles the views of both Clement and Origen, who envision a hierarchy of spiritual development that allows them to account for differences among believers but also to model ongoing transformations for the believer.

The combination of fluidity (action) and fixity (essence) in the *Tripartite Tractate* makes it "difficult to reconcile the teaching of this text with patristic reports of Valentinian soteriology which speak of being 'saved by nature' (Clement of Alexandria, *Strom.* 2.3.10, 2; *Exc. Theod.* 56.3)"[32] or the rigid "doctrine of natures" alleged by Origen in his *On First Principles*. I agree with Attridge and Pagels's assessment that "it is likely that those accounts reflect a misunderstanding (or a caricature) on the part of Church Fathers of Valentinian theology."[33] Thomassen reasons that "the Valentinians could have responded to those who reproached their pre-destinationist 'saved by nature' view by saying that nature, or essence, is intimately tied to the actions by which it is expressed, so that it is not nature that justifies behavior but in fact behavior that reveals one's nature."[34] But if actions determine essence for the *Tripartite Tractate*, then it is not behavior that reveals one's nature, but behavior that *produces* one's nature, as a distillation of one of the three natures inherent in all humans. Even though it is valuable for scholars to make thematic and theological connections across different early Christian texts, the preservation of the category "Valentinian" can serve to reinforce the perception that these texts are sectarian and heterodox in contrast to those of Clement and Origen.

## Becoming: The *Gospel of Philip*'s Message of Transformation

The *Gospel of Philip* is a collection of short teachings and sayings of Jesus that are not placed within a narrative structure. That is, it is structurally more like the *Gospel of Thomas* than it is like the canonical narrative gospels.[35] Although difficult to interpret given its lack of continuous narrative, many of its small units concern themselves with the transformations entailed in becoming and being an insider, often within the context of ritual practices: "Acquiring rebirth, the Name of God, and resurrection through the baptismal and anointing ceremonies is the *beginning* of the initiate's transformative experiences."[36] If anything holds this wide-ranging collection of materials together, it is the theme of progressive transformation. Ethnoracial language is among the wide array of ways of marking differences among humans (and human distinctiveness from other kinds of beings).[37]

Christianness and salvation are not only portrayed in and through change (the individual must undergo profound transformation to become a Christian, Christ, bridegroom, or perfect) but also through stability or essence. That is, the fluidity of identity that the text communicates in passages about ritual, language, and salvation history is grounded in the notion that there are different kinds of beings (for example, humans versus animals; living versus dead; slave versus free, child versus adult; Christian versus Hebrew; or Roman, Greek, Jew, barbarian, and Christian; God versus "ruling powers").[38]

The terms of group identification that appear in the *Gospel of Philip*, such as "Christian," "apostle," "perfect," "Hebrew," "Jew," and "gentile" are not static.[39] I mean this in two senses: they have different rhetorical functions in different units,[40] and most contexts also stress or imply that none of these categories is fixed. Despite the different sources from which the material in the *Gospel of Philip* is drawn,[41] the passages that employ such terminology function to reinforce persistent themes of progressive transformation accomplished by faith, ritual action, ingestion, and visual perception.

Transformation of one's mode of existence is a thematic concern that permeates the entire Gospel. The *Gospel of Philip* uses the juxtaposition between fixed and fluid throughout to exhort its readers to change and to destabilize apparent ontological antitheses while also proclaiming the fundamental reality of both the Pleroma and the ideal form of being.[42] By juxtaposing materials drawn from a number of early Christian perspectives that articulate available modes of existence and the relationship between them in different ways, the Gospel produces powerful yet unstable readings of the simultaneously fixed and fluid character of humanity.

The non-narrative character of the *Gospel of Philip* enhances the force of this double-sided perspective, as the opening of the Gospel vividly shows:

A Hebrew makes another (*tamie*) Hebrew, and such a person is called 'proselytos.' But a proselyte does not make another proselyte.

(*GosPhil* 51.29–32)[43]

The slave only seeks to be free, but does not hope to inherit the estate of his master. But the son is not only a son but lays claim to the inheritance of the father. Those who are heirs to the dead are themselves dead, and they inherit the dead. Those who are heirs to what is living are alive, and they are heirs to both what is living and dead. . . . If he who is dead inherits what is living he will not die.

(*GosPhil* 52.2–10, 13–14)

A gentile (*ethnikos rome*) does not die, for he has never lived in order that he may die. He who has believed in the truth has found life, and this one is in danger of dying, for he is alive. . . . When we were Hebrews we were orphans and had only our mother, but when we became Christians we had both father and mother.

(*GosPhil* 52.15–18, 21–24)

This opening sequence to the Gospel introduces differences among humans: Hebrew/proselyte, slave/(free) son, dead/living, gentile/believer, Hebrews/

Christians. Contrasts among humans and between humans and other kinds of beings in the *Gospel of Philip* serve similar rhetorical functions in their respective units—either to exhort the reader to self-transformation or to explain (and classify) the transformations that have occurred (or failed to occur) cosmologically, historically, and individually.

The opening (*GosPhil* 51.29–52.35) consists of "a series of potentially independent units . . . each involving one or more pairs of antithetical terms. . . . These units have been arranged in such a way as to suggest a chain of loosely analogous relationships between each antithesis and the next."[44] These pairs do not function merely to state what characterizes the differences between the elements of a given pair. A number of these sayings also comment on the fluidity or permeability between the elements of a given pair. Take, for example, the last unit: "When we were Hebrews we were orphans, with (only) our mother, but when we became Christians we got father and mother" (52.21–24). In this passage, Hebrew/Christian form the antithetical pair, characterized by the absence or presence of a father, respectively. But the phrasing makes clear that a Hebrew can (and has) become a Christian.[45]

"Hebrew" appears as an identity category in four contexts in the *Gospel of Philip*, always to designate a group that contrasts with that of the implied reader or the ideal of the text. We have encountered two of these contexts already. In the first, a "Hebrew" is one who can create one like her/himself—a sibling—but not a child; that is, the power of the "Hebrew" is limited, although not absent (a "Hebrew" can replicate but not procreate). In the second context, close on its heels, "Hebrew" is defined as one who only has a mother—in contrast to a "Christian." These two identities are closely linked, however, since Hebrews can be transformed into Christians by acquiring a "father." Jeffrey Siker interprets this clear instance of fluidity between Hebrew and Christians to mean that, for the *Gospel of Philip*, "Hebrews" must not be an ethnoracial term, in contrast to "Jew," which appears twice in the Gospel. In my view, this is untenable and based primarily on the assumption that "race" is itself immutable so an indication of mutability must signal the absence of ideas about race.[46] As I have shown throughout this book, early Christians and their contemporaries neither viewed race as immutable nor distinguished sharply between religious and ethnoracial identities.

Nonetheless, Siker's suggestion that "Hebrews" may be functioning as an intra-Christian term has merit. That is, "Hebrews" may serve to define one category of insiders in a way that is simultaneously ethnoracial and religious. The third context aligns "Hebrew" with a negative connotation of "apostle," indicating that it is being applied to people who might consider themselves or be considered "insiders" and/or "Christians": "Mary is the virgin whom the forces did not defile. Her existence is anathema to the Hebrews, meaning the apostles and the apostolic persons" (*GosPhil* 55.28–30). For Siker, this clinches his argument that "Hebrew" functions throughout the Gospel as an intra-Christian term that refers to "non-gnostic Christians."[47] The fourth context, discussed below, refers to one who fails to receive "the Lord" at baptism as "still a Hebrew," suggesting once again that "Hebrew" indicates a person on the "before" side of a transformative process.[48] If this is the case, then we have an instance of ethnic reasoning being used to internally differentiate members of the Church: instead of psychic and pneumatic *genē* as in the *Tripartite Tractate*, here we have "Hebrew" and "Christian."

While I think it is plausible to interpret "Hebrew" in correlation with what other some other texts designate as the "called" or believing "psychics," Hebrew/Christian does not encompass all types of believers for the *Gospel of Philip*. One passage suggests that one can progress from being a Christian to being a Christ (67.21–27), another says that insiders have "become Christ" (61.34–35), and the "perfect" and the "child of the bridal chamber" seem to occupy the pinnacle of the believing register, especially in the latter portion of the Gospel.[49] One might also read the language as polemical: the Gospel might refute the right of some to call themselves "Christian" by labeling them "Hebrews" instead. While this might seem to confirm Clement's accusation that "Valentinians" divide Christians into different levels (those who have faith and those who have knowledge), the Gospel nonetheless depicts the boundary between "Hebrew" and "Christian" as porous.

In the final portion of the Gospel, transformation is discussed in terms of becoming one of the perfect, from the state of being imperfect—a change effected primarily through acquiring gnosis, although also variously described in terms of changing one's *genos*,[50] weeding,[51] and being emancipated.[52] One of the most striking articulations of the double-sided character of the text's soteriological framework appears near its conclusion:

Human beings mix (*share*) with human beings, horses mix with horses, donkeys mix with donkeys: members of a species (*genos*) mix [with] their fellow members. Just so, it is with spirit (*pneuma*) that spirit mixes, and rational faculty (*logos*) with rational faculty, and light has intercourse [with light]. If [you (sg.)] *become* human, it is [human beings] that [will] love you; if you *become* [spirit], spirit will join with you; [if] you *become* rational faculty, rational faculty will mix with you; if [you] *become* light, light will have intercourse with you: if you *become* the upper (one of those who belong above), the upper will rest upon you. If you *become* a horse or a donkey or calf or dog or sheep or any of the other animals, wild or domesticated, neither human being nor spirit nor rational faculty nor light will love you; neither the upper nor the inner can repose in you, and you will have no share in them.

(*GosPhil* 78.25–79.13, largely following Layton's translation; my emphasis)

One could not hope for a clearer expression of how mutability operates in relation to ideas about fixity. In this excerpt, species distinctions are understood as real and as having soteriological implications—for example, members of animal species have no access to salvation (the domain of the "upper" and the "inner"). Nonetheless, the passage also clearly views the boundaries between species as breachable—one can change one's *genos*,[53] either to one's benefit or loss, not unlike Origen's view of the possibilities entailed in human free will. And like the *Tripartite Tractate*, the *Gospel of Philip* links one's actions with one's "essence." Jorunn Jacobsen Buckley offers a complementary reading of this same passage: "The enumerated relationships depend on the addressed person's achievements, his capacity to transform from the human to other, transcendent levels. . . . In the quoted passage, it is not a matter of the human being approximating the level of spirit, thought, etc., but of actively becoming these entities."[54] Changing one's *genos* has important consequences, as this passage indicates, because it means that one becomes able to attract and mix with others of one's newly acquired *genos*. Being able to mix with others of one's *genos* means being able to produce more members of that *genos*.

For many passages in the *Gospel of Philip*, crossing the boundary between two modes of existence is a process with two facets. The individual must receive what is necessary to accomplish the transformation (that is, "the lord"). Reception is not merely a passive action, however, since receptivity is predicated on the individual's preparation and inclination (that is, "faith"). Salvation can only occur in and through transformations that the individual mindfully seeks or actively undertakes.

Even though the last quarter of the text elaborates this process most fully, the importance of this preparation and its consequences are articulated in a range of ways in earlier passages, including with reference to faith, ethnoracial identity, ritual, visual perception, and salvation. For example:

Faith receives, love gives. [No one can receive] without faith, no one can give without love. Thus in order to receive we believe, and in order to love we give. For if one gives without love, one has no profit from what one has given. *Anyone who has received something other than the lord is still a Hebrew* (*hebraios eti*).

(*GosPhil* 61.36–62.6; my emphasis)

In this passage, faith is depicted as a necessary prerequisite to being able to "receive the lord." The consequences of having faith or not are located in ethnoracial terms, yet the phrase "still a Hebrew" for those who do not receive the lord implies that receiving the lord transforms the individual into something other than a Hebrew. While the text may be read here as suggesting that some claim to be what they are not, it distinctly imagines that an individual can be transformed through a combination of his or her efforts and the reception of spiritual substance.

While the previous passage uses the concept of remaining a "Hebrew" to mark a failure in this transformative process, another passage speaks of this process in terms of becoming Christian:

Anyone who goes down into the water and comes up *without having received anything* and says, 'I am a Christian,' has borrowed the name. But one who received the Holy Spirit has the gift of the name. Anyone who has received a gift will not have it taken away. But one who has borrowed something will have it taken back.

(*GosPhil* 64.22–29; my emphasis)

The process of transformation imagined in both passages requires the individual to receive something ("the lord," "the Holy Spirit") in order for the transformation to be successful.

In the passage above, reception appears to happen (or not) in the context of baptism. Other passages in the Gospel value the ritual of anointing (chrism) over that of baptism, as the following passage indicates:

The chrism is superior to the baptism, for it is from the word 'chrism' that we are called 'Christians,' certainly not because of the word 'baptism.' And it is because of the chrism that the 'Christ' has his name. For the father anointed the son, and the son anointed the apostles, and the apostles anointed us. The one who has been anointed possesses everything. S/he possesses the resurrection, the light, the cross, the holy spirit. The father gave him this in the bridal chamber; he merely accepted (the gift). The father is in the son and the son in the father. This is [the] kingdom of heaven.

(*GosPhil* 74.12–24)

In this passage, we find a convergence of the notion that a communal identity can be produced simultaneously through ritual (anointing) and lineage (a version of apostolic succession). The lineage is established through the ritual, and to it is attributed the name of the group, "Christians."

The *Gospel of Philip* always uses the term "Christian" in a positive sense;[55] nonetheless, it also exhorts its readers to become "perfect," a "Christ," a "child" (of the perfect human being), and a "child of the bridegroom." The following passage suggests the possibility of further levels of transformation available beyond "Christian": "If someone does not acquire [the names of the Father, Son, and Holy Spirit], the name too will be taken from them. But if one gets them in the chrism of [ . . . ] of the force of the cross, which the apostles called right and left. For this person is no longer a Christian but rather is a Christ" (67.21–27).[56]

The Gospel not only calls individuals to prepare themselves for transformation but also speaks about the agents of transformation. Although the "lord," "holy spirit," and "anointed one (Christ)" are among the key agents of transformation in the Gospel, humans can also be such agents. We find this in the Gospel's opening statement: "A Hebrew makes (*tamie*) another Hebrew, who is called a 'proselyte.' But a proselyte does not make another proselyte" (*GosPhil* 51.29–32).[57] The meaning of "Hebrew" (and proselyte) in this passage is unclear but, as the opening statement of the Gospel, it anticipates subsequent passages that speak about like producing like and distinguish between creating and begetting, especially the following passage, which distinguishes between those who can make others like themselves and those who cannot: "The heavenly person has many offspring, more than the earthly. . . . A parent makes (*tamie*) a child and a young child is powerless to make children. For one who has (recently) been begotten (*jpō*) cannot beget (children): rather, a child begets siblings, not children." (58.17–18, 22–26).[58]

The latter portion of the text includes instructions to readers about the roles that humans can play in producing other perfect beings (through love [*GosPhil* 78.12–24], begetting [81.14–34], and evaluating the soul's condition in one's students [81.1–14]). Discerning the Gospel's interest both in exhorting individuals to change and in addressing agents of transformation, we can explain the prevalence of passages that offer the apparently contrasting views that: (1) one can transform oneself (through faith, gnosis, or what one ingests) or be transformed (by chrism, food); and (2) like produces like. The *Gospel of Philip* offers a rather Lamarckian notion of identity—that is, you can acquire characteristics during your life that you then pass on, so that, having been transformed, you can produce others like yourself. Transmission can happen in the form of a "kiss" or through the ritual of anointing or chrism, which produces an apostolic lineage.

■

We do not know the relationship between the Christians who composed the *Tripartite Tractate* and the *Gospel of Philip*, let alone with the Christians with whom Clement and Origen were in competition. Nonetheless, these texts are valuable because they show that the categorical assertion of a "doctrine of natures" or of the notion of a *genos* of "naturally" saved persons belies the fluidity and complexity of available Christian understandings of anthropology and their relation to salvation.

To conclude this section, it is worth turning briefly to evidence preserved by Clement. As noted at the beginning of the chapter, among Clement's surviving works is a notebook of quotations by and remarks about the Christian teacher Theodotos. The *Excerpts of Theodotos* offers a site for examining how Clement massaged the thought of other Christians in order to portray and critique a Christian anthropology of salvation as "fixed," even though we cannot always be certain of when he is citing rival views and when he is stating his own.[59]

Near the opening of this notebook, Clement makes a note that suggests more fluidity than fixity to Theodotos's teaching. He records the teaching that when Jesus said, upon his death, "Father, I deliver my spirit (*pneuma*) into your hands" (Luke 23:46), what he meant was that he was delivering the "pneumatic seeds" that he had collected, as was his role in the drama of cosmic rescue and salvation. These pneumatic seeds are the "elect" (*Exc. Theod.* 1.1–2). Clement then seems to add his own comment to this teaching: "The elect seed we call 'sparks' brought to life by the *logos*, 'pupil of the eye,' 'mustard seed,' and 'yeast,' which unifies by faithfulness the *genē* that seem to be divided" (*Exc. Theod.* 1.3). Clement's comment seems to affirm the idea of pneumatic or elect seeds. The question is whether this pneumatic seed exists in all, or whether it can be gained or lost. Clement's rendering of this teaching suggests that he characterizes its anthropology of salvation as limiting the pneumatic seed to Theodotos and his followers, who define themselves as having this seed by nature. His presentation of Theodotos's threefold distinction of humans into pneumatic, psychic, and hylic would seem to support this. But Clement's notes on Theodotos suggest a more complicated picture, one in fact much closer to his own views.[60]

Throughout the notebook there are a number of passages that suggest a fluid if not also universal understanding of the human capacity for salvation. The distinction between "psychic" and "pneumatic" is not fixed but rather seems to designate the kind of difference that Clement sees between those who have the desire to respond to the *logos* and those who have the full capacity to respond. Similarly, the pneumatics are portrayed as able to transform the psychics, much as Clement envisions the task of the Christian "Gnostic" to be to instruct and transform ("beget") other Christians.

# Conclusion

The similarities among the Christian views represented by Theodotos, the *Tripartite Tractate*, the *Gospel of Philip*, Clement, and Origen do not mean that all early Christians were the same, after all. Rather, it suggests that ethnic reasoning could be used not only to define membership as an insider (being an insider is being a member of a new people, a saved *genos*, etc.) but also as a polemical device to assert the validity one's own position in a context of multiple Christian options.[61] Attention to ethnic reasoning across traditional scholarly lines of classification, such as gnostic/nongnostic or heretical/orthodox, reveals that early Christians found the dialectical understanding of ethnicity/race valuable for formulating their various and competing positions about Christianness and the process of becoming a Christian. For those inclined to still give more weight to Clement and Origen because of their retrospective place in church tradition, it is crucial to underscore that Clement and Origen use ethnic reasoning polemically to support their interpretations of scripture and to counter Christian rivals, but they nonetheless rely upon ethnoracial concepts for their own definitions of Christianness.

Texts cannot serve as windows onto ancient social formations, and few scholars believe it is possible to deduce a community solely from a text. That said, when a text frames its discussion as if there were a community behind it—whether by appealing to a collective ritual, a "school," or a people—it is possible to say that the text rhetorically invokes a social group or groups. We can examine texts for the social ideals they conjure even if we cannot establish precise relations between a text and the social groups it addresses or calls into being. Ethnic reasoning is an effective rhetorical device for those seeking to gain authority for their visions of Christianness in part because they can use it to persuade readers to think of themselves and others using collective categories.

My analysis suggests that early Christians sometimes used ethnic reasoning for polemical purposes, manipulating the fixed/fluid dynamic of ethnoracial discourse to differentiate among forms of Christianness that were, in many cases, quite similar to each other. One of the issues lurking in the intra-Christian arguments about anthropology has to do with the scope and access to salvation—the charge that certain Christians were teaching that some people were intrinsically saved while others are intrinsically excluded seems to pose a direct threat to universalizing proclamations of Christianness. Early Christians not only had to discuss what it means to make universal claims (that is, that salvation is for all humans), but they also had to negotiate rival Christian claims to speak about these universals. Allegations of soteriological fixity were rhetorically powerful because they made the accused seem sectarian in a field of otherwise universalizing claims. Modern scholars have too often understood these allegations as descriptive of rival Christian views and neglected to unpack the contours of universalizing claims.

# 5

**■**

# "From Every Race of Humans"

## Ethnic Reasoning, Conversion, and Christian Universalism

C hristian universalism and race/ethnicity/peoplehood are usually understood to belong on opposing sides, especially in interpretations of texts such as Galatians 3:28: "There is neither Jew nor Greek, neither slave nor free, male and female: for you are all one in Christ Jesus." This verse is often used to reconstruct an inclusive and egalitarian impulse in the Jesus movement and early Christian communities.[1] In such reconstructions, universalism is defined over and against race/ethnicity/peoplehood as that which transcends these categories. I am arguing instead that saying that Christianity is open to all was not mutually exclusive with defining Christians as members of an ethnic or racial group. In many early Christian texts, defining Christians as members of a people reinforces rather than conflicts with assertions of Christian universalism.

This chapter draws together elements of early Christian arguments that we have seen in earlier chapters, especially appeals to the mutability of ethnicity, to show how early Christians used ethnic reasoning to construct universalizing arguments. Approaching race and ethnicity as characterized by a double-sided discourse of fixity and fluidity allows us to see how universalizing arguments can in fact be dependent upon—have embedded within them—ideas of race and ethnicity. By construing Christianness as having an "essence" (a fixed content) that can be acquired, early Christians could define conversion as both the transformation of one's ethnicity and the restoration of one's true identity. And by portraying this transformation as available to all, Christians universalized this ethnoracial transformation.

I have shown throughout this book that many early Christians defined themselves as members of a people, often distinguishing themselves by their religious practices. For example, Clement of Alexandria affirms this by quoting an earlier Christian source, the *Preaching of Peter*, "Do not worship . . . as the Hellenes . . . neither worship as the Jews. But we, who worship [God] in a new way, in the third way (*genei*), are Christian" (*Strom.* 6.39.4, 41.2, 6).[2] Hellene, Jew, and Christian are functionally equivalent categories of "peoples," where peoplehood is marked by modes of worship and attitudes toward "the one Lord."

Ethnic reasoning allowed Christians not only to describe themselves as a people, but also to depict the process of becoming a Christian as one of crossing a boundary from membership in one race to another. Clement explains the above quotation by stating that: "Accordingly then, those from the Hellenic training and also from the law who accept faith are gathered into the one *genos* of the saved people (*laos*): not that the three peoples are separated by time, so that one might suppose [they have] three different natures, but trained in different covenants of the one Lord" (*Strom.* 6.42.2). Clement elaborates the tripartite division contained in the *Preaching of Peter* but shifts the emphasis from what indexes their differences (how they worship) to what they share: a common ground in "the one Lord."[3] Clement does not use this common ground to dissolve all the differences among Hellenes, Jews, and Christians. Rather, he uses this common ground to define Christians as a distinct people constituted out of former members of the Hellenes and Jews. Christians are the *genos* of the *saved*. Members of the first two peoples remain distinct because of their religious practices but are eligible through "training" in a different covenant to become members of the third people, "the one *genos*" saved by faith.[4] Thus what we might conceive of as a religious process, conversion, could be simultaneously imagined as a process of ethnic transformation.

For Clement, transformation from one category to another is neither a movement from one religious identity to another nor one from an ethno-racial identity to a religious one. "Religion" and "ethnicity" or "race" are mutually constituting here, not oppositional. Christianness is potentially universal not because Christians do not constitute a people, but rather because Clement attributes to the Christian people two key attributes: superiority as the "one saved *genos*" and accessibility via "faith."

If ethnicity is understood as mutable, then it is possible to argue not only that one can change ethnicity but that one should. Some Christians equate the Christian *genos* with the human race as a whole, rendering it a potentially universal category. For Clement, transformation in the direction of Hellene or Jew to Christian is privileged. The text does not encourage the reader to ask whether it is possible to imagine a Christian becoming a Hellene or a Jew, nor does it address whether Greekness ("Helleneness") and Judeanness might be equally accessible through transformation of one's mode of practice and attitudes. The universalizing potential of the category "Christian" instead implicitly positions Hellene and Jew as finite and inferior.

This chapter is divided into two major sections. In the first half, I explore the three main ways in which early Christians make universalizing claims, illustrating how ethnic reasoning contributes to each. In the second half, I turn to consider the implications of ethnic reasoning for how we interpret early and modern claims about Christian universalism and for how we interpret the concept of conversion.

## Three Aspects of Christian Universalism

In analyses of early Christianity, "universalism" usually includes three main ideas: the ability for anyone to become a Christian (regardless of background), the aspiration to win over all humans as members, and the ideal that Christianity consists of a unified set of beliefs and practices. Early Christians make such claims. All three aspects of universalism could be expressed using ethnic reasoning.

### Universal Access to Membership

Early Christians could use ethnic reasoning to indicate the openness of membership by emphasizing both the fundamental connections among apparently different groups of humans and the possibility of crossing ethnoracial boundaries. These arguments belong to a kind of ethnic discourse that Jonathan Hall has dubbed "aggregative" because they serve to bring ethnic groups together.[5] In addition to the example from Clement given above, in the previous chapter we have already seen a good example of this from Origen's *On First Principles*: "Many of the present Egyptians and Idumaeans who have come near Israel will, when they have borne more fruit, 'enter into the church of the Lord,' no longer being reckoned as Egyptians or Idumaeans but for the future becoming Israelites." (3.1.23).

In this example, actions (coming near Israel, bearing fruit, and entering into the church of the Lord) effect an ethnic transformation. In chapter 1, I showed that religion could function to emphasize the potential fluidity of ethnoracial affiliation. Looking at the matter from a slightly different angle, we can say that because of this perceived fluidity, early Christians and their contemporaries could imagine a change in religiosity as an ethnoracial transformation. This approach challenges conventional ways of thinking about religious conversion.

Studies of conversion usually either tacitly or explicitly define this transformative concept as mutually exclusive with ethnicity and race because they are viewed as "fixed." If ethnicity/race are understood as only "fixed" (for example, by birth), then it is impossible to imagine their connection to conversion. But as we have seen in Judith, 1 Peter (chapter 1), Justin's *Dialogue with Trypho* (chapter 3), Origen's *On First Principles*, and the *Tripartite Tractate* (chapter 4), conversion can be imagined in terms of change from one *ethnos/genos/laos* to another, effected through a change in one's religious beliefs and practices, which may also entail the acquisition of new ancestors (such as Abraham). As Justin says, by changing religious attitudes and practices, people of "of various colors (*poikilos*) and appearances (*polyeidos*) from every human *genos*" become members of another people (*Dial.* 134.5). While it might remain useful to speak about conversion as religious transformation, we cannot impose a rigid distinction between conversion and other kinds of social transformations. Religious, civic, and ethnoracial communities were closely interconnected, including in conceptualizations of Christianness.

## Aspirations of Universal Scope

By viewing ethnicity or race as subject to change, Christians could also assert that if anyone *can* change to become a member of the Christian race, then all *ought* to. We have seen a good example of this in Justin's *Apologies* in chapter 2. In the *Apologies*, Justin links all humans, implying that all share an essence that gives us the capacity to become members of this new people equated with Christians. He claims that all humans have a "seed" of the *logos*—which he equates with Christ—implanted in us (2 *Apol.* 8.1).

Even though all humans have a "*logos* seed" and are thus potentially Christian, one must nonetheless activate this potential through specific training, resulting in proper actions and beliefs. He claims that Christ came "for the conversion (*allagē*) and restoration (*epanagogē*) of the human race" (1 *Apol.* 23.2). In Justin's view, humanity requires conversion and restoration for two main reasons: first, he asserts that the people who had transmitted the truth about the *logos*, the Jews, went astray; and second, although all humans have the *logos* implanted in them, most peoples have not had access to unsullied teachings about the truth. So although the *logos* is a fixed and universal essence, it has not been fully realized in most humans.

This logic implies that Christians are the true form of humanity, while all other ethnic/racial differences correlate with degrees of imperfect knowledge of the *logos*.

Justin's view that Christ was the historical incarnation of the preexistent *logos* allows him to claim that "[Christ] is the *logos* of which every human *genos* partakes. Those who lived in accordance with the *logos* are Christians, even though they were called godless, such as, among Greeks, Socrates and Heraclitus and others like them; among the barbarians, Abraham, Ananiah, Azariah, and Mishael, and Elijah and many others . . . " (*1 Apol.* 46.2). Conversion is not only framed as the activation and perfection of the *logos* seed already in one's soul; it also transforms people from their imperfect, particular ethnicity to the one unifying, universal one—Christian. Openness of membership and ideally universal scope were thus comprehensible in ethnic terms, not just in contrast to them.

Another second-century source, the *Acts of Andrew*, illustrates how the double-sided dynamic of ethnicity/race as fixed and fluid informed early Christian portrayals of conversion, including as potentially and ideally universal.[6] The character of Andrew in the *Acts of Andrew* employs kinship and ethnoracial language to refer to those who share his views and way of life, or those whom he is exhorting to do so: insiders are members of a happy or blessed (*makarion*) *genos* (33.4 [1]), a saved (*sōzomenon*) *genos* (50.5 [18]), and his siblings and children. Membership in this happy, saved *genos* is attained by remembering one's true nature (the fixed element) upon hearing Andrew's words and by responding by adopting an ascetic ethos (the fluid element).

Andrew defines himself as an apostle whose job is not to teach but to "remind everyone who is akin (*sungenēs*) to these words" (*AA* 47.1–3 [15]). This phrasing appeals to the notion of a primordial, preexistent essence in each person that Andrew's presence helps to activate, rather than a new identity that Andrew helps his listeners to create. But Andrew's speeches make clear that action is required, even for those who are related to him and his teachings. Kinship with Andrew is demonstrated by the transformations that occur in a recipient of Andrew's words. Individuals are reckoned as members of the saved *genos* if they recognize their "own nature" and act upon it. The fluidity obvious in conversion is thus rhetorically tempered by an appeal to the underlying "nature" and kinship between Andrew's followers and himself.[7] Similarly, Andrew depicts the character of this happy, saved *genos* as one of immutability, immovability, rest, and stability.[8] Nonetheless, it is only through change that one can achieve this immovable state. In the *Acts of Andrew*, this required change includes the rejection of sexual contact. As Andrew puts it, the soul requires training and discipline in order to accomplish this goal. While conversion is framed in terms of remembering one's kinship with Andrew and his teaching, we should bear in mind that the ascetic ideal he promotes is one that would have been countercultural in this social and historical context. For most listeners, Andrew's exhortation to "stand fast" presupposes a prior significant departure from prevailing social norms, especially regarding sexual behavior.

Andrew's conversations with one of his followers, Maximilla, exemplify the transformative power of his teaching, while kinship imagery affirms their fundamental connection. Maximilla seeks Andrew's advice about how to handle herself in relation to her husband, Aegeates, who is not only pressuring her to have sex with him but also threatening to torture or kill Andrew if she refuses. Andrew urges her to stand firm in her resolve to "resist the whole allure of sexual intercourse, because you wish to be separated from a polluted and foul way of life." This encouragement suggests that the gap between insiders and outsiders is wide—no less than the extremes of a pure versus a polluted way of life. So he urges her to "endure all [Aegeates'] torments . . . and you will see him wholly paralyzed and wasting away from you and from *all your kin*" (*AA* 37.15–17 [5], my emphasis).[9] Since appeals to kinship pervade this narrative, we need to ask about whether some people are necessarily excluded from kinship with Andrew. That is, does this kinship language connote a non-universal vision of Christianity? What is the scope of the concept of *genos*, whether qualified as "happy" (*makarion*) (33.4 [1]) or "redeemed" (*sōzomenos*) in the *Acts of Andrew*? Does it refer to a limited group of humans who are, by nature, akin to Andrew?

Although some characters in the *Acts of Andrew* are portrayed negatively, such as Aegeates, it is by no means clear that any humans are intrinsically unable to become members of the saved *genos*. The saved *genos* is rather constituted by those who successfully "struggle against many pleasures" and reject the false friendship offered by the devil. Membership seems contingent on learning the "plan of salvation" and acting in accordance with it. While clearly not equivalent with the entire human *genos*, because some humans remain ensnared by false friendship with evil, the saved *genos* is potentially available to all humans.[10] Andrew's concluding speech suggests this, as he links his own apostolic actions to cosmic struggles that have ramifications far beyond the purview of the present:

> [The devil] carried on his work for so long that humanity forgot to recognize it, whereas he (the devil) knew: that is, on account of his gift he [was not seen to be an enemy]. But when the mystery of grace was lighted up, and the counsel of (eternal) rest was made known and the light of the word appeared and it was proved that the redeemed race (*sōzomenos genos*) had

to struggle against many pleasures, then enemy himself was scorned, and
. . . he began to plot against us with hatred and enmity and arrogance. And
this he practices: not to leave us alone until he thinks to separate us (from
God). For then indeed the one who is a stranger (*allotrios*) to us was without care; and he pretended to offer us a friendship such as was worthy of
him. And he had no fear that we whom he had led astray should revolt
from him. However the possession of the plan of salvation, which enlightened us (like a light), has [made his enmity] not stronger [but clearer]. . . .
Since therefore, siblings, we know the future, let us awake from sleep, not
being discontented, not cutting a fine figure, nor bearing in our souls his
marks which are not our own, but being lifted up wholly in the whole
world, let us await with joy the end and take flight from him.

(*AA* 50.1–15, 18–23 [18])

Genesis 2–3 and personified evil offer the primary points of reference for
this cosmic framework. Andrew's earlier conversation with Maximilla
about the effects of her resistance to Aegeates especially elaborates the allu-
sions to Genesis:

And I rightly see in you Eve repenting and in myself Adam being converted: for what she suffered in ignorance my words are now setting right again
in your soul, because you are converted (*epistrephousa*): and what the mind
suffered which was brought down with her and was estranged from itself, I
put right with you who know that you yourself are being drawn up. For you
yourself who did not suffer the same things have healed her affliction; and
I by taking refuge with God have perfected his (Adam's) imperfection: and
where she disobeyed, you have been obedient; and where he acquiesced,
there I flee; and where they let themselves be deceived, there we have
known. For it is ordained that everyone should correct his own fall.

(*AA* 37.20–29 [5])

This passage, especially the last sentence, reinforces the reading that all humans must transform themselves to gain salvation, but also that everyone
potentially can. Both the passage above referring to the correction of Adam
and Eve and the passage from the conclusion about the activity of the devil suggest that each human has the capacity to be misled or to gain salvation.
It also suggests that individual actions contribute to the redemption of humanity as a whole. Thus, even a text that may initially appear to offer a non-
universalizing vision of salvation and Christian membership actually uses
ethnic reasoning and kinship imagery to define conversion as an ideal for
all humans.

## Universalism as Unification of Christianity

The third aspect of early Christian universalism is often referred to as its impulse toward catholicity. The idea that Christianity was or sought to be a unified whole from the outset is a powerful ideal invoked not only by modern but also by early Christians. Keith Hopkins rightly cautions us against taking such claims at face value:

> The frequent claim that scattered Christian communities constituted a single church was not a description of reality in the first two centuries C.E., but a blatant yet forceful denial of reality. What was amazing was the persistence and power of the ideal in the face of its unachievability, even in the fourth century.[11]

In other words, although many early Christians claim to speak on behalf of all Christians, such universalizing claims are idealizing, not descriptive. Most scholars and many others who have watched recent cable or public television productions on Christian origins now operate within a consensus that diversity and difference characterize the groups that we collectively study under the heading early Christianity. Those aspects of Christianity that are asserted as universally true (such as Jesus's resurrection) were themselves only produced through internal struggles and debates.[12] Early Christians used ethnic reasoning as one means by which to undertake these struggles for authoritative meaning, practices, and identities.

As we have seen in the previous chapter, race and ethnicity became battleground concepts for rivalries among Christians before legalization. Some Christians accused other Christians of formulating exclusive, fixed ideas of membership—membership in an elect, limited group—in contrast to other Christians whose membership criteria were unlimited and open. So-called gnostics were said to speak of themselves as belonging to a "naturally" elect or saved race which gave them access to special spiritual knowledge and power. Many modern scholars have missed the fact that antignostic Christians *also* defined themselves as belonging to a people, race, or ethnicity—one that can be joined. Importantly, "gnostic" texts *also* indicate that individuals can acquire membership, so their understandings of peoplehood are far more fluid than their rivals let on. That is, one way to assert universalism on behalf of one's particular preferred version of Christianity is to "racialize" rival forms, construing them as exclusive and limited. The presence of this logic in early Christian texts indicates a kind of prehistory to modern racial thinking, where particularity and "race" appear to be linked even while the racialized logic embedded in universal claims is masked.

The second-century visionary text the *Shepherd of Hermas* offers another kind of example of how ethnic reasoning could function to assert the ideal of unity among Christians. The narrative uses ethnic reasoning both to depict Christianity as a universal phenomenon drawn from a broad range of different peoples and to manage diversity among Christians. In *Hermas*, the believing community is imagined as a single people whose differences should be eradicated upon joining and forming this community; color symbolism functions in the text to reinforce the ideal of uniformity among members.[13] Since *Hermas* views differences among insiders as a problem, it does not necessarily offer a comforting model for contemporary Christians.

Complex ethnoracial language suffuses the longest unit of the third (and final) portion of *Hermas* (the *Similitudes*). Although the dating and compositional history of this prophetic and visionary text has been debated, "no other noncanonical writing was as popular before the fourth century."[14] Near the end of this long work, our protagonist Hermas receives a vision of a gigantic tower being built on a very large rock in a plain: "[The angel] showed me a great plain surrounded by twelve mountains; each mountain had a different appearance" (*Herm. Sim.* 9.1.4). The twelve mountains encircling the plain provide most of the stones for the tower Hermas watches being built. This tower is interpreted both as the church and as a people, the "race of the righteous (*to genos tōn dikaiōn*)" (9.17.5).

Hermas's angelic guide tells him that the mountains represent "the tribes (*phylai*) that inhabit the whole world" (9.17.1). Hermas then asks why the mountain (and thus, the peoples) differ from one another. His guide replies, "'Listen,' he said, 'these twelve tribes (*phylai*) that inhabit the whole world are twelve peoples (*ethnē*), but they are various in understanding and thinking. As you saw the various mountains, so they are, and such are the differences of mind and way of thinking among the peoples (*ethnē*)'" (9.17.2). Although the mountains are glossed as peoples, the text never links any specific group with a specific mountain, leaving it to the reader to make any such connections.

In *Hermas*, these differences are indicated by climate, fauna, and the variety and quality of vegetation on the mountain, and also by color. The mountains are described in a roughly hierarchical fashion, with color-coded designations reserved for the extremes.[15] Prior to becoming part of the tower, the stones quarried from these mountains are said to be of many different colors (9.4.5), even though the text only specifies an overall color for the first and twelfth mountains: "The first was black as pitch, the second was bare without vegetation, and the third was full of thorns and thistles . . ."

(9.1.5), "and the twelfth mountain was all white, and its appearance was joyful, and the mountain was in itself very beautiful" (9.1.10). The color imagery in this context not only seems to carry some value judgment about the quality of the mountains but also serves to emphasize the magnitude and wonder of the building project. As we soon learn, most stones—regardless of their source—become "bright with a single color," white, once they are placed into the growing tower.

The tower stuns Hermas: "it was built as if it were all one stone, without a single joint in it, and the stone appeared as if it had been hewn out of a rock; it seemed to me to be a single stone" (9.9.7). This oneness is especially conveyed by the transformation of the stones into one color.[16] The angel explains this transformation in terms of response to God: "all the *ethnē* that dwell under heaven, when they heard and believed, were called after the name of God. So when they received the seal they had one understanding and one mind, and their faith became one, and their love one" (9.17.3–4).

For this text, Christianity is universal because its membership consists of people from the whole world, represented by the twelve mountains. Furthermore, the *unity* of Christianity is conveyed by the resulting tower—a single, uniform, monochrome edifice. But despite this vision of the tower as a unified whole, composed from all manner of people/stones, it turns out that this is not entirely the case. A few stones do not change color when placed in the tower and have to be removed:

> Stones of different colors were brought from all the mountains, hewn out by the men and given to the virgins. The virgins carried them through the gate and turned them over for the building of the tower. When the multicolored stones were put into the building, they all became white, and changed their various colors. But some stones that the men had supplied for the building did not become bright, but stayed as they were . . .
>
> (*Herm. Sim.* 9.4.4–6)

This lack of transformation is immediately explained as a result of incorrect procedure: the unchanging stones were not handed over to the virgins nor brought through the gate (9.4.6). The correct procedure is to place the stones "by the side of the tower, that the virgins may bring them in through the gate and give them over for the building. For if . . . they are not brought in by the hands of these virgins through the gate they cannot change their colors" (9.4.8). These dozen virgins are interpreted as "holy spirits" and "the powers of the son of God" (9.13.2). Proper conversion entails passing through their hands, which the angel also describes in baptismal terms: "if you receive only the name but do not receive clothing from them, you will gain nothing" (9.13.2). The intended effect of baptism is then described in language consistent with the tower: "all the stones . . . that you saw contributing to the tower's construction, which were given by their [the virgins'] hands and remained in the tower, had been clothed in the power of these virgins. This is why you see the tower having become one solid stone with the [foundation] rock" (9.13.4–5).

But even following the correct procedure still does not guarantee a unified whole. After the stones have turned gleaming white in the tower, they are tested. Some prove "rotten" (*Herm. Sim.* 9.5.2), either cracking or becoming discolored.[17] These imperfect stones are removed from the tower and replaced (9.6.6–7).[18] The problem of difference *within* Christianity now commands our attention, not the question of how Christianity is a unity produced from a prior diversity.

Color imagery in this context functions to highlight tensions in the universalizing vision between a unifying ideal for the tower/church and the differences among members.[19] As the discolored and cracked stones indicate, any stone that fails to gleam whitely spells trouble. The individual Christians for whom the rejected stones stand are identifiable both as members of lawless *genē* and as individual consecrated Christians who have given themselves over to vices.[20] Those who do not maintain harmony with the new whole "were cast out from the race of the righteous (*tou genous tōn dikaiōn*) and became again what they had been before, only worse" (*Herm. Sim.* 9.17.5).

To understand why some stones are cast out of the righteous race after having joined it, Hermas queries his instructor about the character of each mountain-nation. Remember that, until this point, the mountains have been described as the plurality of peoples from which the tower is built. But this time the mountains represent rival forms of Christianness, with the connection left unclear as to how these actually relate to the various peoples from whom the church is constituted. The angel explains the mountains now as various types of insiders—both good kinds and bad:[21] "From the first mountain, the black one, are such believers as these: apostates and blasphemers against the Lord, and betrayers of the servants of God. For these there is no repentance, but there is death, and for this case they also are black, for their race (*genos*) is lawless" (9.19.1). Each mountain is described in turn, with the twelfth mountain producing the most pure believers— once again, only the first and twelfth mountain are associated with a specific color. There is no question that whiteness is contrasted with blackness in this text as good to bad, even though whiteness and blackness cannot be presumed to carry the same freight that they have acquired in modern definitions of race.[22]

What makes the interpretation of the mountains so challenging is that they are multivalent, standing both for the many peoples from which the church is built *and* for the many kinds of believers of which the church consists, on a spectrum from unacceptable to perfect. The text uses the mountains to grapple with two distinct issues: that of the diversity of the backgrounds of those who join the movement and internal diversity among Christians. Not only does the text speak of the mountains as different peoples who together constitute the church, but it also describes Christians as constituting a race (of the righteous) and classifies Christians in racialized language, according to the quality of their allegiance and beliefs.

While the text seems to leave open the possibility of membership in the church/tower for most "tribes," it focuses more on the problem of what happens once one is a member, not upon entrance requirements for membership per se. Except for the few stones initially excluded on procedural grounds, it is only once each stone has become part of the tower that the problems begin. In this vision, universality is equated with uniformity—all its elements should be white stones that fit seamlessly together. Any internal differences can threaten the integrity of the whole.

What is left unexplained, however, is the extent to which the reader ought to draw any causal connections between one's pre-Christian ethnicity and one's likely success or failure at becoming the best kind of Christian.[23] The text does not make any explicit correlation between the levels of interpretation of the mountains as pre-Christian peoples and as types of Christians, in contrast to some modern interpretations of Christian origins that correlate between "racial type" and "heresy" or "orthodoxy."[24]

Nonetheless, the narrative does hint that certain people are "naturally" suited to membership in the "righteous *genos*" by virtue of their origins. This perspective is introduced when the angel tells Hermas about the stones quarried as replacements for the rejected ones. Until this point in the narrative, we have only encountered stones quarried from the twelve mountains or from the mysterious "certain deep place" that represents biblical ancestors (the first and second generations of "righteous men" [*andres dikaioi*]), prophets of God, and the prophets and teachers of "the proclamation of the son of God" (*Herm. Sim.* 9.15.4).[25] Now we learn that the replacement stones are quarried from the plain in which the tower is being constructed. Hermas asks about the origins of these stones. As it turns out, "the stones that are taken from the plain . . . are the roots (*rizai*) of the white mountain [the twelfth one]" (9.30.1). Construed as the origins of the most positively valued mountain, these stones are not at risk of turning "black" once they are in the tower, as some of the stones quarried from other sources might; instead, the stones from the plain "have been found to be white, both past and future believers, for they are of the same *genos*. Blessed is this *genos*, because it is innocent" (9.30.3). The text seems to suggest that some people, by *genos*, are "naturally" part of this tower. Even if one translates *genos* here as "kind" or "type," this explanation is still in the mode of ethnic reasoning, since it creates a historical lineage for some Christians and seems to rely on the notion of inherent, heritable characteristics, especially as they bear upon religious worthiness.[26]

This portion of *Hermas* thus contains two ways of thinking about race/ethnicity: Christianness is either incipient (or fixed: *genos* of the stones from the plains) or created (or fluid: through the transformation of *ethnos* from other mountains). Although both elements of the double-sided character of ethnic reasoning are present in *Hermas*, an emphasis on mutability predominates. The bulk of the unit stresses the creation of the Christian *genos* out of a diverse array of other *ethnē*, *phylai*, and *genē* by means of transformation; even the stones from the plain must be incorporated into the tower by the correct procedure (via the virgins).

The "root" stones are not incorporated into the tower until after it is well under construction. The assertion that there is a *genos* of believers that extends to a time before Christ, no matter how paradoxical that might seem,[27] could form part of a defense against accusations that Christianity is a new (and therefore illegitimate) phenomenon. But rhetorically, the explanation of these latecomers as genealogically linked to the white mountain may instead function to authorize some of the newest members of the righteous *genos* whose credentials (especially if they hold leadership positions in the community) may be perceived as needing support.

The *Shepherd of Hermas* clearly illustrates how universalizing claims serve intra-Christian functions. When it comes to envisioning membership in the righteous *genos*, internal differences are viewed as a problem. While universalism need not be defined in terms of homogeneity,[28] in *Hermas* the universal ideal is characterized by uniformity. For example, the third mountain is associated with believers who are "rich and mixed up with various affairs of business" (9.22.1). As a result, they "do not cleave to the servants of God but are choked by their work and go astray" (9.22.2). For these believers, attitudes toward wealth and perhaps ethics put them in tension with the values promulgated by the text for the community. In contrast, the description for insiders from the fifth mountain uses language common to antignostic polemic; the believers of this mountain are "slow to learn and arrogant (*authadēs*), . . . wishing to know everything (*panta ginōskein*) and yet they know nothing at all (*ouden holōs ginōskousi*). Because of this arrogance of theirs, they lack knowledge (*synesis*—this term functions as a pun here, because it also means "union"); blind folly (*aphrosynē mōra*) has entered into them" (9.22.1–2). The description continues by ridiculing these believers for exalting themselves as wise teachers when they are in fact senseless. By claiming the vantage point of the true universal church, the narrative marginalizes rival Christians (who might *also* claim to speak for all Christians) as rotten members who must be cast out of the righteous race or "repent" by conforming to the teachings and practices that represent the text's point of view. This suggests a historical context of lively intra-Christian competition.[29]

My basic argument so far is that early Christian texts do not support the view that Christian universalism is antithetical to Christian self-definition as a people. Whether presenting Christianity as a movement open to all, ideal for all humans, or ideally unified and uniform, early Christians used ideas about the fluidity and fixity of ethnicity and race to formulate these claims. When speaking about the movement's openness, early Christians like Justin and the authors of the *Acts of Andrew* and the *Shepherd of Hermas* emphasize the fluidity of ethnicity/race by depicting conversion as changing one's ethnicity especially through new beliefs, way of life, ritual practices, and the acquisition of new ancestors. When speaking about Christianity as a group ideally encompassing all humans and internally unified, Christians tend instead to articulate a fixed aspect of ethnicity/race in relation to its potential fluidity. By claiming that humans share some universal characteristic, like Justin's notion of a *logos* seed in all humans, or a shared common ancestor (like Adam or Noah), followers of Jesus could formulate universalizing visions of the future of their people by imagining a way for the original unity of humanity to be reunited in the destiny of a single people. The *Shepherd of Hermas* stresses that the Christian community ought to be a monolithic, seamless whole—signs of variation or internal fluidity are grounds for exclusion.

## Prismatic Considerations: Implications of Ethnic Reasoning for Christian Universalism

Universal claims are neither intrinsically liberating nor oppressive, but can serve both possible ends, depending upon who is making them, in what contexts, and to what ends. Regina Schwartz has sagely noted that "Universalism comes in different shapes, as an ideal of genuine toleration, as an effort to protect universal human rights, and as a kind of imperialism that insists that we are all one and that demands an obliteration of difference."[30] Universalism can easily entail idealization of certain aspects of humanity over and against an "other" defined as separate or less than human; racism lurks "*both* on the side of the universal and the particular."[31]

In this half of the chapter, I explore two major implications of seeing that early Christians used ethnic reasoning to make universalizing claims: first, we need to interpret both ancient and modern Christian universalizing claims in their particular contexts; and second, as suggested in the first half of the chapter, we need to take a closer look at the concept of "conversion," especially for how scholars have defined and used it to reconstruct early Christians in relation to their contemporaries.

## The Importance of Context

Universal claims are always particular. They are made in specific contexts and represent specific interests in the name of all. What is interesting about universal claims is how they are developed, whom they serve, and with what implications. But this is not merely a question of what early Christians attempt, but also what *we* in the present make of their attempts, and how we value universalism and engage our own kinds of universal claims. Attention to context requires that we locate early Christians and their modern interpreters (Christian or not) as participants in their larger social and political landscapes. When early Christians claim that their distinctiveness is the ideal culmination of humanity, they are not unique—Romans and Greeks regularly make such claims as well. To support these points, we will take a brief look first at Roman universalization strategies and then at two examples of how geographical context informs early Christian universalizing claims.

**Romanness as *Humanitas*** Early Christian authors write during the ongoing formulation and enactment of an imperial project that made extensive use of universalizing rhetoric.[32] One of the key terms in this project of Roman universalization is *humanitas*. As Greg Woolf has described it, "*humanitas* encapsulated what it meant to be a Roman." This broad concept, often translated as "civilization," could function simultaneously as a universal ideal and a marker of difference, even among "Romans." This double function is characterized by the view that elite men best embodied *humanitas* even while "it encapsulated a set of ideals to which all men might aspire."[33]

Romans attribute the invention of *humanitas* to the Greeks. While positioning "Greek culture as the first stages of a universal process," Romans claim that they are the legitimate heirs and bearers of this process (marked by *humanitas*), whereas Greeks have become degenerate.[34] To define Romanness in terms of *humanitas*, then, requires arguments somewhat analogous to those some early Christians formulate to define themselves as distinct from *Ioudaioi* while claiming as their own the scriptures that most Christians shared with them. Without needing to claim any direct Christian dependency upon Roman arguments, it is striking how some Christian claims seem to echo this logic in positioning Christians in relation to Jews.

Also important for our purposes, *religio* is one of the building blocks for the construction, display, and negotiation of Romanness.[35] During the early Roman imperial period, associations between cultic practices and peoplehood undergo a shift. Although religious practices continue to be correlated with race/ethnicity/civic membership throughout the imperial period, Augustan cultic innovations lay the groundwork for a universalizing rhetoric that serves to hold together the diverse and regionally operated cults, especially ruler cults.[36] As Aelius Aristides glowingly declares about Roman rule in the middle of the second century:

> Indeed, the poets say that before the rule of Zeus everything was filled with faction, uproar, and disorder, but that when Zeus came to rule, everything was put in order. . . . So too, in view of the situation before you [that is, before Antoninus Pius] and under you, one would suppose that before your empire everything was in confusion, topsy-turvy, and completely disorganized, but that when you took charge, the confusion and faction ceased and there entered in *universal order* and a glorious light in life and government and the laws came to the fore and the altars of the gods were believed in.
>
> (*Or.* 26.103, my emphasis)[37]

Aristides here emphasizes the universal order established by the empire in its political structure, laws, and religious practices. A little earlier in the speech, he praises Romans for encompassing the "whole world in their government, either as citizens or as those who are governed [see *Or.* 26.58–61]. Rome had brought the nations together; the inhabited world had become like one city [see *Or.* 26.36]."[38]

Aristides' political vision of one city expanding to rule the entire world foregrounds civic membership—not ethnoracial membership. But the spread of Rome's power blurred the lines between civic identity and ethnoracial identity, and religious practices helped to mark and redefine both citizenship and ethnic belonging. Christians likewise capitalize on this blurriness, refracting imperial discourse by avowing their citizenship in a different city (heavenly Jerusalem), under a different ruler, and by construing themselves as a people. In both civic and ethnic self-conceptions, religious practices serve as a primary vehicle for performing membership.

When early Christians employ universalizing ethnic reasoning, they can be understood as attempting to negotiate alternative universalizing discourses, especially with respect to ideas about Romanness produced in and through the Roman imperial cult.[39]

In chapter 2, I suggested that we can learn valuable insights from examining how cities, provinces, and other local groups defined themselves in relation to Roman imperial power and Roman understandings of identity. We can extend these insights to understanding universal claims. In redefining Greekness in the imperial period, some "Greeks" developed universalizing arguments that preserved Greekness as the apex of humanity. These claims relied on the assertion that specific cultural forms associated with Greeks, *paideia* and philosophy, were quintessentially "Greek."[40] Nonetheless, "Greekness," like Christianness or other collective identities, still had to be claimed and negotiated in local, particular contexts.[41] Comparing two Christian contemporaries, Tertullian of Carthage and Clement of Alexandria, helps to highlight the significance of context for Christian self-definition and the place of ethnic reasoning in universalizing claims. While Tertullian negotiates Christianness especially in relation to Romanness, Clement's context calls for a closer comparison between Christians and "Greeks."[42]

**Tertullian in Carthage and Clement in Alexandria** Clement and Tertullian were active at the turn of the second and third centuries C.E., and were both prolific Christian authors who lived in very different cultural and political contexts—Clement settled in Alexandria, the largest city in the eastern half of the Roman Empire, which was run semi-independently (though officially controlled by a provincial Roman administrator); its elites spoke Greek. Tertullian lived in Carthage, a large provincial capital in North Africa, in the Western part of the empire. Carthage was run as a Roman province more directly than Alexandria. The lingua franca in Carthage was Latin.

Clement argues for the universal character of Christianity by depicting it as both distinct from but the logical culmination of both Jewishness and Greekness. Clement refers scarcely at all to Romans, instead implicitly positioning Christians as the superior people, characterized by their distinctive religiosity and formed from "Greeks and barbarians," "Greeks and Jews," or "Jews and gentiles." Tertullian, on the other hand, argues that Christians are the best representatives of the Romans—that is, model citizens—in large part because of the way of life produced by their religious practices. He claims that Christians get denounced by Romans as a "third race" (Jews, Romans, Christians) and vehemently rejects this classification, insisting that Christians are not a distinct people because of their religious practices.

Despite these important differences, both Clement and Tertullian use ethnic reasoning. Both need to locate Christianness in relation to existing ways of explaining human differences. Tertullian inhabits a context in which the imperial interests of defining Romanness require him to frame his definition of Christianness explicitly in relation to Romanness. Clement, in contrast, can ignore the category of "Roman," and writes as if he is addressing "Greeks" or gentile Christians.[43] He favors the longstanding totalizing distinctions between Jew/gentile and Greek/barbarian to recast these pairs as a collective whole that together comprise both the source of all Christians and that which is not-Christian.[44]

We have already examined a number of examples from Clement's writing in which he explicitly designates Christians as a *genos*, *laos*, or *ethnos* (see above, as well as chapter 2), so I shall focus here on Tertullian's views. Tertullian argues strenuously *against* the identification of Christians as a third (*tertium*) *genus*. He implies that it is non-Christians who label Christians as a third type of human (*tertium genus*): "We are indeed said to be the 'third type' of humanity" (*Ad Nationes* 1.8). Tertullian refutes this designation in part by insisting upon a contrast between religion (*religio*) and people (*natio*), challenging the application of the term *genus* to those who follow a set of religious practices. Tertullian tries to detach religious from ethnic affiliation so that Christian "religious" distinctiveness cannot be interpreted as ethnic/racial/national distinctiveness. Whether or not he accurately represents the way non-Christians speak about Christians, Tertullian indicates that at least some readers would have understood that the boundaries between *natio*, *genus*, and *religio* were blurrier than Tertullian wants to claim here.

For Tertullian, distinctiveness as a *natio* would put Christians at a disadvantage—Christians could be singled out as a group apart, and thus be more vulnerable to persecution. His rhetorical strategy is to position Christians as the best representatives of the Roman Empire, the followers of the God who makes possible the success of the empire—they are not a distinct *natio* but the true *natio*. His solution relies on ethnic reasoning. He aims to define Christians as members of a *natio*, but one that aligns with and potentially encompasses *Romanitas*. This is a radical move, insofar as it politicizes Christianity even while appearing to downplay differences between Christianness and Romanness.

Were Christians recognized by non-Christians as an "ethnicity"? Tertullian suggests that "third *genus*" is a term used for Christians by non-Christians (see especially *De Scorpiace* 10), at least in Carthage. Specifically, he implies that Christians were being called a *genus* or *natio* on the basis of religious difference. Tertullian finds this problematic; it is not clear that others did. Indeed, we have seen that other early Christians, especially those writing in Greek, including Athenagoras, Aristides, and Clement, all portray religiosity as constitutive of ethnicity, including for Christians.[45] If local Roman citizens expected their adoption of the religious practices of Rome to mark them off from others as specifically Roman, then the religious distinctiveness of Christians would very likely have had a political connotation that Tertullian wishes to minimize, if not remove.

The administrative and cultural differences between Carthage and Alexandria help to account for some of the differences between Clement and Tertullian. As a colony, Carthage contained a small group of elites who were Roman citizens, as well as many other non-Romans, elites and non-elites alike. It was in such communities that Romans encouraged and more systematically established Roman religious cult practices outside of Rome itself. Religious activity offered a means for Roman citizens of this and other colonies to reaffirm their Roman status in contrast to their noncitizen peers.[46] Non-Roman inhabitants of a Roman colony would have had to work out the significance of their religious practices in light of the highly stratified and politicized standard set by those engaged in "creative imitation of Rome itself."[47]

In Alexandria, the relation between religion and imperial control was expressed differently, although we still see a close connection between ethnicity and religious practices.[48] "Hellenism" became the marker used by those classed in this category as a means to provide "their own social gradations with the total group."[49] Clement writes for people who have surrounded themselves with things Greek, who speak Greek, who are at least passingly familiar with Homer, Euripides, and the veneration of Greek deities, and who are quite keenly aware of Alexandria's fashionable culture. "Greek" social customs, religious practices, and pedagogy are presumed to be the standard against which Clement's audience will measure his teachings.[50]

One significance of these examples is that that classicists and ancient historians interested in ethnicity and cultural identity can no longer exclude early Christianity a priori from consideration—it is not feasible to continue to accept a definition of Christianity as a new kind of religion, detached from traditional social and political cultures and centered on belief. Instead, early Christians, like their contemporaries, viewed their religiosity as complexly interconnected with other facets of cultural identity, including ethnicity/race, political identity, and ethics.

A number of pre-Constantinian Christians used culturally available understandings of ethnic, national, and civic belonging to legitimize particular versions of Christianness as the universal and most authentic manifestation of humanity. We may recognize that pre-Constantinian (and indeed many post-Constantinian) Christian claims to be universally representative of all Christians are patently untrue, but we need also to explore how we reconstruct the social structures and practices entailed in the specific universal claims that appear across early Christian writings. For the period before Christianity was legalized, Christian universal claims are intelligible in light of the ways that a range of "minority groups" in the Roman world negotiated their relation to the imperial power structure. Nonetheless, we can see that pre-Constantinian sources contain precisely the kind of double-edged rhetoric of openness and restrictiveness that could be used for oppressive ends once Christianity gained political and social power.

**Modern Contexts for Universalizing Claims about Early Christians** In the modern period, universalizing claims about early Christians also have different connotations according to the context of use. In the hands of modern scholars and Christians, universal claims can function in a range of ways: to reinforce a sense of contemporary Christian unity, to call attention to and problematize contemporary Christian plurality, and to mobilize "Christian" values in contrast to "secular" or nationalist claims in service of supranational goals.

Assertions that Christianity has had from its beginnings a universalizing, racially inclusive mandate have been central both to mainstream academic scholars and to marginalized voices seeking social, political, and religious reform. For mainstream scholars, race has served as the primary criteria by which one can classify Christianity as a special kind of religion, not linked to race.[51] Marginalized voices, by contrast, have often shown how Christianity participates (tacitly or explicitly) in racism, and call for reforms that will allow Christianity to achieve its original racially inclusive ideal.[52]

The mainstream approach makes race an out-of-bounds topic for Christianness—something that does not properly belong to its domain. Marginalized voices, by contrast, make race central, with a view toward intra-Christian critique and reform. I am challenging both of these interpretive streams by arguing that early Christians used ethnic reasoning to develop universalizing claims about Christianness. My goals are more compatible with the approaches to Christian universalism taken by marginalized voices because I support a conceptualization of universalism that emphasizes the value of differences—not their obliteration.[53]

Unfortunately, most modern universalizing claims about Christian origins also depend on ideas about race to reconstruct earliest Christianity as universal in explicit contrast to Judaism, as in this example:

> Christianity was originally just one among many sects of Judaism that flourished in the first century C.E. It differed most from those other sects in

its *universalism, which contrasted sharply with the separatist nationalism* that dominated Jewish sectarianism after the Maccabean revolt.[54]

Separatist nationalism evokes an identity with closed borders (however defined), and universalism one with flexibility. My approach challenges the view that early Christian universalism was formulated by declaring Judaism the religion of a people and Christianity not. I am not saying that both Christianity and Judaism *were* distinct racial groups. Instead, in at least the first three centuries C.E., self-definition in terms of ethnic reasoning was valuable for all of those who sought to secure the meanings of Jewishness and Christianness, including claiming that their identity was open to all and best for all.

Reading early and modern Christian communities and texts as embedded in particular contexts allows us to examine universal claims on a case by case basis for the type of universal vision employed. We can evaluate in which cases universalism seems to foster obliteration of difference, and in which cases it might provide a context for engagement that does not erase difference and instead provides a "common forum in which to negotiate a shared agenda and to foster the possibility of dialogue."[55]

## Rethinking Conversion

A dynamic approach to race/ethnicity helps to show why and how early Christians used ethnic reasoning to help depict conversion as possible and ideal for all. It also suggests that conversion is a socially embedded process intertwined with other forms of cultural identity and not simply a private matter of faith or conscience. We need to view conversion as a social process that entails the crossing of social boundaries. These boundaries may be understood as religious but also as ethnic and racial.

The ability to convert to Christianity might seem to be a hallmark of its universal character. At least since the early modern period, however, the conversion of certain groups and individuals, notably Jews and colonial subjects, has been a matter of considerable anxiety for Christians. Golden Age Spain as well as late nineteenth- and early twentieth-century Europe and its African and Asian colonies have been geopolitical contexts in which Christianity's universalism has run up against the suspicion that not all people can join this universal ideal.[56] The explanation for this anxiety is sometimes expressed in terms of intent and motivation (conversion can only occur when truly intended), but this seemingly reasonable concern has also competed with the racist view that some people may be constitutionally less likely to have this purity of intent in their conversion.

But even defining conversion in terms of intent is problematic because it casts conversion as a personal and private process rather than as a socially and politically mediated one. This individualized and belief-centered understanding of conversion has also informed interpretations of early Christian conversion. In his influential study of ancient conversion, Arthur Darby Nock imagines conversion as an intensely individual experience, encompassing a complete change of one's orientations and commitments. Nock limits this phenomenon to Christianity, Judaism, and philosophical schools, with individual cases allowed for mystery cults. As a result, he excludes most forms of ancient religiosity. Underlying this division are not only assumptions about the "core" of religiosity (that would be present in conversion) but also about how to classify religions. Nock largely interprets Christianity against the backdrop of the two-part definition discussed in chapter 1. That is, Nock views most ancient religions as characterized by practice, not belief, and as interwoven with their social contexts (including civic and ethnic identifications). The assumption of the primacy of practice and context reinforces Nock's view that people did not "convert" to traditional religions, even when they adopted the veneration of new deities or became members of a new cult. He calls such changes "adhesion," not conversion.[57]

Nock's approach to conversion has been challenged and revised in important ways in the last few decades. Thomas Finn, for example, has convincingly argued that practices, especially initiation rituals like baptism and anointing, are central to early Christian conversion. Conversion was not simply a matter of interior conviction, but was accomplished through a process of instruction and action.[58] This insight obviously corrects Nock's overemphasis on belief and individual conviction. Finn makes two other important arguments: that conversion should not be theorized as a one-time change, and that conversion could occur *within* the same religious cult or community (as increased commitment, spiritual development, or a higher level of initiation).[59] These two related points further revise Nock's framework because they include traditional religious piety and cults in the scope of conversion and help us to explain the attention given in a number of groups to ongoing perfection and change even after becoming an insider.

Wayne Meeks and John Curran have also contributed to the critique of Nock's model by questioning both his emphasis on the individual and the strength of commitment presupposed. Meeks suggests that conversion to Christianity needs to be considered in terms of social factors, not simply individual ones.[60] Almost twenty years later, John Curran still considers "this social context of conversion . . . one of the most overlooked dimensions of the whole subject" in interpretations of early Christianity.[61] Building on Meeks, Curran argues that political factors as well as the social dynamics of the Roman "*familia* and *clientela*" structured the conditions of conversion and its effects.[62] Both seek to temper an understanding of conversion as primarily or essentially a personal matter of faith that entails a total transformation of one's worldview and life. Certainly, the apocryphal acts and the martyr narratives seem rhetorically preoccupied with depicting the familial and civic hue and cry against converts—especially well-born female ones such as Thekla and Perpetua. Curran suggests that concerns expressed in early Christian texts about the strength of commitment to Christianity should lead us to question a model of conversion as an interior, personal decision to commit to a different way of life—in chapter 1, we have seen just such a concern registered about wavering Christians in the *Acts of the Martyrs of Lyon and Vienne*.

To insist on the centrality of social context in interpreting the meaning and effects of conversion does not require viewing doctrinal or theological factors as irrelevant. But it does suggest that concerns over doctrine and theology may reflect the interests of competing teachers and would-be authority figures as much as the interests of converts. Attending to the social context of conversion allows us to see ethnic reasoning as one of a cluster of strategies for imagining what it means to become and be a Christian.[63] For example, Maximilla's struggle with her husband Aegeates in the *Acts of Andrew* is clearly interpreted as a consequence of having joined the *makarion genos*—the text portrays conversion as an act with both individual and social consequences.

These valuable revisions to Nock's model resituate Christianness in important ways relative to other ancient forms of identification by emphasizing practice, process, context, and variability of kinds of membership. The shift in analysis of conversion that Curran and Meeks advocate—from a focus on personal belief to a focus on social context—belongs to a larger trend in rethinking definitions of "religion" and especially how "religion" is defined in relation to other dimensions of human life. Meeks anticipates, for example, Gauri Viswanathan's call for the "need to historicize conversion not only as spiritual but also a political activity."[64]

> Why . . . does history throw up so many instances of conversion movements accompanying the fight against racism, sexism, and colonialism? What might be the link between the struggles for basic rights and the adoptions of religions characterized as minority religions? . . . What possibilities for alternative politics of identity might be offered by conversion as a gesture that crosses fixed boundaries between communities and identities?[65]

In her study of conversion in modern England and India, Viswanathan illuminates the modern conceptual frameworks that inform both the study of conversion in antiquity and the modern period. She notes, following Ta-lal Asad, that the structuring of "religion" as marginal to secular society in modernity—that is, as primarily about belief and as the domain of the in-dividual, in contrast to "secular society" and "rational institutionality"—long occluded the constitutive role of "religion" to the "secular." Although there is no oppositional construct "secular society" placed against "reli-gion" in antiquity, early Christianity has frequently been invested with the attributes of "modern" religion, especially as characterized by individual-ized belief.

While Meeks, Curran, and Viswanathan helpfully encourage us to think of conversion as a sociopolitical process, ethnicity is still usually defined as incompatible with conversion, because the former is viewed as fixed where-as religious identity is seen as potentially fluid. A dynamic approach to eth-nicity/race allows us to see that the boundaries between communities and identities are not fixed, although it may be rhetorically, politically, and the-ologically useful to present them as fixed. Moreover, this approach also al-lows us to inquire into the contexts where it may be rhetorically, political-ly, and theologically useful to present conversion as incommensurate with ethnicity or race.

In late nineteenth- and early twentieth-century Germany, arguments about conversion to Christianity were an especially volatile site for imagin-ing the relationship between religious and racial identities for both Jews and Christians, as Sander Gilman has shown. Throughout most of the nine-teenth century, conversion to Christianity was offered by Christians and by some Jews as the dominant model for trying to "remedy" Jewish difference. By the end of the nineteenth century, with the rise of "scientific" biologized explanations for Jewish difference, "conversion was no longer seen as a vi-able alternative."[66] But theory contravened social practice:

> The Jews of Europe were converting. . . . Indeed, the highest rate of con-version among German-speaking Jews seemed to be in Freud's Vienna. At exactly the moment when it was felt that Jewish integration into the Aryan world was impossible, the reality was that there was a sense that this bio-logical integration was occurring and that the hope of the mid-nineteenth-century assimilationists . . . would be realized. The greater the potential re-ality became, the more intensely the theoretical possibility was denied.[67]

This example shows how a "fixed" definition of "race" was invoked in a spe-cific historical context to combat a much more fluid social reality.

In the study of antiquity, debates about the relationship between Chris-tianity and Judaism continue to be waged partly in terms of conversion.

Specifically, the ongoing debates about whether or not Jews actively sought converts are partly about how to understand the relationship between religion and ethnicity/race. While this debate is far too broad-ranging to discuss here,[68] what is important for our purposes is how conversion gets defined in relationship to ethnicity.

Shaye Cohen represents an important and influential perspective in suggesting that for conversion to Judaism to be possible (let alone the notion of an active Jewish mission), belonging has to be imagined in something other than "ethnic" terms. Cohen has advanced the argument that during the last few centuries before the common era, Judaism shifted from being primarily an "ethnic" identity to a "cultural" or religious identity.[69] These terms are primarily meant to indicate a shift to the possibility of conversion to Judaism. As such, they calcify an understanding of ethnicity as one that precludes conversion; only if identity is defined in "cultural" terms is conversion thought to be possible. Cohen puts this view very clearly:

> Ethnic (or ethno-geographic) identity is immutable. . . . However, in the century following the Hasmonean rebellion two new meanings of "Judaeans" emerge: Judaeans are all those, of whatever ethnic or geographic origins, who worship the God whose temple is in Jerusalem (a religious definition), or who have become citizens of the state established by the Judaeans (a political definition). In contrast with ethnic identity, religious and political identities are mutable: gentiles can abandon their false gods and accept the true God, and non-Judaeans can become citizens of the Judaean state.[70]

I find convincing his argument that Judaean self-definition changed during the Hasmonean period, partly through adapting Greek concepts of *politeia* (or citizenship). But characterizing this change as a shift from immutable to mutable conceptualizations of membership too sharply distinguishes between ethnicity and religion/political identity and ignores the double-sided character of identity discourses and practices in all periods (even if fixity is foregrounded at some moments and fluidity privileged at others).[71]

This kind of framework is also troubling for how early Christian/Jewish relations can be interpreted in its light. John North, for example, follows the position that there was a significant Jewish effort to convert gentiles during the second and third centuries C.E., which posed a source of competition for Christians in their own mission.[72] Like Cohen, this characterization of Jewish/Christian competition relies on a sharp distinction between religion and ethnicity: as North puts it, "the Jews . . . have become a religion not an ethnic group."[73] It is as members of a religion, not an ethnicity, that Jews are seen to compete with Christians. This position not only defines ethnicity over and against religion but also implies that ethnic membership cannot be imagined in universalizing terms.

To nuance this position, Joshua Levinson offers a helpful analysis of early rabbinical views, arguing for two dominant paradigms for identity in rabbinical texts: genealogical and covenantal. Both construct Jewishness as what he calls a "fictive ethnicity." These paradigms have different emphases. In the genealogical, "inside and outside are established according to biological descent"; in the covenantal, "identity is established by the acceptance of a certain institutionalized belief system."[74] Levinson does not cast the former as "ethnic" and the latter as "religious"; instead, *both* paradigms help to constitute ethnicity, sometimes in conflict and other times intertwined.[75] Although the genealogical paradigm foregrounds fixity by appeal to descent, Levinson shrewdly notes that:

> Both paradigms present identity as belated rather than indigenous. Whether the decisive moment is the revelation at Sinai or the birth of the twelve tribes, identity is achieved only through a detergent process, by the natural body purging itself of foreign elements. This belatedness, which stresses the acquired nature of identity, would seem to indicate a certain anxiety concerning the inconstancy of identity, which undermines the very distinctions [between insider and outsider] these texts work so hard to construct.[76]

In other words, both genealogical and covenantal arguments about identity look to the past for authorization while nonetheless incorporating fluidity/transformation into the past.

Even though non-rabbinical forms of Judaism flourished alongside emerging rabbinical ones in the first few centuries C.E., Levinson's analysis of rabbinical negotiations of identity offer an important point of comparison with the self-understandings classified as early Christian. Neither rabbinical nor early Christian texts speak with a single voice; nonetheless, emerging Christians also deploy something like these two paradigms, defining membership genealogically as well as covenantally, thereby producing their own versions of ethnicity. As we saw earlier in this chapter, Clement defines membership in the saved *genos* as the result of training in a specific "covenant of the Lord."

Early Christians drew on two kinds of biblical traditions that craft universalizing claims about how the people of Israel is both distinct and yet related to other peoples. One variety stresses "universal siblinghood," as available in readings of Genesis, generally appealing to genealogies in the process (tracing siblinghood to Adam or Noah). The second tradition is covenantal in that it emphasizes an attachment to Yahweh as that which defines membership in Israel, such as in Isaiah.[77] Without needing to hypothesize about specific historical connections between Justin Martyr and rabbis, it is clear that the *Dialogue with Trypho* engages both genealogical arguments and "covenantal" ones to assert that crossing the boundary to become a Christian is simultaneously an ethnic and religious move.

It is not surprising to find Christians using ethnic reasoning to depict conversion as possible and ideal for all. As we saw in much of chapter 2, a rhetoric of restoration and realizing one's potential portrays conversion in terms of regaining or achieving one's true humanity. However, that is not to say that all treatments of conversion use ethnic reasoning or imply ethnoracial change. Imagery for conversion in antiquity ranges widely, including: enslavement (to God), freedom, enfranchisement (as citizen of heaven), purification, enlightenment, resurrection, and rebirth.[78] All contain the idea of transformation from one status or mode of existence to another even if not all connote ethnoracial transformation.

# Conclusion

Early Christian universalizing claims can be fruitfully understood in terms of local attempts to negotiate and construct collective identities in a complex socio-rhetorical landscape. In depicting Christianness as the universal ideal of humanity, early Christians often do so by speaking of Christians as a people distinct from other kinds of peoples. This produces a tension: Christianness is depicted as distinct from other forms of identity yet also asserted as the ideal or most authentic form of humanness.[79] Some early Christian authors try to grapple with this paradox by reasoning that what makes Christianness appear distinct is that most people are deluded into taking as real the current kinds of categorical distinctions by race or people. Nonetheless, these same Christians depend upon such preexisting ideas about human difference to imagine Christians as a people of which all ethnic groups are potentially and ideally members.

My focus has been upon early Christian *collective* self-definition in ethnic/racial terms. Gay Byron has shown that ethnic and color differences were used by a number of early Christians, both before and after legalization, to speak about individuals and groups who embody both Christian inclusion (for example, the Ethiopian eunuch in Acts 8:26–40 and the Ethiopian Moses in the *Apophthegmata patrum*) and exclusion (for example, the young black man in the *Life of Melania the Younger*).[80] I am convinced by Byron's interpretation of the divisive and often damaging effects of what she calls "ethno-political rhetorics" in both ancient texts and modern interpretations. For Byron, the negative and positive rhetorical functions of ethnic and color difference in early Christian texts put the lie to assertions of early Christian universalism: "No longer can one claim that the early Christians were oriented around a universalist worldview."[81] To the extent that she means that *no longer can one claim that early Christians understood themselves solely in terms of the transcendence of ethnic and color differences*, I am in complete agreement. But I do not think this demonstrates an absence of early Christian universalizing. Instead, I have argued that early Christians often developed universalizing arguments using ethnic reasoning, defining themselves as an ethnic or racial whole composed of, in Justin's words, humans "of every race." Nonetheless, even if some early Christians promote a universalist worldview, appeals to ethnic differences have functioned in Christian discourse to demarcate the limits of authentic Christianness.

Rereading early Christian universalizing arguments provides us with a critical opportunity to reflect on the effects of interpretive frameworks that have largely construed early Christian efforts at self-definition, especially universalizing claims, in sharp contrast to ethnoracial self-definition. I see a few implications for contemporary Christian communities and those who study race and ethnicity. For those especially interested in race and ethnicity, I am making a twofold argument: on the one hand, even though race and ethnicity are modern concepts, features of these concepts have prehistories worth taking seriously. On the other hand, we need more studies of how interpretations of early Christianity are racialized in the modern period. I also hope to encourage more nuanced examinations of how universal claims in contemporary forms of Christianity may covertly encode racism and ethnocentrism. This understanding needs to take place in the context of recent history—not just of Christianity and its interpretation, but also of the ways that concepts of race and ethnicity have been intertwined with analyses and material practices of "religion."

# Epilogue

By arguing for the prevalence of early Christian ethnic reasoning and by resisting interpretations of early Christianity as a movement that sought to transcend all ethnic and racial differences, I am not claiming that Christianity is fundamentally racist. Many early Christian texts do claim that individuals from all backgrounds can become Christian and gain salvation. When a text does so by portraying Christianness in terms of belonging to a people, we need to be alert to the context and conditions for such a description.

Even if one wants to insist that being a member of some "Christian people" is qualitatively different than being Jewish, Greek, Roman, Egyptian, and so on, it is not sufficient to state that Christians formed a "religion" in contrast to a "race" or "ethnicity."[1] Many early Christians described the consequences of belief in Christ (even though the kinds of belief varied widely) as acquiring membership in a people. When various believers in and followers of Christ (however understood) used ethnic reasoning, they were continuing a longstanding practice of viewing religious practices and beliefs as intertwined with collective identifications that overlap with our modern concepts of race and ethnicity, as well as nationality and civic identity.[2]

I have argued not only that many ancient Christians employed ethnic reasoning in the process of defining themselves but also that *modern* varieties of ethnic reasoning have informed prevailing reconstructions of early Christian texts and history. Modern ethnic reasoning makes its appearance especially in preoccupations with Christian essences and origins as well as in attempts to distinguish early Christian rhetoric from modern racist and anti-Jewish Christian interpretations and practices. In the former instance, ethnic reasoning is embedded in the methodology even if ethnicity and race are never explicitly mentioned. That is, Christian origins become racialized through organic metaphors that construct the content of Christianness and the differences between Christians and non-Christians and among Christians in essential terms.[3] In the latter instance, ethnicity and race are foregrounded as problematic concepts but treated as a later historical contamination of Christianity; rhetorically, such discussions of race and ethnicity rely on a plot of "pure origin and subsequent decline" for Christian history.

I agree with those who, like Karen King, advocate that we need "to abandon the two most pervasive narrative structures for telling the story of Christian origins: the plot of pure origin and subsequent decline and the plot of progress from primitive state to progressive development."[4] As I argued in the introduction, these plot lines reinforce racial and gendered ways of thinking even as they mask them, because they imagine and reconstruct the history of Christianity in terms of (non-Foucauldian) genealogies. In giving up these narrative structures,

> it would no longer be possible to divide the phenomena into two and only two types (orthodoxy and heresy), nor into linear trajectories of diverse forms of Christianity, nor into a set of coherent and internally consistent, but mutually exclusive and antagonistic, "varieties of Christianity" (however diverse). In each case the coherence of the phenomenon established by these approaches is the effect of scholarly discourses, not the practices of first- to fourth-century writers and readers.[5]

King does not mean that scholars should get away from our own categories and describe ancient Christianity as it "really was." The problem is not that scholarly discourses establish the coherence of "Christianity" per se, but rather that scholars too often fail to examine the motives behind and the implications of the historical mappings and reconstructions we produce— when we acknowledge our creative roles at all.[6] The process of historical interpretation and reflection is far messier.

While not a panacea for Christian anti-Judaism or racism, the prismatic approach I advocate calls for attention to the interconnections among our own commitments and values, the ways we have been trained to think and interpret, and the goals and ideologies of ancient texts.[7] This kind of approach allows us to examine how modern scholarly discussions have been burdened by their own modern "ethno-political rhetorics,"[8] while also proposing how one can read the ancient ethnic reasoning. Such readings of ancient rhetoric will always be refracted through our own perspectives and cultural locations.

The conceptualization that I have adopted in this book of race and ethnicity as being characterized by both fixity and fluidity suits the prismatic approach because it highlights the shapeshifting instantiations of these complexly interrelated concepts without insisting that they have any intrinsic essence. "Religion" shares this shapeshifting quality with ethnicity and race. There are no intrinsic borders among these concepts.

One of the reasons why I have deliberately blurred the possible distinctions between race and ethnicity in this study is because it allows us to see how ethnic reasoning functions in constructions of Christian identity to speak both about boundaries between Christians and non-Christians and about internal differences between Christians. Ancient understandings of "race" and "ethnicity" were important for the ways that early "Christians" devised their internal and external boundaries.

Furthermore, I have argued that modern understandings of race and ethnicity have informed our reconstructions of ancient Christian self-definition and modern discussions about what Christianity is and should be. Together, the ways that race and ethnicity get used in the modern period with reference to Christianity share important features with ancient heresiological discourse, with its goals of establishing normative boundaries. In the modern period, "race" and "ethnicity" have sometimes featured in discussions of boundaries between Christians and non-Christians—especially in discussions of how Christianity differs from Judaism and in colonial contexts where Christian universalizing aims to convert all humans have run up against racist questions about how to classify particular colonized groups. But "race" and "ethnicity" are also invoked in discussions of internal diversity *among* Christians—often to argue that racial or ethnic divisions among Christians (and indeed among all humans) are incompatible with Christianity.[9]

Exploring early Christian self-definition through ethnic reasoning does not require that one classify forms of Christianity into two types (orthodox/heretical), although it can illuminate ways in which early Christians developed this binary discourse. Ethnic reasoning could function as polemic, to divide alleged insiders from outsiders, as it could to unify diverse constituents under the umbrella of "Christian," "the saved *genos*," the "true Israel," or other such collective categories. Ethnic reasoning is not a hallmark of "heterodoxy" or "heresy." Nonetheless, *modern* forms of ethnic reasoning have helped to perpetuate this apparently "purely theological" binary. Modern interpreters perpetuate both a heresy/orthodoxy binary and the idea that ethnicity/race are fixed, by defining heterodox or heretical positions as those that allegedly limit salvation to a few and the "orthodox" (or "proto-orthodox") position as universally available.[10]

Examining ethnic reasoning also does not require tracing linear trajectories among forms of Christianity or reconstructing early Christian diversity in terms of coherent but distinct forms. I have consciously avoided such taxonomies in this book. If anything, my emphasis on how early Christians could use ethnic reasoning might risk giving the impression of an underlying sameness. This is not my goal. There was no single, unified, original form of early Christianity. Indeed, there has never been a single form of Christianity. What I wish to highlight is that ethnic reasoning was a flexible and widely used tool of self-fashioning for those whom we study as early Christians (whether or not they called themselves "Christian"). These folks defined themselves in a range of ways, including as members of a people. But not all early Christians agreed about what kind of people they composed, or what kinds of characteristics and behaviors constituted membership in this people. That is, if we find ethnic reasoning in an early Christian text, we should not presume that its author or readers understood themselves as members of the same Christian people as the author and readers of all other early Christian texts that employ ethnic reasoning.

This study focuses on the historical period before the legalization of Christianity in 313 C.E. A number of people have asked me what happens to ethnic reasoning after legalization—does it disappear or change? Certainly, the fourth century is an important turning point for Christians because legalization brings with it the possibility of consolidating social power behind claims to embody authentic Christianness. Ethnic reasoning continues to feature in late Antique intra-Christian polemic, honed in heresiological discourse to mark inauthentic Christians from true ones.[11] More important for this study is the fact that modern forms of ethnic reasoning will continue to play a role in Christian self-understandings and scholarly reconstructions. We need to confront ethnic reasoning in order to overcome both racism and Christian anti-Judaism. While it is not sufficient to say that early Christians transcended or ignored ethnic/racial categories or ways of thinking, neither are we condemned to specific modern instantiations of ethnic and racial divisions among Christians or between Christians and non-Christians.

# Notes

## Preface

1.  See Shawn Kelley, *Racializing Jesus: Race, Ideology, and the Formation of Modern Biblical Scholarship* (New York: Routledge, 2002), esp. 211–222.
2.  The notion of prismatic vision is inspired by Donna Haraway's proposed metaphor of diffraction. See Donna Haraway, *Modest_Witness@Second_Millenium. FemaleMan©_Meets_OncoMouse™: Feminism and Technoscience* (New York: Routledge, 1997), 16.
3.  Ibid.
4.  Elisabeth Schüssler Fiorenza, *Rhetoric and Ethic: The Politics of Biblical Studies* (Minneapolis: Fortress, 1999), 199. While the entire book outlines and illustrates the "ethics of interpretation," she offers a useful appendix highlighting its main features (195–198). Her *Jesus and the Politics of Interpretation* (New York: Continuum, 2000) offers a book-length "application" of the ethics of interpretation to scholarship on the historical Jesus.
5.  Simon Goldhill, *Who Needs Greek? Contests in the Cultural History of Hellenism* (Cambridge: Cambridge University Press, 2002), 11. Emphasis in original.
6.  In the preface to his book, Shawn Kelley notes that his study of racialized scholarly discourses has been inspired both by a concern about American antiblack racism and Nazi anti-Semitism (Kelley, *Racializing Jesus*, ix–xi). Despite being framed in binary terms, North American race relations have never simply been one of black/white. The racializing of indigenous Americans has also been central, as has more regionally specific racialization of other cultural groups (including Mexicans, Chinese, Japanese, and Irish). See Scott Malcomson, *One Drop of Blood: The American Misadventure of Race* (New York: Farrar, Strauss, Giroux, 2000).
7.  On the relationship between "race" and "ethnicity," discussed in more detail below, see Werner Sollors, "Foreword: Theories of American Ethnicity," in *Theories*

*of Ethnicity: A Classical Reader*, ed. Werner Sollors (New York: New York University Press, 1996), xxix–xxxv; Karen Brodkin, *How Jews Became White Folks and What That Says about Race in America* (New Brunswick, N.J.: Rutgers University Press, 1998), 189 n. 1; and Robert Bartlett, "Medieval and Modern Concepts of Race and Ethnicity," *Journal of Medieval and Early Modern Studies* 31 (2001): 39–42. On taking the present as starting point, see Elisabeth Schüssler Fiorenza, *Rhetoric and Ethic*, 11, 28, 49; and Vincent Wimbush, "Introduction: Reading Darkness, Reading Scripture," in *African Americans and the Bible: Sacred Texts and Social Textures*, ed. Vincent Wimbush with the assistance of Rosamond C. Rodman (New York: Continuum, 2000), 9–19.

8. On some reasons for this marginalization, see Elisabeth Schüssler Fiorenza, *Bread Not Stone: The Challenge of Feminist Biblical Interpretation* (Boston: Beacon, 1984); and Fernando F. Segovia, "Racial and Ethnic Minorities in Biblical Studies," in *Ethnicity and the Bible*, ed. Mark Brett (1996; repr. Boston: Brill, 2002), 469–492.

9. Denise K. Buell, "Race and Universalism in Early Christianity," *JECS* 10:4 (2002): 429–468.

10. Denise K. Buell, "Rethinking the Relevance of Race for Early Christian Self-Definition." *HTR* 94 (2001): 449–476.

# Introduction

1. *Ep. Diog.* 1.1. Some of the ideas in the introduction are developed from Denise Kimber Buell, "Rethinking the Relevance of Race for Early Christian Self-Definition," *HTR* 94 (2001): 449–458, 473–476.

2. Frank M. Snowden Jr., *Before Color Prejudice: The Ancient View of Blacks* (Cambridge: Harvard University Press, 1983), 99.

3. Anthony D. Smith, *The Ethnic Origins of Nations* (Oxford: Blackwell, 1986), 35.

4. Rosemary Radford Ruether, "Sexism and God-Language," in *Weaving the Visions: New Patterns in Feminist Spirituality*, ed. Judith Plaskow and Carol P. Christ (San Francisco: Harper and Row, 1989), 156.

5. Guy G. Stroumsa, *Barbarian Philosophy: The Religious Revolution of Early Christianity* (Tübingen: Mohr [Siebeck], 1999), 83.

6. See Jonathan Hall, *Ethnic Identity in Greek Antiquity* (Cambridge: Cambridge University Press, 1997), 35–37; and "γένος," in *A Greek Lexicon*, compiled by Henry George Liddell and Robert Scott, revised and expanded by Henry Stuart Jones with Robert McKenzie, et al., 9th ed. (1940; repr., Oxford: Clarendon, 1990), 344.

7. For example, when early Christians discuss themselves in a context that makes "Christians" analogous with "Greeks," "Romans," and/or "Egyptians," I see ethnic reasoning at work.

8. In this universalizing context, the term modern term "race" is more useful than "ethnicity," since the former includes universalizing connotations ("human

race") whereas "ethnicity" connotes only particularity. Thanks to David Konstan for this important observation.

9. This effect complements Daniel Boyarin's goals in *Dying for God: Martyrdom and the Making of Christianity and Judaism* (Stanford: Stanford University Press, 1999), 1–19; Daniel Boyarin, "Justin Martyr Invents Judaism," *Church History* 70 (2001): 427–461; and Daniel Boyarin, *Border Lines: The Partition of Judaeo-Christianity* (Philadelphia: University of Pennsylvania Press, 2004). See also Charlotte Fonrobert, "The *Didascalia Apostolorum*: A Mishnah for the Followers of Jesus," *JECS* 9.4 (2001): 483–509.

10. Judith Lieu's important book *Christian Identity in the Jewish and Graeco-Roman World* (Oxford: Oxford University Press, 2004) was released after this book was completed. Her approach and arguments complement my own closely both in her attention to Christian self-definition in context and specifically her discussion of ethnicity as one form of Christian self-definition. See especially, 20–21, 98–146, 239–268, 305–310. See also Elizabeth A. Castelli and Hal Taussig, "Drawing Large and Startling Figures: Reimagining Christian Origins by Painting like Picasso," in *Reimagining Christian Origins: A Colloquium Honoring Burton L. Mack*, ed. Elizabeth A. Castelli and Hal Taussig (Valley Forge, Penn.: Trinity Press International, 1996), 12–13.

11. Antony Spawforth, "Shades of Greekness: A Lydian Case Study," in *Ancient Perceptions of Greek Ethnicity*, ed. Irad Malkin (Washington D.C.: Center for Hellenic Studies/Cambridge: Harvard University Press, 2001), 375–400. See chapter 2 below for further discussion of the Lydians.

12. Walter Bauer's regional approach commands the greatest influence in this regard, but there are divergent analyses of regionalism. The contingent, particular formations of Christianness may be placed in an interpretive model where Christianity, though local, particular, and "ethnic" in inception, improves by moving above and beyond the particular considerations of social context (as if this is possible) to achieve a universal form. This idea seems embedded in Brock's distinction between religious and "national" communities in Sebastian P. Brock, "Christians in the Sasanian Empire: A Case of Divided Loyalties," in *Religion and National Identity: Papers Read at the Nineteenth Summer Meeting and the Twentieth Winter Meeting of the Ecclesiastical History Society*, ed. Stuart Mews (Oxford: Basil Blackwell, 1982), 15–19. Even Bauer's own analysis relies upon ethnic stereotypes to explain regional variations, privileging Rome as the cultural site where what became orthodoxy could properly flourish (unlike the syncretism that characterized the Syrian and Egyptian context). See Walter Bauer, *Orthodoxy and Heresy in Earliest Christianity*, trans. Philadelphia Seminar on Christian Origins (Mifflintown, Penn.: Sigler, 1971), 230. Steven Grosby offers a related approach, asking about the lingering effects of "primordial" ties upon Christians, by which he means especially those of kinship and territory. See Steven Grosby, "The Category of the Primordial in the Study of Early Christianity and Second-Century Judaism," *History of Religions* 36 (1996): 140–163.

13. This is the argument J. B. Lightfoot makes in *Saint Paul's Epistle to the Galatians*.

*A Revised Text with Introduction, Notes, and Dissertations*, 7th ed. (London: Macmillan and Co., 1881).

14. Ann Laura Stoler, "Racial Histories and their Regimes of Truth," *Political Power and Social Theory* 11 (1997): 198.

15. Irad Malkin, "Introduction," in *Ancient Perceptions of Greek Ethnicity* (Washington D.C.: Center for Hellenic Studies/Cambridge: Harvard University Press, 2001), 15.

16. Stoler, "Racial Histories," 186.

17. Malkin, "Introduction," 6, 15–16; and Stoler, "Racial Histories," 198–200.

18. Gerd Baumann, *The Multicultural Riddle: Rethinking National, Ethnic, and Religious Identities* (New York: Routledge, 1999), 90.

19. Ibid., 91.

20. Baumann views putative claims to common descent as a hallmark of ethnicity. More vaguely, he views appeals to moral absolutes as a hallmark of religion. Both are used to formulate communal rights claims, but they draw their boundaries differently (7). Both are co-opted by the authorizing rhetoric of the nation state, but in contrasting ways. The distinction between ethnicity and nationality becomes flattened to the extent that nationality functions as an "unmarked" ethnicity (with its mark revealed by the identification of some internal groups as "other, minority" groups), whereas religion is apparently rejected by the secular rhetoric of the state even while it covertly produces its own "civil religion."

21. Ibid., 24, 54.

22. Ibid., 141 n. 1, 143–158.

23. Within classics and ancient history, one of the most eloquent spokespersons for such a view is Jonathan Hall. See Hall, *Ethnic Identity*, 17–33; and Jonathan Hall, *Hellenicity: Between Ethnicity and Culture* (Chicago: University of Chicago Press, 2002), 9–17.

24. See David M. Schneider, "What Is Kinship All About?" in *Kinship Studies in the Morgan Centennial Year*, ed. Priscilla Reining (Washington D.C.: Anthropological Society of Washington, 1972), esp. 44–47.

25. Ibid., 50–60.

26. Susannah Heschel, *Abraham Geiger and the Jewish Jesus* (Chicago: University of Chicago Press, 1998), 276 n. 116. For an English translation of Renan's work, see Ernest Renan, *Life of Jesus*, trans. Charles Edwin Wilbour (New York: Carleton, 1864).

27. Heschel, *Abraham Geiger*, 156.

28. Ernest Renan, *Oeuvres complètes*, ed. Henriette Psichari, 10 vols. (Paris, 1947–1961), 5:1142; cited from Heschel, *Abraham Geiger*, 156, 277 n. 129.

29. See Vincent Wimbush, "Reading Texts as Reading Ourselves: A Chapter in the History of African-American Biblical Interpretation," in *Reading from this Place, vol. 1: Social Location and Biblical Interpretation in the United States*, ed. Fernando Segovia and Mary Ann Tolbert (Minneapolis: Fortress, 1995), 103–108.

30. The modern racial landscape of Christianity in North America has been adduced to demonstrate a failure in early Christian universalistic and egalitarian ideals.

The fact that mainline Protestant Christian churches remain among the most racially segregated spaces in America reveals a gaping chasm between the assertion of such ideals and concrete social arrangements of Christianity. See Bradford J. Verter, "Furthering the Freedom Struggle: Racial Justice Activism in the Mainline Churches Since the Civil Rights Era," in *The Quiet Hand of God: Faith-Based Activism and The Public Role of Mainline Protestantism*, ed. Robert Wuthnow and John H. Evans (Berkeley: University of California Press, 2002), 181–212. It is necessary to ask whether and how this ideal, in the hands of the white Christians, has rendered assertions of Christian universalism complicit with racism. Michael Emerson and Christian Smith view this complicity as arising from Protestant ideals of individualism that obscure the systemic character of racism. By insisting on the nonracist character of Christianity and viewing racism as an individual rather than systemic problem, white evangelicals often view themselves as nonracist and lack the strategies to tackle racism on an institutionalized and cultural level. See Michael Emerson and Christian Smith, *Divided by Faith: Evangelical Religion and the Problem of Race in America* (Oxford: Oxford University Press, 2000). This problem within modern American Christianity is part of a larger American problem. As Patricia Williams has argued, even well-intentioned assertions of America's colorblindness do not create the condition of colorblindness (that is, do not function as performative utterances) but rather signal a hysterical refusal to see precisely the extent to which colorblindness is not the case and function to impede the achievement of a society in which race, especially marked in terms of "color," no longer matters. See Patricia Williams, "The Emperor's New Clothes," in *Seeing a Color-Blind Future: The Paradox of Race* (New York: Noonday, 1997), 3–16.

31. Mary Beard, John North, and Simon Price, *Religions of Rome*, 2 vols. (Cambridge: Cambridge University Press, 1998), 1:276.

32. "The left-wing myth asserts that Jews are an anachronistic religious and national group . . . opposed to universal egalitarianism and internationalism." Katherina von Kellenbach, *Anti-Judaism in Feminist Religious Writings* (Atlanta: Scholars Press, 1994), 42.

33. To question the definition of Jewish/Christian differences in ethnic terms may seem strange to Christians, but it may also be unsettling for Jews. There is considerable debate among Jews as to how to speak about Jewishness with respect to "religion," "race," and "ethnicity." Nonetheless, strengthening and maintaining Jewishness in the wake of attempted genocide is often construed in biological terms—that is, in light of the topics of family, marriage, and childbearing (rather than, say, in terms of conversion). This emphasis on the biological continuity of Jewishness is an understandable response to the terrible biological reasoning that was used as a basis for anti-Jewish discrimination and murder. Biological explanations of Jewishness (or other identity categories) result from historically and culturally specific circumstances rather than demonstrations of essential truth about identity. The meanings of Jewishness, like blackness, whiteness, and Christianness, are not fixed but are produced, revised, and debated in specific contexts. My thanks to Ann Braude for raising this issue.

34. For example, James Cone forcefully critiques white theologians for not taking race and America's history of racism into account when articulating and analyzing their theologies. See James Cone, *Risks of Faith: The Emergence of a Black Theology of Liberation, 1968–1998* (Boston: Beacon, 1999), 130–133.

35. Denise Eileen McCoskey, "Answering the Multicultural Imperative: A Course on Race and Ethnicity in Antiquity," *Classical World* 92 (1999): 553 n. 1. It is worth noting, however, that a number of influential works on identity in classical antiquity were published in the twentieth century that used the category of "race," often by authors writing in a context where contemporary race relations were pressing (Snowden and American civil rights; Saddington and South African apartheid). See for example, A. N. Sherwin-White, *Racial Prejudice in Imperial Rome* (Cambridge: Cambridge University Press, 1967); Frank Snowden Jr., *Blacks in Antiquity: Ethiopians in the Greco-Roman Experience* (Cambridge: Harvard University Press, 1970); Frank Snowden Jr., *Before Color Prejudice*; and D. B. Saddington, "Race Relations in the Early Roman Empire," *ANRW* II.3 (1975): 112–137. Classicists may begin to revisit the concept of race (and racism) in light of Benjamin Isaac's book *The Invention of Racism in Classical Antiquity* (Princeton, N.J.: Princeton University Press, 2004), which was published after this book was completed. Isaac argues for the presence of "proto-racism" in classical sources.

36. C. Loring Brace et al., "Clines and Clusters Versus 'Race': A Test in Ancient Egypt and the Case of a Death on the Nile," *Black Athena Revisited*, ed. Mary Lefkowitz and Guy M. Rogers (Chapel Hill: University of North Carolina Press, 1996), 162.

37. In some scholarship in classics, "cultural identity" is beginning to be suggested as a replacement for "ethnicity," if ethnicity is defined as connoting "fixity." Thus the rationale is somewhat analogous with that of using "ethnicity" instead of "race."

38. This section is adapted from Buell, "Race and Universalism," 432–441. Molly Myerowitz Levine notes that this dismissal of race as anachronistic has been a central feature of criticism of Bernal's work. See Levine, "The Marginalization of Martin Bernal," *Classical Philology* 93 (1998): 347, 351. Two essays published in a collective rebuttal of Bernal's work especially exemplify this trend: Kathryn Bard, "Ancient Egyptians and the Issue of Race," in *Black Athena Revisited*, 104–111; and C. Loring Brace et al., "Clines and Clusters," 162.

39. William Chester Jordan, "Why 'Race'?" *Journal of Medieval and Early Modern Studies* 31 (2001): 169.

40. Ibid., 168–169.

41. Audrey Smedley, like Jordan, distinguishes race from ethnicity primarily in terms of change. Race, she asserts, is held to be immutable, whereas ethnicity has long been perceived to be mutable. See Audrey Smedley, *Race in North America: Origin and Evolution of a Worldview*, 2nd ed. (Boulder, Colo.: Westview, 1999), 8, 28–35.

42. Race is the keystone idea for an ideology that appeals to immutability to justify social inequalities. "Race" and "ethnicity" can function in particular socio-

historical moments to signify different things (that is, while sometimes used interchangeably, they can also function distinctly).

43. Gay L. Byron, *Symbolic Blackness and Ethnic Difference in Early Christian Literature* (New York: Routledge, 2002). See also David Brakke, "Ethiopian Demons: Male Sexuality, the Black-Skinned Other, and the Monastic Self," *Journal of the History of Sexuality* 10 (2001): 501–535. Both Byron and Brakke foreground the ancient link between Ethiopianness and black skin.

44. Stoler, "Racial Histories," 197.

45. Ibid.

46. Ibid., 198.

47. Ibid., 197. In this passage she is also referring to George Stocking, *Race, Culture, and Evolution: Essays in the History of Anthropology* (Chicago: University of Chicago Press, 1986), 234–269.

48. Peter Harrison, *"Religion" and the Religions in the English Enlightenment* (Cambridge: Cambridge University Press, 1990), 120–121.

49. Sixteenth- and seventeenth-century British writers, for example, especially spurred by the "discovery of America," drew from the Bible to pose questions about how to classify its inhabitants: Were they human? If so, were they (and how were they) descended from Adam? If not from Adam, then how did they fit into the scheme of salvation and sacred history? This is discussed in more detail in Harrison, *"Religion" and the Religions*.

50. Harrison, *"Religion" and the Religions*, 109.

51. For example, seventeenth-century interpreters not only attributed to Cain the origin of "false religion" but also argued that "Cain's progeny began to intermarry with those of more pure stock" thereby further corrupting authentic religion (Harrison, *"Religion" and the Religions*, 105). Readings of Noah and his descendants reinforced this pattern, with specific correlations made to religious and racial differences: "A long-standing tradition had it that religious corruption re-emerged in the sons of Noah, and in particular in the person of Ham, 'who it's likely,' said Bishop Simon Patrick, 'carried much of the Spirit of Cain with him into the Ark.' Soon Ham's offspring were to manifest the symptoms of their hereditary affliction" (106). Augustine's writings were influential here, as he had argued that "Ham prefigured the heretics, while Noah's other two sons, Shem and Japheth, represented the Jews and Greeks respectively" (106).

52. Eugene D. Genovese argues that it was white southern theological liberals, rather than conservatives, who conjoined scientific racism with biblical interpretation to support the notion that race-based slavery was sanctioned by scripture. See Eugene D. Genovese, *A Consuming Fire: The Fall of the Confederacy in the Mind of the White Christian South* (Athens: University of Georgia Press, 1998), esp. 84–85. See also Randall C. Bailey, "Academic Biblical Interpretation among African Americans in the United States," in *African Americans and the Bible: Sacred Texts and Social Textures*, Vincent Wimbush, ed., with the assistance of Rosamond C. Rodman (New York: Continuum, 2000), 700; David M. Goldenberg, "The Curse of Ham: A Case of Rabbinic Racism?" in *Struggles in the*

*Promised Land: Toward a History of Black-Jewish Relations in the United States,* ed. Jack Salzman and Cornel West (New York: Oxford University Press, 1997), 32; David M. Goldenberg, *The Curse of Ham: Race and Slavery in Early Judaism, Christianity, and Islam* (Princeton: Princeton University Press, 2003); and Regina Schwartz, *The Curse of Cain: The Violent Legacy of Monotheism* (Chicago: University of Chicago Press, 1997), 103–106.

53. Harrison, *"Religion" and the Religions*, 108. One writer, Glanvill, named Ham as the progenitor not just of idolaters but of apes. Harrison notes, "This judgment . . . highlights again the tendency to see sin and its first offspring—idolatry—as having a biological and inherited basis. Sin results in degeneracy. The ultimate degeneracy results in the loss of humanity. Neither does Glanvill's view seem so far-fetched in the light of discussions about whether the American natives were human or not" (108).

54. See, for example, Valerie Babb, *Whiteness Visible: The Meaning of Whiteness in American Literature and Culture* (New York: New York University Press, 1998), 16–45; and Matthew Jacobson Frye, *Whiteness of a Different Color: European Immigration and the Alchemy of Race* (Cambridge: Harvard University Press, 1998), 171–172. Frye notes that European Christian colonists in North America in the seventeenth and eighteenth centuries also classified Jewish differences in terms of religion rather than race (3–4, 171–72).

55. Peter van der Veer, *Imperial Encounters: Religion and Modernity in India and Britain* (Princeton: Princeton University Press, 2001), 13.

56. Gauri Viswanathan, *Outside the Fold: Conversion, Modernity, and Belief* (Princeton: Princeton University Press, 1998).

57. Furthermore, Jonathan Hall notes that, in some post–World War II scholarship, "ethnicity" was substituted for "race" without a significant change in meaning (Hall, *Ethnic Identity*, 19–20).

58. A spate of recent classics publications with "ethnicity" or "ethnic" in their titles gives one indication of this consensus. Note, for example, Koen Goudriaan, *Ethnicity in Ptolemaic Egypt* (Amsterdam: Gieben, 1988); Per Bilde et al., eds., *Ethnicity in Hellenistic Egypt* (Aarhus, Denmark: Aarhus University Press, 1992); Jonathan Hall, *Ethnic Identity*; Walter Pohl, ed., *Strategies of Distinction: The Construction of Ethnic Communities, 300–800* (Leiden: Brill, 1998); Stephen Mitchell and Geoffrey Greatex, eds., *Ethnicity and Culture in Late Antiquity* (London: Duckworth and the Classical Press of Wales, 2000); Irad Malkin, ed., *Ancient Perceptions of Greek Ethnicity* (2001).

59. Jonathan Z. Smith has been the most eloquent spokesperson for this insight. See his "A Matter of Class: Taxonomies of Religion," *HTR* 89 (1996), 387–403; and his "Classification," in *Guide to the Study of Religion*, ed. Willi Braun and Russell T. McCutcheon (London: Cassell, 2000), 35–44.

60. Werner Sollors, "Foreword: Theories of American Ethnicity," in *Theories of Ethnicity: A Classical Reader*, ed. Werner Sollors (New York: New York University Press, 1996), xxxv.

61. Ibid.

62. Irene Silverblatt's research explores the overlap and intersection between religious, ethnoracial, national, and gendered categories in the context of colonial Peru. She notes, for example, how "Portugese" often functions as a synonym for "Jew" in Spanish colonial discourse. Irene Silverblatt, "Race, Religion, and the Modern/Colonial World: Spanish Cultural Politics and the Inquisition in Seventeenth-Century Peru" (public lecture, Radcliffe Institute for Advanced Study, Cambridge, Mass., Sept. 2001). See also Irene Silverblatt, "New Christians and New World Fears in Seventeenth-Century Peru," in *From the Margins: Historical Anthropology and Its Futures,* ed. Brian Keith Axel (Durham, N.C.: Duke University Press, 2002), 95–121.

63. Although not all modern scholars agree with Stoler about how to characterize race, many recent sociological and anthropological studies of ethnicity also show how individual and group practices display mutability even when ethnicity is articulated as a "given" aspect of identity. See, for example, Anthony D. Smith, *Ethnic Origins of Nations,* 211 (cited approvingly by Malkin, "Introduction," 16); Gerd Baumann, *The Multicultural Riddle,* esp. 91–94; Mary Waters, *Ethnic Options: Choosing Identities in America* (Berkeley: University of California Press, 1990); G. Carter Bentley, "Ethnicity and Practice," *Journal for the Study of Comparative Society and History* 29 (1987): 24–55; Charles F. Keyes, "The Dialectics of Ethnic Change," in *Ethnic Change,* ed. Charles F. Keyes (Seattle: University of Washington, 1981), 3–30.

64. See now Lieu, *Christian Identity,* 98–146, and also 309. That ethnicity and "cultural identity" are increasingly contrasted seems to me an analogous move to the one I have just described for the distinction between race and ethnicity. In the contrast between ethnicity and cultural identity, ethnicity often gets reductively linked to notions of descent ("real" or "imagined"—another problematic divide) in contrast to cultural identity's definition as a category defined by the acquisition and performance of rather fluid cultural norms. Ethnicity and race should be interpreted as facets of cultural identity, not in opposition to it. See Denise Kimber Buell, "Race and Universalism in Early Christianity," *JECS* 10:4 (2002): 438–439.

65. Greg Woolf, "Becoming Roman, Staying Greek: Culture, Identity and the Civilizing Process in the Roman East," *Proceedings of the Cambridge Philological Society* n.s. 40 (1994): 130.

66. Ibid., 12.

67. Andrew Wallace-Hadrill, "To Be Roman, Go Greek: Thoughts on Hellenization at Rome," in *Modus Operandi: Essays in Honour of Geoffrey Rickman,* ed. Michel Austin, Jill Harries, and Christopher Smith (London: Institute of Classical Studies, School of Advanced Study, University of London, 1998), 85–86.

68. Two especially good recent collection of essays that span classical and Roman antiquity are: *Being Greek under Rome: Cultural Identity, the Second Sophistic and the Development of Empire,* ed. Simon Goldhill (Cambridge: Cambridge University Press, 2001); and Malkin, *Ancient Perceptions of Greek Ethnicity.*

69. Hall, *Hellenicity,* 15.

70. Stoler notes that antiracist motivations partly explain the trend to expose race's immutability as a false idea. While not criticizing antiracist motivations, she critiques those who attack the immutability of race for assuming that "if we can disprove the credibility of race as a scientific concept, we can dismantle the power of racism itself—that racisms rise and fall on the scientific credibility of the concept of race" (Stoler, "Racial Histories," 196). Not only have these debunking efforts stunningly failed to eradicate modern racisms, but, as Stoler further notes, they offer a flattened picture of historical formations of race and racism, by implying that race used to be "a clear concept, and that past racisms were dependent on it. Contra that prevailing wisdom . . . colonial concepts of 'race' have had more the consistency and constancy of the Milky Way—perceptible boundaries from a distance but made up of a moving constellation of parts of changing intensity—and less the fixity of a southern star" (197). In this passage, Stoler is specifically alluding to the views of Howard Winant.

71. In reflecting on the reception to her essay "Racial Histories and Their Regimes of Truth," Ann Stoler remarks that her argument about the resiliency of racial logic because of its double-sided character has largely been ignored. I find wholly persuasive her emphasis on the importance of this argument: "I argued that scholars have failed to appreciate the power of essentialist thinking. Racial essences are not made up of a fixed and finite set of features but rather an interchanging and malleable range of them. . . . The crucial point is that racial systems combine elements of fixity and fluidity in ways that make them both resilient and impervious to empirical, experiential counterclaims. I would still hold that how people imagine race to be secured should be the subject of sustained analysis." In Stoler, "Reflections on 'Racial Histories and Their Regimes of Truth' " in *Race Critical Theory: Text and Context*, ed. Philomena Essed and David Theo Goldberg (Oxford, Mass.: Blackwell, 2002), 420.

72. See, for example, van der Veer, *Imperial Encounters*. As Bruce Lincoln has recently shown, religion and language converge in the production of race/ethnicity/nation in modern definitions of "myth"; see his *Theorizing Myth: Narrative, Ideology, and Scholarship* (Chicago: University of Chicago Press, 1999).

73. See, for example, Richard Hingley, *Roman Officers and British Gentlemen: The Imperial Origins of British Archaeology* (New York: Routledge, 2000).

74. Nancy Leys Stepan and Sander L. Gilman, "Appropriating the Idioms of Science: The Rejection of Scientific Racism," in *The "Racial" Economy of Science: Toward a Democratic Future*, ed. Sandra Harding (Bloomington: Indiana University Press, 1993), 178.

75. Ibid., 175.

76. Hall, *Ethnic Identity*, 13.

77. Ibid., 4–16.

78. Schwartz, *The Curse of Cain*, 126.

79. See, for example, Karen Brodkin, *How the Jews Became White Folks and What That Says about Race in America* (New Brunswick, N.J.: Rutgers University Press, 1998), 55–76, 178–179.

80. Regina Schwartz gives a good example of how political context and intellectual traditions converged to produce a strong and long-standing interpretive approach to the [Hebrew] Bible. She argues that the influence of Romanticism and German nationalism upon historical-critical approaches to biblical interpretation has meant that "even when the Bible embraces multiplicity and even when its version of history is marked by disruptions, biblical scholarship . . . has insisted upon establishing continuity" (Schwartz, *The Curse of Cain*, 124). She explains, "In the nineteenth-century, historical-critical scholarship saw itself as part of a larger Germanic historiographic tradition. . . . The chief assumptions of that tradition— that history charts development, that its focus should be the development of the nation (the German nation in particular), and that the nation should be understood as an individual entity with its own unfolding spirit, its own internal laws of development—will govern biblical interpretation" (124–25).

81. Cited in Cornelius P. Tiele, *Elements of the Science of Religion*, 2 vols. (New York: Scribner's Sons, 1897), 1:42.

82. This distinction echoes the earlier sixteenth- and seventeenth-century British distinctions between "religions of revelation" and "natural religion" (see Harrison, *"Religion" and the Religions*, 39).

83. Tiele, *Elements*, 1:125–26.

84. Ibid., 1: 45; 1:124–126. See also Crawford Howell Toy, *Judaism and Christianity: A Sketch of the Progress of Thought from Old Testament to New Testament* (Boston: Little, Brown, and Co., 1891), 1–45, esp. 30–34.

85. In the modern period, race and ethnicity sometimes have been viewed as constituent elements of Christianness, often to serve unabashedly white, "Anglo-Saxon" (in the United States) or "Aryan" (in Germany) goals. James Moorhead shows that, in the late nineteenth and early twentieth centuries, some white Americans promoted an ideal of universalism that interpreted these ideals as embodied in white ("Anglo-Saxon") Protestant Christianity. For its proponents, this message combined a long history of national rhetoric of American chosenness with a specific understanding of who represents this chosenness and a paradoxical assertion that this group's values embodied universal values. Even if the heyday of this rhetoric has passed, its legacy persists in both international policies and intranational race relations. See James H. Moorhead, "The American Israel: Protestant Tribalism and Universal Mission," in *Many Are Chosen: Divine Election and Western Nationalism*, ed. William R. Hutchison and Martmut Lehmann (Minneapolis: Fortress, 1994), 145–166, esp. 151–154 and 165–166.

86. Schwartz, *The Curse of Cain*, 141–42.

87. Ibid., 142. Schwartz concludes this discussion by underscoring the epistemological and ethical implications of her reading: "A Bible that suggests that identity is a question rather than an answer, provisional and not reified, fails to underwrite nationalism, imperialism, and persecutions of the Other, in part because it fails to make any clear claims about who the Other is. But if I have offered a more politically congenial Bible (for some) than the one the heirs of German historicism have given us, it is not an invitation to authorize it, for to seek such

authority—even for the insight that history is ruptured and collective identity pro-visional—is, as I have tried to show, to seek foundation in shifting sand" (142).

88. Arthur Darby Nock, *Conversion: The Old and the New in Religion from Alexan-der the Great to Augustine of Hippo* (1933; repr., Baltimore: Johns Hopkins Uni-versity Press, 1988), 4–5, 14.

89. Nock theorizes that an individual can, via migration or intercultural contact (such as through travel or trade), take on new religious practices that fall into this first category. But he defines this process as adhesion, not conversion. For Nock, conversion differs from adhesion in requiring a complete transformation and exclusive allegiance. He imagines adherence as supplemental or additive, as signaling no fundamental change in one's identity. Nock, *Conversion*, 6–7, 13–16. I discuss conversion in more detail in chapter 5.

90. Nock, *Conversion*, 187–190.

91. This way of thinking is indebted to scientific discourses with their privileging el-ements/fundamental units/atomism. In the study of religion writ large the best-known example would be Durkheim's elementary forms (which also has a tele-ological dimension).

92. For excellent discussion of some of the history of scholarship on this question, see Susannah Heschel, "Jesus as Theological Transvestite," in *Judaism Since Gen-der*, ed. Miriam Peskowitz and Laura Levitt (New York: Routledge, 1997), 188–199; and Halvor Moxnes, "Jesus the Jew: Dilemmas of Interpretation," in *Fair Play: Diversity and Conflicts in Early Christianity: Essays in Honour of Heik-ki Räisänen*, ed. Ismo Dunderberg, Christopher Tuckett, and Kari Syreeni (Lei-den: Brill, 2002), 83–103.

93. This is borne out in the work of scholars such as Ernst Renan, H. S. Chamber-lain, and Walter Grundmann (see for example, Heschel, *Abraham Geiger*, 156; and Moxnes, "Jesus the Jew," 88–89).

94. Jonathan Z. Smith, for example, argues that many modern scholars of Christian origins replicate patterns established by the ancient Greek writer Herodotus in studies of "the relations of early Christianity to the religions of Late Antiquity." Herodotus and later historiographers and ethnographers wrote to classify the re-lations among races and nations. Smith does not call attention to this slippage between ancient ethnography and modern assertions about Christianity, but he implies that scholars are modeling Christianity in terms of peoplehood. He claims that scholars rely especially on the notion of Christian "autochthony" to support the notion of Christian uniqueness: "This concept of self-generation, in the Herodotean enterprise, is always conjoined to a second *topos*, the notion of 'borrowing.' Thus the Egyptians are dependent on no one for their customs and borrow no foreign practices (*Histories* 2.79, 91); the Persians, objects of scorn for both the Greeks and the Egyptians, borrow from everyone. . . . For secondary cultures, such as Greece, everything depends on pedigree, on borrowing from a prestigious primary centre. Thus, taking up Egyptian propagandistic claims, Herodotus writes that the 'younger' Greeks borrowed freely from the 'older' Egyptians (e.g., 2.4, 43, 49, 50, 57, 58, 81, 82) with no suggestion that this implies

a necessarily negative evaluation." Jonathan Z. Smith, *Drudgery Divine: On the Comparison of Early Christianities and the Religions of Late Antiquity* (Chicago: University of Chicago Press, 1990), 45–46. In writing about Christian origins, if scholars do not claim autochthony for Christianity, then they trace Christianity's pedigree to "a prestigious centre. In this model, Israel appears in the role of the Herodotean Egypt. The Catholic Church, or in more recent treatments, 'Greco-Oriental syncretism,' plays the part of Persia" (46). Smith's comparison between ancient ethnography or historiography and modern accounts of Christian origins is provocative and illuminating to the extent that he indirectly shows how modern scholars construct Christian history as the history of a people. But Smith's example also has an important limitation, because one need not make Herodotus the precedent for modern scholarship. Early Christian authors certainly do adapt the ethnographic and historiographic models of at least non-Greek authors. See Frances Young, "Greek Apologists of the Second Century," in *Apologetics in the Roman Empire: Pagans, Jews, and Christians*, ed. Mark Edwards, Martin Goodman, and Simon Price in association with Christopher Rowland (Oxford: Oxford University Press, 1999), 92–99; and Arthur Droge, *Homer or Moses? Early Christian Interpretations of the History of Culture* (Tübingen: Mohr [Siebeck], 1989), 11, 13. But it might be better to say that modern scholars read early Christian adaptations of ancient ethnographies through the lens of social evolution and modernist assumptions about progress. As a result, modern scholarship has produced a view of Christianity as a new species of religion, an evolutionary advance over earlier forms (most especially Judaism), but novel in breaking the connection between religion and race or nation.

95. For an analysis of how metaphors of sexual reproduction inform Clement of Alexandria's approach to early Christian identity and polemics, see Denise K. Buell, *Making Christians: Clement of Alexandria and the Rhetoric of Legitimacy* (Princeton: Princeton University Press, 1999).

96. See both Smith, *Drudgery Divine*; and Karen L. King, "Translating History: Reframing Gnosticism in Postmodernity," in *Tradition und Translation: Zum Problem der Interkulturellen Übersetzbarkeit religiöser Phänomene. Festschrift für Carsten Colpe zum 65. Geburstag*, ed. Christoph Elsas et al. (Berlin: De Gruyter, 1994), 264–277.

97. See for example Margaret MacDonald, *Early Christian Women and Pagan Opinion: The Power of the Hysterical Woman* (Cambridge: Cambridge University Press, 1996); Ross S. Kraemer, *Her Share of the Blessings: Women's Religions Among Pagans, Jews, and Christians in the Greco-Roman World* (New York: Oxford University Press, 1992), 157–173; and Shelly Matthews, *First Converts: Rich Pagan Women and the Rhetoric of Mission in Early Judaism and Christianity* (Stanford: Stanford University Press, 2001).

98. For example, Castelli and Taussig, "Drawing Large and Startling Figures," 9–12.

99. This is not unlike the way that ideas about *religion* ground and structure our notion of the secular (Kathleen Sands, "Tracking Religion . . . " (public lecture, Radcliffe Institute for Advanced Study, Cambridge, Mass., Feb. 2001). See also

Janet R. Jakobsen with Ann Pellegrini, "World Secularisms at the Millennium," *Social Text* 64 (2000): 1–27.

100. This historical sequencing is by no means comprehensively accepted, but Katharina von Kellenbach identifies it as one of the three "rules of formation" of Christian discourse about Judaism (Kellenbach, *Anti-Judaism in Feminist Religious Writings*, 41). A model of the historical codevelopment of Christianity and rabbinic Judaism is favored by others (Alan Segal and Daniel Boyarin, for example). Even though the formulations and implications of this model remain less widely developed, my work should be read as contributing to this scholarly direction.

101. This question of Christianity's success emerges from a simplified appropriation of evolutionary logic.

102. Jonathan Z. Smith argues that this negative teleology, from pure origins to corrupted forms of Christianity via "mixing" with Greek and Roman religions, was favored especially by Protestant biblical scholars and served an anti-Catholic function (Smith, *Drudgery Divine*). Beard, North, and Price also note how obsession with finding pristine origins (genealogy) and a story of decline and syncretism (negative teleology) have dominated traditional interpretations of Roman religion. If we can remove "all the 'foreign,' non-Roman elements that are clearly visible in the religion of (say) the late Republic," we can discover the authentic core of Roman religion (Beard, North, and Price, *Religions of Rome*, 1:10). They rightly reject this approach (14, 16) and advocate instead a model that tries to account for change and continuity by starting from an analysis of already developed religious institutions in the republican period. They reason that by starting *in media res* they have fuller documentation about the organization and practice of Roman religion; combined with the principle that "the structural features of an religion change only slowly" (17), they strive to find nuanced explanations for how changes in perceptions of religion as well as changes in structure take place over time, before and after this arbitrary starting point. While this alternative risks overstating continuity, it is a definite improvement on earlier patterns.

103. Recent important complications to this have been offered by Boyarin and Fonrobert (see note 9, above). Other criticisms of particular hypotheses about a historical "break" between Christianity and Judaism appear earlier: Reuven Kimelman, "Birkhat Ha-Minim and the Lack of Evidence for an Anti-Christian Jewish Prayer in Late Antiquity," in *Jewish and Christian Self-Definition, vol. 2: Aspects of Judaism in the Greco-Roman Period*, ed. E. P. Sanders, A. I. Baumgarten, and Alan Mendelson (Philadelphia: Fortress, 1981), 226–244; Wayne A. Meeks, "Breaking Away: Three New Testament Pictures of Christianity's Separation from Jewish Communities," in *"To See Ourselves as Others See Us": Christians, Jews, "Others" in Late Antiquity*, ed. Jacob Neusner and Ernst Frerichs (Chico, Calif.: Scholars, 1985), 93–116; and Adam H. Becker and Annette Yoshiko Reed, eds., *The Ways That Never Parted: Jews and Christians in Late Antiquity and the Early Middle Ages* (Tübingen: Mohr [Siebeck], 2003), esp. 2–24.

104. For example, see Jeffrey Siker, *Disinheriting the Jews: Abraham in Early Christian Controversy* (Louisville, KY: Westminster/John Knox, 1991), 189–192.

105. See most recently, Elisabeth Schüssler Fiorenza's two books, *Jesus and the Politics of Interpretation*, 48–51; and *Rhetoric and Ethic*, 48–49, 145–148, 191. See also the important programmatic essay by Castelli and Taussig, "Drawing Large and Startling Figures," 3–20.

106. Johannes Roldanus examines how these motifs of citizen of heaven and strangers in this world develop in early Christian writings partly in light of the exegesis of four Christian Testament passages: Gal. 4:26; Phil. 3:20; Heb. 11:9–16; and 1 Pet. 1:17, 4:4. See Johannes Roldanus, "Références patristiques au 'chrétiens-étranger' dans les trois premiers siècles," *Cahiers de Biblia Patristica* 1 (1987): 27–52.

107. *A Diognète*, ed. and trans. Henri-Irénée Marrou, 2nd ed. (Paris: du Cerf, 1965), 131.

108. The author of the *Epistle to Diognetus* also metaphorically depicts Christians' place in the world as "what the soul is in the body" (6.1). This metaphor offers another way to explain how Christians can be a *genos*, yet also be geographically dispersed: "The soul is spread through all the members of the body, and Christians throughout the cities of the world" (6.2). By extension, the author claims that Christians are not of the world, but are necessary to it; hatred of Christians is explained by analogy with the hatred of the pleasure-seeking flesh for the soul. And finally, Christians, like the soul, only grow stronger when punished.

109. See for example, Rowan Greer, "Alien Citizens: A Marvelous Paradox," in *Civitas: Religious Interpretations of the City*, ed. Peter S. Hawkins (Atlanta: Scholars, 1986), 39–56.

# 1. "Worshippers of So-Called Gods, Jews, and Christians"

1. In his introduction to a recent collection of essays primarily by classicists, Simon Goldhill has called attention to this lack: "religious affiliation is a question rapidly growing in importance" and can provide a vital context for illuminating "that slow process of Christianization." See Simon Goldhill, "Introduction. Setting an Agenda: 'Everything is Greece to the wise,' " in *Being Greek under Rome: Cultural Identity, the Second Sophistic and the Development of Empire*, ed. Simon Goldhill (Cambridge: Cambridge University Press, 2001), 24–25.

2. Within the study of early Christianity, Judith Lieu offers an important exception. See her *Christian Identity in the Jewish and Graeco-Roman World* (Oxford: Oxford University Press, 2004); and "Race of the God-Fearers," *JTS* n.s. 46 (1995): 483–501. See also David M. Olster, "Classical Ethnography and Early Christianity," in *The Formulation of Christianity by Conflict Through the Ages*, ed. Katharine B. Free (Lewiston, N.Y.: Mellen, 1995), 9–31.

3. The Greek version of Aristides's *Apology* additionally subdivides the first group into three more recognizable groups: Chaldeans, Greeks, and Egyptians. Aristides

does not provide any principle by which this further division is made, although Helmut Koester notes that the text draws on well-known distinctions from Jewish apologetics. See Helmut Koester, *Introduction to the New Testament. Vol. 2: History and Literature of Early Christianity* (New York: de Gruyter, 1982), 341. The first race is functionally equivalent to "gentile," which can be subdivided further into particular nations. Because Greeks form only one of the subdivision of this first *genos*, Judith Lieu cautions against overstating the parallels between the Greek version of Aristides's *Apology* and the threefold divisions of humanity (that is, Greeks, Jews, and Christians) found in other early Christian texts such as the *Preaching of Peter*, *Epistle to Diognetus*, and the *Tripartite Tractate*. See Judith Lieu, *Image and Reality: The Jews in the World of the Christians in the Second Century* (Edinburgh: T&T Clark, 1996), 167–168. But the parallel may in fact hold, since Philo of Alexandria and Paul both use the terms "Greek" and "gentile" as almost interchangeable, even if they do not equate Greeks with all gentiles.

4. Indeed, translators of this text did not take this tripartite division for granted. Both the Syrian and Armenian versions of the *Apology* say that there are four kinds of humanity: Barbarians, Greeks, Jews (Syrian) or Hebrews (Armenian), and Christians. See Aristide, *Apologie*, introduction, critical edition, French translation, and commentary by Bernard Pouderon and Marie-Joseph Pierre with Bernard Outtier and Marina Guiorgadzé (Paris: du Cerf, 2003).

5. In the introduction.

6. Jonathan Friedman, "Notes on Culture and Identity in Imperial Worlds," in *Religion and Religious Practice in the Seleucid Kingdom*, ed. Per Bilde et al. (Aarhus, Denmark: Aarhus University Press, 1990), 23.

7. Irad Malkin, "Introduction," in *Ancient Perceptions of Greek Ethnicity*, ed. Irad Malkin (Cambridge: Harvard University Press, 2001), 6.

8. Ibid., 5–6. See also Rosalind Thomas, "Ethnicity, Genealogy, and Hellenism in Herodotus," in *Ancient Perceptions of Greek Ethnicity*, 213; and Suzanne Saïd, "The Discourse of Identity in Greek Rhetoric from Isocrates to Aristides," in *Ancient Perceptions of Greek Ethnicity*, 275.

9. Because this passage is the earliest surviving Greek passage recognizable as a definition of Greekness, it is tempting to invest it with an authority and stability that belies its own rhetoricity. Jonathan Hall, for example, has noted that Herodotus's appeal to shared sanctuaries and sacrifices might have seemed quite an unlikely basis for asserting collective Greekness. Because of the diversity of religious cults and deities worshipped, religion could easily be used to describe the differences among Greeks. See Jonathan Hall, *Ethnic Identity in Greek Antiquity* (Cambridge: Cambridge University Press, 1997), 45.

10. Carla Antonaccio has explored fifth-century B.C.E. speeches about the colonists of Sicily. In one of these, Hermocrates defines the Sicilian colonists from the mainland on the basis of the land they now occupy: "In essence, Hermocrates asserts a new identity and homeland against the old ethnicity of Dorian and Ionian. In the face of a common threat, he argues that this new identity should override other ethnic, political, or civic identities and interests" (Carla Antonaccio,

"Ethnicity and Colonization," in *Ancient Perceptions of Greek Ethnicity*, 120). In this context, the negotiation of colonial identity, both in relation to the colonized and to the homelands, motivates appeals to territory.

11. Rosalind Thomas comments that this approach is not much used by Herodotus, but is central for the Hippocratic text *Air, Waters, Places* (Thomas, "Ethnicity, Genealogy, and Hellenism in Herodotus," 217). D. B. Saddington notes that climatic theories of ethnoracial difference remain important during the Roman imperial period. See his "Race Relations in the Early Roman Empire," *ANRW* II.3 (1975): 113.

12. For example, Ptolemy insists that the inhabitants of Coele Syria, Idumaea, and Judaea are "bold, godless (*atheoi*), and scheming" (*Tetr.* 2.3). A more extended example from this second-century C.E. text gives a sense of the broad range of characteristics Ptolemy attributes to regionally specific astral influences. He divides the world into four quadrants, and this description of the middle portion of the southeastern quadrant encompasses multiple *ethnē*: "Accordingly those who live in these countries [Cyrenaica, Marmarica, Egypt, Thebais, the Oasis, Troglodytica, Arabia, Azania, and Middle Ethiopia], because they are all subject to the occidental rule of the five planets, are worshippers of the gods, superstitious, given to religious ceremony and fond of lamentation; they bury their dead in the earth, putting them out of sight, on account of the occidental aspect of the planets; and they practice all kinds of usages, customs, and rites in the service of all manner of gods. Under command they are humble, timid, penurious, and long-suffering, in leadership courageous and magnanimous; but they are polygamous and polyandrous and lecherous, marrying even their own sisters, and the men are potent in begetting, the women in conceiving, even as their land is fertile. Furthermore, many of the males are unsound and effeminate of soul, and some even hold in contempt the organ of generation, through the influence of the aspect of the maleficent planets in combination with Venus occidental" (*Tetr.* 2.3).

13. Maud W. Gleason, *Making Men: Sophists and Self-Representation in Ancient Rome* (Princeton: Princeton University Press, 1995), 33.

14. Ibid. She is referring to Polemo as epitomized by Adamantius (Adamantius 2.31, 1.382–83F).

15. It might strike some readers as very odd that Egyptians should be excluded from a city in Egypt. But this puzzle can partly be solved by understanding that, since its founding by Alexander the Great, Alexandria had a strange relationship to the rest of the country, as its moniker "Alexandria by (*ad*) Egypt" suggests. Although containing a diverse and cosmopolitan population, it was culturally associated with Hellenism. To further complicate matters, it is worth knowing that when Rome subsumed Egypt politically, it declared that all who were not citizens of Alexandria, Ptolemais, and Naucratis would count as Egyptian for imperial purposes, including taxation. Not surprisingly, this decision did not correspond to existing practices of ethnic self-definition in Egypt, which were already fairly fluid. See, for example, Roger S. Bagnall, "Greeks and Egyptians: Ethnicity, Status,

and Culture," in *Cleopatra's Egypt: Age of the Ptolemies*, curated by Robert S. Bianchi (New York: The Brooklyn Museum, 1988), 21–27; and Willy Clarysse, "Some Greeks in Egypt," in *Life in a Multi-Cultural Society: Egypt from Cambyses to Constantine and Beyond*, ed. Janet H. Johnson (Chicago: The Oriental Institute of the University of Chicago, 1992), 51–56.

16. *P. Giss.* 40 ii; trans. Naphtali Lewis.

17. This sentence also addresses those who are not covered by the expulsion edict: "[the ones to be prevented from entering Alexandria are] not those who converge upon Alexandria out of desire to view the glorious city or come here in pursuit of a more cultured existence or on occasional business" (*P. Giss.* 40 ii; trans. Naphtali Lewis).

18. *P. Giss.* 40 ii; trans. Naphtali Lewis.

19. David Konstan, "*To Hellēnikon ethnos*," in *Ancient Perceptions of Greek Ethnicity*, 30. As Konstan rightly emphasizes, "In themselves, common traits, whether recognized as such or not, do not constitute an ethnic self-awareness. Rather, ethnicity arises when a collective identity is asserted on the basis of shared characteristics" (30).

20. Ibid., 33, 36. Rosalind Thomas offers an important complementary analysis of Herodotus's use of ethnic claims that highlights how Herodotus emphasizes mutable facets of ethnicity (Thomas, "Ethnicity, Genealogy, and Hellenism in Herodotus," 218–228).

21. See Ewan Bowie, "Greeks and their Past in the Second Sophistic," in *Studies in Ancient Society*, ed. Moses Finley (London: Routledge, 1974), 166–209; Antony Spawforth, "Shade of Greekness: A Lydian Case Study," in *Ancient Perceptions of Greek Ethnicity*, 375–400; and Rebecca Preston, "Roman Questions, Greek Answers: Plutarch and the Construction of Identity," in *Being Greek Under Rome*, 86–117.

22. See especially Andrew Wallace-Hadrill, "To Be Roman, Go Greek: Thoughts on Hellenization at Rome," in *Modus Operandi: Essays in Honour of Geoffrey Rickman*, ed. Michael Austin, Jill Harries, and Christopher Smith (London: Institute of Classical Studies, 1998), 79–91.

23. See for example, Shaye J. D. Cohen, *The Beginnings of Jewishness: Boundaries, Varieties, Uncertainties* (Berkeley: University of California Press, 1999); and Erich S. Gruen, *Heritage and Hellenism: The Reinvention of Jewish Tradition* (Berkeley: University of California Press, 1998).

24. Hall, *Ethnic Identity*, 40.

25. See for example, Gerd Baumann, *The Multicultural Riddle: Rethinking National, Ethnic, and Religious Identities* (New York: Routledge, 1999).

26. Hall, *Ethnic Identity*, 24.

27. David Konstan, "Defining Ancient Greek Ethnicity," *Diaspora* 6 (1997): 109.

28. Hall, *Ethnic Identity*, 19, 25, 40.

29. Greg Woolf writes: "Romans did not conceive of their identity as underwritten by a unique language or a common descent in the same way that some others (including Greeks) did, and their traditions of origin stressed the progressive incor-

poration of outsiders. Roman identity as based to an unusual degree on membership of [*sic*] a political and religious community with common values and *mores* (customs, morality, and way of life)." See Woolf, "Becoming Roman, Staying Greek: Culture, Identity and the Civilizing Process in the Roman East," *Proceedings of the Cambridge Philological Society* n.s. 40 (1994): 120. See also Woolf, *Becoming Roman: The Origins of Provincial Civilization in Gaul* (Cambridge: Cambridge University Press, 1998); and Simon Swain, *Hellenism and Empire: Language, Classicism, and Power in the Greek World, A.D. 50–250* (Oxford: Clarendon, 1996).

30. See Andrew Wallace-Hadrill, "*Mutatio morum*: The Idea of a Cultural Revolution," in *The Roman Cultural Revolution*, ed. Thomas Habinek and Alessandro Schiesaro (Cambridge: Cambridge University Press, 1997), 3–22.

31. Nicole Loraux's *Born of the Earth: Myth and Politics in Athens*, trans. Selina Stewart (Ithaca: Cornell University Press, 2000) not only argues that Athenians define themselves in terms of place and lineage, but also that this definition serves to define males in contrast to females, such that the Athenian *genos* relies on but does not count females for its existence and perpetuation.

32. For example, as David Konstan discusses, Pericles' funeral oration defines Athenian identity in terms of common values and way of life, not genealogy (Thucydides 2.35–46; in Konstan, "*To Hellēnikon ethnos*," 35–36). Five centuries later, Favorinus provocatively claims "to show the Greeks of Hellas that education can produce the same results as birth" (*Corinthian Oration* 28). He elsewhere delights in calling himself a Gaul who knew Greek—as if this were an unlikely combination—but in the *Corinthian Oration*, Favorinus invokes the image of one who seeks "at all cost not to seem Greek but to be Greek too" (25), suggesting that the results that education might effect are ethnoracial (discussed in Gleason, *Making Men*, 16; see also 144, 150).

33. Hall, *Ethnic Identity*, esp. 28–32.

34. Regina Schwartz, *The Curse of Cain: The Violent Legacy of Monotheism* (Chicago: University of Chicago Press, 1997), 12.

35. Arthur D. Nock, *Conversion: The Old and the New in Religion from Alexander the Great to Augustine of Hippo* (1933; repr., Baltimore: Johns Hopkins University Press, 1988), 18–19.

36. Mary Beard, John North, and Simon Price note: "In the late Republic and into the first century A.D., there seems to have been a general assumption at Rome that each foreign race had its own characteristic religious practices." See Mary Beard, John North, and Simon Price, *Religions of Rome,* 2 vols. (Cambridge: Cambridge University Press, 1998), 1:121.

37. See D. B. Saddington, "Race Relations in the Early Roman Empire," 115.

38. For example, see Juvenal *Satires*; Plutarch *On Isis and Osiris* 71 [379D4–E15]; Josephus *Against Apion* 1.225.

39. See my more extended interpretations of this passage in Denise K. Buell, "Rethinking the Relevance of Race for Early Christian Self-Definition," *HTR* 94 (2001): 461–462; and Denise K. Buell, "Race and Universalism in Early Christianity," *JECS* 10:4 (2002): 429–432, 441–442.

40. Clement interprets this passage not only as a means to distinguish among Greeks, Jews, and Christians, but also to argue for their unification—as Christians—through the adoption of Christian beliefs and practices: "Accordingly then, those from the Hellenic training and also from the law, who accept faith are gathered into the one *genos* of the saved people (*laos*): not that the three peoples are separated by time, so that one might suppose [they have] three different natures, but trained in different covenants of the one Lord" (*Strom.* 6.42.2).

41. Cited in Malkin, "Introduction," 6. From Robert Parker, *Cleomenes on the Acropolis: An Inaugural Lecture Delivered Before the University of Oxford on 12 May 1997* (Oxford: Clarendon, 1998), 12.

42. Nancy Jay, *"Throughout Your Generations Forever": Sacrifice, Religion, and Paternity* (Chicago: University of Chicago Press, 1992).

43. Ibid., 37 (and see also 30–46). Jay notes that: "Social paternity and biological paternity may, and often do, coincide, but it is social paternity that determines patrilineage membership . . . Sacrifice cannot be infallible evidence of begetting and therefore obviously cannot constitute biological paternity. It is the social relations of reproduction, not biological reproduction, that sacrificial ritual can create and maintain. Where the state and the social relations of production are not separable from patrilineally organized social relations of reproduction, the entire social order may be understood as dependent on sacrifice" (36–37). Throughout the book, she underscores the gendered implications of such a social system, noting that it creates social relations around "fathers" and "sons" (socially, if not biologically), bypassing women and maternity. Taking a different approach, Gianna Pomata uses Greek and Roman medical literature about procreation to show that while Romans did hold a view of kinship linked to notions of "shared blood," only men were thought to be able to produce the relationship of kinship by shared blood (*agnatio*), which had civic, legal consequences. Women could only produce a "natural" form of kinship (*cognatio*) without such consequences. See Gianna Pomata, "Blood Ties and Semen Ties: Consanguity and Agnation in Roman Law," in *Gender, Kinship, Power: A Comparative and Interdisciplinary History*, ed. Mary Jo Maynes et al. (New York: Routledge, 1996), 43–64. The sacrificial system in both Greek and Roman cultures concerned (and Jay would say helped to create as well as signify) relations of *agnatio* only.

44. Chapter 3 explores how Justin Martyr adapts this tradition.

45. Judith was most likely composed in the mid-second century B.C.E.

46. Josephus explains the differences and enmity between Jews and Egyptians as stemming not only from bitterness over former power differences ("the domination of our ancestors [*progonoi*] over their country") but also the differences between their forms of piety (*eusebeia*) (*Against Apion* 1.224).

47. Cohen, *The Beginnings of Jewishness*, 132–138.

48. See Denise K. Buell, "Ethnicity and Religion in Mediterranean Antiquity and Beyond," *Religious Studies Review* 26 (2000): 247.

49. Naomi Janowitz, "Rethinking Jewish Identity in Late Antiquity," in *Ethnicity*

*and Culture in Late Antiquity,* ed. Stephen Mitchell and Geoffrey Greatex (London: Duckworth and the Classical Press of Wales, 2000), 213–214.

50. As Jonathan Friedman describes it, "traditional ethnicity . . . is based on membership defined by the practice of certain activities including those related to genealogical descent. . . . Ethnic affiliation can easily be changed or complemented by geographical mobility or by change in social reference. Where a member of a group changes residence he is adopted or adopts the local ancestors and gods and becomes a practicing member of the new community. Here the social group is more like a congregation than a biological unit. This does not mean that identity is a mere question of social roles or membership as we understand it, i.e. as an externality that does not touch our inner selves. On the contrary, personal identity in such societies is not independent of the social context but almost entirely defined by it" (Friedman, "Notes on Culture and Identity in Imperial Worlds," 27).

51. Tim Whitmarsh, "'Greece is the World,'" in *Being Greek Under Rome,* 273.

52. Even though Jonathan Hall and I disagree about precisely how to define ethnicity, he too argues that "ethnicity is a *specific type* of cultural identity" (emphasis in original). For Hall, what makes ethnicity different from other possible types of ethnicity "is the fact that the symbols on which it draws revolve around notions of fictive kinship and descent, common history, and a specific homeland. See Jonathan Hall, *Hellenicity: Between Ethnicity and Culture* (Chicago: University of Chicago Press, 2002), 17.

53. While 1 Peter uses the term "Christian" as one of self-identification, my use of scare quotes is intended to remind readers that this term's meaning needs to be argued for, not presumed.

54. John Elliott's study of 1 Peter is valuable for its argument about the centrality of the concepts of resident alien (*paroikos*) and visiting stranger (*parepidēmos*), concepts that discursively locate Christianness in terms of kinship, civic, and ethnoracial categories. See John H. Elliott, *A Home for the Homeless: A Sociological Exegesis of 1 Peter, Its Situation and Strategy* (Philadelphia: Fortress, 1981), 23, 25, 118–150, 284.

55. The Greek version specifies that this is the preaching of the "true Gospel" spread by the twelve disciples after Jesus's ascension (*Apol.* 15.2).

56. See Marcel Simon, *Verus Israel: Étude sur les relations entre chrétiens et juifs dans l'empire romain (135–425)* (Paris: Éditions de Boccard, 1964), 136.

57. Caroline Johnson Hodge, "'If Children, Then Heirs'": A Study of Kinship and Ethnicity in Paul's Letters (Ph.D. Dissertation, Brown University, 2002), 55–137; 178–222. See also Denise K. Buell and Caroline Johnson Hodge, "The Politics of Interpretation: The Rhetoric of Race and Ethnicity in Paul," *JBL* 123 (2004): 235–252.

58. The initial depiction of Judith does locate her genealogically as a descendant of Israel (Jth. 8:1) but the overwhelming emphasis is on her piety. The presence of the genealogy only reinforces the dynamic movement between fixed (in this case, communicated in the genealogy) and fluid in conceptualizations of ethnicity/race.

59. For an example of saved *genos*, see *Acts of Andrew* 50.5 (18); for an example of righteous *genos*, see *Shepherd of Hermas Sim.* 9.17.5; for an example of immovable *genea*, see *Apocryphon of John* (NHC III, 1) 33.3, (BG 8505, 2) 65.2; for an example of true *genos*, see *Gospel of Philip* 76.3; for an example of holy *laos*, see Justin, *Dial.* 119.3; for an example of special *laos*, see Clement, *Strom.* 6.106.4–107.1.

60. Josephus attributes this view tracing Jews to Egyptian ancestry to his enemy Apion (*Against Apion* 2.28). For places where Josephus rejects this view, see *Against Apion* 1.75, 104, 252, 278; 2.8. He relies on the work of Manetho, who wrote a history of Egypt for one of the early Ptolemies, for support.

61. A century earlier, Diodoros of Sicily recounts with some skepticism Egyptian claims that they are the ancestors of Jews and Athenians. Religious practices, notably circumcision (in the case of Jews) and the veneration of Demeter (in the case of Athenians) are among the factors offered as "proof" for these claims (see Diodorus 1.28.1–29.6).

62. Woolf, *Becoming Roman*, 55.

63. Indeed the very establishment of regionally organized cults was itself a departure from city-run cults, as Steve Friesen writes: "no Greek or Roman cults, either for rulers or for others, had been organized on a regional basis [before the early Augustan period]. The unprecedented spread of such institutions in the second century indicates that new social relationships were in formation." See Steven J. Friesen, *Twice Neokoros: Ephesus, Asia and the Cult of the Flavian Imperial Family* (Leiden: Brill, 1993), 144.

64. J. B. Rives argues that it is only under the Emperor Decius in the middle of the third century that Romans implement a religious system that is universal by insisting on a unifying cultic act. See J. B. Rives, "The Decree of Decius and the Religion of the Empire," *Journal of Roman Studies* 89 (1999): 135–154.

65. This important point is made by Simon Price, who argues that studies of Roman imperial cult have too often looked through Christianizing lenses with the result that "inflates the importance of the imperial cult and posits a stark choice between Christ and the Caesars, between religion and politics" S. R. F. Price, *Rituals and Power: The Roman Imperial Cult in Asia Minor* (Cambridge: Cambridge University Press, 1984), 15.

66. Religious "reform" is often justified in terms of restoring what already exists within the tradition. Much more controversial are those changes that are proposed or viewed as innovations, which seem to risk transforming the community's identity altogether. Feminist theologians have repeatedly faced charges that their calls for changes within religious communities will result in such a break from tradition—that Christianity will cease being Christianity or Judaism Judaism, etc. Judith Plaskow offers a sensitive discussion of the stakes of such arguments in her ground-breaking *Standing Again at Sinai: Judaism from a Feminist Perspective* (New York: Harper and Row, 1990).

67. Beard, North, and Price, *Religions of Rome*, 1:212.

68. This portrayal of the fluidity of Romanness (or perhaps any collective identity)

can be extended to other domains as well, as Eve d'Ambra emphasizes: "Works of art commissioned by patrons of varying social ranks or in farflung regions of the empire reflect the extraordinary receptivity to diverse influences that characterizes Roman art and culture as a whole. This quality is also evident in the political character of the empire, which grew through conquest and assimilated its former enemies as residents or citizens of the empire. Not only were geographical boundaries fluid, but the rigid social order had loopholes: it permitted owners to free their slaves and confer Roman citizenship on them. . . . In a society driven by demonstrations of power and wealth, it is striking that there were styles and standards appropriate across the social spectrum. What defined the Roman character and allowed a person to pass as a Roman was never simply given. It had to be tested, challenged, and sorted out through the system that granted rank and status to citizens according to factors such as birth, wealth, and accomplishments, which occasionally clashed with one another." See Eve d'Ambra, *Roman Art* (Cambridge: Cambridge University Press, 1998), 13.

69. Beard, North, and Price, *Religions of Rome*, 1:150. They note that these attempts correlate with the rise of theoretical discourses about "religion."

70. Similarly, in the Hebrew Bible, "idolatry" functions both to mark foreignness and illegitimate religious worship (including that of Israelite insiders). The meaning and application of the term *superstitio* shifted over time. Where the label *superstitio* had previously connoted improper or excessive religious practices, including in Roman cults, by the second century C.E. its primary connotation shifted to participation in non-Roman cults that were deemed improper or excessive in their practices. Thus *superstitio*, as the converse of *religio*, shifts from having as its primary meaning something *Romans* risk doing by improper or excessive religious observances of Roman deities to a characteristic of *non-*Romans: "Tacitus, for example, refers to the Druids' prophecy that Rome would fall to the Gauls as 'an empty *superstitio*' (*Histories* IV.54.4). Egyptian and Jewish rituals too were branded with the same label. According to Tacitus again, the people of Alexandria 'subject to superstitions' worshipped the god Serapis above all; while his extremely hostile account of Jewish customs observes that this race was 'prone to *superstitio*, and opposed to religious practices' (*Histories* IV.81.2; V.13.1). . . . At the same time, these foreign cults were seen as potential forces of political subversion: Druids prophesied the downfall of Rome and the Jews actually did revolt against Rome" (Beard, North, and Price, *Religions of Rome*, 1:221–222)

71. This function of religion for the internal regulation of a people suggests that early Christian heresiological arguments may have been understood in the context of ethnoracial self-definitions. I consider this implication in chapter 4.

72. I thus depart from Hall on this point, who explicitly minimizes the possible discursive relevance of religion (Hall, *Ethnic Identity*, 21–24, 40).

73. We know little about Athenagoras, apart from his surviving works; this one situates itself somewhere between 166–180 by its address to the emperors Marcus Aurelius (d. 180) and Commodus (who was made Caesar in 166 and joint

Augustus in 177). My discussion of the *Embassy* is adapted from Buell, Rethinking the Relevance of Race," 462–464.

74. Frances Young, "Greek Apologists of the Second Century," in *Apologetics in the Roman Empire: Pagans, Jews, and Christians*, ed. Mark Edwards et al. (Oxford: Oxford University Press, 1999), 92 (my emphasis). Young is speaking of second-century Christian literature in Greek; without claiming to be comprehensive, she classifies the following works as apologetic: Justin Martyr, *First* and *Second Apology, Dialogue with Trypho*; Tatian, *Oration to the Greeks*; Athenagoras, *Embassy, Epistle to Diognetus*; Theophilus, *To Autolycus* (82–90). I agree with Young's view that apologetics is not a literary genre but a rhetorical strategy that can appear in any number of literary forms (91). I interpret the primary readers of this "fight" to be those with some relationship to Christian teachings and practices rather than the emperors and imperial officials to whom they are often ostensibly addressed.

75. See also Frances Young, "Greek Apologists of the Second Century," 103.

76. Woolf, *Becoming Roman*, 214–215.

77. Other Christian authors of this period, like the anonymous writer of the *Epistle to Diognetus*, assert instead that Christians share customs with their neighbors even though their true allegiances lie elsewhere (namely, heaven or the kingdom of God).

78. Athenagoras's comparison of Christianness with civic allegiances indicates that the lines between civic identity and ethnicity are blurry. This fuzziness does not indicate category confusion so much as it indicates the importance of not imposing clear distinctions among categories that were more nested than bounded. Because Romanness develops out of and maintains its civic ties to a particular city even while it takes on universal, imperial connotations, it blurs the lines between civic, racial, and national/imperial identities. Religious practices were central to the way that at least the elites of some cities negotiated their allegiances with the Roman Empire while preserving a sense of distinctiveness. For example, see Douglas Edwards on Aphrodisias in *Religion and Power: Pagans, Jews, and Christians in the Greek East* (Oxford: Oxford University Press, 1996), 58; and Steve Friesen on Ephesos in *Twice Neokoros*.

79. Judith Perkins, *The Suffering Self* (New York: Routledge, 1995).

80. See Daniel Boyarin, *Dying for God: Martyrdom and the Making of Christianity and Judaism* (Stanford: Stanford University Press, 1999), 109. Boyarin rightly emphasizes the importance of distinguishing between the setting of martyr texts and their dates of composition (113, 119). Although the latter cannot always be established with certainty, many are only preserved in fourth- and fifth-century texts, as Boyarin notes. See Elizabeth A. Castelli, *Martyrdom and Memory: Early Christian Culture Making* (New York: Columbia University Press, 2004).

81. Lieu, "Race of the God-Fearers," 485–488, 492; and Lieu, *Image and Reality*, 83–86. Lieu translates *genos* as "race" and *ethnos* as "nation."

82. Lieu, "Race of the God-Fearers," 491–493; see also 494–497; and Lieu, *Image and Reality*, 84–85. She writes: "The sense of being a race or people is one proudly

held in Jewish literature from the Maccabean period, often in a context of suffering and persecution. The threat from the Assyrians is directed against 'the race of Israel' (Jdt. 6:2, 5, 19; 8:20, 32; 11:10), while Judith herself prays, 'may your whole nation (*ethnos*) and every tribe know that you are God . . . and there is none other who shields the race (*genos*) of Israel' (9:14)" (Lieu, "Race of the God-Fearers," 491). And in the Maccabean literature, she notes that "their suffering and celebration of deliverance is as a nation (2 Macc. 10.8; 11.25, 27; 4 Macc. 4.19) or race (2 Macc. 6.12; 12.31; 14.8); in particular the martyrs pray on behalf of the whole race who, through their death, will soon experience the mercy of God (2 Macc. 7.16, 37, 38)" (Lieu, *Image and Reality*, 84).

83. Lieu, *Image and Reality*, 85.

84. Although attention to ethnic reasoning shapes my analysis, the implications of this focus supports Daniel Boyarin's arguments that the discourse of martyrdom, "far from being evidence for Christian influence on Judaism or the opposite, is most plausibly read as evidence for the close contact and the impossibility of drawing sharp and absolute distinctions between these communities or their discourses throughout this period (of the second through fourth centuries)" (Boyarin, *Dying for God*, 117).

85. The original date of composition remains unknown. See Herbert Musurillo, *Acts of the Christian Martyrs: Volume II* (Oxford: Clarendon, 1972), xx.

86. Greg Woolf, *Becoming Roman*, 225. See also Duncan Fishwick, *The Imperial Cult in the Latin West: Studies in the Ruler Cult of the Western Provinces of the Roman Empire* (Leiden: Brill, 1987).

87. Greg Woolf, *Becoming Roman*, 38, 40, 216–217, 222, 231. Woolf writes that "the rise of Lyon to effective capital of the Three Gauls was due largely to the success of the neighboring sanctuary" (217). See also Paul Zanker, *The Power of Images in the Age of Augustus*, trans. Alan Shapiro (Ann Arbor: University of Michigan Press, 1988), 302.

88. Greg Woolf, *Becoming Roman*, 225, 235.

89. Ibid., 216.

90. I do not mean to imply, however, that the late second-century narrative setting is identical to the time, writing, or concerns of the author and readers of the text.

91. To avoid misunderstanding, let me stress that I am not arguing about the historical validity of the account—that is, whether or not Sanctus actually made such an assertion. Rather, I am underscoring what is at least a literary rhetorical strategy.

92. See Stephen Benko, *Pagan Rome and the Early Christians* (Bloomington: Indiana University Press, 1984), 1–24.

93. While confession of the name denoted guilt, denial did not automatically denote innocence in Pliny's eyes. Those who denied affiliation with the name had to reinforce it through ritual action.

94. Other texts studied as early Christian do not use the name "Christian," however, opting instead for other collective terms of self-identification (for example, the elect, Hebrews, etc.). This is worth noting since it suggests that the importance of

the name "Christian" does not apply to every individual or group in the second and third centuries that might now be classified by scholars as "early Christian."

95. Daniel Boyarin, *Dying For God*, 95.

96. Herbert Musurillo, the editor and translator of the most widely used Greek-English edition of the Christian martyr acts, refers to this verse in a slightly different way: "Foremost, of course, is the portrayal of the martyrs' courage in the face of the most vicious torture and humiliation, a courage shared by both sexes, by both slave and free, as though in fulfillment of Paul's pronouncement in Galatians (3:28), *For you are all one in Christ Jesus*" (Musurillo, *Acts of the Christian Martyrs*, lii).

97. There are other texts that become prooftexts as well: notably, Matthew 28:19 ("Go therefore and make disciples of all *ethnē*, baptizing them . . . "); Acts 2:1–21 (Pentecost; especially vv. 5–11 interpreted with reference to all people, not just Jews of the diaspora); Acts 10:1–48 (Cornelius; especially Peter's speech in verses 34–35: "Truly I perceive that God shows no partiality, but in every nation any one who fears him and does what is right is acceptable to him"); and Acts 17:26 (Paul's speech: "And [God] made one every *ethnos* of humanity . . . ").

98. See also Recension C of *The Martyrdom of Saints Justin, Chariton, Charito, Evelpistus, Hierax, Paeon, and Valerian* (*Acts of the Christian Martyrs* 2:54–61). In this version, unlike recensions A and B, the trial and executions are prefaced not only by comments about the wickedness of the emperor (Antoninus) and the arresting official (Rusticus), but also by comments about the backgrounds of the Christians arrested: "Now the saints did not have the same native city (*patris*), for they came from different places. But the favor of the spirit bound them together and taught them to think as siblings and to have only one head, Christ" (1.2). As in the case of the *Acts of the Martyrs of Lyon and Vienne*, in this recension the first thing that Rusticus asks them is "what they are called, where they come from (*hothen eien*), and what their kind of piety (*ti to sebas*) they practice. They confessed that they were Christians and made clear to him what their calling was, and said that their only city was God's, the free city, the heavenly Jerusalem, whose craftsman and creator was God. They said to him: 'What advantage is it for you, o tyrant, to know the names of our earthly cities?' " (*M. Just.* 1.3). This response provokes Rusticus to demand to Justin that he "sacrifice to the immortal gods and fulfill the imperial edicts" (1.4).

99. This varies somewhat from Daniel Boyarin's view that this phrasing is parallel not to "Ioudaios eimi" but rather the declaration of the *Shemaʿ* (Boyarin, *Dying for God*, 188), because he sees both functioning equivalently as "a ritualized and performative speech act associated with a statement of pure essence [that] becomes the central action of the martyrology. In rabbinic texts this is the declaration of the oneness of God via the recitation "Hear O Israel." For Christians, it is the declaration of the essence of self: "I am a Christian." In both, this is the final act of the martyr's life. For Christian texts, this is new with the *Martyrium Polycarpi*. For rabbinic Jews, it begins with the stories about Polycarp's contemporary, Rabbi Akiva" (Boyarin, *Dying for God*, 95; see also 121). For Boyarin,

claiming to be a Christian differs fundamentally from claiming to be a Jew because the former is illegal and the latter not: "it would have made as much sense to forbid someone to be a Jew as it would to forbid her to be a Greek" (188). While this difference is correct, given that the name "Jew" was never the target of persecution per se, his conclusion preserves the rift between ethnicity and religiosity in Christianity that I am holding up for question. By interpreting what they share in common as religious identities (Boyarin interprets, with Shaye Cohen, the one instance that appears parallel with the "Christianus sum," in 2 Macc. 6:6, which refers to a moment when "people could not confess themselves to be Jews" as meaning that they could not confess their Jewish practices [189]), Boyarin seems to exclude the possibility that the identity being claimed in the assertion "Christianus sum" is simultaneously a religious and ethnic one.

100. The wavering Christians are noteworthy. Their presence in the narrative may seem less dramatic than the vivid tortures endured by Sanctus, Blandina, and some of the other steadfast Christians, but they are no less significant to the overall plot. They embody the fluidity of collective identification, both in their wavering and in their reaffiliation. John Curran also emphasizes the importance of less-than-committed converts to Christianity in analyzing the phenomenon of conversion. See John Curran, "The Conversion of Rome Revisited," *Ethnicity and Culture in Late Antiquity*, 4–12.

101. This text is the earliest dated document from the Latin church (Musurillo, *Acts of the Christian Martyrs*, xxii).

102. The offer by a Christian to instruct a Roman official in true religion is a trope in martyr narratives (for example, see *M. Poly.* 10.2).

103. See also *M. Poly.* 8.2; 9.2–3.

104. J. B. Rives insists on these point for the Carthaginian context. See J. B. Rives, *Religion and Authority in Roman Carthage from Augustus to Constantine* (Oxford: Clarendon, 1995), 169–170. Rives also helpfully underscores the internal diversity of Christianity in second- and third-century Carthage, which the *Acts of the Scillitan Martyrs* does not indicate (Rives, *Religion and Authority*, 227–234). For another good example of internal Christian diversity noted in a martyr text, see the *Martyrdom of Polycarp*, which indicates tensions among New Prophecy (also known as "Phyrgian" and Montanist) Christians and the Christians identified with Polycarp and his followers (*M. Poly.* 4.1).

105. Keith Hopkins, *A World Full of Gods: The Strange Triumph of Christianity* (New York: Free Press, 1999), 80 (my emphasis).

106. John North, "The Development of Religious Pluralism," in *The Jews Among Pagans and Christians In the Roman Empire*, ed. Judith Lieu, John North, and Tessa Rajak (New York: Routledge, 1992), 178.

107. Ibid., 187.

108. Michael Penn calls attention to this in his study of early Christian kissing. Penn suggests that "For early Christians, Athenagoras's work does not remain an apologetic description but becomes a ritual script. By following his instructions, participants could perform Christian righteousness." See Michael Penn,

"Performing Family: Ritual Kissing and the Construction of Early Christian Kinship," *JECS* 10 (2002): 172.

109. Lieu, "Race of the God-Fearers," 493–500.

110. Katharina von Kellenbach, *Anti-Judaism in Feminist Religious Writings* (Atlanta: Scholars Press, 1994), 41.

111. See for example, Rosemary Radford Ruether, *Faith and Fratricide: The Theological Roots of Anti-Semitism* (New York: Seabury, 1974), 239–245.

112. Beard, North, and Price, *Religions of Rome*, 1:42–43.

113. As Rudolf Bultmann puts it: "Primitive Christianity is quite uninterested in making the world a better place, it has no proposals for political or social reform. All must do their duty to the State. But they have no direct political responsibilities. After all, the Christian is a 'citizen of heaven' (Phil. 3.20)." See Rudolf Bultmann, *Primitive Christianity in Its Contemporary Settting*, trans. R. H. Fuller (1956; repr., New York: Meridian, 1966), 206.

114. For example, see North, "Development of Religious Pluralism," 180–181.

115. See also Buell, "Race and Universalism," esp. 441–468.

116. Discussing Roman reactions to Bacchic worship in Rome, Beard, North, and Price write: "By the first decade of the second century [B.C.E.], this form of group cult, at odds with traditional modes of behaviour, was well established and widespread in Italy. . . . It was the group cult, depending on voluntary adherence, that was in the end to bring the most radical changes to Roman religious life. The Bacchic groups of Italy were the first example of the problems that could arise; later groups were to become more and more independent, to develop their own ideas and value-systems, to be more and more deeply in conflict with the established social and family structures"(Beard, North, and Price, *Religions of Rome*, 1:98). They describe the membership of the Bacchic cult group as having "cut across all the usual boundaries between social groups, for we know of devotees amongst slaves and free, among Romans, Latins, and allies, men and women, country people and city-dwellers, rich and poor." (93–94).

117. Guy G. Stroumsa, *Barbarian Philosophy: The Religious Revolution of Early Christianity* (Tübingen: Mohr [Siebeck], 1999), 60.

118. As Jonathan Z. Smith has shown, this devaluing of ritual practices needs to be understood in the modern context of Protestant anti-Catholicism within scholarly interpretive frameworks, especially in the eighteenth and nineteenth centuries. See Jonathan Z. Smith, *Drudgery Divine: On the Comparison of Early Christianities and the Religions of Late Antiquity.* (Chicago: University of Chicago Press, 1990), 1–35, 55–62.

## 2. "We Were Before the Foundation of the World"

1. Arthur J. Droge, *Homer or Moses? Early Christian Interpretations of the History of Culture* (Tübingen: Mohr [Siebeck], 1989), 196. Christian ethnic reasoning ex-

tends far beyond the limited instances of the phrase "third race"; this is only one particularly striking articulation.

2. For a discussion of Jewish, Greek, and Egyptian predecessors, see Droge, *Homer or Moses?*, 1–48. The remainder of the work examines the historiographical strategies of selected early Christian authors in greater detail (Justin Martyr, Tatian, Theophilus of Antioch, and Clement of Alexandria).

3. Rachel Moriarty also explores how early Christians created a historical tradition, viewing early Christians as different from other ancient groups who actually "had" a past while Christians created a tradition "to help provide Christians with the past they lacked." See Rachel Moriarty, " 'The Faith of Our Fathers': The Making of the Early Christian Past," in *The Church Retrospective: Papers Read at the 1995 Summer Meeting and the 1996 Winter Meeting of the Ecclesiastical History Society*, ed. R.N. Swanson (Woodbridge, Suffolk: Boydell, 1997), 6. See now also Judith Lieu, *Christian Identity in the Jewish and Graeco-Roman World* (Oxford: Oxford University Press, 2004), 62–97.

4. Christopher P. Jones shows that this use of kinship in ancient political discourse was especially important during the Hellenistic period. Although he refrains from linking these arguments to ethnicity, his study repeatedly calls attention to the ways that appeals to kinship affected collective self-understandings and social-political practices. See Christopher P. Jones, *Kinship Diplomacy in the Ancient World* (Cambridge: Harvard University Press, 1999), esp. 2–5, 66–80, 94–99.

5. In making this distinction, I am adapting Jonathan Z. Smith's discussion of "uniqueness" in the study of Christian origins. See Jonathan Z. Smith, *Drudgery Divine: On the Comparison of Early Christianities and the Religions of Late Antiquity* (Chicago: University of Chicago Press, 1990), 36–53.

6. On all three points, see Smith, *Drudgery Divine*, 38–46. Elisabeth Schüssler Fiorenza offers the most comprehensive analysis of the limitations of interpreting the person and teachings of Jesus as ontologically unique. See Elisabeth Schüssler Fiorenza, *Jesus and the Politics of Interpretation* (New York: Continuum, 2000). For a recent discussion of the gospel genre, see Helmut Koester, *Ancient Christian Gospels: Their History and Development* (Philadelphia: Fortress, 1990). For an extensive analysis of the category of eschatology, see Melanie Johnson-DeBaufre, "It's the End of the World As We Know It" (Th.D. Diss., Harvard Divinity School, 2002).

7. David M. Olster, "Classical Ethnography and Early Christianity," in *The Formulation of Christianity by Conflict Through the Ages*, ed. Katharine B. Free (Lewiston, N.Y.: Mellen, 1995), 9–12.

8. Frances Young, "Greek Apologists of the Second Century," in *Apologetics in the Roman Empire*, ed. Mark Edwards, Martin Goodman, and Simon Price (New York: Oxford University Press, 1999), 103.

9. Indeed, this can be an explicit goal of historical-critical scholarship. One example of this is the use of historical criticism to demonstrate a precedent for women in leadership positions in the early church. On the other hand, appeal to historical

*disjuncture* has been used to argue for reform as well (for example, to extend rights to gay men and lesbians and to oppose slavery).

10. Shawn Kelley, *Racializing Jesus: Race, Ideology, and the Formation of Modern Biblical Scholarship* (New York: Routledge, 2002).

11. Averil Cameron, *Christianity and the Rhetoric of Empire: The Development of Christian Discourse* (Berkeley: University of California Press, 1991), 24.

12. Ibid., 24–25.

13. Young, "Greek Apologists," 103, my emphasis.

14. Ibid., 101.

15. To give due credit to Young, despite seeing Christian ethnic reasoning as enabling a definition of religion distinct from ethnicity, she offers an undeveloped but provocative conclusion. She suggests that after the legalization of Christianity, this trend changed dramatically "when the power relations were reversed and Christianity itself turned into an ethnic tradition" (Young, "Greek Apologists," 104).

16. Michel Foucault, *Politics, Philosophy, Culture: Interviews and Other Writings, 1977-1984*, trans. Alan Sheridan and others, ed. with and introduction by Lawrence D. Kritzman (New York: Routledge, 1988), 262. Cited in Robert Young, *White Mythologies: Writing History and the West* (New York: Routledge, 1990), 87.

17. This view has been formulated by a range of critical theorists. See for example Elisabeth Schüssler Fiorenza, *But She Said: Feminist Practices of Biblical Interpretation* (Boston: Beacon, 1992), 87–96; Michel de Certeau, *The Writing of History*, trans. Tom Conley (New York: Columbia University Press, 1988), 1–102; and Dipesh Chakrabartry, *Provincializing Europe: Postcolonial Thought and Historical Difference* (Princeton: Princeton University Press, 2000), 108–113.

18. Two things (at least) show this: first, the considerable variation in the name given to the collective identity (not necessarily "Christian," but also "Hebrew" and "the immoveable *genea*," among others); and second, considerable debate over what it means to be a member of any of these collective identities.

19. For example, see Young, "Greek Apologists," 92–93; Droge, *Homer or Moses?*, 9–11; and Arthur Darby Nock, *Conversion: The Old and the New in Religion from Alexander the Great to Augustine of Hippo* (Baltimore: Johns Hopkins University Press, 1988), 251.

20. See *Apology* 19.2; 21.1–2, 6.

21. The text also notes that the mothers of Abraham's children differ, but it foregrounds as more significant the difference in Abraham's knowledge of God.

22. In this respect, *Recognitions* differs significantly from Paul's interpretation of Genesis in Galatians 4, where he stresses the saliency of the difference in status of Sarah (free) and Hagar (slave) for the character of Abraham's two lineages.

23. F. Stanley Jones, in his translation of the Pseudo-Clementine Homilies, *An Ancient Jewish Christian Source on the History of Christianity: Pseudo-Clementine Recognitions 1.27–71* (Atlanta: Scholars, 1995), 160.

24. See Denise K. Buell, "Race and Universalism in Early Christianity," *JECS* 10:4 (2002): 446–450.

25. See Buell, "Race and Universalism," *JECS* 10:4 (2002): 450–453.

26. Erich S. Gruen, "Jewish Perspectives on Greek Culture and Ethnicity," in *Ancient Perceptions of Greek Ethnicity*, ed. Irad Malkin (Washington D.C.: Center for Hellenic Studies/Cambridge: Harvard University Press, 2001), 362 (see 1 Macc. 12:20–23); see also Erich S. Gruen, "The Purported Jewish-Spartan Affiliation," in *Transitions to Empire: Essays in Greco-Roman History, 360–146 B.C., in Honor of E. Badian*, ed. Robert W. Wallace and Edward M. Harris (Norman, Okla.: University of Oklahoma Press, 1996), 254–269.

27. Jones, *Kinship Diplomacy*, 72–80.

28. Paul is here using a form of aggregative ethnic construction. See Jonathan Hall, *Ethnic Identity*, 47–51; see also 40–44. See also Denise Buell, "Ethnicity and Religion in Mediterranean Antiquity and Beyond," *Religious Studies Review* 26 (2000): 248–249. This insight has since been developed in detail in Caroline Johnson Hodge, " 'If Sons, Then Heirs': A Study of Kinship and Ethnicity in Paul's Letters" (Ph.D. Diss., Brown University, 2002), 182–222. See also Stanley K. Stowers, *A Rereading of Romans: Justice, Jews, and Gentiles* (New Haven: Yale University Press, 1994), esp. 99, 107, 227, 239, 249.

29. Hodge, " 'If Sons, Then Heirs,' " 107–112, 117–123.

30. While the next chapter explores how Justin does this in the *Dialogue with Trypho*, see also Jeffrey Siker's more comprehensive study: Jeffrey Siker, *Disinheriting the Jews: Abraham in Early Christian Controversy* (Louisville, KY: Westminster/John Knox, 1991).

31. Justin Martyr *1 Apol.* 32.3; 53.2.

32. *1 Apol.* 31.7; 40.7; 50.12; see also 32.4; 39.3; 53.3.

33. In his *Apology*, Tertullian invokes both the fluidity and fixity of identity to craft a universalizing argument for Christianity that recalls those of Justin's *logos* theology. While Justin argues that all humans have the *logos* implanted in them, and are thus potentially Christian (and Christianness is the fullest expression of humanity), Tertullian claims that the human soul is "in its very nature Christian (*animae naturaliter Christianae*)" (*Apol.* 17.6); this assertion of the fixity of Christian essence in all human souls is balanced by the position that "Christians are made not born (*fiunt, non nascuntur Christiani*)" (18.4). That is, while all humans are potentially Christian, some kind of transformation must occur before one realizes this potential.

34. Droge, *Homer or Moses?*, 72 (see 69–79); emphasis in original.

35. Citations are taken from the Nag Hammadi Library copy of the text. One other copy has survived, in the Papyrus Berolinensis 8502, 3 (BG). These two copies are very similar. The critical edition I have used is by Douglas Parrott, which also contains editions of the other manuscripts, and the two surviving manuscripts of a closely related text, *Eugnostos*. See *Eugnostos and the Sophia of Jesus Christ*, in *The Coptic Gnostic Library: A Complete Edition of the Nag Hammadi Codices. Vol. 3*, ed. Douglas M. Parrott (1991; repr., Leiden: Brill, 2000).

36. See Buell, "Race and Universalism," 446–450.

37. Elsewhere, Celsus makes the charge (via the Jewish interlocutor) that Christian teaching is unoriginal because it is derived from Jewish law and doctrine

(*Against Celsus* 2.4; 2.5). For example, Origen writes "[Celsus's] Jew disparages as stale stuff the doctrine of the resurrection of the dead and of God's judgment giving reward to the righteous but fire to the unrighteous. He thinks that he can overthrow Christianity by saying that in these matters Christians teach nothing new" (2.5). Celsus also used the charge of lack of novelty with respect to the organization of Jesus's teachings—specifically, his selection of apostles which Celsus compares to the organization of other philosophical sects (1.62) and the figure of Jesus as a teacher (2.8). See Buell, "Race and Universalism," 450–453.

38. Having linked all humanity to Seth, Theophilus explains the subsequent division of humanity as a consequence of two main factors: God's division of the languages in response to the tower (of Babel), and migration.

39. *TriTrac* 133.67; and 132.4–15 and 132.28–133.14. The critical edition of the *Tripartite Tractate* that I am working from is *The Tripartite Tractate*, in *The Coptic Gnostic Library: A Complete Edition of the Nag Hammadi Codices, Vol. 1*, ed., trans., and critical notes by Harold W. Attridge and Elaine H. Pagels (1985; repr., Leiden: Brill, 2000).

40. "Left" is linked with "hylic" and "right" with "psychic." The fact that the first human is described as a mixture of all three components provides a basis for mitigating against the view that the differences between these three *genē* are necessary and original to humans. Instead, all three components are "native" to humans. As Pagels and Attridge observe, this tripartite understanding of the human soul is a "traditional doctrine of Platonism"; they further note, "there is no reason to assume that the souls of subsequent human beings differ from that of the first member of the race. This suggests that, for the *TriTrac* at least, the tripartition of human beings, mentioned in 118.14–58, is not determined by the constitution of different types of human souls. All souls are composed of all three types of substance deriving from the intermediate world" (XXIII: 412). So also Einar Thomassen in his commentary on the *Tripartite Tractate*, *Le Traité Tripartite*, critical ed., introduction and commentary by Einar Thomassen, trans. by Louis Painchaud and Einar Thomassen (Québec: Les Presses de l'Université Laval, 1989), 428.

41. "Le mot genos (118:22.28.37; 119:9) . . . évoque non pas les constituantes génétiques des individus, mais des qualities religieuses, c'est-à-dire éthiques et intellectuelles" (Thomassen, *Le Traité Tripartite*, 428).

42. Thomassen, *Le Traité Tripartite*, 412; see also 446.

43. Attridge and Pagels, "The Tripartite Tractate," XXIII: 447, my emphasis.

44. François Hartog, *Memories of Odysseus: Frontier Tales from Ancient Greece*, trans. Janet Lloyd (Chicago: University of Chicago Press, 2001), 6.

45. Ibid., 163.

46. Ibid., 176.

47. Ibid.

48. Ibid.

49. Greg Woolf, "Becoming Roman, Staying Greek: Culture, Identity and the Civilizing Process in the Roman East," *Proceedings of the Cambridge Philological Society* n.s. 40 (1994): 57–59.

50. Hartog, *Memories of Odysseus*, p. 163.

51. Ibid., 195.

52. Aaron Johnson has demonstrated that Eusebius continues the kind of genealogical arguments we have seen in pre-Constantinian Christian ethnic reasoning. In his examination of Eusebius's *Praeparatio Evangelica*, Johnson shows how Christians are constructed as an *ethnos*. See Aaron P. Johnson, "Identity, Descent, and Polemic: Ethnic Argumentation in Eusebius's *Praeparatio Evangelica*," *JECS* 12 (2004): 23–56.

53. Marianne Palmer Bonz, *The Past as Legacy: Luke-Acts and Ancient Epic* (Minneapolis: Fortress, 2000), see esp. 39.

54. Antony Spawforth, "Shades of Greekness: a Lydian Case Study," in *Ancient Perceptions of Greek Ethnicity*, 375–400.

55. Spawforth makes the important point that modern scholars need to be cautious when using the concept of "Greekness" since it "impose[s] a misleading uniformity on the regionally and culturally differentiated populations of the Greek-speaking east" (Spawforth, "Shades of Greekness," 375).

56. There is a considerable body of scholarship on the forms of and explanations for "archaism" or the "classicizing" tendency that characterizes second- and third-century C.E. Greek and Roman understandings and (in the case of "Greeks") practices of "Greekness." The most influential study in recent times has been Ewan L. Bowie's "Greeks and their Past in the Second Sophistic," *Past and Present* 46 (1970): 3–41, reprinted in *Studies in Ancient Society*, ed. Moses Finley London: Routledge, 1974, 166–209. See also Ewan L. Bowie, "Hellenes and Hellenism in Writers of the Second Sophistic," in *ΕΛΛΗΝΙΣΜΟΣ: Quelques Jalons pour une Histoire de l'Identité Grecque, Actes de Colloque de Strasbourg 25–27 octobre 1989*, ed. Suzanne Saïd (Leiden: Brill, 1991), 182–204; and David Konstan, "*To Hellēnikon ethnos*: Ethnicity and the Construction of Ancient Greek Identity," in *Ancient Perceptions of Greek Ethnicity*, 29–50, esp. 36–43. On the importance of this definition of Greekness for Roman self-definition, see Greg Woolf, "Becoming Roman," 116–143; and Andrew Wallace-Hadrill, "To Be Roman, Go Greek: Thoughts on Hellenization at Rome," in *Modus Operandi: Essays in Honour of Geoffrey Rickman*, ed. Michel Austin, Jill Harries, and Christopher Smith (London: Institute of Classical Studies, School of Advanced Study, University of London, 1998), 79–91.

57. Spawforth, "Shades of Greekness," 380–383.

58. Ibid., 383. Strabo *Geography* 12.1.3; 13.4.5.

59. Spawforth, "Shades of Greekness," 376.

60. Ibid., 384.

61. Ibid., 379.

62. Ibid., 385.

63. Ibid., 385–386.

64. Ibid., 386. He continues: "This extraordinary claim was a source of particular pride, it seems, and explains why the Sardians preferred to give the name 'Hellas' to the Roman province of Achaia in public inscriptions" (386–387). For further

analysis of the Sardian epigraphy see Peter Herrmann, "Inschriften von Sardis," *Chiron* 23 (1993): 233–248.

65. Spawforth, "Shades of Greekness," 387. Christopher Jones also makes this point about intracity rivalries while emphasizing that Sardian claims were consistent with a long legacy of city-state "kinship diplomacy," now adapted to the imperial context (Jones, *Kinship Diplomacy*, 117–118). On these rivalries in Asia Minor, see also Steven J. Friesen, *Twice Neokoros: Ephesus, Asia and the Cult of the Flavian Imperial Family* (Leiden: Brill, 1993).

66. Jones notes that during another context of rivalry, this time especially between Sardis and Smyrna in bids for the right to house a temple of Tiberius, Livia, and the senate, Sardians appealed to their kinship with and descent from Etruscans. They argued that "Etruria had been colonized by the Lydian prince Tyrrhenus" (Jones, *Kinship Diplomacy*, 109). Jones goes on to say that it is not a surprise "that Etruria was worth claiming as kindred territory. Its history was intimately connected with that of Rome, and many members of the ruling class had Etruscan connections by birth or marriage. At the time of the Sardian plea, one of these influential Etruscans was none other than Tiberius' all-powerful minister, Sejanus" (110). Although Sardis lost the bid for the temple, Jones suggests it was not due to suspicion about the arguments from kinship but rather other factors such as geographical location that prevailed (110).

67. For Diodorus's skepticism, see 1.2.9.5.

68. Elias Bickerman, "Origines Gentium," *Classical Philology* 47 (1952): 78.

69. "Under the double impact of Greek power and Greek science, the barbarians, mostly ignorant of their own primitive history, as soon as they had become a bit hellenized, accepted the Greek schema of *archaiologia*. The Romans recognized Aeneas, the Callaeci acknowledge Teucer as their ancestors. The Tarentines, being colonists from Lacedaemon, 'by flattery' attributed the same origin to their powerful Samnite neighbors, exactly as some centuries later the Roman senate called the Aedui in Gaul 'brothers and relations.' By Cato's time, the Spartan descent of the Sabini (Samnites) already had become a part of the latter's national tradition. In the time of the Athenian domination, and, then again, after Alexander the Great, kinship with the dominant race was a trump not to be neglected" (Bickerman, "Origines Gentium," 73–74).

70. Bickerman, "Origines Gentium," 74–75. For more recent studies of this phenomenon, see Spawforth, "Shades of Greekness," esp. 384–392; Erich S. Gruen, "The Purported Jewish-Spartan Affiliation," in *Transitions to Empire*, 254–269; and Erich S. Gruen, "Jewish Perspectives on Greek Culture and Ethnicity," in *Ancient Perceptions of Greek Ethnicity*, 347–373.

71. Indeed, this is a point that Tertullian stresses in arguing that Christianity can and should be a universal movement (*Apology* 1.6.7; see also 18.4).

72. Irad Malkin, "Introduction," *Ancient Perceptions of Greek Ethnicity*, 18.

73. Ibid., 19.

74. Ibid.

75. Ibid. My emphasis.

76. Ann Laura Stoler, "Racial Histories and their Regimes of Truth," *Political Power and Social Theory* 11 (1997): 192.

## 3. "We, Quarried from the Bowels of Christ, Are the True *Genos* of Israel"

1. Mary Beard, John North, and Simon Price, *Religions of Rome*, 2 vols. (Cambridge: Cambridge University Press, 1998), 1:276.

2. See also, for example, J. B. Rives: "Judaism was in one key respect hardly suitable as a model for the creation of a common religious identity in the empire. Despite the fluctuating importance of proselytism, *Judaism remained essentially an ethnic religion*, the religion of a people, as it has continued to this day. *There was*, however, *another tradition* within the Roman Empire *which*, although sharing many features with Judaism, was *emphatically not an ethnic religion. This was of course Christianity.*" J. B. Rives, *Religion and Authority in Roman Carthage from Augustus to Constantine* (Oxford: Clarendon, 1995), 267. Emphasis mine.

3. The rabbinic innovation of the principle of matrilineal descent vividly illustrates how ways of reckoning descent are historically contingent. See Shaye Cohen, *The Beginnings of Jewishness: Boundaries, Varieties, Uncertainties* (Berkeley: University of California Press, 1999), 263–307.

4. The critical edition I have consulted is: Iustini Martyris, *Dialogus cum Tryphone*, ed. Miroslav Marcovich (Berlin: De Gruyter, 1997).

5. See Daniel Boyarin, *Border Lines: The Partition of Judaeo-Christianity* (Philadelphia: University of Pennsylvania Press, 2004), which was published after this book was completed; his interpretation of Justin's *Dialogue* is used to illuminate and rethink rabbinical discourse. Boyarin views belief in the *logos* as the primary basis for Christian distinctiveness in the *Dialogue*. Boyarin argues that Justin appeals to belief in the *logos* to craft a "religious identity" on theological grounds (39). In my reading, this religious identity is simultaneously an ethnic one—it is misleading to distinguish between "religious" and "ethnic" in the *Dialogue*.

6. *Dial.* 44.1; see also 125.5 (where the ancestor in question is Jacob), 135.5–6, 140.2, and 25.1, which make a related point.

7. This claim is more fully elaborated in his two *Apologies*, especially through the concept of the *logos* being implanted in all human souls.

8. These first two techniques closely resemble those of historical ethnography we have seen in chapter 2. Justin draws from scripture to posit a universal human origin via Noah. And when linking Christians to Abraham and Jacob, Justin adapts the lineages privileged by other Jews for their own self-identification distinct from the rest of humanity.

9. *Dial.* 44.4.

10. Trypho poses questions that lead Justin to comment on the diversity of Christian views and practices. For example, see *Dial.* 34.8–35.8 (eating meat sacrificed to idols and the identification of authentic teachers); 47.1–3 (observing Mosaic

law and believing in Christ); 48.1–4 (the nature of Christ); and 80.1–5 (the future of Jerusalem and resurrection of the dead).

11. Judith Lieu also notes that this characterizes Trypho's Judaism. See Judith Lieu, *Image and Reality: The Jews in the World of the Christians in the Second Century* (Edinburgh: T&T Clark, 1996), 148.

12. Marcel Simon, *Verus Israel: A Study of the Relations Between Christians and Jews in the Roman Empire (135–425)*, trans. H. McKeating (French orig. 1964; Oxford: Oxford University Press, 1986), xii–xviii, 63–64, 111, 135, 146–155, 271–305, 369. This view is the one adopted in Lieu, *Image and Reality*, 118, 121, 128, 286; and Graham Stanton, "Justin Martyr's *Dialogue with Trypho*: Group Boundaries, 'Proselytes' and 'God-fearers,' " in *Tolerance and Intolerance in Early Judaism and Christianity*, ed. Graham N. Stanton and Guy G. Stroumsa (Cambridge: Cambridge University Press, 1998), 273, 275. This view has been criticized by Miriam S. Taylor, *Anti-Judaism and Early Christian Identity: A Critique of the Scholarly Consensus* (Leiden: Brill, 1995).

13. Throughout the lengthy *Dialogue*, Justin only uses forms of the term *Ioudaioi* (always in plural) seven times; *Christianos* (in singular and plural forms) appears twenty-three times (see *Dialogus cum Tryphone*, 336, 339). English translations frequently supply "Christian" and "Jew" where it does not appear in the Greek, giving the impression that these categories are clearer and more widely used than they actually are.

14. Although I disagree with Graham Stanton's view that "tight social boundaries" divide Jews and Christians in Justin's day, he quite rightly notes that the *Dialogue* is developed on the presupposition that boundaries between Jews and Christians are permeable. Chapter 8 introduces the main body of the text with Trypho and Justin exhorting each other to be persuaded to adopt their respective requirements for membership (Stanton, "Justin Martyr's *Dialogue*," 266–267).

15. As Daniel Boyarin puts it: "while both early rabbinic texts and Justin's text are busy producing both a border between 'Jews' and 'Christians' and concomitantly one between the orthodox and the 'heretics,' these borders are actually not so clear as the 'authors' of these texts would want us to believe. Instead, then, of thinking of Justin . . . as reacting to a 'Jewish' model or, on the other hand, understanding the Rabbis as reacting to a Christian development, I would rather propose a complex process of mutual self-definition, of testing of borders and boundaries, definitions of what could be shared and what would be differential between the nascent formations that would, by the fourth century, truly become separate religions." Daniel Boyarin, "Justin Martyr Invents Judaism," *Church History* 70 (2001): 455–456. Seth Schwartz has recently offered a provocative challenge to focusing on the rabbis, arguing that what he calls the "late antique revival of Judaism" that begins in the fourth century C.E. was in not "in any way a product of rabbinic influence, though the revival may in the long run have contributed to the rabbis' medieval rise." Seth Schwartz, *Imperialism and Jewish Society, 200 B.C.E. to 640 C.E.* (Princeton: Princeton University Press, 2001), 16.

16. See Lieu, *Image and Reality*, 278–279. See also Ross S. Kraemer, "Jewish Tuna and

3. "We, Quarried from the Bowels of Christ, Are the True *Genos* of Israel"

Christian Fish: Identifying Religious Affiliation in Epigraphic Sources," *HTR* 84 (1991): 141–162.

17. Boyarin convincingly notes that appeal to belief in the *logos* (which Justin equates with Christ) is not, in fact, unique to Christians. See Boyarin, *Border Lines*, 38. The Pseudo-Clementine *Recognitions*, a text that does not use the term "Christian" and almost never uses the term "Jew," similarly insists that belief in Jesus as the eternal Christ is the only factor that separates the "people" or "nation" (1.43.2). The Syriac version states, "For concerning this alone is there a difference between us who believe in Jesus and those among our people who do not believe"; the Latin, "For only in this regard does there seem to be a difference between us who believe in Jesus and the unbelieving Jews." See F. Stanley Jones, *An Ancient Jewish Christian Source on the History of Christianity: Pseudo-Clementine* Recognitions 1.27–71 (Atlanta: Scholars, 1995), 73. It is worth noting, however, that practices are at issue for both Justin and Pseudo-Clement. While the latter repeatedly condemns sacrifices, Justin especially criticizes circumcision.

18. See *Dial.* 48.1–49.1, where Justin notes that Christians differ in their views of Christ's nature: "there are some of our race (*genos*) who confess that he is the Christ but claim that he is of human origin. I disagree with these, and would not agree even if it were the majority, who share my opinion, were to" (48.4). The Pseudo-Clementine *Recognitions* attributes to Peter the idea that the Christ is a human whom God appointed as "the chief over humans" (1.45.2).

19. Peter Richardson, Jeffrey Siker, and Judith Lieu are important exceptions to this blind spot. Each note briefly that Justin defines Christians as a race or people in this text. See Peter Richardson, *Israel in the Apostolic Church* (Cambridge: Cambridge University Press, 1969), 11; Jeffrey S. Siker, *Disinheriting the Jews: Abraham in Early Christian Controversy* (Louisville, KY: Westminster/John Knox, 1991), 174–74; and Lieu, *Image and Reality*, 136.

20. Although he never cites Paul, Justin seems to build upon Paul's arguments from Romans 9:6–8: "For not all who are descended from Israel belong to Israel, and not all are children of Abraham because they are his descendants; but 'through Isaac shall your descendants be named' [Gen. 21:12]. This means that it is not the children of the flesh who are the children of God, but the children of the promise are reckoned as his descendants." But, unlike Paul, Justin formulates Christians as a distinct *genos*, even while also identifying Christians as the true Israel. See Caroline Johnson Hodge, " 'If Children, Then Heirs' (Rom. 8:17 and Gal. 4:7): A Study of Kinship and Ethnicity in Romans and Galatians" (Ph.D. Diss., Brown University, 2002), 112–117; 178–222.

21. *Dial.* 119.3–5.

22. *Dial.* 123.8.

23. *Dial.* 44.1, 119.3–5.

24. *Dial.* 64.2–3, 116.3, 120.2, 139.5.

25. *Dial.* 11.5; see also 123.8, 125.5, 135.3.

26. *Dial.* 116.3.

27. *Dial.* 119.3; see also 123.1, 124.1, 134.4.

28. *Dial.* 123.6, 130.3, 135.5–6.

29. *Dial.* 119.3–5.

30. *Dial.* 138.2.

31. For example, see *Dial.* 123.4–8, 135.4–6.

32. Tessa Rajak, "Talking at Trypho: Christian Apologetic as Anti-Judaism in Justin's *Dialogue with Trypho the Jew*," in *Apologetics in the Roman Empire*, ed. Mark Edwards, Martin Goodman, and Simon Price, in association with Christopher Rowland (New York and Oxford: Oxford University Press, 1999), 73.

33. As Peter Richardson and Judith Lieu note, Justin is the earliest extant Christian writer to call Christians "Israel" (Richardson, *Israel in the Apostolic Church*, ix; and Lieu, *Image and Reality*, 136). That is, unlike Paul, Justin uses the term "Christian" as a category distinct from *Ioudaios*.

34. Disobedience is quite a different criterion for defining a people than "seed," 'blood," or lineage. Disobedience (and its converse obedience) is far more likely to serve as a marker of the fluidity of membership in a people than as a marker of fixity, unless defined as an invariable trait of a group. Justin repeatedly cites prophetic admonitions that God can revoke Israel's chosenness for disobedience as proof that Christians are now God's chosen (or the true Israel).

35. In other words, this competition extends to intra-Christian competition as well.

36. James Kugel writes that ancient exegetes of this last verse long interpreted this non-people to be the Samaritans (e.g., Sir. 50:25–26). Paul anticipates Justin in identifying the non-people with gentiles (Rom. 10:19; see also 11:11). See James L. Kugel, *Traditions of the Bible: A Guide to the Bible As It Was at the Start of the Common Era* (Cambridge: Harvard University Press, 1998), 423–424, 884. Clement of Alexandria offers a similar interpretation, explicitly drawing upon Paul's interpretation, to identify the non-people as gentiles (*Strom.* 2.43.1–4).

37. Justin's citation of Isaiah 62:12 takes it out of context. In Isaiah, the "holy people" are the reestablished Zion, Jerusalem (see Is. 62:12).

38. Recalling Justin, Clement of Alexandria also links faithfulness to a specific genealogical and ethnoracial identity: "If 'Abraham's faith was counted to him as righteousness,' and we are, through what we have heard, the seed of Abraham, then we too must have faith. We are Israelites, not through physical marks, but because we have been open to persuasion through what we have heard" (*Strom.* 2.28.4).

39. The title of this section alludes to Daniel Boyarin's article on Justin, which in turn references Wayne Meeks's critique of the *Birkhat ha-minim* as a red herring in Johannine scholarship in addressing questions of the relationship between the Jesus followers and other Jews (see Boyarin, "Justin Martyr Invents Judaism," 430).

40. See also *Dial.* 125.5 and 140.2. *Dial.* 25.1 does not use the phrase "according to the flesh" but refers to those who use appeals to be the children (*tekna*) of Abraham in order to "receive even a small part of the divine inheritance with us."

41. Nonetheless, we should not equate a "neutral" statement with a literal or factual statement. What counts as descent or kinship "according to the flesh" is always context-specific and subject to revision or challenge. For example, such descent may be reckoned through the mother, the father, or both; or descent may require social institutions and practices (such as legal marriage or sacrifice) in

order to be recognized at all. Furthermore, it may be possible to acquire such descent through adoption or other social rituals.

42. This argument echoes Paul's views, despite Justin's lack of explicit dependence upon Paul. For an analysis of Paul's views, see Hodge, "If Sons, Then Heirs."

43. Justin's contrast is not identical with that found in Pauline and some early Christian writings, where descent *kata sarka* is paired with descent *kata pneumatikon*. The primary difference is that Justin does not emphasize "spirit" as his key for interpreting scripture or defining truth. Nonetheless, what these pairings share in common is an unequal binary pairing and a link between type of descent and authenticity of biblical interpretation.

44. "Circumcision of the flesh is the only mark by which you can be clearly distinguished from other humans" (*Dial.* 16.3; see also 92.3). As Justin points out (23.5), circumcision is a gender-specific practice, so obviously the only Jews who could be identified by circumcision would be male Jews.

45. For example, see *Dial.* 11.5 and 23.4.

46. *Dial.* 23.5.

47. For an excellent discussion of rabbinic self-definition articulating this point, see Joshua Levinson, "Bodies and Bo(a)rders: Emerging Fictions of Identity in Late Antiquity," *HTR* 93 (2000), esp. 344–348.

48. See chapter 5 for further discussion of universalizing arguments such as these.

49. Appealing to a passage in Jeremiah about God's plans to "make a new covenant with Israel" (Jer. 31:31–34) as evidence that Christ embodies this new covenant and that Christ's followers embody Israel, Justin writes: "If, therefore, God predicted that he would make a new covenant, and this for a light to the gentiles (*ethnē*), and we see and are convinced that, through the name of the crucified Jesus Christ, people have turned to God, leaving idolatry and other sinful practices behind them and have kept the faith (*homologia*) and practiced piety (*eusebeia*) even to death, then everyone can clearly see from these deeds (*erga*) and the accompanying powerful miracles that he [Christ] is indeed the new law, the new covenant, and the expectation of those who, from every people (*ethnē*), have awaited the blessings of God. We have been led to God through this crucified Christ, and we are the true spiritual Israel, and the descendants of Judah, Jacob, Isaac, and Abraham, who, though uncircumcised, was approved and blessed by God because of his faith and was called the father of many peoples (*ethnē*)" (*Dial.* 11.4–5).

50. We find Justin using this logic in relation to circumcision as well: "You who have the circumcision of the flesh are in great need of our circumcision" (*Dial.* 19.3).

51. This is the view Justin later attributes to Jews (*Dial.* 123.1). Someone might have understood circumcision to have the effect of making Justin (or any previously uncircumcised male) a descendant of Abraham *kata sarka*, but this is not the sole criteria for salvation.

52. Earlier in the *Dialogue*, he states that Christians "are instructed to forget the ancient customs (*ethoi*) of our ancestors" (63.5). See also his extended interpretation of Jacob's marriages, where Leah is interpreted as "your people" and Rachel as "our Church" (134.3): "Jacob served Laban for his spotted and speckled sheep. Christ served his service even as far as the cross, *for men of various colors and ap-*

*pearances out of every nation*, purchasing them by blood and the mystery of the cross. Leah's eyes were weak, and in truth, very weak are the eyes of your souls. *Rachel stole the gods of Laban, and hid them until this present day, and similarly for us, have our ancestral and material gods perished"* (134.5, my emphasis).

53. It is unnecessary to posit a distinct social group like "god-fearers" in order to support this reading, although such a group is compatible with this idea.

54. *Dial.* 47.2–3, 48.4, 80.2.

55. *Dial.* 35.2–8, 80.3, 4, 82.1–4. He also speaks of Jews "in name only" (80.4).

56. Trypho says that he knows "that there are many who profess faith in Jesus and are considered to be Christians, yet they claim there is no harm in eating meats sacrificed to idols" (*Dial.* 35.1). Justin's reply primarily concerns false teachers and false doctrine rather than this specific issue.

57. *Dial.* 48.1. After Justin acknowledges that some of his *genos* think Jesus is the Christ but merely human (48.4), Trypho follows up by stating that he finds this view more reasonable than Justin's.

58. *Dial.* 80.1.

59. On illegitimate Christians, see *Dial.* 35.2–6, 80.3–4. See also Boyarin, "Justin Martyr Invents Judaism," 453–456.

60. See *Dial.* 11.5, 135.3.

61. See *Dial.* 119.3–5, 138.2–3.

62. *Dial.* 134.6; see also 119.4.

63. For example, " 'His name is forever; above the sun shall it spring up; and all the peoples (*ethnē*) shall be blessed in him' (Psalms 72:17). But if all the *ethnē* are blessed in the Christ, and we out of all the *ethnē* believe in this man, then he is the Christ and *we they that have been blessed by him*. The sun indeed God had given formerly for worship . . . yet one cannot find any who ever endured death because of belief in the sun. *But one can find people of every race (pantos genos anthrōpōn) who, because of the name of Jesus, have endured, and do endure, sufferings of all kinds for not denying him*. . . . Now in his first coming, which was without honor and form, and was despised, he yet showed so much brilliancy and might that in no single people (*genos*) is he unknown: so that *some among every one have repented of the old evil manner of life belonging to each race (genos)."* (*Dial.* 121.1–2, 3, my emphasis).

64. For example, *Dial.* 124.4.

65. Garth Fowden, *Empire to Commonwealth: Consequences of Monotheism in Late Antiquity* (Princeton: Princeton University Press, 1993), 70.

# 4. "A *Genos* Saved by Nature"

1. Ann Laura Stoler, "Racial Histories and their Regimes of Truth," *Political Power and Social Theory* 11 (1997): 198. For a more extended discussion, see introduction and chapter 1.

2. The concepts "gnosticism" and "gnostic" continue to receive scrutiny and criticism. The relationship of the texts classified as "gnostic" to Christianness is

problematic, in part because "gnostic" functions as shorthand for "difference" from "standard" Christianness, even when it is recognized that no such "standard" existed in the time when these texts were composed. Furthermore, even among those who use the term heuristically, there is debate over which texts ought to be comprehended by the term. Bentley Layton favors keeping the term in play and classifying texts according to their use of Greek cognates related to gnosis. See for example, Bentley Layton, "Prolegomena to the Study of Gnosticism," in *The Social World of Early Christians: Essays in Honor of Wayne Meeks* (Minneapolis: Fortress, 1995), 338–344. Michael Williams argues for getting rid of "gnostic" and "gnosticism" as terms of classification at all. See Michael Williams, *Rethinking "Gnosticism": An Argument for Dismantling a Dubious Category* (Princeton: Princeton University Press, 1996). Karen L. King, while insisting on the modernity of these terms, offers a more nuanced analysis of the challenges and implications of the terms of scholarly classification. See Karen King, *What Is Gnosticism?* (Cambridge: Harvard University Press, 2003), esp. 149–190.

3. For example, Gedaliahu Stroumsa writes, "The Gnostics, who were fundamentally different from common humanity and who did not share its fate throughout history, considered themselves to belong to a race or seed that was different, being both immovable (ATKIM, *asaleutos*) and eternal." Gedaliahu Stroumsa, *Another Seed: Studies in Gnostic Mythology* (Leiden: Brill, 1984), 100.

4. King thoroughly analyzes the discourse of "gnosticism" in relation to "heresy" in King, *What is Gnosticism?* (see esp. chapter 2).

5. For example, Henry Alan Green cites Irenaeus to support an interpretation of gnosticism as a "stratified system that closely resembles a caste system. This system of stratification is a hierarchical ordering of salvation with inferior and superior grades that are eternally sustained. This hierarchical ordering is seen as being ontologically determined and anthropologically present in this world. Caste membership is by ascription only." Henry Allen Green, "Suggested Sociological Themes in the Study of Gnosticism," *Vigiliae Christianae* 31 (1977): 177.

6. James E. Davison, while suggesting that Clement in some ways resembles Valentinian Christians (who are sometimes categorized as "gnostic"), nonetheless seems to accept this characterization of Valentinian anthropology: "the Valentinians distinguished between three kinds of people—material (hylic), animal (psychic), and spiritual (pneumatic). The differences among them are absolute." James Davison, "Structural Similarities and Dissimilarities in the Thought of Clement of Alexandria and the Valentinians," *Second Century* 3 (1983), 206. This interpretation of the threefold classification leads Davison to conclude that one of the three major ways in which Clement differed from the Valentinians was that Clement had a universal vision for salvation, thinking that "all can be saved" while the Valentinians had an elitist vision: "As God has limited his relationship to the unwilled universe to the placing of pneumatic seed within it, his activity in the world is also confined within a very narrow range. Divine activity is exhausted in redeeming the 'elect' " (215–216). Davison does not consider the possibility that "Valentinian" is itself a problematic category.

7. King, *What Is Gnosticism?* King also critiques the view that "gnostics are saved by nature" (see 191–200).

8. Luise Schottroff, "*Animae naturaliter salvandae*: Zum Problem der himmlischen Herkunft des Gnostikers," in *Christentum und Gnosis*, ed. Walter Eltester (Berlin: Töpelmann, 1969), 65–97.

9. For example, see Elaine Pagels's insightful study of Irenaeus's tendentious anti-Valentinian rhetoric. Elaine Pagels, "Conflicting Versions of Valentinian Eschatology: Irenaeus's Treatise vs. The Excerpts from Theodotus," *HTR* 67 (1974): 35–53. Pagels draws attention to how Irenaeus repeatedly portrays the Valentinians' idea of pneumatic seed in a divisive and deterministic manner, masking the unifying function of the seed and the transformative potential attributed to psychics elsewhere in Irenaeus's writings as well as in the *Excerpts of Theodotus*.

10. *The Apocryphon of John* (all four extant MS traditions), *The Sophia of Jesus Christ, Gospel of the Egyptians, The Three Steles of Seth*, and *Zostrianos*. See Michael Williams, *The Immovable Race: A Gnostic Designation and the Theme of Stability in Late Antiquity* (Leiden: Brill, 1985), 1–4.

11. Williams, *Immovable Race*, 158–185. See also David Brakke, "The Seed of Seth at the Flood; Biblical Interpretation and Gnostic Theological Reflection" in *Reading in Christian Communities: Essays on Interpretation in the Early Church*, ed. Charles A. Bobertz and David Brakke (Notre Dame: University of Notre Dame Press, 2002), 41–62.

12. "The Tripartite Tractate," ed., trans., and critical notes by Harold W. Attridge and Elaine H. Pagels, in *The Coptic Gnostic Library: A Complete Edition of the Nag Hammadi Codices, Vol. 1* (1985; repr., Leiden: Brill, 2000) XII:184–190. See also the discussion in chapter 2 above.

13. The scare quotes here mean that I do not think these categories transparently correspond to any social group or set of texts. The relationship between "Valentinian" and "gnostic" is a matter of dispute. Valentinus was a well-known early Christian teacher whose students and successors are referred to in ancient texts as either the followers of Valentinus or the school of Valentinus. But ancient sources also indicate that, as was the case with Clement and Origen who were also teachers, Valentinus carved out his authority as a teacher in the context of imagining a larger Christian community in which not all members were his students. The desire to distinguish Valentinians from gnostics may function to rehabilitate Valentinians within the spectrum of early Christian diversity, but it leaves intact the construct of "gnostic" and still positions Valentinians as an "offshoot" of this category. Bentley Layton, for example, offers a view very similar to that of the second-century heresiologist Irenaeus. Both view Valentinus as having developed a system out of "gnostic" materials. Layton writes: "the structure of the Gnostic type of myth also has striking parallels in Valentinian mythography, just as Irenaeus (*Adv. Haer.* 1.11.1) states that the Valentinian *hairesis* derived historically from the Gnostic *hairesis*. But many aspects of Valentinian mythography are also significantly different from Schenke's Gnostic type of myth, so that Valentinus and his followers can best be kept apart as a distinct

mutation, or reformed offshoot, of the original Gnostics." In Layton, "Prolegomena to the Study of Ancient Gnosticism," 343. It is important to note, however, that Irenaeus explicitly seeks to discredit the Christianity articulated by Valentinus and his followers, and to offer his own as the authoritative one. A central way that Irenaeus can discredit Valentinians is to claim that they are the "descendants" of "heretics" and thus heretics themselves, not the authentic Christians they understand themselves to be. Irenaeus ends the first book of his five-volume treatise (*Against all Heresies*), which has Valentinians as its special target (see 1.1.2), by making this argument explicit: "It was necessary to prove that, as their very opinions and regulations show, those who are of the school of Valentinus derive their origin from such mothers, fathers, and ancestors [i.e., Gnostics]" (1.31.3). Irenaeus clearly communicates that he represents those who derive their origin from better ancestors—who can trace their authority to God—by stating that his humble aim is to "convert" Valentinians back to the truth. He says that he writes "with the hope that perchance some of them, exercising repentance and returning to the only creator, and for the shaper of the universe, may obtain salvation and that others may not henceforth be drawn away by their wicked, although plausible, persuasions . . . " (1.31.3). For further discussion of the implications and problems of classifying Valentinus and Valentinians, see King, *What Is Gnosticism?*, 154–156, 162–164.

14. The very mention of insiders and outsiders raises the question of social groups and their relation to the surviving texts. See the conclusion of this chapter for further discussion.

15. Although Clement is traditionally associated with an "official" school of the main Alexandrian church, there is no basis for either a single "main" Alexandrian church or an "official" school in his day.

16. Indeed, as David Brakke has noted, the model of study circles—of Christian teachers with their students—seems to have been the most ancient form of Christian organization in Alexandria. See David Brakke, "Canon Formation and Social Conflict in Fourth-Century Egypt: Athanasius of Alexandria's Thirty-Ninth *Festal Letter*," *HTR* 87 (1994): 399–405.

17. The quotation in this section's heading is from *Strom.* 2.115.2.

18. I have only selected a few of the many possible examples to illustrate my points. Another fruitful context for study would be Clement's critique of so-called Valentinian ideas in the larger context of discussing martyrdom and death (see *Strom.* 4.89.1–94.4).

19. Not only was the practice of adoption widespread in antiquity, but the idea of being adopted as a son of God is used by Philo and Paul to speak about the consequences of righteous action. Philo states that only the wise person like Abraham can become God's friend: "For wisdom is God's friend rather than his slave. And thus he says plainly of Abraham, 'shall I hide anything from my friend Abraham?' (Gen. 18:17). The one who has this portion has passed beyond the bounds of human happiness. This one alone is well-born, for he has registered God as his father and become by adoption his only son . . . " (Philo, *On Sobriety*

55–56). See also Rom. 8:23 and 9:4; Gal. 4:5; and Eph. 1:5. Irenaeus also plays with fixed and fluid meanings of sonship: " 'Son' . . . has a twofold meaning: one in the order of nature, because he was born a son; the other, in that he was made so . . . whether with respect to his creation or by the teaching of his doctrine. For when any person has been taught from the mouth of another, he is termed the son of him who instructs him, and the latter [is called] his father. According to nature . . . we are all sons of God, because we have all been created by God. But with respect to obedience and doctrine we are not all the sons of God; those only are so who believe in him and do his will. And those who do not believe, and do not obey his will, are sons and angels of the devil, because they do the works of the devil. . . . For as, among humans, those sons who disobey their father, being disinherited, are still sons in the course of nature, but by law are disinherited . . . so in the same way is it with God—those who do not obey him are disinherited by him and have ceased to be his sons" (*Adv. Haer.* 4.41.2–3). This passage comes after Irenaeus's strong objection to the notion that humans have different natures and that some are by nature good or bad. He emphasizes that all humans have free will, and the equal capacity to be good or bad. Unlike Clement, Irenaeus insists that all humans are God's children "by nature." Although this assertion qualifies him for status as a "founder of a heresy" according to Clement's argument, Irenaeus makes clear that being God's son "by nature" is not sufficient to ensure salvation. One must also become a son by action—a view shared by Clement. This is a sleight of hand argument because it implies that his rivals offer more limited and fixed interpretations of salvation—either appealing to a natural relation to God for only a few or by appealing to intrinsically good or bad natures (thereby denying free will or the relevance of action). Nonetheless, Irenaeus is able to preserve his own idea of fixity—all are "by nature" sons of God—while insisting that the kinship that really matters for the purposes of salvation must be acquired (is fluid). He implicitly denies that his rivals could hold an equally subtle understanding of the relation between kinship and salvation. Luther Martin, for example, suggests that adoption is the model for understanding how many become "Sethites," the saved "insiders" of the *Apocalypse of Adam*. See Luther Martin, "Genealogy and Sociology in the *Apocalypse of Adam*," in *Gnosticism and the Early Christian World: In Honor of James M. Robinson*, eds. James E. Goehring, et al. (Sonoma, CA; Polebridge, 1990), 34–35.

20. Clement further notes that Adam is an example of one who did not make a good choice, in contrast to Noah, Abraham, and the younger son of Isaac (Jacob) (*Strom.* 2.98.3–99.3).

21. See note 19 above for how closely this resembles Philo's reference to adoption.

22. See for example, *Strom.* 3.70.1–2, 6.39.4–42.2, 6.106.4–107.1.

23. For a thorough discussion, see Denise Buell, *Making Christians: Clement of Alexandria and the Rhetoric of Legitimacy* (Princeton: Princeton University Press, 1999) esp. 50–68, 117–179.

24. See for example, *Strom.* 3.1.1, 3.29.3, 3.59.3.

25. Physiognomy, the study of the character from behavior, voice, and looks, was well established in antiquity and adapted by Christians in their characterizations of holy people. See Maud Gleason, *Making Men: Sophists and Self-Presentation in Ancient Rome* (Princeton: Princeton University Press, 1995); and Georgia Frank, *The Memory of the Eyes: Pilgrims to Living Saints in Late Antiquity* (Berkeley: University of California Press, 2000), 134–170.

26. This section may also indicate competition over how to interpret Paul, since Origen is alluding to Romans 9:20–21.

27. This translation follows the Greek text. In the Latin, the text differs, reading: "enter into the Church of the Lord, on the day of revelation, they become vessels of honor." Clement of Alexandria also describes the highest level of Christian, the gnostic Christian, as one who has also become an Israelite (*Strom.* 4.169.1). In her notes to the French-Greek critical edition, Annewies van den Hoek notes Philo's likely influence on this imagery. See Clément d'Alexandrie, *Les Stromates: Stromate IV*, introduction, critical text, and notes by Annewies van den Hoek, Claude Mondésert, trans. (Paris: du Cerf, 2001), 338 n. 3.

28. Origen omits the category of "psychics" or soul-endowed, which is usually associated with "Valentinian" anthropology. This omission is also found in the *Valentinian Exposition* (NHC XI, 2), which only includes a twofold division of pneumatic and "fleshly" (*sarkikos*). See Einar Thomassen, "The Valentinianism of the *Valentinian Exposition* (NHC XI, 2)," *Muséon* 102 (1989): 233–235. Elaine Pagels notes that the catchphrase "those who introduce the doctrine of natures" is especially used by Origen when criticizing Valentinians. See Elaine Pagels, "A Valentinian Interpretation of Baptism and Eucharist—And its Critique of 'Orthodox' Sacramental Theology and Practice," *HTR* 65 (1972): 154.

29. Before the 1945 discovery of the Nag Hammadi Library, scholars had to reconstruct ideas attributed to "Valentinian" Christians primarily from citations embedded within the writings of their Christian rivals, including Clement and Origen. For an English translation of this collection, see *The Nag Hammadi Library in English*, revised ed., James Robinson, ed. (San Francisco: Harper and Row, 1977).

30. Wesley Isenberg, "The Gospel According to Philip," in the *Coptic Gnostic Library, Vol. II* (1989; repr. Leiden: Brill, 2000), 131. Thus, it cannot be presumed that Clement or Origen knew these writings. I am not arguing for any causal connections among these texts.

31. *TriTrac* 133.67, 132.4–15, and 132.28–133.14.

32. From Attridge and Pagels's notes to *The Tripartite Tractate*, in *The Coptic Gnostic Library: A Complete Edition of the Nag Hammadi Codices. Vol. 1.* Ed., trans., and critical notes by Harold W. Attridge and Elaine H. Pagels. (1985; repr., Leiden: Brill, 2000): XXIII:446.

33. Ibid.

34. From Einar Thomassen's commentary in *Le Traité Tripartite*. Ed., introduction, and commentary by Einar Thomassen, Louis Painchaud and Einar Thomassen, trans. (Québec: Les Presses de l'Université Laval, 1989), 428–429.

35. It is interesting that the *Gospel of Philip* follows the *Gospel of Thomas* in the Nag Hammadi library. As Isenberg notes, "this resemblance may have suggested the sequence to the copyist of the Coptic manuscript." See Wesley Isenberg, "The Gospel According to Philip," 138.

36. April de Conick, "The True Mysteries: Sacramentalism in the *Gospel of Philip*," *Vigiliae Christianae* 55 (2001): 237 (my emphasis).

37. Of all the texts contained in the surviving Nag Hammadi collection, only the *Gospel of Philip* and the *Testimony of Truth* use the term "Christian" as an insider term. See Martha Lee Turner, *The Gospel According to Philip: The Sources and Coherence of an Early Christian Collection* (Leiden: Brill, 1996), 7, 146.

38. For example, "If you say, 'I am a Jew,' no one will tremble. If you say, 'I am a Roman,' no one will be bothered. If you say, 'I am a Greek—or a barbarian, a slave, free' no one will be disturbed. If you [say], 'I am a Christian,' the [ . . . ] will shake" (*GosPhil* 62.26–32). While this passage uses ethnoracial and status language to differentiate Christians from others, other passages speak about the transformation of the individual as changing one's collective identification: "When we were Hebrews we were orphans, with (only) our mother, but when we became Christians we got father and mother" (52.21–24).

39. Martha Turner writes, "The terms 'Christian,' 'apostle,' 'perfect,' 'Hebrew,' 'Jew,' and gentile' are all restricted to the first three quarters of the *Gospel According to Philip*" (Turner, *Gospel According to Philip*, 146). Turner proposes that the *GosPhil* be viewed in two major chunks. The first three quarters of the text (up to 77.15) is collected from at least three major early Christian traditions (those of "Thomas" Christianity, "classic" gnosticism, and "Valentinian" Christianity), whereas the material from 77.15 to the end is drawn from one source or viewpoint, which she characterizes as a "primitive" Valentinian one, very close to the teachings of the *Gospel of Truth* (see Turner, *Gospel According to Philip*, 184–205). She asserts that "themes, interests, and approaches which characterize the first three-quarters of the document vanish when we cross that divide . . . [and] something like a single voice emerges" (135). Because Turner reads the interests of the collector largely through the last quarter of the document, she deems the absence of most of these collective terms as a sign of their overall insignificance (259): "The issues of group identity to which they point are of interest to at least some of the sources of that material; these are absent from the final quarter of the document." (146).

Turner acknowledges that the term "the perfect" does appear in the final quarter of the text, as a category of identification which readers are exhorted to become. Her distinction between the use of "perfect" in the first three quarters of the text and the final quarter is puzzling and rather forced. She says that in the first three quarters it has an "initiatory" sense, whereas in the final quarter it has a "moral" sense (155). While Turner may well be correct that the final portion of the text comes from a distinct source, the various uses of *teleios* across the text are more consistent than any other term of self-identity.

Turner's suggestion that "modes of existence" are central to the entire gospel is generally persuasive (although she masks her own interpretive contributions by attributing her reading to the "compiler's" intent.) In her view, the compiler chose materials that could address "two interrelated problems—the origin and nature of evil in the world, and the nature of the highest possibilities open to human beings" (261). She further suggests that the "collector" selected this material for positive use (not simply to rebut it): "The collector of the *Gospel According to Philip* . . . seems to have had little or no interest in refuting the material collected: while he or she could hardly have agreed with every opinion expressed, each excerpt seems to have been selected for its positive value" (258). It follows from her hypothesis, then, that any use of identity terms, including ethnoracial ones, must be comprehensible as relevant to addressing these problems. It makes more sense that the author/compiler viewed these collective terms of identification in the first three quarters of the text as consonant with the ideas conveyed in different language later in the Gospel than that these concepts cease to be relevant. If the author has one (or more) underlying concerns or questions that have motivated this selection of diverse materials, and especially if we agree that these concerns pertain at least to modes of existence, then Turner's categorical distinction about the relevance of terms of collective identity for the first three quarters and not for the last quarter is illogical. She mistakes the absence of terms such as "Hebrew" for the absence of the function they serve. The function of these identity categories in the first three quarters of the text are fulfilled in the last quarter by terms such as "the perfect" and pairings such as "bridegroom" and "child of the bridegroom."

40. Turner, *Gospel According to Philip*, 146. In particular, she notes that "apostle" appears with both strongly positive and strongly negative connotations in the Gospel. The *Gospel of Philip* contains two negative uses of the term "apostle," the first of which links it also to "Hebrew": "Her [Mary's] existence is anathema to the Hebrews, meaning the apostles and apostolic persons" (55.28–30); and the second links the apostles with "the fallen nature of Sophia" (152): "The apostles said to the disciples, 'May all of our offerings get salt!' They were referring [to wisdom] as 'salt.' Without it, no offering is acceptable. Now wisdom [is] barren, [without] offspring. For this reason, [she] is called '[ . . . ] . . . of the salt.' Wherever [ . . . ] can [ . . . ] like them, the Holy Spirit [ . . . ], [and] many are her offspring" (*GosPhil* 59.27–60.1). Turner also notes passages that seem to attribute ideas unproblematically to apostles (62.7, 67.24, 73.8) and one very positive one: "it was because of chrism (anointing) that the Christ (the anointed) was named, for the Father anointed the Son; and the Son anointed the apostles, and the apostles anointed us. Whoever has been anointed has everything . . . " (74.15–18) (151–154).

41. There is scholarly consensus that the *Gospel of Philip* draws from a range of different sources but considerable disagreement about how to read it. A number of scholars focus on its constituent units while others seek to interpret it as a unified whole. Proponents of composite structure: Hans-Martin Schenke, Isenberg, A. H. C. van Eijk, and Martha Lee Turner. Proponents of treating the text as a unified whole: J.-E. Ménard, Robert McL. Wilson, Y. Janssens, G. S. Gasparro, S.

Giversen, and Jorunn Jacobsen Buckley. The two main interpretive options—
the "florilegium" (notebook collecting a list of sayings from disparate sources)
versus coherent, systematic (Valentinian) unity—offer a false choice. That the
text shares some features with other ancient writing collections, of which there
is a wide variety, does not contraindicate coherency. That the text's coherency
can be read in divergent ways (from an emphasis on sacraments to links with
Jewish mysticism to Valentinian theology) indicates both the inevitable role of
the interpreter in the process and the interpretive fungibility of the non-
narrative structure. I find convincing the view that the author drew from a range
of earlier Christian traditions and produced a text whose non-narrative composition can sustain many readings.

42.  Jorunn Jacobsen Buckley has developed a complementary analysis of the
Gospel's understanding of language (especially of names). She writes: "Once
[the author] has broken down the habitual scheme of dichotomies, the author is
ready to inform his readers that names are as 'unreal' as conventional categories
of opposition. Names do not capture reality; contrasting concepts have no external—only illusory—referents. Virtually in the same breath, the writer de-
stroys conceptual dualism and the naïve idea of correspondence between names
and referents, whether palpable or purely mental. On closer inspection, however, the author has annulled one kind of dualism, but he introduces another, by
denying the 'correspondence theory' regarding names. So, in the case of names,
there is a true, though deceptive, dualism: an almost jaunty dialectic is at work.
Very neatly, the *Gospel of Philip* has undermined two traditional—but to the text
philosophically immature—modes of understanding. However, the two kinds of
polemics are related, even providing the same message. This is so because the
ideas of 'original nature,' of 'the indissoluble eternal' ones 'exalted above the
world' relate to the teaching about names. Just as the dualistic concepts hide the
'original nature,' so deceptive names do refer, however obliquely, to the immutable reality in the upper world. The *Gospel of Philip* in both cases proposes a
synthetic, but paradoxical, view in which customary dualistic and nominalistic
modes of though are given a jolt." Jorunn Buckley, "Conceptual Models and
Polemical Issues in the Gospel of Philip," *ANRW* II 22.5 (1998): 4174–4175.

43.  The rest of the brief unit is fragmentary, but may imply that the contrast is between beings that make others like themselves and beings that do not: "exist just
as they . . . and make others like themselves, while . . . simply exist" (*GosPhil*
51.33–52.1).

44.  Turner, *The Gospel According to Philip*, 242. As Turner notes, "while pairs of opposites are not infrequent in the material contained in the Gospel according to
Philip, this section is by a very wide margin the densest concatenation of paired
oppositions anywhere in the document" (244). She provides a helpful schemat-
ic chart of these passages (242–244).

45.  This passage also recalls the *Excerpts of Theodotos*. Clement's notes speak not
only of seed as having been sown into psychics and pneumatics, but also distinguishes between seed in gendered terms. Early in the notebook, Clement speaks

about Sophia having produced male and female seed, "elect" and "called" respectively, which are different but ultimately both reunited with the *logos* (*Exc. Theod.* 21.1–3). The difference between them is glossed later in the text in terms of parentage: the "male" seed is produced by Sophia together with her male counterpart, whereas the "female" seed is produced by Sophia alone (i.e., her feminine component: see 39–40). In the last portion of the text, the plan of salvation is described as the savior's descent to gather up and transform those who "were *children of the female only*" (68); slightly later: "so long then, they say, as the seed is yet unformed, it is the *offspring of the female*, but when it was formed, it was changed to a man and becomes a son of the bridegroom" (79). The *Excerpts of Theodotos* does not use a Hebrew/Christian distinction and refers more explicitly to cosmological prehistory, but the similarities between baptismal, bridal chamber, and transformation indicate a similar way of thinking.

46. The passage that Siker uses to support this position showcases how we scholars bring our own lenses to any reading because of the fragmentary nature of the surviving manuscript. This passage contains tantalizing terms and phrases, including: "elect *genos*," "true *genos*," "Christians," "Greeks," and "Jews" (*GosPhil* 75.30–32). For Siker, the presence of the term "Jew" is highly significant. He suggests that it must have a categorically different meaning from "Hebrew" because of the passage that Christians were once Hebrews. Although Siker rightly cautions that this passage is so fragmentary as to be subject to all manner of reconstructions according to the sense that the modern editor finds most reasonable, he follows Welsey Isenberg's reconstruction: "No Jew [was ever born] to Greek parents [as long as the world] has existed. And [as a] Christian [people], we [ourselves do not descend] from the Jews." Jeffrey Siker, "Gnostic Views on Jews and Christians in the Gospel of Philip," *Novum Testamentum* 31 (1989): 278. Siker supports his preference as follows: "elsewhere in the Gospel of Philip the affirmation is not that Gnostic-Christians were 'Jews,' but that they were once 'Hebrews,' which appears to have a *religious* significance, unlike 'Jews,' which refers to a *race or class*" (278 n. 5, my emphasis). Siker and Isenberg seem to read the distinction between "Jews" and "Christians" in this text as immutable, which is only supportable through the textual emendation and insertion in the fragmentary passage and based on a modern notion that race is immutable. Furthermore, these scholars correlate these terms with historical social groups, which seems far from secure.

47. Siker, "Gnostic Views," 277.

48. Martha Turner also entertains the possibility that Hebrew designates "another kind of Christian" in the other three passages in which the term appears (Turner, *The Gospel According to Philip*, 151).

49. For passages referring to the perfect, see *GosPhil* 76.23–36 and 80.1–22; for child of the bridal chamber, see *GosPhil* 86.4–18.

50. *GosPhil* 78.25–79.13.

51. *GosPhil* 83.8–25; or being weeded: 85.29–31 (cf. Matt. 15:13).

52. *GosPhil* 83.25–84.13; 85.24–29.

53. While this passage classifies all humans as members of one *genos*, other passages differentiate among kinds of humans.

54. Buckley, "Conceptual Models and Polemical Issues," 4170.

55. "Christian" appears seven times in the *Gospel of Philip*. Turner parses its appearances as follows: four times as positive term of self-designation (52.21–24, 62.26–34, 74.13–14, 75.25–76.2) (Turner, *The Gospel According to Philip*, 147–148); twice in ways "which question other people's claim to this term" and have to do with baptism (148–49); and once in such a degraded portion of the manuscript that it is too "lacunose" to interpret (74.24–75.1) (150). Of the two examples she cites pertaining to baptism, I think the polemic is only clear in the first (64.22–29), and even here, the polemic clearly positions "Christian" as a term claimed by the *Gospel of Philip* for insiders. In the second instance, the passage's reference to "no longer a Christian but a Christ" (67.19–27) does not need to be read as rejecting a positive sense of the term "Christian," as I have noted. Finally, I agree with Turner that the tantalizing passage in which Christian appears in the same unit as *Ioudaioi* and the phrase "the true *genos*" is too incomplete to interpret definitively.

56. See also *GosPhil* 61.34–35.

57. The fragmentary end of this unit seems to contrast things that "make others" (perhaps meaning others like themselves) with things that "simply exist." It is too fragmentary, however, to make draw any definitive analysis.

58. See also "A horse sires (*jpō*) a horse, a man begets a man, a god brings forth a god" (*GosPhil* 75.25–27). This passage reinforces an understanding of "Hebrews" as an "insider" of a lower rank, recalling the opening passage in which a Hebrew is said to be able to replicate (that is, to be able to make another Hebrew).

59. We also do not know the contexts from which Clement draws his citations.

60. Elaine Pagels makes this point with respect to Irenaeus. She notes that Irenaeus distinguishes between two types of humans—those who will be saved and those who will not (Pagels, "Conflicting Versions," 51). Although he stresses that the Valentinians divide humans into three kinds, she convincingly argues that Irenaeus misconstrues the fluidity between the Valentinian "psychic" and "pneumatic" (44–53).

61. For a discussion of Valentinian polemic against non-Valentinians, see Elaine Pagels, "A Valentinian Interpretation of Baptism and Eucharist," 153–169.

# 5. "From Every Race of Humans"

1. For analysis of this verse and Paul's use of ethnic reasoning, see Denise K. Buell and Caroline Johnson Hodge, "The Politics of Interpretation: The Rhetoric of Race and Ethnicity in Paul," *JBL* 123 (2004): 235–252.

2. The critical edition consulted for the sixth book of Clement's *Strōmateis* is Clément d'Alexandrie, *Les Stromates: Stromate VI*, introduction, critical ed., trans., and notes by Patrick Descourtieux (Paris: Éditions du Cerf, 1999). I read this passage to make different points in Denise K. Buell, "Rethinking the Relevance

of Race for Early Christian Self-Definition," *HTR* 94 (2001): 461–462. This interpretation is adapted from Denise Buell, "Race and Universalism in Early Christianity," *JECS* 10:4 (2002): 429–431.

3. See Buell, "Rethinking the Relevance of Race," 462.

4. Throughout his corpus, Clement of Alexandria portrays Christians as a *periousios laos* ("special" or "abundant people;" Ex. 19:5) who have been formed out of those from "either" or "both" race(s) by which he means "Jews" or "Greeks" (or "gentiles") or "barbarians" and "Greeks" (where Jews are including under the category of barbarian). See for example, *Strom.* 3.70.1–2, 6.13.106.4, 6.17.159.8–9, and *Prot.* 12.120.2. Clement asserts quite programmatically, "Of humans, all are either Greek or barbarian," a point which he uses to claim the universality of the Christian God (*Strom.* 5.133.8).

5. For a more extended discussion of aggregative ethnic reasoning, see Buell, "Race and Universalism," 441–445.

6. See *Acta Andreae*, edited with French translation by Jean-Marc Prieur (Brepols: Turnhout, 1989). The Greek manuscript known as Vatican, gr. 808 (BHG 95) contains the relevant ethnoracial terms discussed in this section. I have followed Prieur's numbering of sections; the latter number corresponds to the Vat. 808 ms. This narrative does not use the term "Christian" for insiders.

7. The text contains another perspective, represented by Stratocles, one of Andrew's followers. Stratocles seems to understand himself not to have been reminded of his own saved nature so much as to have received vital "seeds" from Andrew necessary for salvation: "*when you were the sower I received the seeds of the words of salvation. And for these to sprout and grow up there is need of no other than yourself*, most blessed Andrew. And what else have I to say to you than this, servant of God? I need the great mercy and help that comes from you, *to be able to be worthy of the seed I have from you*, which will only grow permanently and emerge into the light if you wish it and pray for it and for my whole self" (*AA* 44.9–16 [12], my emphasis). Andrew's words of salvation are described as "seeds" that he implants in the souls of his hearers. For more on this agricultural trope, see Denise K. Buell, *Making Christians: Clement of Alexandria and the Rhetoric of Legitimacy* (Princeton: Princeton University Press, 1999), 31–78. Despite Andrew's claim that he reminds, not teaches, this passage portrays his words as capable of producing a new life, not merely as a catalyst for an already incipient one. Here, conversion is likened to the slow process of cultivation, not just a sudden awakening or realization of one's true nature.

8. See for example, Andrew's closing speech: "Siblings, I was sent as an apostle by the Lord into these parts, of which my Lord thought me worthy, not indeed to teach anyone, but to remind everyone who is akin (*sungenēs*) to these words that they live in transient evils while they enjoy their harmful delusions. From which things I always exhorted you to keep clear and to press toward the things that are permanent and to take flight from all that is transient. For you see that not one of you stands firm, but everything, including human ways, is changeable. And this is the case because the soul is untrained and has gone astray in nature (*ph-*

*ysis*) and retains pledges corresponding to its error. I therefore hold blessed (*makarios*) those who obey the words preached to them and who through them see, as in a mirror, the mysteries of their own nature, for the sake of which all things were built." (*AA* 47 [15]).

9. Andrew further exhorts Maximilla to "keep yourself, from now on, chaste and pure, holy, undefiled, sincere, free from adultery, unwilling for relationship with him who is a stranger to us, unbent, unbroken, tearless, unhurt, immovable in storms, undivided, free from offense, and without sympathy for the works of Cain. For if you do not give yourself over, Maximilla, to the things that are the opposites of these, I shall rest, being thus compelled to give up this life for your sake, that is for my own sake. But if I, who am perhaps even able to help others akin to me (*sungeneis*) through you, am driven away from here and if you are persuaded by your relationship with Aegeates and by the flatteries of his father, the serpent, to return to your earlier ways, know that I shall be punished on your account until you would understand that I spurned life for the sake of a soul that was unworthy" (*AA* 40.5–17 [8]). This passage associates insiders and outsiders not only with kinship language (kin versus strangers) but reinforces the danger of the outsiders by linking them with the biblical troublemakers of Cain (an insider gone bad) and the serpent (who seeks to make insiders into outsiders). In response to this rather strong-armed appeal to an ethics of mutual accountability, Maximilla departs. The narrative describes her resolve to follow Andrew's advice in a striking manner which echoes Stratocles' view that Andrew has sown transformative seeds in him: "For when she had heard what he had answered her and had been in some way impressed by it and had become what the words signified (*genomenē touto hoper hoi logoi edeiknuon*), she went out, neither rashly nor without set purpose, and went to the praetorium" (46.2–5 [14]). For an analysis of the performative effects of language in this passage, see Laura Nasrallah, " 'She Became What the Words Signified': The Greek Acts of Andrew's Construction of the Reader-Disciple," in *The Apocryphal Acts of the Apostles*, ed. François Bovon (Cambridge: Harvard University Press, 1999), 233–258.

10. Michael A. Williams, *The Immovable Race: A Gnostic Designation and the Theme of Stability in Late Antiquity* (Leiden: Brill, 1985): 181–182.

11. Keith Hopkins, "Christian Number and Its Implications," *JECS* 6 (1998): 207.

12. The struggle over the concept of resurrection has been vividly shown by Elaine Pagels, *Gnostic Gospels* (1979; repr., New York: Vintage, 1981), 3–32.

13. My interpretation of *Hermas* is adapted from Buell, "Race and Universalism," 453–461, 466. For a broad-ranging examination of color symbolism in early Christian texts see Gay L. Byron, *Symbolic Blackness and Ethnic Difference in Early Christian Literature* (New York: Routledge, 2002).

14. Carolyn Osiek, *Shepherd of Hermas: A Commentary.* Ed. Helmut Koester. (Minneapolis: Fortress, 1999), 1.

15. Byron notes that *Hermas* uses color symbolism to define vices and virtues; blackness epitomizes vice while whiteness signifies virtue. This symbolism becomes even more vivid later in this unit, where two groups of women are distinguished

by their white and black clothing (*Herm. Sim.* 9.15.1–3) and the first and twelfth mountains are correlated with bad and perfect believers (9.19.1). See Byron, *Symbolic Blackness*, 67–69.

16. The *Gospel of Philip* also uses this metaphor of color transformation. Although the terms of the analogy differ, this example also features the transformation of various colors into white: "The Lord went into the dye works of Levi. He took seventy-two different colors and threw them into the vat. He took them all out white. And he said, 'Even so has the son of man come [as] a dyer' " (*GosPhil* 63.25–30).

17. In Hermas's vision, the "Lord of the tower" arrives to do this testing: "He felt each stone and he held a staff in his hand and hit each individual stone used in the building. And as he struck, some of them became as black as pitch, and some rotten, and some with cracks, and some short, and some neither white nor black, and some rough and not fitting in with the other stones and some with many stains" (*Herm. Sim.* 9.6.3–4).

18. The replacement stones are subsequently explained as the "roots" of the twelfth mountain. See below for further discussion. It is also important to note that not all of the stones that fail the test are permanently excluded from the tower. The text gives two levels of explanation for this: in the vision, the rejected stones are cleaned (*Herm. Sim.* 9.7.2, 6) and those that are successfully cleaned are put back into the tower; in the subsequent interpretation of the vision, the rejected stones are explained as Christians who have succumbed to various sins (9.13.6–9) and are able to rejoin the tower if they repent (9.14.1–2).

19. See also Byron, *Symbolic Blackness*, 66–67, 69.

20. The rejected stones, although they "all bore the name of the Son of God, and they also received the power of the virgins . . . were made disobedient by the women whom you saw clothed in black clothing. . . . When they saw them they desired them, and put on their power, and put off the clothing and power of the virgins" (*Herm. Sim.* 9.13.7, 8).

21. The spectrum of varieties of believers and unbelievers is consistent with the classifications of people given throughout the rest of the text. As Osiek notes, the mountains correlate with "the following kinds of people: 1. Apostates, blasphemers, and betrayers (*Herm. Sim.* 19.1); 2. Hypocrites and false teachers (19.2); 3. Wealthy and those choked with business concerns (20); 4. Doubleminded (21); 5. Slow learners and arrogant (22); 6. Quarrelers (23); 7. Simple, without guile (24); 8. Apostles and teachers (25); 9. Bad pastors and deniers (26); 10. Bishops and givers of hospitality (27); 11. Those who suffer for the name (28); 12. Innocent ones (29)" (Osiek, *Shepherd of Hermas*, 244).

22. See *Herm. Sim.* 9. 19–29 and *Herm. Vis.* 4.3.2–5. See also Byron, *Symbolic Blackness*, 66–67, and David Brakke, "Ethiopian Demons: Male Sexuality, the Black-Skinned Other, and the Monastic Self," *Journal of the History of Sexuality* 10 (2001): 501–535.

23. Unlike Origen and Clement, the *Shepherd of Hermas* gives no attention to the religious customs of the mountain/races when they are interpreted as the pre-Christian sources for the Christian race. Nevertheless, because the description of

the nation mountains explains ethnic variation among non-Christians in terms of "differences of mind and way of thinking" (*Herm. Sim.* 9.17.2), this text produces an unsteady connection between the nations from which Christians come and the quality of their beliefs.

24. A vivid example of this logic appears in the nineteenth-century British scholar J. B. Lightfoot's study of Paul's Letter to the Galatians, reprinted multiple times in the second half of the nineteenth century. In this work, Lightfoot uses the ethnoracial background of the Galatians (read as Celtic/Gallic) to explain the tone of Paul's letter and the Galatians' "backsliding" from Paul's Gospel. Lightfoot uses the notion that religious attitudes form part of one's ethnoracial character that is transmitted from one generation to the next to describe the Galatians as racially unsuited to preserve Paul's Gospel. He also projects this "innate racial failing" forward into Christian history: "The fragmentary notices of its subsequent career reflect some light on the temper and disposition of the Galatian Church in St. Paul's day. To Catholic writers of a later day indeed the failings of its infancy seemed to be so faithfully reproduced in its mature age, that they invested the Apostle's rebuke with a prophetic import. Asia Minor was the nursery of heresy, and of all the Asiatic Churches it was nowhere so rife as in Galatia. The Galatian capital was the stronghold of the Montanist revival, which lingered on for more than two centuries, splitting into diverse sects, each distinguished by some fantastic gesture or minute ritual observance. Here too were to be found Ophites, Manichaeans, sectarians of all kinds." See J. B. Lightfoot, *Saint Paul's Epistle to the Galatians. A Revised Text with Introduction, Notes, and Dissertations*; 7th ed. (London: Macmillan, 1881), 32–33.

25. Because modern readers are especially attuned to the construction of Christian universal claims over and against an understanding of Jewishness as particular, it is worth noting the invisibility of Judaism in *Hermas* as well as the absence of the term "Christian" for insiders. While the text is clearly indebted to biblical imagery (twelve mountains as twelve *phylai*, and perhaps also the sense of a special lineage of Christians exemplified by the blessed *genos* of the roots of the white mountain), it appropriates this imagery without explicit reference to Jews or Israel. The clearest connection appears in the interpretation of the foundation stones for the tower, from the "certain deep place," which include the first and second generation of "righteous men" and the "prophets of God"; these biblical figures are not, however, explicitly tied to Israel.

26. This imagery may be an adaptation of the notion of a priestly lineage within Israel (see for example, Lev. 21:7; Josephus, *Against Apion* 1.30–36). Thanks to Caroline Johnson Hodge for this observation.

27. As we have seen above, Justin also makes an argument for Christians before Christ, using the concept of a lineage produced by the *logos spermatikos* (2 *Apol.* 8.1–3; 13.2–6).

28. Clement of Alexandria, for example, uses the image of a symphony to depict diversity within an overarching unity in the *logos* (*Prot.* 9.88.2–3). See Buell, "Race and Universalism," 448.

29. Although possible, such a context need not be limited to the second-century Roman setting that Osiek suggests: "Depending on the date of the final edition of the text, it is possible that Valentinus, Cerdo, Marcion, and Marcellina had all arrived in Rome and were teaching there, as was Justin. References to false, evil, and would-be teachers, and differences with regard to the morality of the flesh indicate theological tensions in the church" (Osiek, *Shepherd of Hermas*, 22).

30. Regina Schwartz, *The Curse of Cain: The Violent Legacy of Monotheism* (Chicago: University of Chicago Press, 1997), 88.

31. Etienne Balibar, "Racism and Nationalism," in *Race, Nation, Class: Ambiguous Identities*, by Etienne Balibar and Immanuel Wallerstein, trans. Chris Turner (London: Verso, 1991), 54 (emphasis in original). Like Stoler's concept of race, Balibar understands theoretical racism as consisting of "the ideal synthesis of transformation and fixity, or repetition and destiny. The 'secret,' the discovery of which it endlessly rehearses, is that of a humanity eternally leaving animality behind and eternally threatened with falling into the grasp of animality. That is why, when it substitutes the signifier of culture for that of race, it has always to attach this to a 'heritage,' and 'ancestry,' a 'rootedness,' all signifiers of the imaginary face-to-face relations between man and his origins" (57). Balibar convincingly argues that, in the discourse of nationalism, this theoretical racism produces both supernationalism and supranationalism or universalism. On the latter, he writes: "there actually is a racist 'internationalism' or 'supranationalism' which tends to idealize timeless or transhistorical communities such as the 'Indo-Europeans,' 'the West,' 'Judaeo-Christian civilization,' and therefore communities which are at the same time both closed and open, which have no frontiers or whose only frontiers are . . . 'internal' ones, inseparable from the individual individuals themselves or . . . from their 'essence.' In fact these are the frontiers of an ideal humanity. Here the excess of racism over nationalism . . . stretches it out to the dimensions of an infinite totality" (61–62).

32. This section is adapted from Buell, "Race and Universalism," 462–464.

33. Greg Woolf, *Becoming Roman: The Origins of Provincial Civilization in Gaul* (Cambridge: Cambridge University Press, 1998), 55. I take his use of "men" in this citation as a sign of the gendered limits of this universal ideal even though he does not comment on this point.

34. Ibid., 57; see 56–58.

35. Ibid., 55.

36. Indeed the very establishment of regionally organized cults was itself a departure from city-run cults, as Steve Friesen writes: "no Greek or Roman cults, either for rulers or for others, had been organized on a regional basis [before the early Augustan period]. The unprecedented spread of such institutions in the second century indicates that new social relationships were in formation." Steven J. Friesen, *Twice Neokoros: Ephesus, Asia and the Cult of the Flavian Imperial Family* (Leiden: Brill, 1993), 144.

37. Cited from Friesen, *Twice Neokoros*, 151. Translation by Charles Behr, *P. Aelius Aristides: The Complete Works* (Leiden: Brill, 1981), 2:96.

38. Friesen, *Twice Neokoros*, 154–155.

39. Jaś Elsner suggests that it is not only Christians who engage in this kind of resituating (his primary example is Pseudo-Lucian's *On the Syrian Goddess*, but he also extends this to Philostratus's *Life of Apollonius of Tyana*) See "Describing Self in the language of Other: Pseudo (?) Lucian at the Temple of Hierapolis," in *Being Greek under Rome: Cultural Identity, the Second Sophistic and the Development of Empire*, ed. Simon Goldhill (Cambridge: Cambridge University Press, 2001), 159–162. To what extent can we view Christian universalism as a discourse that mimics and refracts imperial discourse and practices in seeking to produce a collective subject-position with alternative universal ideals? Andrew Jacobs suggests that postcolonial theory may shed light on this question. See Andrew Jacobs, *Remains of the Jews: The Holy Land and Christian Empire in Late Antiquity* (Stanford: Stanford University Press, 2004).

40. These pursuits paradoxically could potentially confer on one the status of world citizen. For example, see Simon Swain, "Defending Hellenism: Philostratus, *In Honour of Apollonius*," in *Apologetics in the Roman Empire: Pagans, Jews, and Christians*, ed. Mark Edwards, Martin Goodman, and Simon Price, in association with Christopher Rowland (Oxford: Oxford University Press, 1999), 157–196.

41. For a terrific example of local negotiation of Greekness in Asia Minor, see Antony Spawforth, "Shades of Greekness: a Lydian Case Study," in *Ancient Perceptions of Greek Ethnicity*, ed. Irad Malkin (Washington D.C.: Center for Hellenic Studies/Cambridge: Harvard University Press, 2001), 375–400 (discussed in Chapter 2).

42. Other Christian works would benefit from comparable analysis. For some initial reflections on Justin Martyr's relationship to strategies employed by inhabitants of Asia Minor, see Buell, "Rethinking the Relevance of Race," 464–466.

43. See Denise K. Buell, "Ambiguous Legacy: A Feminist Commentary on Clement of Alexandria's Works," in *The Feminist Companion to Early Gnostic and Patristic Thought*, ed. Amy-Jill Levine (Sheffield: Sheffield Academic Press, forthcoming).

44. For example, "Of humans, all are either Greek or barbarian"—a point Clement uses to claim the universality of the Christian God (*Strom.* 5.133.8). Occasionally, Clement uses the adjective "barbarian" to refer to Christian teachings, but more frequently he insists that Christianity makes barbarians and Greeks into one people (for example, see *Strom.* 6.159.8–9; *Prot.* 12.120.2).

45. As I showed in chapter 1, Athenagoras uses this connection between religion and ethnicity to argue that Christians deserve protection under the law to worship their own God, as the Romans grant to other peoples and cities.

46. Mary Beard, John North, and Simon Price, *Religions of Rome*. 2 vols. (Cambridge: Cambridge University Press, 1998), 1:336. For a comprehensive analysis, see J. B. Rives, *Religion and Authority in Roman Carthage from Augustus to Constantine* (Oxford: Clarendon, 1995).

47. Beard, North, and Price, *Religions of Rome*, 1:333.

48. Because Alexandria was viewed as somewhat distinct from the rest of Egypt, I am commenting only on the situation in Alexandria. For the rest of Egypt, while Ro-

mans did not abolish the traditional and powerful Egyptian priesthoods, they did establish offices and procedures for regulating and overseeing them. Non-Roman religious practices in Egypt—Judaism, the cult of Sarapis, and the traditional Egyptian religion—each offered a vehicle for resistance to imperial control by standing for a group's distinctiveness apart from Romanness, not primarily as a means of negotiation with and adaptation to it. Opposition to Roman rule was expressed and interpreted simultaneously as religious and ethnic rebellion in Egypt, as was the case in Judea. The most striking, although tantalizingly brief, account of such a confluence of religion and ethnicity in rebellion against Rome allegedly occurred in 172–173 C.E. Cassius Dio reports an uprising of Egyptian peasants of the upper Nile delta led by an Egyptian priest (Cassio Dio LXXII.4). In addition, there is the well-known *Oracle of the Potter*, which contains pro-Egyptian and antiforeigner rhetoric couched in religious terms. Beard, North, and Price give examples for Thrace and Gaul as well (Beard, North, and Price, *Religions of Rome*, 1:347–348).

49. Naphtali Lewis, *Life in Egypt Under Roman Rule* (Oxford: Clarendon Press, 1983), 31–32.

50. This paragraph has been adapted from Buell, "Ambiguous Legacy."

51. See William D. Whitney, "On the So-Called Science of Religion," *Princeton Review* (1881): 451: "Christianity belongs in the same class with [religions proceeding from an individual founder: Zoroastrianism, Mohammadanism, and Buddhism], as being an individual and universal religion, *growing out of one that was limited to a race*" (My emphasis). Also: "Most religions limit themselves to a particular people or nationality, and if they spread and are accepted by other nations, it is as part and parcel of the civilisation to which they belong; but these two alone [Buddhism and Christianity] address themselves, not to a single people, but to all men and to every nation in its own language. . . . In short, Buddhism and Christianity are universalistic in character, while all other ethical religions are in the main particularistic." Cornelius P. Tiele, *Elements of the Science of Religion*. 2 vols. (New York: Scribner's Sons, 1897), 1:125–126.

52. In his 1829 *Appeal*, which was banned in the South, the African-American Bostonian businessman David Walker writes: "Surely the Americans must believe that God is partial, notwithstanding his apostle Peter, declared before Cornelius and other that he has no respect for persons [Acts 10:34–35], but in every nation he that feareth God and worketh righteousness is accepted with him. . . . Have not the Americans the Bible in their hands? Do they believe it? Surely they do not. See how they treat us in open violation of the Bible!!" David Walker, "Excerpts from *Appeal to the Coloured Citizens of the World, but in Particular, and Very Expressly, to Those of the United States of America*," in *Afro-American Religious History: A Documentary Witness*, ed. Milton C. Sernett (Durham, N.C.: Duke University Press, 1985), 190–191. Slightly later, he continues: "How can preachers and people of America believe the Bible? Does it teach them any distinction on account of a man's color? Hearken, Americans! To the injunctions of our Lord and Master, to his humble followers: 'And Jesus came and spake

unto them saying, "all power is given unto me in heaven and in earth. Go ye, therefore, and teach all nations, baptizing them in the name of the Father, and of the Son, and of the Holy Ghost, Teaching them to observe all things whatsoever I have commanded you; and lo, I am with you always, even unto the end of the world. Amen." ' [Mt. 28: 18, 19, 20]. . . . Do you understand the above, Americans? We are a people, notwithstanding many of you doubt it." (194).

To use a more recent example, consider the experiences of Korean-American Christian immigrants to the United States: "A large number of Christian immigrants came to the United States from Asia . . . and they have built their own Christian communities and sought a fellowship with the existing U.S. Christian establishment by joining their denominations. However, because they are from cultures very different from the dominant U.S. culture, they have received a very cool reception. . . . The U.S. establishment is not willing to accept culturally different immigrants unless they are totally acculturated into American life. They seem to have forgotten the fact that right from the beginning, the Christian community has been as diverse as twentieth-century America in respect to its cultural mix and ethnic composition. . . . This early Christian community accepted the cultural and ethnic diversity among its membership as a norm; it accepted ethnically as well as culturally diverse gentile Christians into its fellowship without asking them to follow the religious practice of a particular group. Peter realized that this was God's intention (referring to Acts 10:1–11:18)." Chan-Hi Kim, "Reading the Cornelius Story from an Asian Immigrant Perspective," in *Reading from this Place, volume 1. Social Location and Biblical Interpretation in the United States*, ed. Fernando F. Segovia and MaryAnn Tolbert (Minneapolis; Fortress, 1995), 171–172.

53. For example, see Sze-Kar Wan, "Does Diaspora Identity Imply Some Sort of Universality? An Asian-American Reading of Galatians," in *Interpreting Beyond Borders*, ed. Fernando F. Segovia (Sheffield: Sheffield Academic Press, 2000), 128–129.

54. Gillian Feeley-Harnik, *The Lord's Table: Eucharist and Passover in Early Christianity* (Philadelphia: University of Pennsylvania Press, 1981), 55; my emphasis.

55. Wan, "Does Diaspora Identity Imply Some Sort of Universality?", 115.

56. For example, see Scarlett Freund and Teofilo Ruiz, "Jews, *Conversos*, and the Inquisition in Spain, 1391–1492: The Ambiguities of History," in *Jewish-Christian Encounters over the Centuries: Symbiosis, Prejudice, Holocaust, Dialogue*, ed. Marvin Perry and Frederick M. Schweitzer (New York: Peter Lang, 1994), 169–195; Sander L. Gilman, *The Case of Sigmund Freud: Medicine and Identity at the Fin de Siècle* (Baltimore: The Johns Hopkins University Press, 1993), 69; and David Chidester, *Savage Systems: Colonialism and Comparative Religion in Southern Africa* (Charlottesville: University of Virginia Press, 1996), 14–16.

57. Arthur Darby Nock, *Conversion: The Old and the New in Religion from Alexander the Great to Augustine of Hippo* (1933; repr., Baltimore: The Johns Hopkins University Press, 1988), 3–16.

58. Thomas M. Finn, *From Death to Rebirth: Ritual and Conversion in Antiquity* (Mahwah, N.J.: Paulist, 1997), 34–35.

■

59. Ibid., 9, 19, 30, 239.

60. Wayne A. Meeks, *First Urban Christians: The Social World of the Apostle Paul* (New Haven: Yale University Press, 1983), 77.

61. John Curran, "The Conversion of Rome Revisited," in *Ethnicity and Culture in Late Antiquity*, ed. Stephen Mitchell and Geoffrey Greatex (London: Duckworth and the Classical Press of Wales, 2000), 8.

62. Ibid., 7–9.

63. Other sometimes intersecting strategies include conceptualizing conversion as a change in kinship, status, and philosophical affiliation.

64. Gauri Viswanathan, *Outside the Fold: Conversion, Modernity, and Belief* (Princeton: Princeton University Press, 1998), xvii.

65. Ibid., xvi–xvii.

66. Gilman, *The Case of Sigmund Freud*, 69.

67. Ibid., 72, 73.

68. For a recent discussion of this debate, see Miriam S. Taylor, *Anti-Judaism and Early Christian Identity: A Critique of the Scholarly Consensus* (Leiden: Brill, 1995).

69. Shaye Cohen most fully argues for this shift in Shaye Cohen, *The Beginnings of Jewishness: Boundaries, Varieties, Uncertainties* (Berkeley and Los Angeles: University of California Press, 1999), especially 109–139. See also Thomas Finn, "When the exiles returned from Babylonia (beginning in 539 B.C.E.) and built the second temple, a shift in Israelite identity from ethnicity to religion occurred; a Gentile could become a Jew" (Finn, *From Death to Rebirth*, 12–13). Casting ethnicity as the fixed "before" category, in which transformation from outsider to insider is either impossible or can only occur through appeals to kinship and shared descent, also appears in some recent arguments about changing definitions of Greekness. Here too, cultural identity serves as the "after," intended to signal the widening criteria for being defined as Greek in the Hellenistic period. The title of Jonathan Hall's recent book, *Hellenicity: Between Ethnicity and Culture*, nuances this claim slightly by suggesting a blurring rather than a sharp break and helpfully locating ethnicity as one aspect of cultural identity. Nonetheless, he argues for a movement in Hellene self-definition from "ethnic" to a greater emphasis on other cultural factors.

70. Cohen, *The Beginnings of Jewishness*, 109–110.

71. For further analysis of Cohen's work, see Denise K. Buell, "Ethnicity and Religion in Mediterranean Antiquity and Beyond," *Religious Studies Review* 26 (2000): 245–246.

72. Marcel Simon was an early champion of this position (in his *Verus Israel*), which has been more recently forwarded by Martin Goodman.

73. John North, "Development of Religious Pluralism," in *The Jews Among Pagans and Christians in the Roman Empire*, ed. Judith Lieu, John North, and Tessa Rajak (New York: Routledge, 1992), 191.

74. Joshua Levinson, "Bodies and Bo(a)rders: Emerging Fictions of Identity in Late Antiquity," *HTR* 93 (2000): 344.

75. Ibid., 345–346.

76. Ibid., 348.

77. See Schwartz, *The Curse of Cain*, 88. In the latter case, as Regina Schwartz notes, it is attachment to Yahweh that determines membership in a people. This membership is portrayed as mutable—by "attaching" oneself to Yahweh, one can move from being a "foreigner" to one of Yahweh's people: "Let no foreigner who has attached himself to Yahweh say, 'Yahweh will surely exclude me from his people.' . . . For my house will be called a house of prayer for all the peoples" (Is. 56:3, 7).

78. Instead of viewing "rebirth" as a metaphorical nod to the "real" thing, why not view the symbolic function of both birth and rebirth in identity and conversion talk as indicating the "fixity" established through change? What one becomes as a result of birth/rebirth can be framed in multiple ways—kin, coreligionist, and member of an ethnoracial group.

79. See Jon D. Levenson's useful discussion of the different kinds of universalisms that religious traditions formulate. Jon D. Levenson, "The Universal Horizon of Biblical Particularism," in *Ethnicity and the Bible*, ed. Mark G. Brett (Leiden: Brill, 1996), 143–145.

80. Byron, *Symbolic Blackness*, 104–120. See also her clear remarks in the concluding chapter: "No longer is it acceptable to dismiss the possibility that ethnic and color difference played a significant role in . . . early Christianity" (124). "Assumptions about ethnic groups, geographical locations, and color differences in antiquity influenced the way that early Christians shaped their stories about the theological, ecclesiological, and political developments in their communities. As a result, Egyptians/Egypt, Ethiopians/Ethiopia, and Blacks/blackness became associated with the threats and dangers that could potentially destroy the development of a certain 'orthodox' brand of Christianity. In spite of the basic contention that Christianity was to extend to all peoples—even the remote Ethiopians—it is clear that certain groups of Christians were marginalized and rendered invisible and silent through ethnic and color-coded language. . . . Ethnic and color differences came to *symbolize* theological, ideological, and political intra-Christian controversies and challenges" (123, emphasis in original).

81. Byron, *Symbolic Blackness*, 124.

# Epilogue

1. See also Judith Lieu, *Christian Identity in the Jewish and Graeco-Roman World* (Oxford: Oxford University Press, 2004), 310.

2. The distinctions among race, ethnicity, nationality, civic identity, and religious identity today are also often blurry, as evidenced in the way that one's geographical origin or chosen homeplace, one's nationality, and one's assigned or claimed race and ethnicity are often interpreted by others (if not also by oneself) as being inextricably linked with a particular religious identity. In the United

States, being an American citizen cannot be automatically interpreted in terms of membership in a particular religious community. Nonetheless, many Americans make assumptions about religious affiliation based on one's name (an O'Malley is likely to be Catholic while an Ahmed is likely to be Muslim), presumed racial or ethnic background (that a French-Canadian is likely to be Catholic), or a combination of geography and presumed ethnoracial identity (that an African American from the Northeast is likely to be Protestant while an African American from New Orleans is likely to be Catholic).

3.  Shawn Kelley has diagnosed a comparable problem in the scholarship on the historical Jesus, arguing that "much modern biblical scholarship, influenced by German philosophy (especially by Herder, Hegel, and Heidegger), has functioned within the orbit of *völkisch* Romanticism, which is a form of aestheticized and racialized nationalism. In other words, much biblical scholarship has implicitly fallen under the sway of Romantic aesthetic ideology of organicity . . . " Shawn Kelley, *Racializing Jesus: Race, Ideology, and the Formation of Modern Biblical Scholarship* (New York: Routledge, 2002), 216.

4.  Karen L. King, *What Is Gnosticism?* (Cambridge: Harvard University Press, 2003), 233.

5.  Ibid., 233–234.

6.  See Elizabeth Schüssler Fiorenza, *Rhetoric and Ethic: The Politics of Biblical Studies* (Minneapolis: Fortress Press, 1999), especially 17–102, 195–198.

7.  See Schüssler Fiorenza, *Rhetoric and Ethic*, 199–200. This approach also resembles what Kelley, referencing Derrida, describes as a practice of "double-readings—double-readings of the (racialized) heritage of modernity and double-readings of the biblical text itself" (Kelley, *Racializing Jesus*, 222).

8.  Gay L. Byron, *Symbolic Blackness and Ethnic Difference in Early Christian Literature* (New York: Routledge, 2002), 123.

9.  This is a longstanding theme within African American theology (from early-nineteenth-century voices such as Maria Miller Stewart and David Walker to twentieth-century ones such as Reverdy Ransom and Cornel West) and one with continued relevance (see, for example, *Ending Racism in the Churches*, ed. Susan E. Davies and Sister Paul Teresa Hennessee [Cleveland: Pilgrim, 1998]).

10. Karen King has argued that one of the major ways in which scholars have reinscribed early Christian polemical framing devices is to define Christian normativity, heterodoxy, and heresy in relation to Jewishness. "Jewish-Christian" texts are heterodox because they are deemed "too Jewish"; "gnostic" texts are heretical because they are deemed "not Jewish enough" (King, *What Is Gnosticism?*, 4, 38–47, 175–190). According to this logic, so-called normative or orthodox Christianity, like Goldilocks's third attempt at eating, sitting, and sleeping, contains just the right proportions of Jewishness. As King has also noted, Christian relations to non-Jewish "others" have also been instrumental for how early Christians defined themselves and how modern scholars classify forms of Christianness. While "Jew" and "Hellene" or "Roman" (and later "pagan") exemplify "not-Christian" (or potential Christian) in many early Christian texts, so too

have scholars labeled as heterodox (especially "gnostic") forms of Christianness that seem to embody too much Greekness or alleged "pagan" influence. King shows that modern scholars have also defined "gnosticism" in terms of "an outside contamination of pure Christianity" (4), including too much "Hellenistic" influence (55–70) and "oriental" influences (71–109).

11. I do not mean to suggest that the rhetorical functions of ethnic reasoning do not change over time. But I am wary of the claim that in the post-legalization period Christianity becomes a "religion," defined as a category explicitly separated from "ethnicity and language," because, like all tales of origins, this claim deflects attention both from the function of telling such a tale and from the complexity of Christian self-definition before and after legalization. See Daniel Boyarin, *Border Lines: The Partition of Judaeo-Christianity* (Philadelphia: University of Pennsylvania Press, 2004), 202–206. For Boyarin, one crucial function of locating the origins of "religion" in late fourth- and early fifth-century Christian discourse is to support his argument that the rabbis, in response to Christian self-definition as a religion and its creation of the notion of Jewish orthodoxy in the process, rejected this logic such that "Judaism refused to be, in the end, a *religion*" (224, emphasis in original). I agree that the concept of "religion" as culturally disembedded is Christian-inflected, but would argue that this notion exists in tension with rhetorical and material practices, including ethnic reasoning.

# Bibliography

## Ancient Sources

*Acts of the Christian Martyrs.* Volume 2. Introduction, edited, and English translation by Herbert Musurillo. Oxford: Clarendon, 1972.

*The Acts of Andrew and The Acts of Andrew and Matthias in the City of Cannibals.* Introduction, edited, and English translation by Dennis Ronald MacDonald. Texts and Translations 33. Christian Apocrypha Series 1. Atlanta: Scholars, 1990.

*The Acts of Andrew.* Edited and French translation by Jean-Marc Prieur. Corpus Christianorum Series Apocryphorum 6. Brepols: Turnhout, 1989.

Aristides. *Apologie.* Introduction, edited, French translation, and commentary by Bernard Pouderon et al. SC 470. Paris: Éditions du Cerf, 2003.

Athenagoras. *Supplique au Sujet des Chrétiens et sur la résurrection des Morts.* Introduction, edited, and French translation by Bernard Pouderon. SC 379. Paris: Éditions du Cerf, 1992.

Clement of Alexandria. *Opera.* Edited by Otto Stählin. 4 vols. Die griechischen christlichen Schriftsteller der ersten drei Jahrhunderte, 12, 15, 17, 39. Leipzig: Hinrichs, 1905–1909.

——. *Extraits de Théodote.* Introduction, edited, French translation, and notes by F. Sagnard. SC 23. Paris: Éditions du Cerf, 1948.

——. *Protrepticus.* Edited by Miroslav Marcovich. Supplements to Vigiliae Christianae. Texts and Studies of Early Christian Life and Language 34. Leiden: Brill, 1995.

——. *Protrepticus und Paedagogus.* Edited by Otto Stählin. Revised by Ursula Treu, 3rd ed. Vol. 1. Die griechischen christlichen Schriftsteller der ersten Jahrhunderte. 1904. Reprint, Berlin: Akademie Verlag, 1972.

——. *Les Stromates: Stromate II.* Introduction and notes by P. Th. Camelot. French translation by Claude Mondésert. SC 38. Paris: Éditions du Cerf, 1954.

———. *Les Stromates: Stromate IV*. Introduction, edited, and notes by Annewies van den Hoek. French translation by Claude Mondésert. SC 463. Paris: Éditions du Cerf, 2001.

———. *Les Stromates: Stromate VI*. Introduction, edited, French translation, and notes by Patrick Descourtieux. SC 446. Paris: Éditions du Cerf, 1999.

Diodorus of Sicily. In *Diodorus of Sicily in Twelve Volumes*. Vol. 1. Edited and English translation by C. H. Oldfather. Loeb Classical Library. 1933. Reprint, Cambridge, Mass.: Harvard University Press, 1968.

*À Diognète*. Edited and French translation by Henri-Irénée Marrou. 2nd ed. SC 33. Paris: Éditions du Cerf, 1965.

*Eugnostos and the Sophia of Jesus Christ*. In *The Coptic Gnostic Library: A Complete Edition of the Nag Hammadi Codices. Vol. 3*. Edited and English translation by Douglas M. Parrott. 1991. Reprint, Leiden: Brill, 2000.

Irenaeus. *Against All Heresies*. In *Ante-Nicene Fathers, Volume 1. The Apostolic Fathers, Justin Martyr, Irenaeus*. Edited by Alexander Roberts and James Donaldson. 1885. Reprint, Peabody, Mass.: Hendrickson, 1994.

Justin Martyr. *The First and Second Apologies*. English translation by Leslie William Barnard. Ancient Christian Writers 56. New York: Paulist, 1997.

———. *Apologie pour les Chrétiens*. Edited and French translation by Charles Munier. Paradosis 39. Fribourg, Switzerland: Éditions universitaires, 1995.

———. *Dialogue with Trypho*. Translation by Thomas B. Falls. Revised and introduction by Thomas P. Halton. Edited by Michael Slusser. Selections from the Father of the Church 3. Washington D.C.: The Catholic University of America Press, 2003.

———. *Dialogus cum Tryphone*. Edited by Miroslav Marcovich. Patristische Texte und Studien 47. Berlin: De Gruyter, 1997.

*The Gospel According to Philip*. In the *Coptic Gnostic Library: A Complete Edition of the Nag Hammadi Codices. Vol. 2*. Edited by Bentley Layton. English translation by Wesley W. Isenberg. 1989. Reprint, Leiden: Brill, 2000.

Origen. *Contre Celse. Vols. 3 and 4*. Introduction, edited, French translation, and notes by Marcel Borret. SC 147 and 150. Paris: Éditions du Cerf, 1969.

———. *Contra Celsum*. Introduction, English translation, and notes by Henry Chadwick. 1953. Reprint, with corrections. Cambridge: Cambridge University Press, 1965.

———. *Traité des Principes*. 5 vols. Introduction, edited, and French translation by Henri Crouzel and Manlio Simonetti. SC 252, 253, 268, 269, 312. Paris: Éditions du Cerf, 1978–1984.

Philo of Alexandria. *On Sobriety*. In *Works*. Vol. 3. English translation by D. H. Colson and G. H. Whitaker. Loeb Classical Library 247. 1930. Reprint, Cambridge, Mass.: Harvard University Press, 2001.

Pseudo-Clementine Homilies. *An Ancient Jewish Christian Source on the History of Christianity:* Pseudo-Clementine Recognitions *1.27–71*. English translation from the Latin and Syriac by F. Stanley Jones. Society of Biblical Literature Texts and Translations 37. Christian Apocrypha Series 2. Atlanta: Scholars, 1995.

Ptolemy of Alexandria. *Tetrabiblos.* Edited and English translation by F. E. Robbins. Loeb Classical Library. Cambridge, Mass.: Harvard University Press, 1956.

*The Shepherd of Hermas.* In *The Apostolic Fathers Vol. 2.* Edited and English translation by Kirsopp Lake. Loeb Classical Library 25. 1913. Reprint, Cambridge, Mass.: Harvard University Press, 1992.

*Der Hirt des Hermas.* In *Die Apostolichen Vater 1.* Edited by Molly Whittaker. Berlin: Akademie Verlag, 1956.

Tertullian. *Apology.* Edited and English translation by T. R. Glover. Loeb Classical Library 250. 1931. Reprint, Cambridge, Mass.: Harvard University Press, 1998.

Theophilus of Antioch. *Ad Autolycum.* Text and translation by Robert M. Grant. Oxford: Clarendon, 1970.

*The Tripartite Tractate.* In *The Coptic Gnostic Library: A Complete Edition of the Nag Hammadi Codices. Vol. 1.* Edited, translated, and critical notes by Harold W. Attridge and Elaine H. Pagels. 1985. Reprint, Leiden: Brill, 2000.

*Le Traité Tripartite.* Edited, introduction and commentary by Einar Thomassen. French translation by Louis Painchaud and Einar Thomassen. Bibliothèque Copte de Nag Hammadi, Section "Textes" 19. Québec: Les Presses de l'Université Laval, 1989.

# Modern Sources

Allen, Theodore. *The Invention of the White Race.* 2 vols. London and New York: Verso, 1994.

d'Ambra, Eve. *Roman Art.* Cambridge: Cambridge University Press, 1998.

Antonaccio, Carla M. "Ethnicity and Colonization." In *Ancient Perceptions of Greek Ethnicity,* edited by Irad Malkin, 113–157. Washington D.C.: Center for Hellenic Studies/Cambridge, Mass.: Harvard University Press, 2001.

Appiah, K. Anthony, and Amy Gutmann. *Color Conscious: The Political Morality of Race.* Princeton, N.J.: Princeton University Press, 1996.

Babb, Valerie. *Whiteness Visible: The Meaning of Whiteness in American Literature and Culture.* New York: New York University Press, 1998.

Bagnall, Roger S. "Greeks and Egyptians: Ethnicity, Status, and Culture." In *Cleopatra's Egypt: Age of the Ptolemies,* curated by Robert S. Bianchi, 12–27. New York: The Brooklyn Museum, 1988.

Bailey, Randall C. "Academic Biblical Interpretation among African Americans in the United States." In *African Americans and the Bible: Sacred Texts and Social Textures,* edited by Vincent Wimbush with the assistance of Rosamond C. Rodman. 696–711. New York: Continuum, 2000.

Balch, David L. "Attitudes Toward Foreigners in 2 Maccabees, Eupolemos, Esther, Aristeas, and Luke-Acts." In *The Early Church in Its Context: Essays in Honor of Everett Ferguson,* edited by Abraham J. Malherbe, Frederick W. Norris, and James W. Thompson, 22–47. Supplements to Novum Testamentum 90. Leiden: Brill, 1998.

Balibar, Etienne, and Immanuel Wallerstein. *Race, Nation, Class: Ambiguous Identities*. Translation of Balibar by Chris Turner. London: Verso, 1991.

Bard, Kathryn. "Ancient Egyptians and the Issue of Race." In *Black Athena Revisited*, edited by Mary Lefkowitz and Guy M. Rogers, 103–111. Chapel Hill: University of North Carolina Press, 1996.

Bartlett, Robert. "Medieval and Modern Concepts of Race and Ethnicity." *Journal of Medieval and Early Modern Studies* 31 (2001): 39–56.

Baumann, Gerd. *The Multicultural Riddle: Rethinking National, Ethnic, and Religious Identities*. New York: Routledge, 1999.

Bauer, Walter. *Orthodoxy and Heresy in Earliest Christianity*, translated by the Philadelphia Seminar on Christian Origins. German original 1934. ET: Mifflintown, Penn.: Sigler, 1971.

Becker, Adam H., and Annette Yoshiko Reed, eds. *The Ways that Never Parted: Jews and Christians in Late Antiquity and the Early Middle Ages*. Texts and Studies in Ancient Judaism 95. Tübingen: Mohr [Siebeck], 2003.

Beard, Mary, John North, and Simon Price. *Religions of Rome*. 2 vols. Cambridge: Cambridge University Press, 1998.

Benko, Stephen. *Pagan Rome and the Early Christians*. Bloomington: Indiana University Press, 1984.

Bentley, G. Carter. "Ethnicity and Practice." *Journal for the Comparative Study of Society and History* 29 (1987): 24–55.

The Bible and Culture Collective. *The Postmodern Bible*. New Haven, Conn.: Yale University Press, 1995.

Bickerman, Elias J. "Origines Gentium." *Classical Philology* 47 (1952): 65–81.

Bilde, Per, et al., eds. *Ethnicity in Hellenistic Egypt*. Aarhus, Denmark: Aarhus University Press, 1992.

Bonz, Marianne Palmer. *The Past as Legacy: Luke-Acts and Ancient Epic*. Minneapolis: Fortress, 2000.

Bowersock, Glenn W. *Fiction as History: Nero to Julian*. Berkeley: University of California Press, 1994.

Bowie, Ewan L. "Hellenes and Hellenism in Writers of the Second Sophistic." In *ΕΛΛΗΝΙΣΜΟΣ: Quelques Jalons pour une Histoire de l'Identité Grecque, Actes de Colloque de Strasbourg 25–27 octobre 1989*, edited by Suzanne Saïd, 182–204. Leiden: Brill, 1991.

———. "Greeks and their Past in the Second Sophistic." *Past and Present* 46 (1970): 3–41. Reprinted in Moses Finley, ed. *Studies in Ancient Society*, 166–209. London: Routledge, 1974.

Boyarin, Daniel. *Border Lines: The Partition of Judaeo-Christianity*. Divinations: Rereading Late Ancient Religions. Philadelphia: University of Pennsylvania Press, 2004.

———. "Justin Martyr Invents Judaism." *Church History* 70 (2001): 427–61.

———. *Dying for God: Martyrdom and the Making of Christianity and Judaism*. Figurae: Reading Medieval Culture. Stanford: Stanford University Press, 1999.

Brace, C. Loring, et al. "Clines and Clusters Versus 'Race': A Test in Ancient Egypt and the Case of a Death on the Nile." In *Black Athena Revisited*, edited by Mary

Lefkowitz and Guy M. Rogers, 129–164. Chapel Hill: University of North Carolina Press, 1996.

Brakke, David. "Ethiopian Demons: Male Sexuality, the Black-Skinned Other, and the Monastic Self." *Journal of the History of Sexuality* 10 (2001): 501–535.

——. "The Seed of Seth at the Flood; Biblical Interpretation and Gnostic Theological Reflection." In *Reading in Christian Communities: Essays on Interpretation in the Early Church*, edited by Charles A. Bobertz and David Brakke, 41–62. Notre Dame: University of Notre Dame Press, 2002.

——. "Canon Formation and Social Conflict in Fourth-Century Egypt: Athanasius of Alexandria's Thirty-Ninth *Festal Letter*." *HTR* 87 (1994): 395–419.

Brett, Mark G.., ed. *Ethnicity and the Bible*. 1996. Reprint, Boston: Brill, 2002.

Briggs, Sheila. " 'Buried with Christ': The Politics of Identity and the Poverty of Interpretation." In *The Book and the Text: The Bible and Literary Theory*, edited by Regina Schwartz, 276–303. Oxford: Basil Blackwell, 1990.

Brock, Sebastian P. "Christians in the Sasanian Empire: A Case of Divided Loyalties." In *Religion and National Identity: Papers Read at the Nineteenth Summer Meeting and the Twentieth Winter Meeting of the Ecclesiastical History Society*, edited by Stuart Mews, 1–19. Oxford: Basil Blackwell, 1982.

Brodkin, Karen. *How Jews Became White Folks and What That Says about Race in America*. New Brunswick, N.J.: Rutgers University Press, 1998.

Buckley, Jorunn Jacobsen. "Conceptual Models and Polemical Issues in the Gospel of Philip." *ANRW* II 22.5 (1998): 4167–4194.

Buell, Denise K. "Race and Universalism in Early Christianity." *JECS* 10:4 (2002): 429–468.

——. "Rethinking the Relevance of Race for Early Christian Self-Definition." *HTR* 94 (2001): 449–476.

——. "Ethnicity and Religion in Mediterranean Antiquity and Beyond." *Religious Studies Review* 26 (2000): 243–249.

——. *Making Christians: Clement of Alexandria and the Rhetoric of Legitimacy*. Princeton, N.J.: Princeton University Press, 1999.

——. "Ambiguous Legacy: A Feminist Commentary on Clement of Alexandria's Works." In *The Feminist Companion to Early Gnostic and Patristic Thought*, edited by Amy-Jill Levine. Sheffield, UK: Sheffield Academic Press, forthcoming.

Buell, Denise Kimber, and Caroline Johnson Hodge. "The Politics of Interpretation: The Rhetoric of Race and Ethnicity in Paul." *Journal of Biblical Literature*, 123 (2004): 235–252.

Bultmann, Rudolf. *Primitive Christianity in Its Contemporary Setting*. Translated by R. H. Fuller. 1956. Reprint, New York: Meridian Books, 1966.

Byron, Gay L. *Symbolic Blackness and Ethnic Difference in Early Christian Literature*. New York: Routledge, 2002.

Cameron, Averil. *Christianity and the Rhetoric of Empire: The Development of Christian Discourse*. Berkeley: University of California Press, 1991.

Castelli, Elizabeth A. *Martyrdom and Memory: Early Christian Culture Making*. New York: Columbia University Press, 2004.

Castelli, Elizabeth A., and Hal Taussig. "Drawing Large and Startling Figures: Reimagining Christian Origins by Painting Like Picasso." In *Reimagining Christian Origins: A Colloquium Honoring Burton L. Mack*, edited by Elizabeth A. Castelli and Hal Taussig, 3–20. Valley Forge, Penn.: Trinity Press International, 1996.

Certeau, Michel de. *The Writing of History*. Translated by Tom Conley. French original 1975. ET: New York: Columbia University Press, 1988.

Chakrabartry, Dipesh. *Provincializing Europe: Postcolonial Thought and Historical Difference*. Princeton, N.J.: Princeton University Press, 2000.

Chidester, David. *Savage Systems: Colonialism and Comparative Religion in Southern Africa*. Charlottesville: University of Virginia Press, 1996.

Clarysse, Willy. "Some Greeks in Egypt." In *Life in a Multi-Cultural Society: Egypt from Cambyses to Constantine and Beyond*, edited by Janet H. Johnson, 51–56. Studies in Ancient Oriental Civilization 51. Chicago: The Oriental Institute of the University of Chicago, 1992.

Cohen, Edward E. *The Athenian Nation*. Princeton, N.J.: Princeton University Press, 2000.

Cohen, Shaye J. D. *The Beginnings of Jewishness: Boundaries, Varieties, Uncertainties*. Hellenistic Culture and Society XXXI. Berkeley and Los Angeles: University of California Press, 1999.

Cone, James. *Risks of Faith: The Emergence of a Black Theology of Liberation, 1968–1998*. Boston: Beacon, 1999.

Conick, April D. de. "The True Mysteries: Sacramentalism in the *Gospel of Philip*." *Vigiliae Christianae* 55 (2001): 225–261.

Curran, John. "The Conversion of Rome Revisited." In *Ethnicity and Culture in Late Antiquity*, edited by Stephen Mitchell and Geoffrey Greatex, 1–14. London: Duckworth and the Classical Press of Wales, 2000.

Daniélou, Jean. *A History of Early Christian Doctrine Before the Council of Nicaea, Volume Two: Gospel Message and Hellenistic Culture*. Translated, edited, and with a postscript by John Austin Baker. London: Darton, Longman, and Todd/ Philadelphia: Westminster, 1973.

Davison, James E. "Structual Similarities and Dissimilarities in the Thought of Clement of Alexandria and the Valentinians." *Second Century* 3 (1983): 210–17.

Domínguez, Virginia. *People as Subject, People as Object: Selfhood and Peoplehood in Contemporary Israel*. Madison: The University of Wisconsin Press, 1989.

Droge, Arthur J. *Homer or Moses? Early Christian Interpretations of the History of Culture*. Hermeneutische Untersuchungen zur Theologie 26. Tübingen: Mohr [Siebeck], 1989.

Dunn, Geoffrey D. "The Universal Spread of Christianity as a Rhetorical Argument in Tertullian's *adversus Iudaeos*." *JECS* 8 (2000): 1–19.

Edwards, Douglas R. *Religion and Power: Pagans, Jews, and Christians in the Greek East*. New York: Oxford University Press, 1996.

Edwards, Mark, Martin Goodman, and Simon Price, in association with Christopher Rowland, eds. *Apologetics in the Roman Empire: Pagans, Jews, and Christians*. New York: Oxford University Press, 1999.

Elliott, John H. *A Home for the Homeless: A Sociological Exegesis of 1 Peter, Its Situation and Strategy*. Philadelphia: Fortress, 1981.

Elsner, Jaś. "Describing Self in the Language of Other: Pseudo (?) Lucian at the Temple of Hierapolis." In *Being Greek under Rome: Cultural Identity, the Second Sophistic and the Development of Empire*, edited by Simon Goldhill, 123–153. Cambridge: Cambridge University Press, 2001.

Emerson, Michael, and Christian Smith. *Divided by Faith: Evangelical Religion and the Problem of Race in America*. Oxford: Oxford University Press, 2000.

Feeley-Harnik, Gillian. *The Lord's Table: Eucharist and Passover in Early Christianity*. Philadelphia: University of Pennsylvania Press, 1981.

Fishwick, Duncan. *The Imperial Cult in the Latin West: Studies in the Ruler Cult of the Western Provinces of the Roman Empire*. Études Préliminaires aux Religions Orientales dans l'Empire Romain 118. Leiden: Brill, 1987.

Fonrobert, Charlotte. "The *Didascalia Apostolorum*: A Mishnah for the Followers of Jesus." *JECS* 9.4 (2001): 483–509.

Foucault, Michel. *Politics, Philosophy, Culture: Interviews and Other Writings, 1977–1984*. Translated by Alan Sheridan and others. Edited with an introduction by Lawrence D. Kritzman. New York: Routledge, 1988.

Fowden, Garth. *Empire to Commonwealth: Consequences of Monotheism in Late Antiquity*. Princeton, N.J.: Princeton University Press, 1993.

Frank, Georgia. *The Memory of the Eyes: Pilgrims to Living Saints in Late Antiquity*. The Transformation of Classical Heritage 30. Berkeley and Los Angeles: University of California Press, 2000.

Frankenberg, Ruth. *White Women, Race Matters: The Social Construction of Whiteness*. Minneapolis: University of Minnesota Press, 1993.

Freund, Scarlett, and Teofilo Ruiz. "Jews, *Conversos*, and the Inquisition in Spain, 1391–1492: The Ambiguities of History." In *Jewish-Christian Encounters over the Centuries: Symbiosis, Prejudice, Holocaust, Dialogue*, edited by Marvin Perry and Frederick M. Schweitzer, 169–195. New York: Peter Lang, 1994.

Friedman, Jonathan. "Notes on Culture and Identity in Imperial Worlds." In *Religion and Religious Practice in the Seleucid Kingdom*, edited by Per Bilde et al., 14–39. Studies in Hellenistic Civilizations 1. Aarhus, Denmark: Aarhus University Press, 1990.

Friesen, Steven J. *Twice Neokoros: Ephesus, Asia and the Cult of the Flavian Imperial Family*. Religions in the Graeco-Roman World 116. Leiden: Brill, 1993.

Frye, Matthew Jacobson. *Whiteness of a Different Color: European Immigration and the Alchemy of Race*. Cambridge, Mass.: Harvard University Press, 1998.

Geiger, Abraham. *Judaism and Its History: In Two Parts*. Translated by Charles Newburgh. New York: Bloch, 1911.

Genovese, Eugene D. *A Consuming Fire: The Fall of the Confederacy in the Mind of the White Christian South*. Mercer University Lama Memorial Lectures, No. 41. Athens, GA: The University of Georgia Press, 1998.

Gilman, Sander L. *The Case of Sigmund Freud: Medicine and Identity and the Fin de Siècle*. Baltimore: The Johns Hopkins University Press, 1993.

Glaude, Eddie S., Jr. *Exodus! Religion, Race, and Nation in Early Nineteenth-Century Black America*. Chicago: University of Chicago Press, 2000.

Gleason, Maud W. *Making Men: Sophists and Self-Presentation in Ancient Rome*. Princeton, N.J.: Princeton University Press, 1995.

Goldenberg, David M. *The Curse of Ham: Race and Slavery in Early Judaism, Christianity, and Islam*. Princeton, N.J.: Princeton University Press, 2003.

——. "The Curse of Ham: A Case of Rabbinic Racism?" In *Struggles in the Promised Land: Toward a History of Black-Jewish Relations in the United States*, edited by Jack Salzman and Cornel West, 21–51. New York: Oxford University Press, 1997.

Goldhill, Simon. *Who Needs Greek? Contests in the Cultural History of Hellenism*. Cambridge: Cambridge University Press, 2002.

——, ed. *Being Greek Under Rome: Cultural Identity, the Second Sophistic, and the Development of Empire*. Cambridge: Cambridge University Press, 2001.

Gomez, Michael A. *Exchanging Our Country Marks: The Transformation of African Identities in the Colonial and Antebellum South*. Chapel Hill: University of North Carolina Press, 1998.

Goudriaan, Koen. *Ethnicity in Ptolemaic Egypt*. Amsterdam: Gieben, 1988.

Green, Henry Alan. "Suggested Sociological Themes in the Study of Gnosticism." *Vigiliae Christianae* 31 (1977): 169–180.

Greer, Rowan. "Alien Citizens: A Marvelous Paradox." In *Civitas: Religious Interpretations of the City*, edited by Peter S. Hawkins, 39–56. Atlanta: Scholars, 1986.

Grosby, Steven. "The Category of the Primordial in the Study of Early Christianity and Second-Century Judaism." *History of Religions* 36 (1996): 140–163.

Gruen, Erich S. "Jewish Perspectives on Greek Culture and Ethnicity." In *Ancient Perceptions of Greek Ethnicity*, edited by Irad Malkin, 347–373. Washington D.C.: Center for Hellenic Studies/Cambridge, Mass.: Harvard University Press, 2001.

——. *Heritage and Hellenism: The Reinvention of Jewish Tradition*. Berkeley: University of California Press, 1998.

——. "The Purported Jewish-Spartan Affiliation." In *Transitions to Empire: Essays in Greco-Roman History, 360–146 B.C., in Honor of E. Badian*, edited by Robert W. Wallace and Edward M. Harris, 254–269. Norman, Okla.: University of Oklahoma Press, 1996.

Hale, Grace Elizabeth. *Making Whiteness: The Culture of Segregation in the South, 1890–1940*. New York: Pantheon Books, 1998.

Hall, Edith. *Inventing the Barbarian: Greek Self-Definition Through Tragedy*. Oxford: Clarendon, 1989.

Hall, Jonathan M. *Hellenicity: Between Ethnicity and Culture*. Chicago: University of Chicago Press, 2002.

——. *Ethnic Identity in Greek Antiquity*. Cambridge: Cambridge University Press, 1997.

Haraway, Donna. *Modest_Witness@Second_Millenium.FemaleMan©_Meets_OncoMouse™: Feminism and Technoscience*. New York: Routledge, 1997.

von Harnack, Adolf. *Expansion of Christianity in the First Three Centuries*. Translated by James Moffat. 2 vols. 1904–05. Reprint, New York: Arno, 1972.

Harrison, Peter. *"Religion" and the Religions in the English Enlightenment.* Cambridge: Cambridge University Press, 1990.

Hartog, François. *Memories of Odysseus: Frontier Tales from Ancient Greece.* Translated by Janet Lloyd. Chicago: University of Chicago Press, 2001.

——. *The Mirror of Herodotus: The Representation of the Other in the Writing of History.* Translated by Janet Lloyd. Berkeley: University of California Press, 1988.

Herrmann, Peter. "Inschriften von Sardis." *Chiron* 23 (1993): 233–48.

Heschel, Susanna. *Abraham Geiger and the Jewish Jesus.* Chicago: University of Chicago Press, 1998.

——. "Jesus as Theological Transvestite." In *Judaism Since Gender,* edited by Miriam Peskowitz and Laura Levitt, 188–199. New York: Routledge, 1997.

Hingley, Richard. *Roman Officers and British Gentlemen: the Imperial Origins of British Archaeology.* New York: Routledge, 2000.

Hirschman, Marc. "Rabbinic Universalism in the Second and Third Centuries." *HTR* 93 (2000): 101–115.

Hodge, Caroline Johnson. " 'If Children, Then Heirs' (Rom. 8:17 and Gal. 4:7): A Study of Kinship and Ethnicity in Romans and Galatians." Ph.D. dissertation, Brown University, 2002.

Hollinger, David. *Post-Ethnic America: Beyond Multiculturalism.* New York: Basic Books, 1995.

Hopkins, Keith. *A World Full of Gods: The Strange Triumph of Christianity.* New York: Free Press, 1999.

——. "Christian Number and Its Implications." *JECS* 6 (1998): 185–226.

Isaac, Benjamin. *The Invention of Racism in Classical Antiquity.* Princeton, N.J.: Princeton University Press, 2004.

——. *The Near East Under Roman Rule: Selected Papers.* Mnemosyne. Leiden: Brill, 1998.

Jacobs, Andrew S. *Remains of the Jews: The Holy Land and Christian Empire in Late Antiquity.* Stanford: Stanford University Press, 2004.

Jakobsen, Janet R., with Ann Pellegrini. "World Secularisms at the Millennium." *Social Text* 64 (2000): 1–27.

Janowitz, Naomi. "Rethinking Jewish Identity in Late Antiquity." In *Ethnicity and Culture in Late Antiquity,* edited by Stephen Mitchell and Geoffrey Greatex, 205–219. London: Duckworth and the Classical Press of Wales, 2000.

Jay, Nancy. *"Throughout Your Generations Forever": Sacrifice, Religion, and Paternity.* Chicago: University of Chicago Press, 1992.

Johnson, Aaron P. "Identity, Descent, and Polemic: Ethnic Argumentation in Eusebius's *Praeparatio Evangelica.*" *JECS* 12:1 (2004): 23–56.

Johnson-DeBaufre, Melanie. "It's the End of the World as We Know It." Th.D. dissertation, Harvard Divinity School, 2002.

Jones, Christopher P. *Kinship Diplomacy in the Ancient World.* Revealing Antiquity 12. Cambridge, Mass.: Harvard University Press, 1999.

Jordan, William Chester. "Why 'Race'?" *Journal of Medieval and Early Modern Studies* 31 (2001): 165–173.

Kampen, Natalie B. "Gender Theory in Art." In *I, Claudia: Women in Ancient Rome*, edited by Diane E. E. Kleiner and Susan Matheson, 14–25. New Haven, Conn.: Yale University Art Gallery. Distributed by the University of Texas Press, Austin, 1996.

Kamtekar, Rachana. "Distinction without a Difference? Race and *Genos* in Plato." In *Philosophers on Race: Critical Essays*, edited by Julie Ward and Tommy Lott, 1–13. Oxford/Malden, Mass.: Blackwell, 2002.

Kellenbach, Katharina von. *Anti-Judaism in Feminist Religious Writings*. Atlanta: Scholars Press, 1994.

Kelley, Shawn. *Racializing Jesus: Race, Ideology, and the Formation of Modern Biblical Scholarship*. New York: Routledge, 2002.

Keyes, Charles F. "The Dialectic of Ethnic Change." In *Ethnic Change*, edited by Charles F. Keyes, 3–30. Seattle: University of Washington Press, 1981.

Kim, Chan-Hie. "Reading the Cornelius Story from an Asian Immigrant Perspective." In *Reading from this Place, volume 1: Social Location and Biblical Interpretation in the United States*, edited by Fernando F. Segovia and Mary Ann Tolbert, 165–174. Minneapolis: Fortress, 1995.

Kimelman, Reuven. "Birkhat Ha-Minim and the Lack of Evidence for an Anti-Christian Jewish Prayer in Late Antiquity." In *Jewish and Christian Self-Definition, volume 2: Aspects of Judaism in the Greco-Roman Period*, edited by E. P. Sanders, A. I. Baumgarten, and Alan Mendelson, 226–244. Philadelphia: Fortress, 1981.

King, Karen L. *What is Gnosticism?* Cambridge, Mass.: Harvard University Press, 2003.

———. "Translating History: Reframing Gnosticism in Postmodernity." In *Tradition und Translation: Zum Problem der Interkulturellen Übersetzbarkeit Religiöser Phänomene. Festschrift für Carsten Colpe zum 65. Geburtstag*, edited by Christoph Elsas et al., 264–277. Berlin: De Gruyter, 1994.

Koester, Helmut. *Ancient Christian Gospels: Their History and Development*. Philadelphia: Fortress, 1990.

Konstan, David. "*To Hellēnikon Ethnos*: Ethnicity and the Construction of Ancient Greek Identity." In *Ancient Perceptions of Greek Ethnicity*, edited by Irad Malkin, 29–50. Washington D.C.: Center for Hellenic Studies/Cambridge, Mass.: Harvard University Press, 2001.

———. "Defining Ancient Greek Ethnicity." *Diaspora* 6 (1997): 97–110.

Kraemer, Ross Shepard, and Mary Rose D'Angelo, eds. *Women and Christian Origins*. New York: Oxford University Press, 1999.

———. *Her Share of the Blessings: Women's Religions Among Pagans, Jews, and Christians in the Greco-Roman World*. New York: Oxford University Press, 1992.

———. "Jewish Tuna and Christian Fish: Identifying Religious Affiliation in Epigraphic Sources." *HTR* 84 (1991): 141–162.

Kugel, James L. *Traditions of the Bible: A Guide to the Bible As It Was at the Start of the Common Era*. Cambridge, Mass.: Harvard University Press, 1998.

Lapin, Hayim. "Introduction: Locating Ethnicity and Religious Community in Later Roman Palestine." In *Religious and Ethnic Communities in Later Roman Palestine*, edited by H. Lapin, 1–28. Bethesda, MD: University Press of Maryland, 1998.

Layton, Bentley. "Prolegomena to the Study of Gnosticism." In *The Social World of the First Christians: Studies in Honor of Wayne Meeks*, edited by Michael L. White and Larry O. Yarborough, 338–344. Minneapolis: Fortress, 1995.

Lefkowitz, Mary, and Guy M. Rogers, eds. *Black Athena Revisited*. Chapel Hill: University of North Carolina Press, 1996.

Levenson, Jon D. "The Universal Horizon of Biblical Particularism." In *Ethnicity and the Bible*, edited by Mark G. Brett, 143–169. 1996. Reprint, Boston: Brill, 2002.

Levine, Molly Myerowitz. "The Marginalization of Martin Bernal." *Classical Philology* 93 (1998): 345–363.

Levinson, Joshua. "Bodies and Bo(a)rders: Emerging Fictions of Identity in Late Antiquity. *HTR* 93 (2000): 343–372.

Lewis, Naphtali. *Life in Egypt Under Roman Rule*. Oxford: Clarendon Press, 1983.

Lieu, Judith. *Christian Identity in the Jewish and Graeco-Roman World*. Oxford: Oxford University Press, 2004.

——. *Image and Reality: The Jews in the World of the Christians in the Second Century*. Edinburgh: T&T Clark, 1996.

——. "Race of God-Fearers." *JTS* n.s. 46 (1995): 483–501.

Lightfoot, J. B. *Saint Paul's Epistle to the Galatians. A Revised Text with Introduction, Notes, and Dissertations*. 7th ed. London: Macmillan and Co., 1881.

Lincoln, Bruce. *Theorizing Myth: Narrative, Ideology, and Scholarship*. Chicago: University of Chicago Press, 1999.

Loraux, Nicole. *Born of the Earth: Myth and Politics in Athens*. Translated by Selina Stewart. French original 1996. ET: Ithaca: Cornell University Press, 2000.

MacDonald, Margaret Y. *Early Christian Women and Pagan Opinion: The Power of the Hysterical Woman*. Cambridge: Cambridge University Press, 1996.

McClintock, Anne. *Imperial Leather: Race, Gender and Sexuality in the Colonial Contest*. New York: Routledge, 1995.

McCoskey, Denise Eileen. "Answering the Multicultural Imperative: A Course on Race and Ethnicity in Antiquity." *Classical World* 92 (1999): 553–561.

Malcomson, Scott. *One Drop of Blood: The American Misadventure of Race*. New York: Farrar, Strauss, Giroux, 2000.

Malkin, Irad, ed. *Ancient Perceptions of Greek Ethnicity*. Washington D.C.: Center for Hellenic Studies/Cambridge, Mass.: Harvard University Press, 2001.

Martin, Luther. "Genealogy and Sociology in the Apocalypse of Adam." In *Gnosticism and the Early Christian World: In Honor of James M. Robinson*, edited by James E. Goehring et al., 25–36. Sonoma, Calif.: Polebridge, 1990.

Matthews, Shelly. *First Converts: Rich Pagan Women and the Rhetoric of Mission in Early Judaism and Christianity*. Contraversions. Stanford: Stanford University Press, 2001.

Meeks, Wayne A. "Breaking Away: Three New Testament Pictures of Christianity's Separation from Jewish Communities." In *"To See Ourselves as Others See Us": Christians, Jews, "Others" in Late Antiquity*, edited by Jacob Neusner and Ernst Frerichs, 93–116. Chico, Calif.: Scholars, 1985.

Millar, Fergus. "Empire and City, Augustus to Julian: Obligations, Excuses, and Status." *Journal of Roman Studies* 73 (1983): 76–96.

Mitchell, Stephen. "Ethnicity, Acculturation and Empire in Roman and Late Roman Asia Minor." In *Ethnicity and Culture in Late Antiquity*, edited by Stephen Mitchell and Geoffrey Greatex, 117–150. London: Duckworth and the Classical Press of Wales, 2000.

Mitchell, Stephen, and Geoffrey Greatex, eds. *Ethnicity and Culture in Late Antiquity*. London: Duckworth and the Classical Press of Wales, 2000.

Mohrmann, Christine. *Études sur le latin des chrétiens. Tome IV. Latin chrétien et latin medieval*. Stori e Litteratura 143. Rome: Edizioni di Storia e Letteratura, 1977.

Moorhead, James H. "The American Israel: Protestant Tribalism and Universal Mission." In *Many Are Chosen: Divine Election and Western Nationalism*, edited by William R. Hutchison and Hartmut Lehmann, 145–166. Harvard Theological Studies 38. Minneapolis: Fortress, 1994.

Moriarty, Rachel. " 'The Faith of Our Fathers': The Making of the Early Christian Past." In *The Church Retrospective: Papers Reads at the 1995 Summer Meeting and the 1996 Winter Meeting of the Ecclesiastical History Society*, edited by R. N. Swanson, 5–17. Woodbridge, Suffolk: Boydell, 1997.

Morrison, Toni. *Playing in the Dark: Whiteness and the Literary Imagination*. Cambridge, Mass.: Harvard University Press, 1992.

Moxnes, Halvor. "Jesus the Jew: Dilemmas of Interpretation." In *Fair Play: Diversity and Conflicts in Early Christianity: Essays in Honour of Heikki Räisänen*, edited by Ismo Dunderberg, Christopher Tuckett, and Kari Syreeni, 83–103. Leiden: Brill, 2002.

Murray, Robert. *Symbols of Church and Kingdom: A Study in Early Syriac Tradition*. London: Cambridge University Press, 1975.

Nasrallah, Laura. " 'She Became What the Words Signified': The Greek Acts of Andrew's Construction of the Reader-Disciple." In *The Apocryphal Acts of the Apostles*, edited by François Bovon, 233–258. Cambridge, Mass.: Harvard University Press, 1999.

Neusner, Jacob, and Ernst Frerichs, eds. *"To See Ourselves as Others See Us": Christians, Jews, "Others" in Late Antiquity*. Chico, Calif.: Scholars, 1985.

Nock, Arthur Darby. *Conversion: The Old and the New in Religion from Alexander the Great to Augustine of Hippo*. 1933. Reprint, Baltimore: The Johns Hopkins University Press, 1988.

North, John. "The Development of Religious Pluralism." In *The Jews Among Pagans and Christians in the Roman Empire*, edited by Judith Lieu, John North, and Tessa Rajak, 174–193. New York: Routledge, 1992.

Olster, David M. "Classical Ethnography and Early Christianity." In *The Formulation of Christianity by Conflict Through the Ages*, edited by Katharine B. Free, 9–31. Lewiston, N.Y.: Mellen, 1995.

——. *Roman Defeat, Christian Response, and the Literary Construction of the Jew*. Philadelphia: University of Pennsylvania Press, 1994.

Pagels, Elaine H. *Gnostic Gospels*. 1979. Reprint, New York: Vintage, 1981.

——. "Conflicting Versions of Valentinian Eschatology: Irenaeus's Treatise vs. The Excerpts from Theodotus." *HTR* 67 (1974): 35–53.

——. "A Valentinian Interpretation of Baptism and Eucharist—And its Critique of 'Orthodox' Sacramental Theology and Practice." *HTR* 65 (1972): 153–169.

Parker, Robert. *Cleomenes on the Acropolis: An Inaugural Lecture Delivered Before the University of Oxford on 12 May 1997*. Oxford: Clarendon, 1998.

Penn, Michael. "Performing Family: Ritual Kissing and the Construction of Early Christian Kinship." *JECS* 10 (2002): 151–174.

Perkins, Judith. *The Suffering Self*. New York: Routledge, 1995.

Plaskow, Judith. *Standing Again at Sinai: Judaism from a Feminist Perspective*. New York: Harper and Row, 1990.

Pohl, Walter, ed. *Strategies of Distinction: The Construction of Ethnic Communities, 300–800*. Leiden: Brill, 1998.

Pomata, Gianna. "Blood Ties and Semen Ties: Consanguity and Agnation in Roman Law." In *Gender, Kinship, Power: A Comparative and Interdisciplinary History*, edited by Mary Jo Maynes et al., 43–64. New York: Routledge, 1996.

Preston, Rebecca. "Roman Questions, Greek Answers: Plutarch and the Construction of Identity." In *Being Greek Under Rome: Cultural Identity, the Second Sophistic, and the Development of Empire*, edited by Simon Goldhill, 86–117. Cambridge: Cambridge University Press, 2001.

Price, S. R. F. *Rituals and Power: The Roman Imperial Cult in Asia Minor*. Cambridge: Cambridge University Press, 1984.

Raboteau, Albert. "African-Americans, Exodus, and the American Israel." In *African-American Christianity: Essays in History*, edited by Paul E. Johnson, 1–17. Berkeley: University of California Press, 1994.

Rajak, Tessa. "Talking at Trypho: Christian Apologetic as Anti-Judaism in Justin's *Dialogue with Trypho the Jew*." In *Apologetics in the Roman Empire: Pagans, Jews, and Christians*, edited by Mark Edwards, Martin Goodman, and Simon Price, in association with Christopher Rowland, 59–80. New York: Oxford University Press, 1999.

Renan, Ernest. *Life of Jesus*. Translated by Charles Edwin Wilbour. New York: Carleton, 1864.

——. *Oeuvres completes*. 10 vols. Edited by Henriette Psichari. Paris: Colmann-Lévy, 1947–1961.

Richardson, Peter. *Israel in the Apostolic Church*. Society for New Testament Studies Monograph Series 10. Cambridge: Cambridge University Press, 1969.

Rives, J. B. "The Decree of Decius and the Religion of the Empire." *Journal of Roman Studies* 89 (1999): 135–154.

——. *Religion and Authority in Roman Carthage from Augustus to Constantine*. Oxford: Clarendon, 1995.

Roediger, David R. *The Wages of Whiteness : Race and the Making of the American Working Class*. New York: Verso, 1999.

Rokeah, David. *Jews, Pagans, and Christians in Conflict*. Studia Post-Biblica. Jerusalem: Magnes Press, Hebrew University/Leiden: Brill, 1982.

Roldanus, Johannes. "Références patristiques au 'chrétiens-étranger' dans les trois premiers siècles." *Cahiers de Biblia Patristica* 1 (1987): 27–52.

Ruether, Rosemary Radford. "Sexism and God-Language." In *Weaving the Visions: New Patterns in Feminist Spirituality*, edited by Judith Plaskow and Carol P. Christ, 151–162. San Francisco: Harper and Row, 1989.

——. *Faith and Fratricide: The Theological Roots of Anti-Semitism*. New York: Seabury, 1974.

Saddington, D. B. "Race Relations in the Early Roman Empire." *ANRW* II.3 (1975): 112–137.

Saïd, Suzanne. "The Discourse of Identity in Greek Rhetoric from Isocrates to Aristides." In *Ancient Perceptions of Greek Ethnicity*, edited by Irad Malkin, 275–299. Washington D.C.: Center for Hellenic Studies/Cambridge, Mass.: Harvard University Press, 2001.

Sands, Kathleen. "Tracking Religion. . . . " Public lecture delivered at the Radcliffe Institute for Advanced Study, Cambridge, Mass., Februrary 2001.

Schneider, David M. "What Is Kinship All About?" In *Kinship Studies in the Morgan Centennial Year*, edited by Priscilla Reining, 32–63. Washington D.C.: Anthropological Society of Washington, 1972.

Schottroff, Luise. "*Animae naturaliter salvandae*: Zum Problem der himmlischen Herkunft des Gnostikers." In *Christentum und Gnosis*, edited by Walter Eltester, 65–97. BZNW 37. Berlin: Töpelmann, 1969.

Schüssler Fiorenza, Elisabeth. *Jesus and the Politics of Interpretation*. New York: Continuum, 2000.

——. *Rhetoric and Ethic: The Politics of Biblical Studies*. Minneapolis: Fortress, 1999.

——. *But She Said: Feminist Practices of Biblical Interpretation*. Boston: Beacon, 1992.

——. *Bread Not Stone: The Challenge of Feminist Biblical Interpretation*. Boston: Beacon, 1984.

Schwartz, Regina. *The Curse of Cain: The Violent Legacy of Monotheism*. Chicago: University of Chicago Press, 1997.

Schwartz, Seth. *Imperialism and Jewish Society, 200 B.C.E. to 640 C.E.* Jews, Christians, and Muslims from the Ancient to the Modern World. Princeton, N.J.: Princeton University Press, 2001.

Segovia, Fernando F. "Racial and Ethnic Minorities in Biblical Studies." In *Ethnicity and the Bible*, edited by Mark G. Brett, 469–492. 1996. Reprint, Boston: Brill, 2002.

Segovia, Fernando F., and Mary Ann Tolbert, eds. *Reading from this Place, volume 1: Social Location and Biblical Interpretation in the United States*. Minneapolis: Fortress, 1995.

Sherwin-White, A. N. *Racial Prejudice in Imperial Rome*. Cambridge: Cambridge University Press, 1967.

Silverblatt, Irene. "New Christians and New World Fears in Seventeenth-Century Peru." In *From the Margins: Historical Anthropology and Its Futures*, edited by Brian Keith Axel, 95–121. Durham, N.C.: Duke University Press, 2002.

——. "Race, Religion, and the Modern/Colonial World: Spanish Cultural Politics and the Inquisition in Seventeenth-Century Peru." Public lecture delivered at the Radcliffe Institute for Advanced Study, Cambridge, Mass., September 2001.

Siker, Jeffrey S. *Disinheriting the Jews: Abraham in Early Christian Controversy*. Louisville, KY: Westminster/John Knox, 1991.

——. "Gnostic Views on Jews and Christians in the Gospel of Philip." *Novum Testamentum* 31 (1989): 275–288.

Simon, Marcel. *Verus Israel: Étude sur les relations entre chrétiens et juifs dans l'empire romain (135–425)*. Paris: Éditions de Boccard, 1964. ET: *Verus Israel: A Study of the Relations Between Christians and Jews in the Roman Empire (135–425)*. Translated by H. McKeating. Oxford: Oxford University Press, 1986.

Smedley, Audrey. *Race in North America: Origin and Evolution of a Worldview*, 2d ed. Boulder, Colo.: Westview, 1999.

Smith, Anthony D. *The Ethnic Origins of Nations*. Oxford: Blackwell, 1986.

Smith, Jonathan Z. "Classification." In *Guide to the Study of Religion*, edited by Willi Braun and Russell T. McCutcheon, 35–44. London: Cassell, 2000.

——. "A Matter of Class: Taxonomies of Religion." *HTR* 89 (1996): 387–403.

——. "Differential Equations: On Constructing the 'Other.' " Thirteenth Annual University Lecture in Religion. Pheonix, Ariz.: Department of Religious Studies at Arizona State University, 1992.

——. *Drudgery Divine: On the Comparison of Early Christianities and the Religions of Late Antiquity*. Chicago: University of Chicago Press, 1990.

——. "What a Difference A Difference Makes." In *"To See Ourselves as Others See Us": Christians, Jews, "Others" in Late Antiquity*, edited by Jacob Neusner and Ernst Frerichs, 3–47. Chico, Calif.: Scholars, 1985.

Snowden, Frank M., Jr. *Before Color Prejudice: The Ancient View of Blacks*. Cambridge, Mass.: Harvard University Press, 1983.

——. *Blacks in Antiquity: Ethiopians in the Greco-Roman Experience*. Cambridge, Mass.: Harvard University Press, 1970.

Sollors, Werner. "Foreword: Theories of American Ethnicity." In *Theories of Ethnicity: A Classical Reader*, edited by Werner Sollors, x–xliv. New York: New York University Press, 1996.

Spawforth, Antony. "Shade of Greekness: A Lydian Case Study." In *Ancient Perceptions of Greek Ethnicity*, edited by Irad Malkin, 375–400. Washington D.C.: Center for Hellenic Studies/Cambridge, Mass.: Harvard University Press, 2001.

Stanton, Graham. "Justin Martyr's *Dialogue with Trypho*: Group Boundaries, 'Proselytes,' and 'God-fearers.' " In *Tolerance and Intolerance in Early Judaism and Christianity*, edited by Graham N. Stanton and Guy G. Stroumsa, 263–278. Cambridge: Cambridge University Press, 1998.

Stepan, Nancy Leys. *The Idea of Race in Science: Great Britain, 1800–1960*. London: MacMillan; Hamden, Conn.: Archon, 1982.

Stepan, Nancy Leys, and Gilman, Sander L. "Appropriating the Idioms of Science: The Rejection of Scientific Racism." In *The "Racial" Economy of Science: Toward a Democratic Future*, edited by Sandra Harding, 170–193. Bloomington: Indiana University Press, 1993.

Stocking, George. *Race, Culture, and Evolution: Essays in the History of Anthropology.* Chicago: University of Chicago Press, 1986.

Stoler, Ann Laura. "Reflections on 'Racial Histories and Their Regimes of Truth' (A. Stoler)." In *Race Critical Theory: Text and Context,* edited by Philomena Essed and David Theo Goldberg, 417–421. Oxford: Blackwell, 2002.

———. "Racial Histories and their Regimes of Truth." *Political Power and Social Theory* 11 (1997): 183–206.

Stowers, Stanley K. "Greeks Who Sacrifice and Those Who Do Not: Toward an Anthropology of Greek Religion." In *The Social World of the First Christians: Studies in Honor of Wayne Meeks,* edited by Michael L. White and Larry O. Yarborough, 293–333. Minneapolis: Fortress, 1995.

———. *A Rereading of Romans: Justice, Jews, and Gentiles.* New Haven, Conn.: Yale University Press, 1994.

Stroumsa, Guy G. *Barbarian Philosophy: The Religious Revolution of Early Christianity.* Wissenschaftliche Untersuchungen zum Neuen Testament 112. Tübingen: Mohr [Siebeck], 1999.

———. *Another Seed: Studies in Gnostic Mythology.* NHS 24. Leiden: Brill, 1984.

Swain, Simon. "Defending Hellenism: Philostratus, *In Honour of Apollonius.*" In *Apologetics in the Roman Empire: Pagans, Jews, and Christians,* edited by Mark Edwards, Martin Goodman, and Simon Price, in association with Christopher Rowland, 157–196. New York: Oxford University Press, 1999.

———. *Hellenism and Empire: Language, Classicism, and Power in the Greek World,* A.D. 50–250. Oxford: Clarendon, 1996.

Taylor, Miriam S. *Anti-Judaism and Early Christian Identity: A Critique of the Scholarly Consensus.* Studia Post-Biblica 46. Leiden: Brill, 1995.

Thandeka. *Learning to Be White: Money, Race, and God in America.* New York: Continuum, 1999.

Thomas, Rosalind. "Ethnicity, Genealogy, and Hellenism in Herodotus." In *Ancient Perceptions of Greek Ethnicity,* edited by Irad Malkin, 213–233. Washington D.C.: Center for Hellenic Studies/Cambridge, Mass.: Harvard University Press, 2001.

Thomassen, Einar. "The Valentinianism of the *Valentinian Exposition* (NHC XI, 2)." *Muséon* 102 (1989): 225–36.

Tiele, Cornelius P. *Elements of the Science of Religion.* 2 vols. New York: Scribner's Sons, 1897.

Toy, Crawford Howell. *Judaism and Christianity: A Sketch of the Progress of Thought from Old Testament to New Testament.* Boston: Little, Brown and Co., 1891.

Turner, Martha Lee. *The Gospel According to Philip: The Sources and Coherence of an Early Christian Collection.* Nag Hammadi and Manichean Studies 38. Leiden: Brill, 1996.

van der Veer, Peter. *Imperial Encounters: Religion and Modernity in India and Britain.* Princeton, N.J.: Princeton University Press, 2001.

Verter, Bradford J. "Furthering the Freedom Struggle: Racial Justice Activism in the Mainline Churches Since the Civil Rights Era." In *The Quiet Hand of God: Faith-*

*Based Activism and the Public Role of Mainline Protestantism*, edited by Robert Wuthnow and John H. Evans, 181–212. Berkeley and Los Angeles: University of California Press, 2002.

Viswanathan, Gauri. *Outside the Fold: Conversion, Modernity, and Belief.* Princeton, N.J.: Princeton University Press, 1998.

Walker, David. [1829] "Excerpts from *Appeal to the Coloured Citizens of the World, but in Particular, and Very Expressly, to Those of the United States of America.*" In *Afro-American Religious History: A Documentary Witness*, edited by Milton C. Sernett, 188–195. Durham, N.C.: Duke University Press, 1985.

Wallace-Hadrill, Andrew. "To Be Roman, Go Greek: Thoughts on Hellenization at Rome." In *Modus Operandi: Essays in Honour of Geoffrey Rickman*, edited by Michel Austin, Jill Harries, and Christopher Smith, 79–91. London: Institute of Classical Studies, School of Advanced Study, University of London, 1998.

——. "*Mutatio morum*: The Idea of a Cultural Revolution." In *The Roman Cultural Revolution*, edited by Thomas Habinek and Alessandro Schiesaro, 3–22. Cambridge: Cambridge University Press, 1997.

Wan, Sze-Kar. "Does Diaspora Identity Imply Some Sort of Universality? An Asian-American Reading of Galatians." In *Interpreting Beyond Borders*, edited by Fernando F. Segovia, 107–131. The Bible and Postcolonialism 3. Sheffield: Sheffield Academic Press, 2000.

Waters, Mary. *Ethnic Options: Choosing Identities in America.* Berkeley: University of California Press, 1990.

West, Cornel. *The Cornel West Reader.* New York: Basic *Civitas* Books, 1999.

——. "Race and Social Theory." In *Keeping Faith: Philosophy and Race in America*, 251–270. New York: Routledge, 1993. Reprinted in *The Cornel West Reader*, 251–265. New York: Basic *Civitas* Books, 1999.

White, L. Michael, and Larry O. Yarborough, eds. *The Social World of the First Christians: Studies in Honor of Wayne Meeks.* Minneapolis: Fortress, 1995.

Whitmarsh, Tim. " 'Greece is the World.' " In *Being Greek Under Rome: Cultural Identity, the Second Sophistic, and the Development of Empire*, edited by Simon Goldhill, 269–305. Cambridge: Cambridge University Press, 2001.

Whitney, William D. "On the So-Called Science of Religion." *Princeton Review* 57 (May 1881): 429–452.

Williams, Michael A. *Rethinking "Gnosticism": An Argument for Dismantling a Dubious Category.* Princeton, N.J.: Princeton University Press, 1996.

——. *The Immovable Race: A Gnostic Designation and the Theme of Stability in Late Antiquity.* Nag Hammadi Studies 29. Leiden: Brill, 1985.

Williams, Patricia. *Seeing a Color-Blind Future: The Paradox of Race.* New York: Noonday Press, 1998.

Wimbush, Vincent, ed., with the assistance of Rosamond C. Rodman. *African Americans and the Bible: Sacred Texts and Social Textures.* New York: Continuum, 2000.

——. "Reading Texts as Reading Ourselves: A Chapter in the History of African-American Biblical Interpretation." In *Reading from this Place, volume 1: Social*

*Location and Biblical Interpretation in the United States*, edited by Fernando F. Segovia and Mary Ann Tolbert, 95–108. Minneapolis: Fortress, 1995.

Woolf, Greg. *Becoming Roman: The Origins of Provincial Civilization in Gaul.* Cambridge: Cambridge University Press, 1998.

———. "Becoming Roman, Staying Greek: Culture, Identity, and the Civilizing Process in the Roman East." *Proceedings of the Cambridge Philological Society*, n.s. 40 (1994): 116–143.

Young, Frances. "Greek Apologists of the Second Century." In *Apologetics in the Roman Empire: Pagans, Jews, and Christians*, edited by Mark Edwards, Martin Goodman, and Simon Price, in association with Christopher Rowland, 81–104. New York: Oxford University Press, 1999.

Young, Robert. *White Mythologies: Writing History and the West.* New York: Routledge, 1990.

Zanker, Paul. *The Power of Images in the Age of Augustus.* Translated by Alan Shapiro. Ann Arbor: University of Michigan Press, 1988.

# Index of Ancient Sources

# General Index